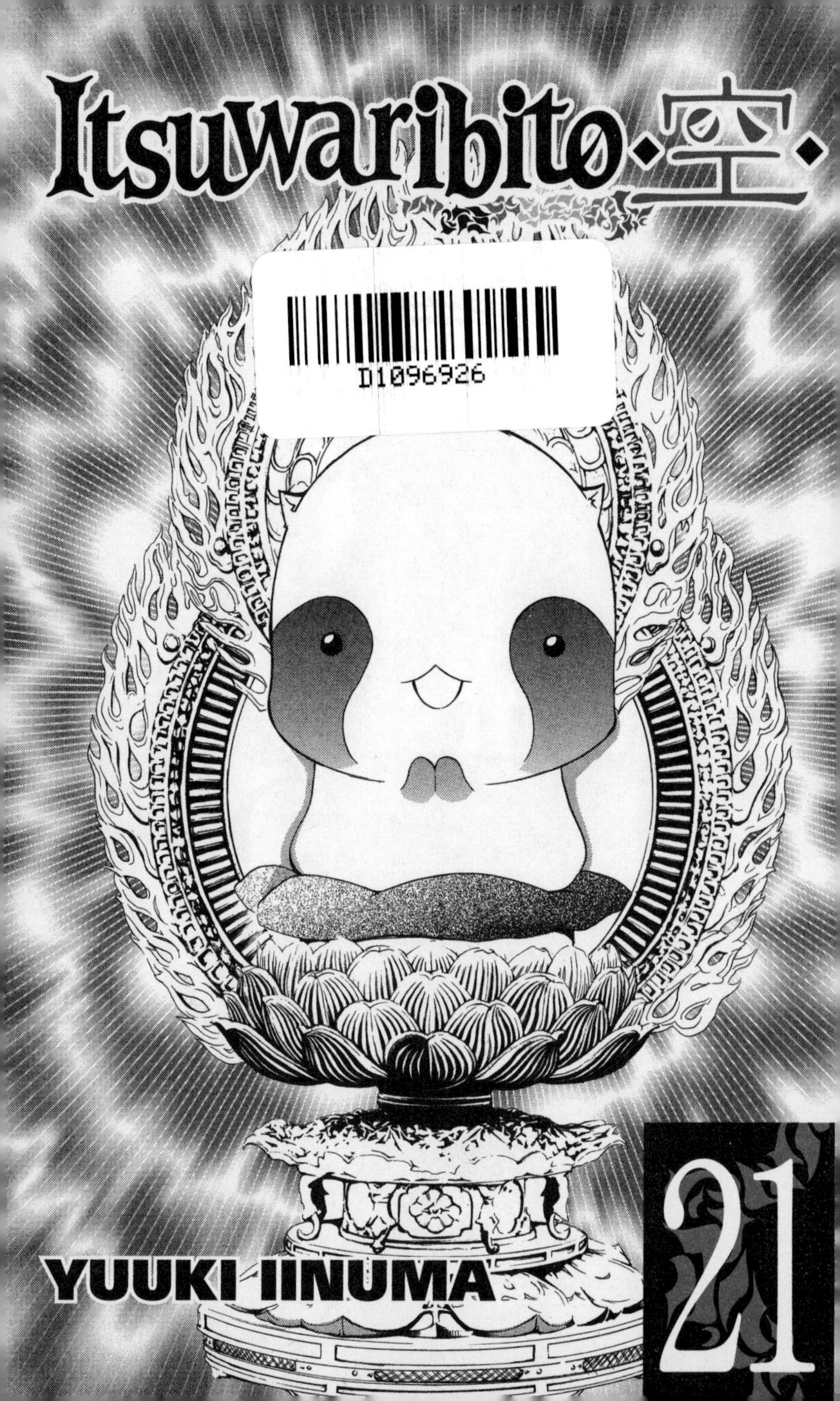
Itsuwaribito·空·
21
YUUKI IINUMA

Contents

Chapter 198 The Truth of the Old Story

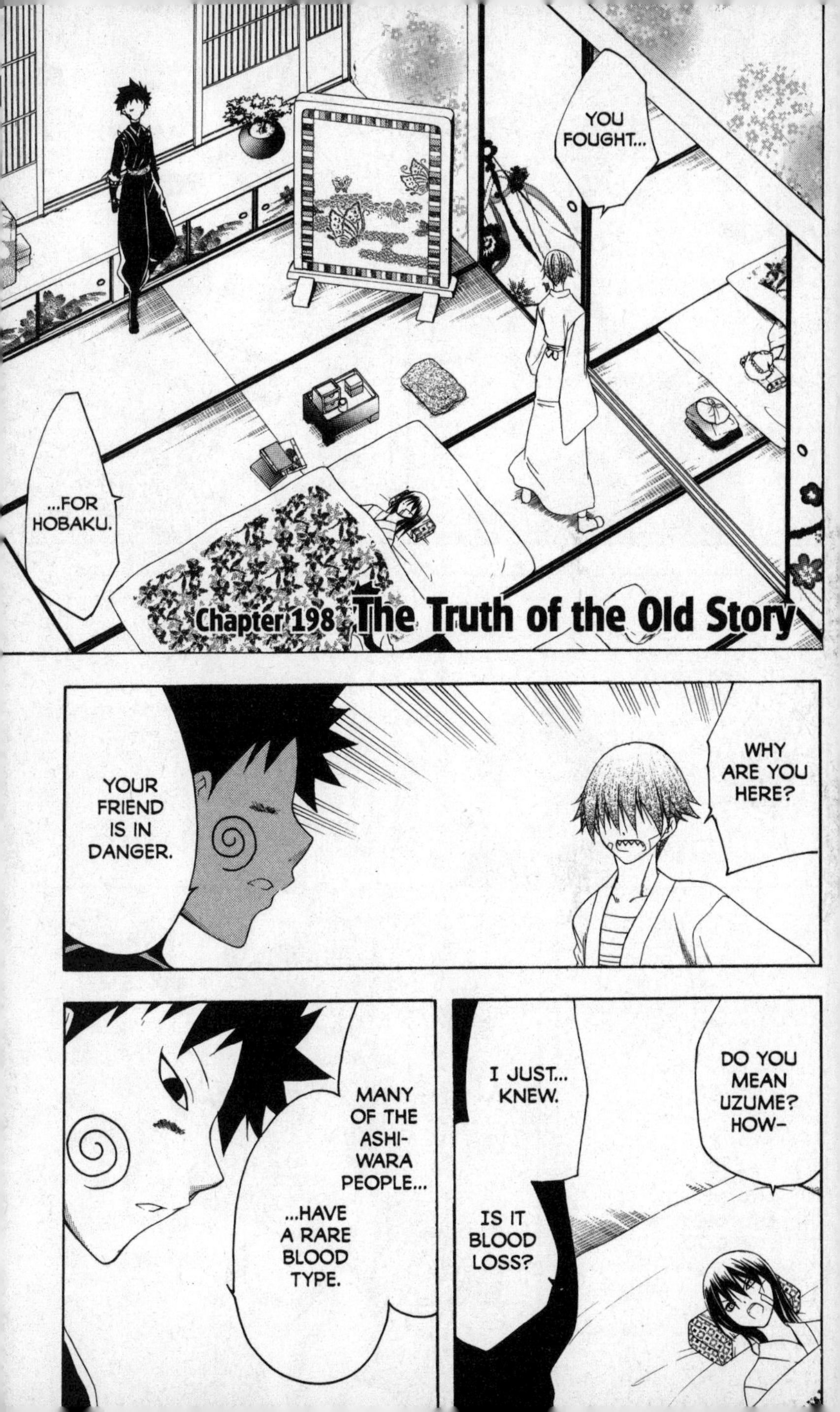

YOU FOUGHT...
...FOR HOBAKU.
Chapter 198 The Truth of the Old Story
WHY ARE YOU HERE?
YOUR FRIEND IS IN DANGER.
DO YOU MEAN UZUME? HOW–
I JUST... KNEW.
IS IT BLOOD LOSS?
MANY OF THE ASHI-WARA PEOPLE...
...HAVE A RARE BLOOD TYPE.

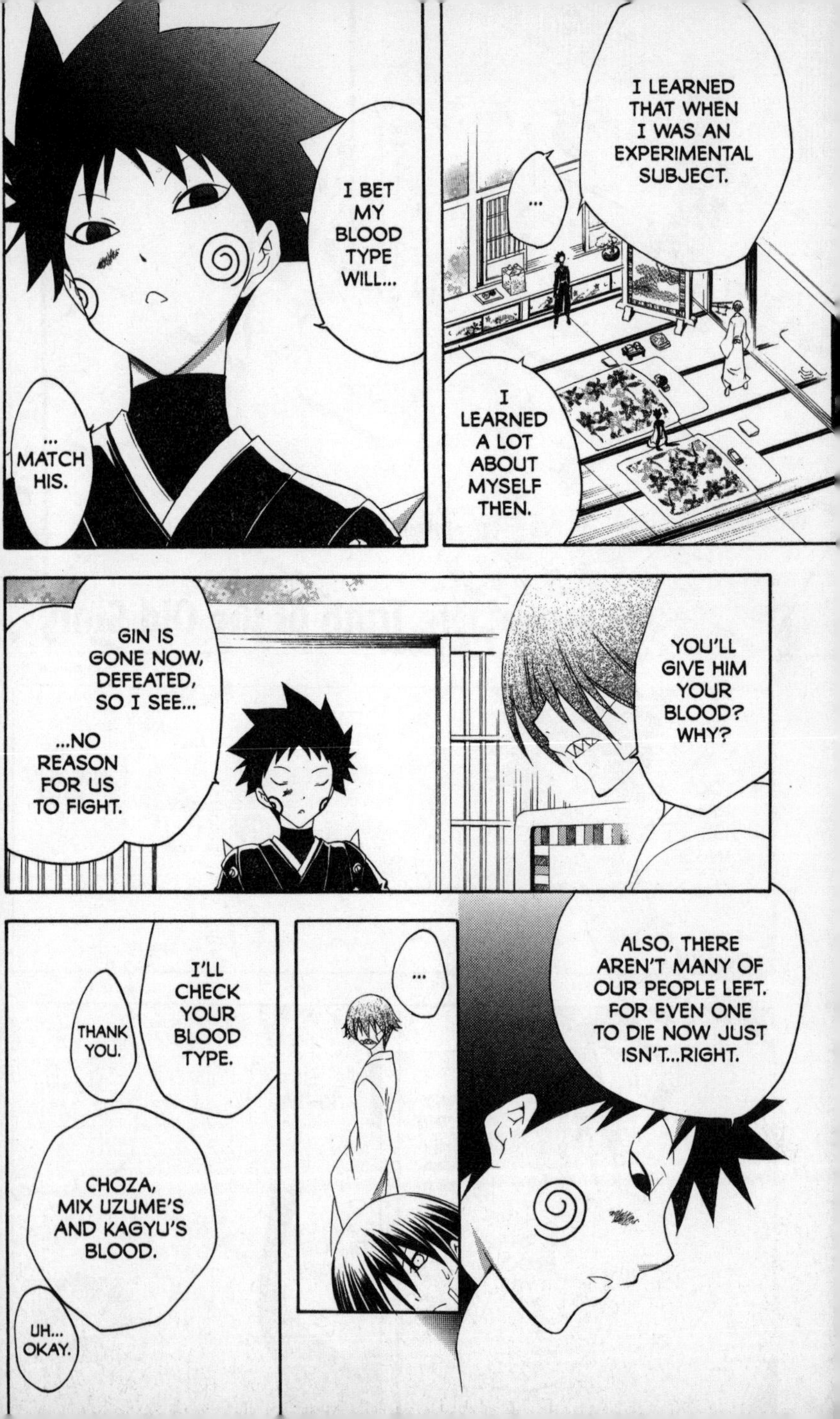
I LEARNED THAT WHEN I WAS AN EXPERIMENTAL SUBJECT.
...
I LEARNED A LOT ABOUT MYSELF THEN.
I BET MY BLOOD TYPE WILL...
...MATCH HIS.
YOU'LL GIVE HIM YOUR BLOOD? WHY?
GIN IS GONE NOW, DEFEATED, SO I SEE...
...NO REASON FOR US TO FIGHT.
ALSO, THERE AREN'T MANY OF OUR PEOPLE LEFT. FOR EVEN ONE TO DIE NOW JUST ISN'T...RIGHT.
...
I'LL CHECK YOUR BLOOD TYPE.
THANK YOU.
CHOZA, MIX UZUME'S AND KAGYU'S BLOOD.
UH... OKAY.

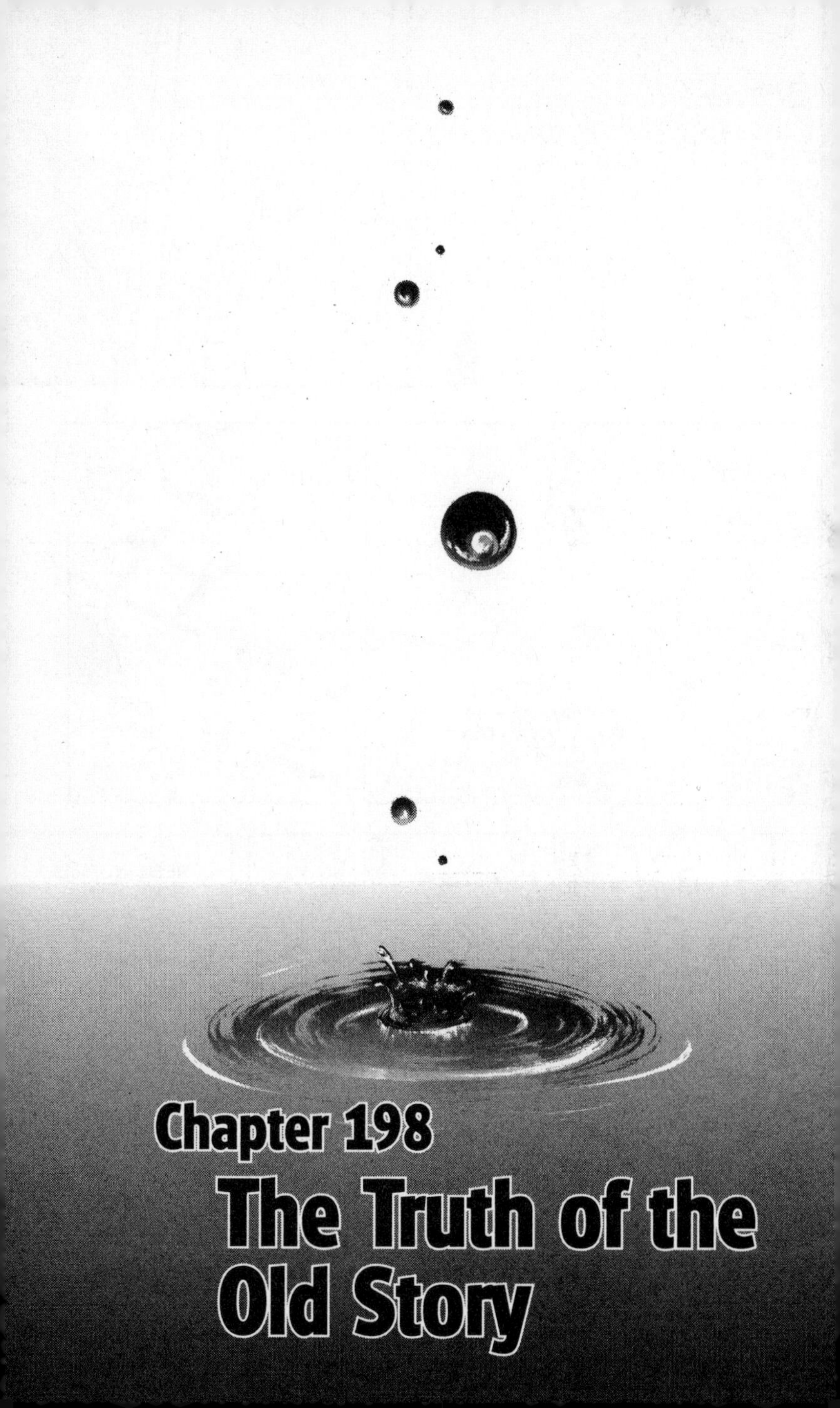

Chapter 198
The Truth of the Old Story

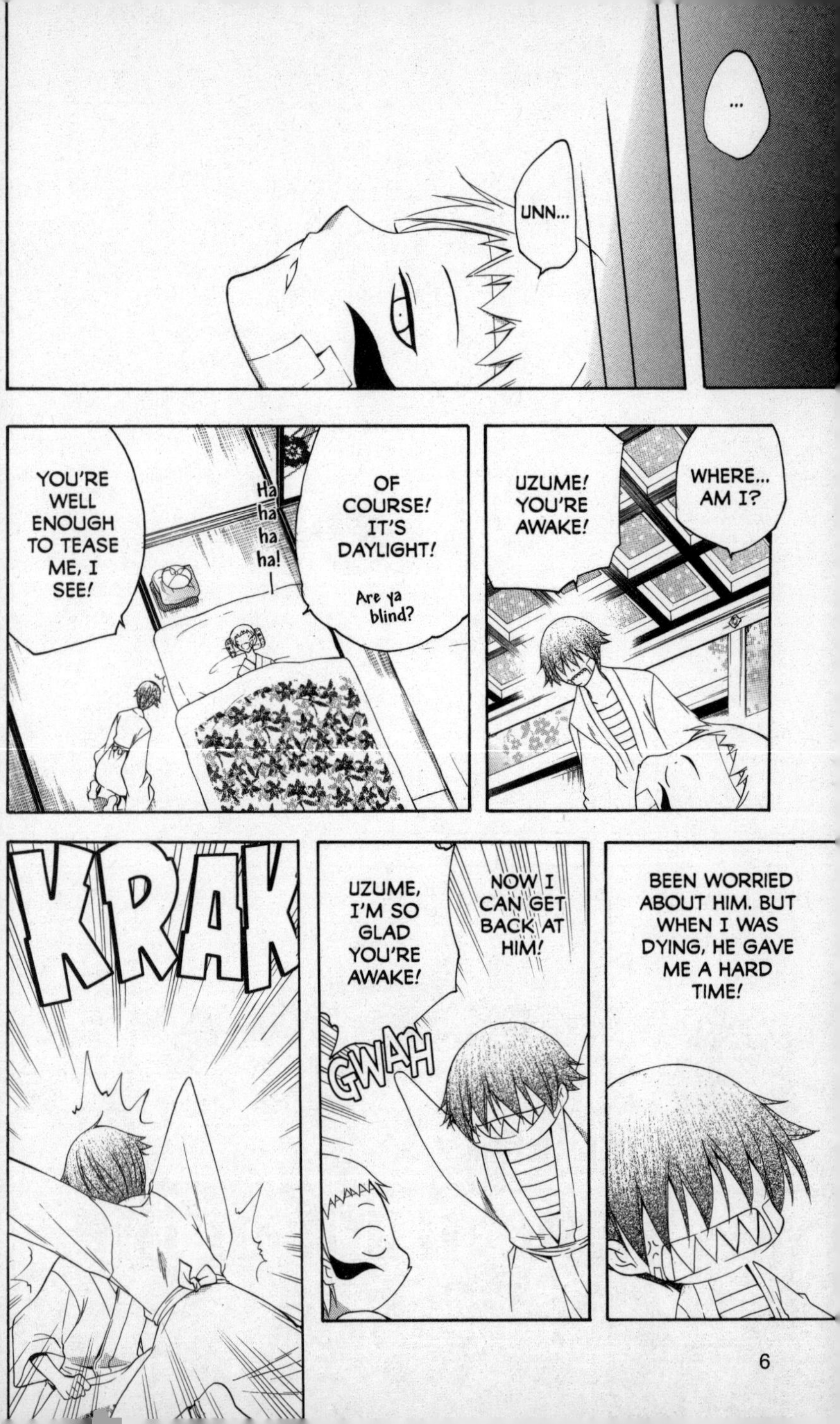
...
UNN...
WHERE... AM I?
UZUME! YOU'RE AWAKE!
OF COURSE! IT'S DAYLIGHT!
Are ya blind?
Ha ha ha ha!
YOU'RE WELL ENOUGH TO TEASE ME, I SEE!
BEEN WORRIED ABOUT HIM. BUT WHEN I WAS DYING, HE GAVE ME A HARD TIME!
NOW I CAN GET BACK AT HIM!
UZUME, I'M SO GLAD YOU'RE AWAKE!
GWAH
KRAK

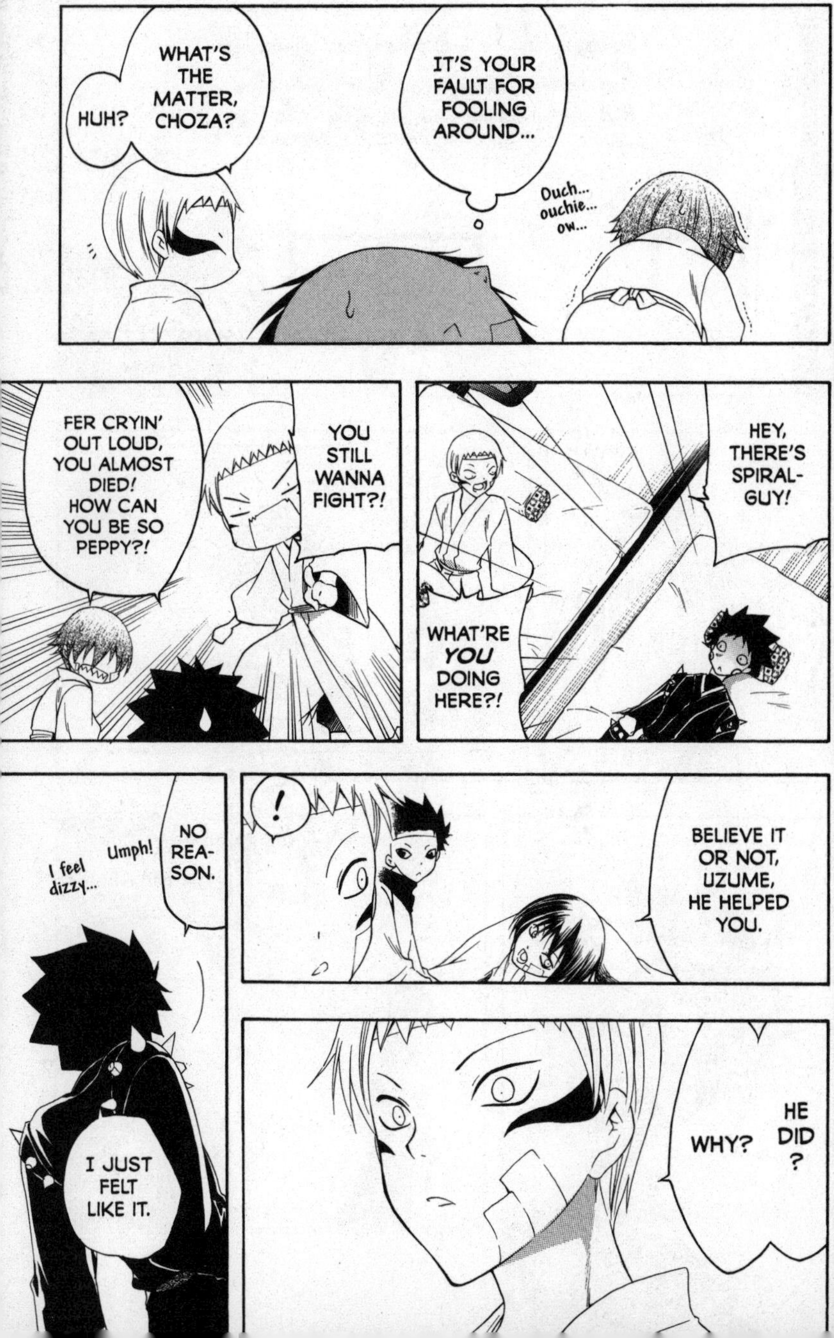
IT'S YOUR FAULT FOR FOOLING AROUND...
Ouch... ouchie... ow...
WHAT'S THE MATTER, CHOZA?
HUH?
HEY, THERE'S SPIRAL-GUY!
WHAT'RE *YOU* DOING HERE?!
YOU STILL WANNA FIGHT?!
FER CRYIN' OUT LOUD, YOU ALMOST DIED! HOW CAN YOU BE SO PEPPY?!
BELIEVE IT OR NOT, UZUME, HE HELPED YOU.
!
HE DID?
WHY?
NO REA-SON.
Umph!
I feel dizzy...
I JUST FELT LIKE IT.

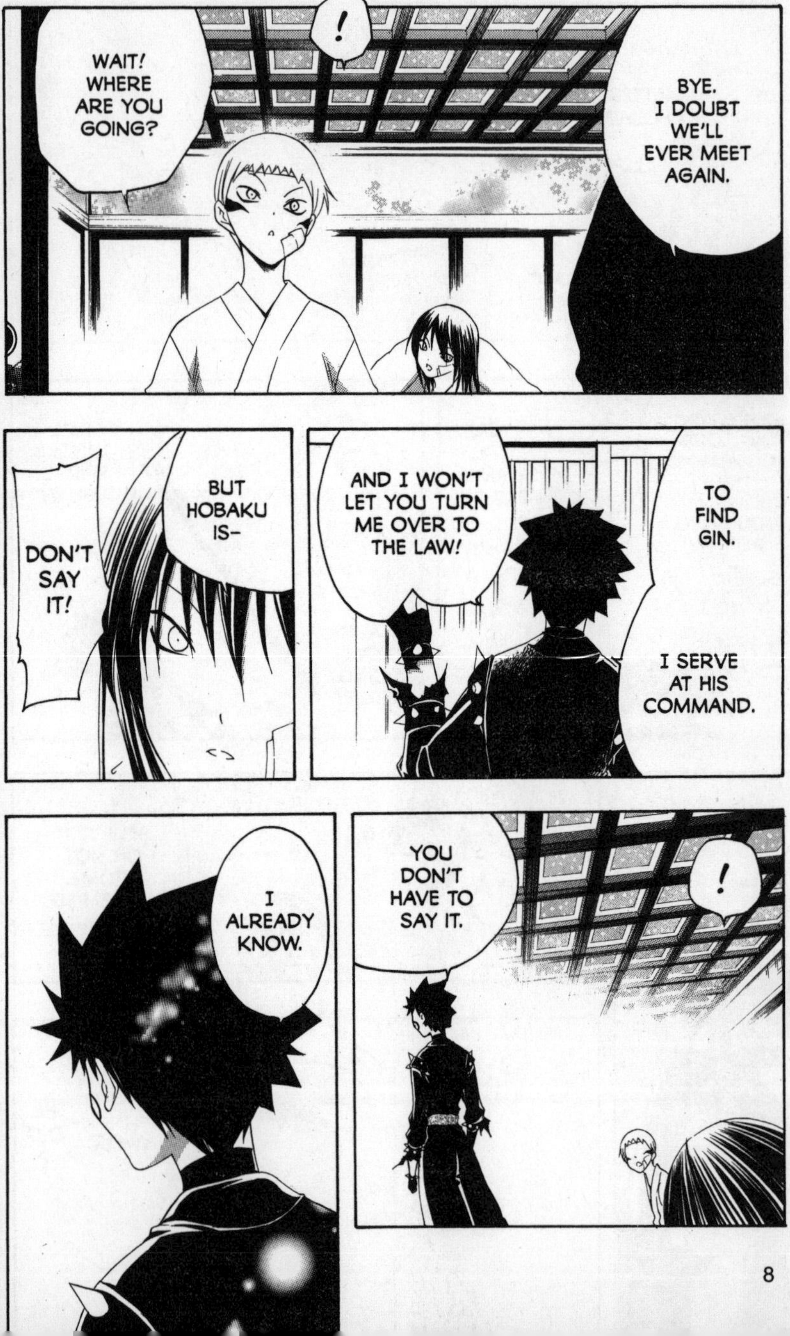
BYE. I DOUBT WE'LL EVER MEET AGAIN.
!
WAIT! WHERE ARE YOU GOING?
TO FIND GIN.
I SERVE AT HIS COMMAND.
AND I WON'T LET YOU TURN ME OVER TO THE LAW!
BUT HOBAKU IS–
DON'T SAY IT!
!
YOU DON'T HAVE TO SAY IT.
I ALREADY KNOW.

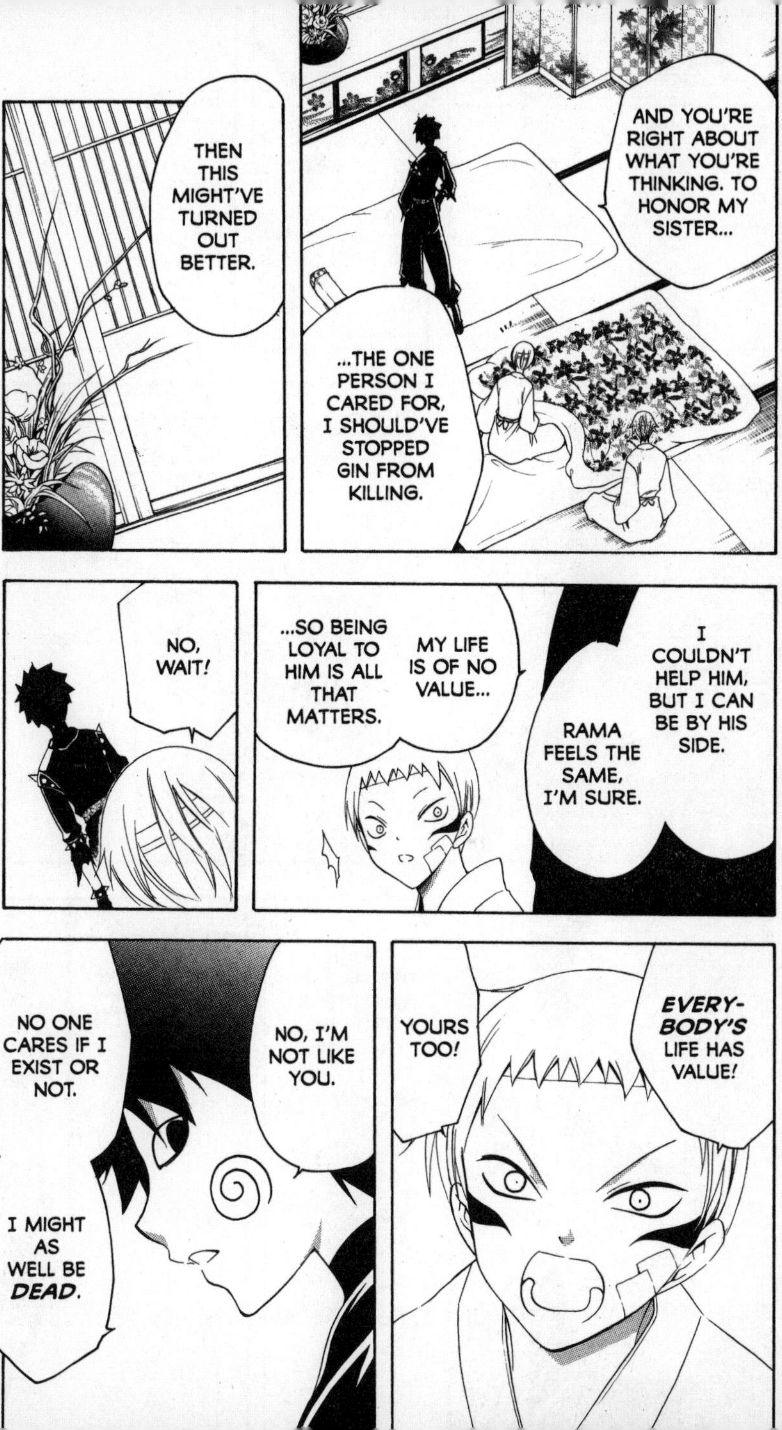
AND YOU'RE RIGHT ABOUT WHAT YOU'RE THINKING. TO HONOR MY SISTER...
...THE ONE PERSON I CARED FOR, I SHOULD'VE STOPPED GIN FROM KILLING.
THEN THIS MIGHT'VE TURNED OUT BETTER.
I COULDN'T HELP HIM, BUT I CAN BE BY HIS SIDE.
RAMA FEELS THE SAME, I'M SURE.
MY LIFE IS OF NO VALUE...
...SO BEING LOYAL TO HIM IS ALL THAT MATTERS.
NO, WAIT!
EVERYBODY'S LIFE HAS VALUE!
YOURS TOO!
NO, I'M NOT LIKE YOU.
NO ONE CARES IF I EXIST OR NOT.
I MIGHT AS WELL BE *DEAD*.

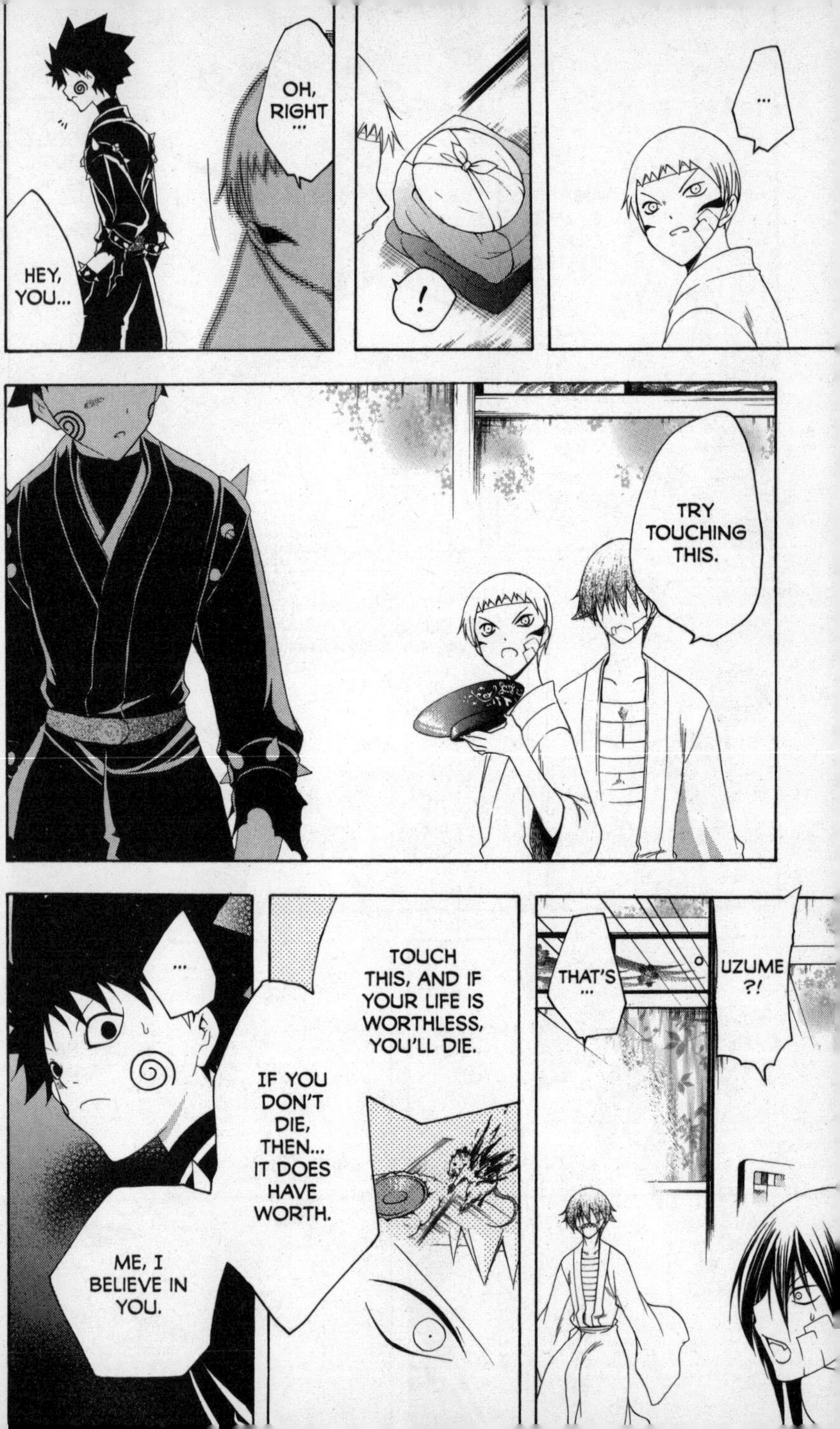
...
!
OH, RIGHT ...
HEY, YOU...
TRY TOUCHING THIS.
UZUME ?!
THAT'S ...
TOUCH THIS, AND IF YOUR LIFE IS WORTHLESS, YOU'LL DIE.
IF YOU DON'T DIE, THEN... IT DOES HAVE WORTH.
...
ME, I BELIEVE IN YOU.

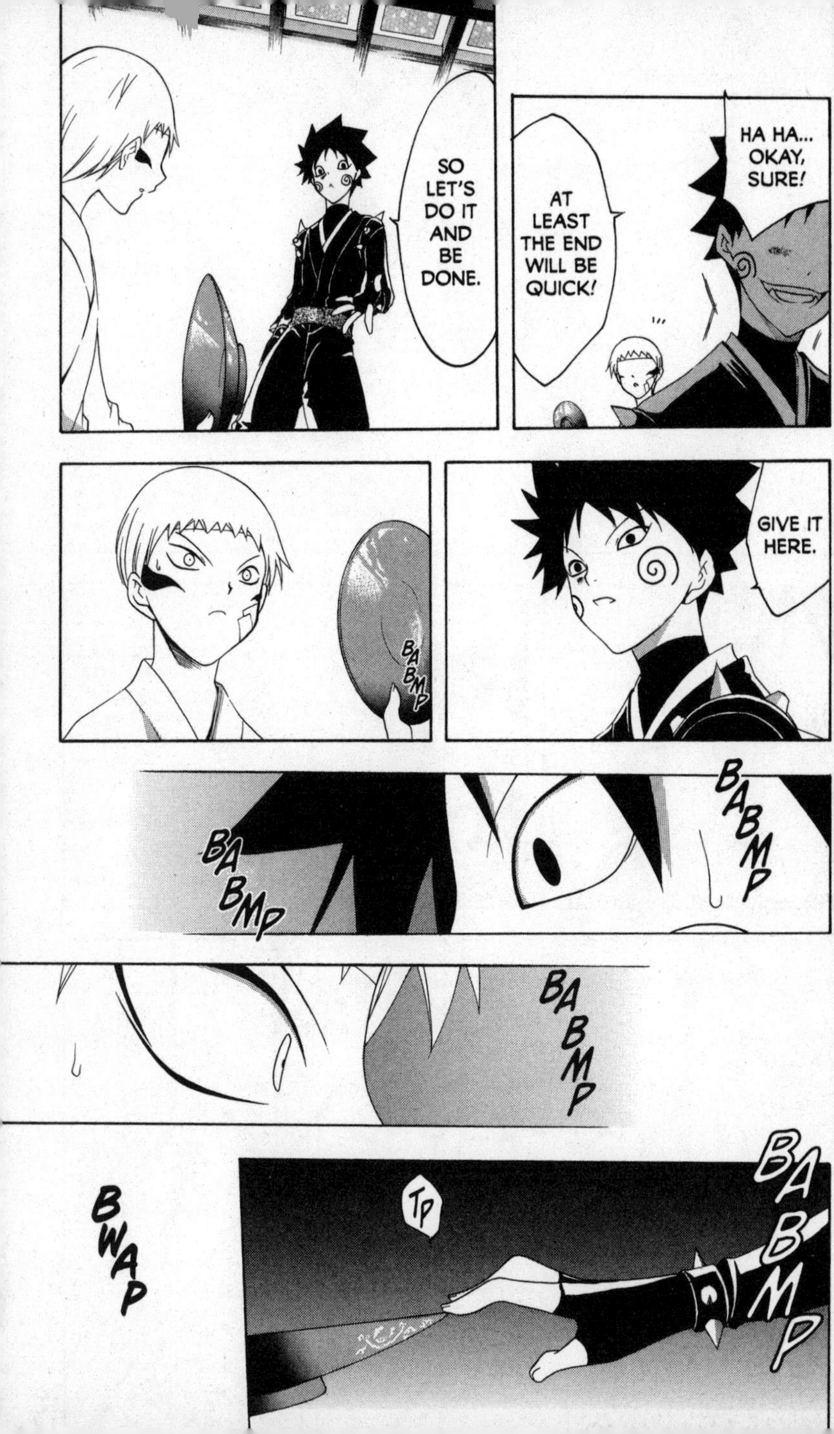
HA HA... OKAY, SURE!
AT LEAST THE END WILL BE QUICK!
SO LET'S DO IT AND BE DONE.
GIVE IT HERE.
BABMP
BABMP
BABMP
BABMP
BABMP
Tp
BWAP

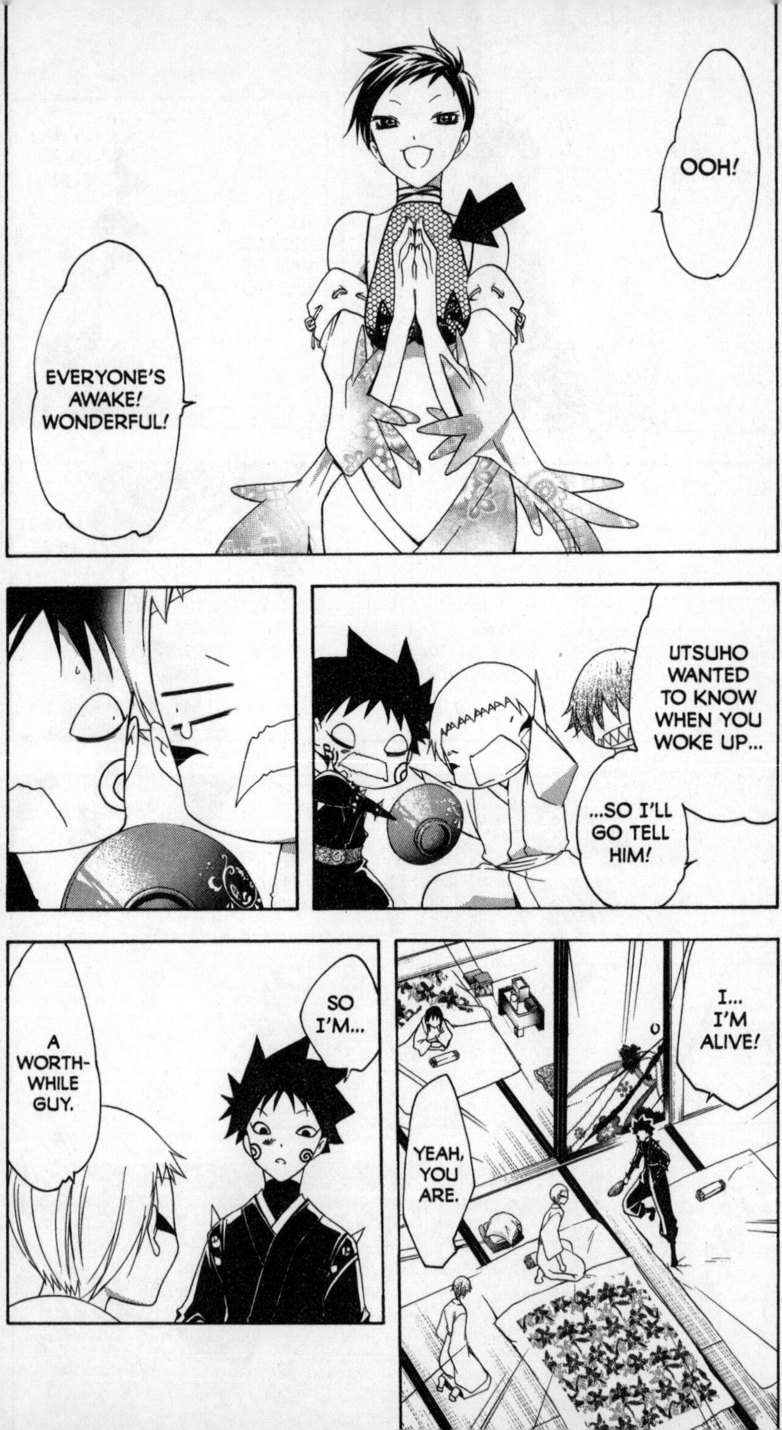
OOH!
EVERYONE'S AWAKE! WONDERFUL!
UTSUHO WANTED TO KNOW WHEN YOU WOKE UP...
...SO I'LL GO TELL HIM!
I... I'M ALIVE!
YEAH, YOU ARE.
SO I'M...
A WORTH-WHILE GUY.

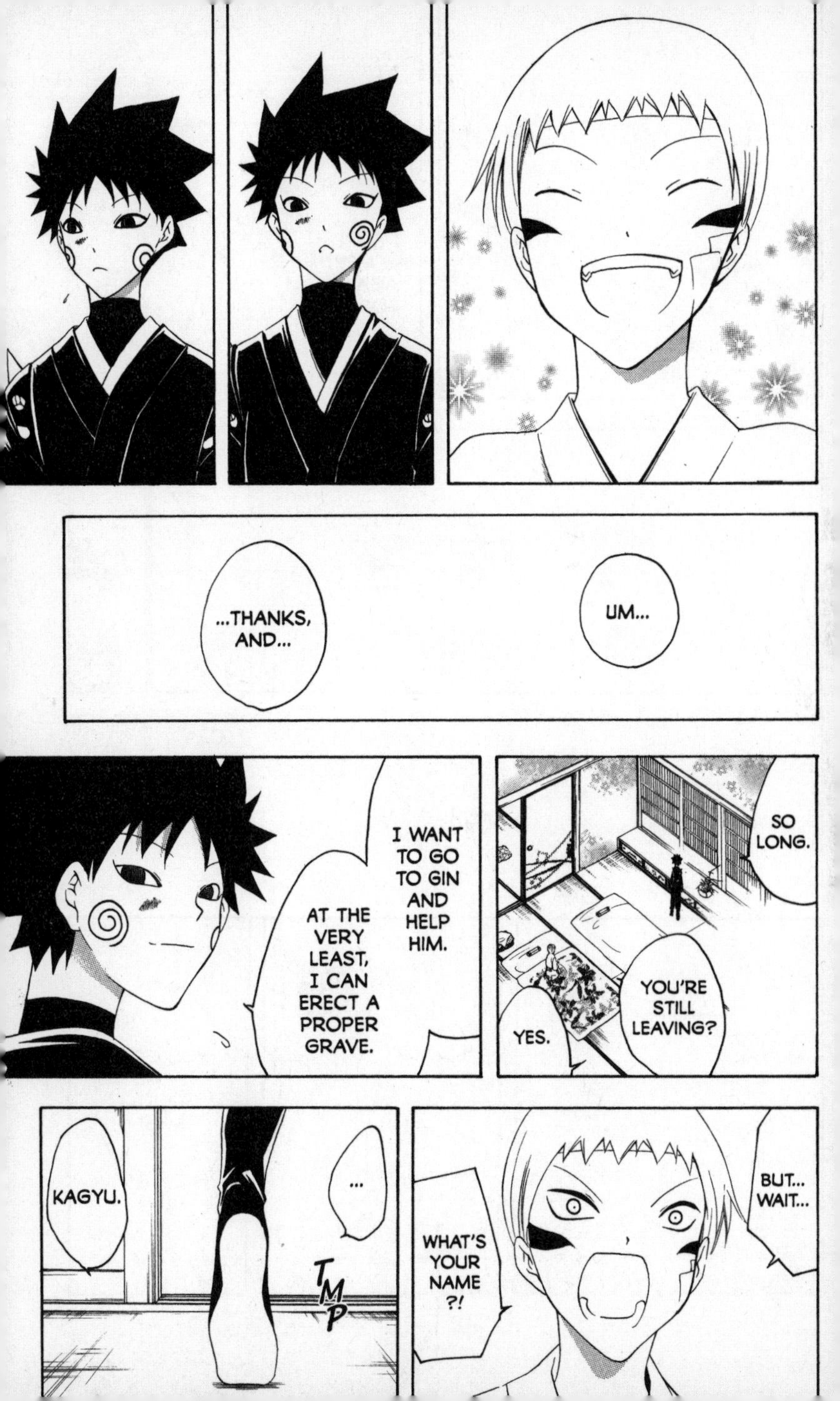
UM...
...THANKS, AND...
SO LONG.
YOU'RE STILL LEAVING?
YES.
I WANT TO GO TO GIN AND HELP HIM.
AT THE VERY LEAST, I CAN ERECT A PROPER GRAVE.
BUT... WAIT...
WHAT'S YOUR NAME ?!
...
TMP
KAGYU.

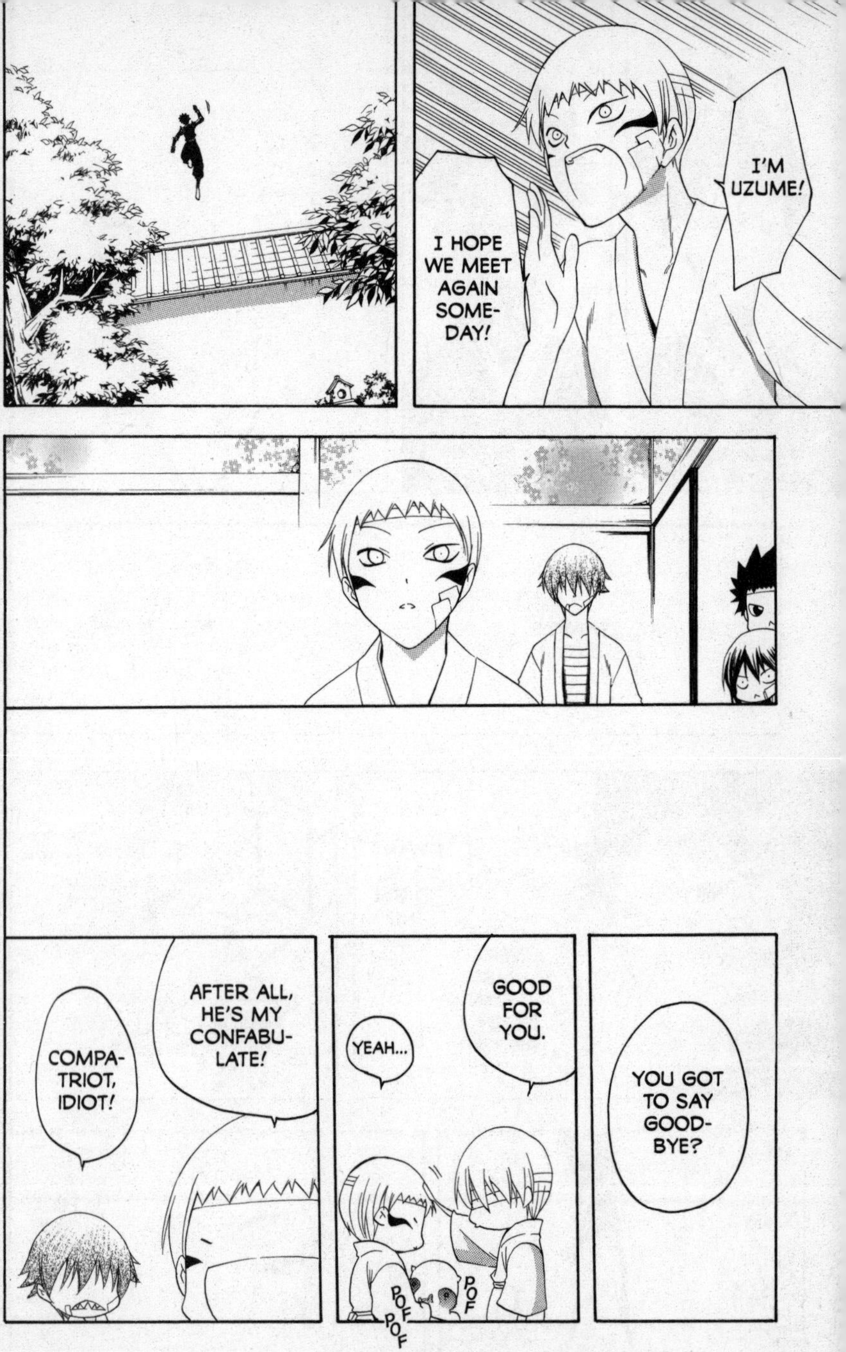
I'M UZUME!
I HOPE WE MEET AGAIN SOME-DAY!
YOU GOT TO SAY GOOD-BYE?
GOOD FOR YOU.
YEAH...
POF POF
POF POF
AFTER ALL, HE'S MY CONFABU-LATE!
COMPA-TRIOT, IDIOT!

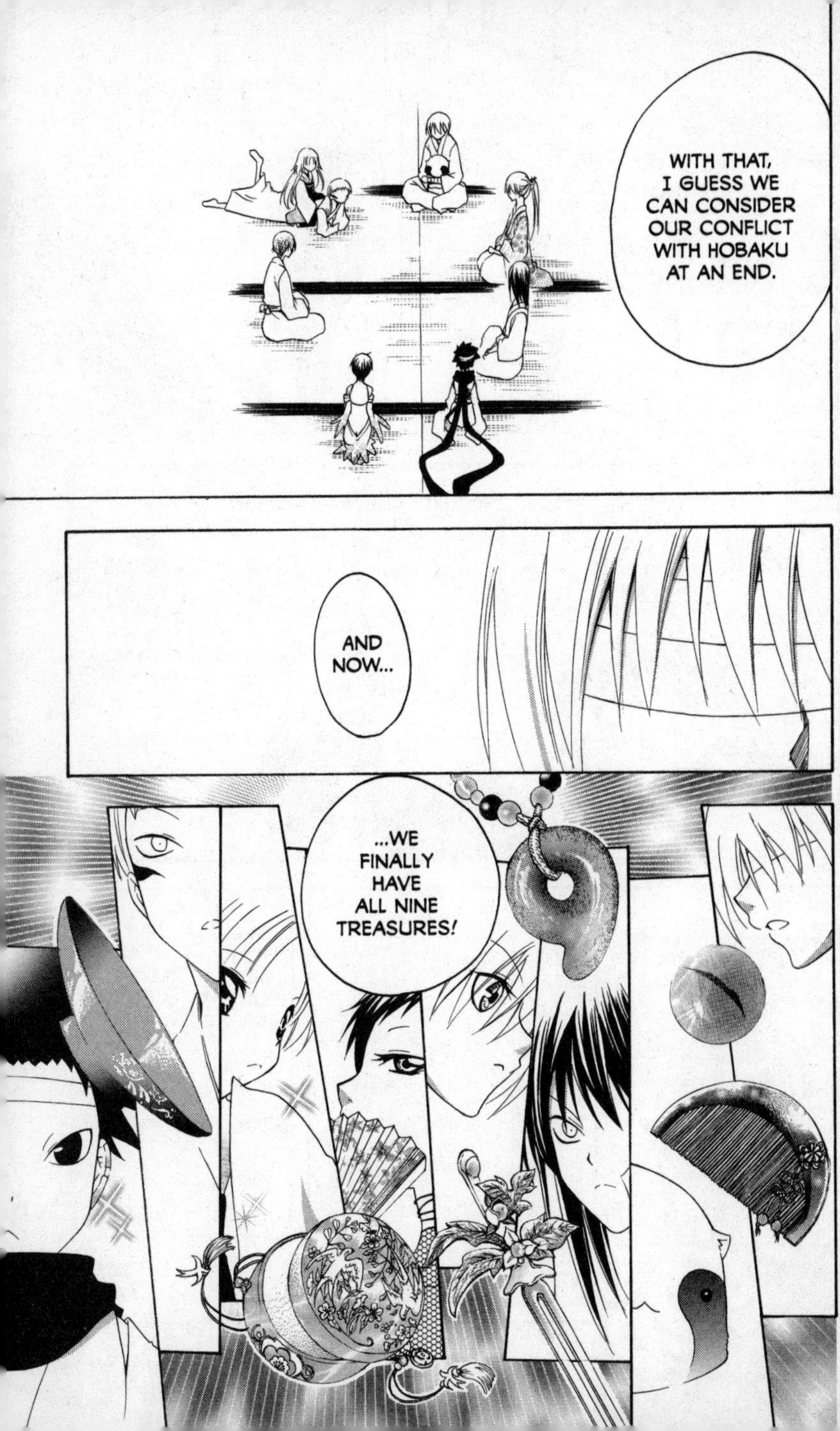
WITH THAT, I GUESS WE CAN CONSIDER OUR CONFLICT WITH HOBAKU AT AN END.
AND NOW...
...WE FINALLY HAVE ALL NINE TREASURES!

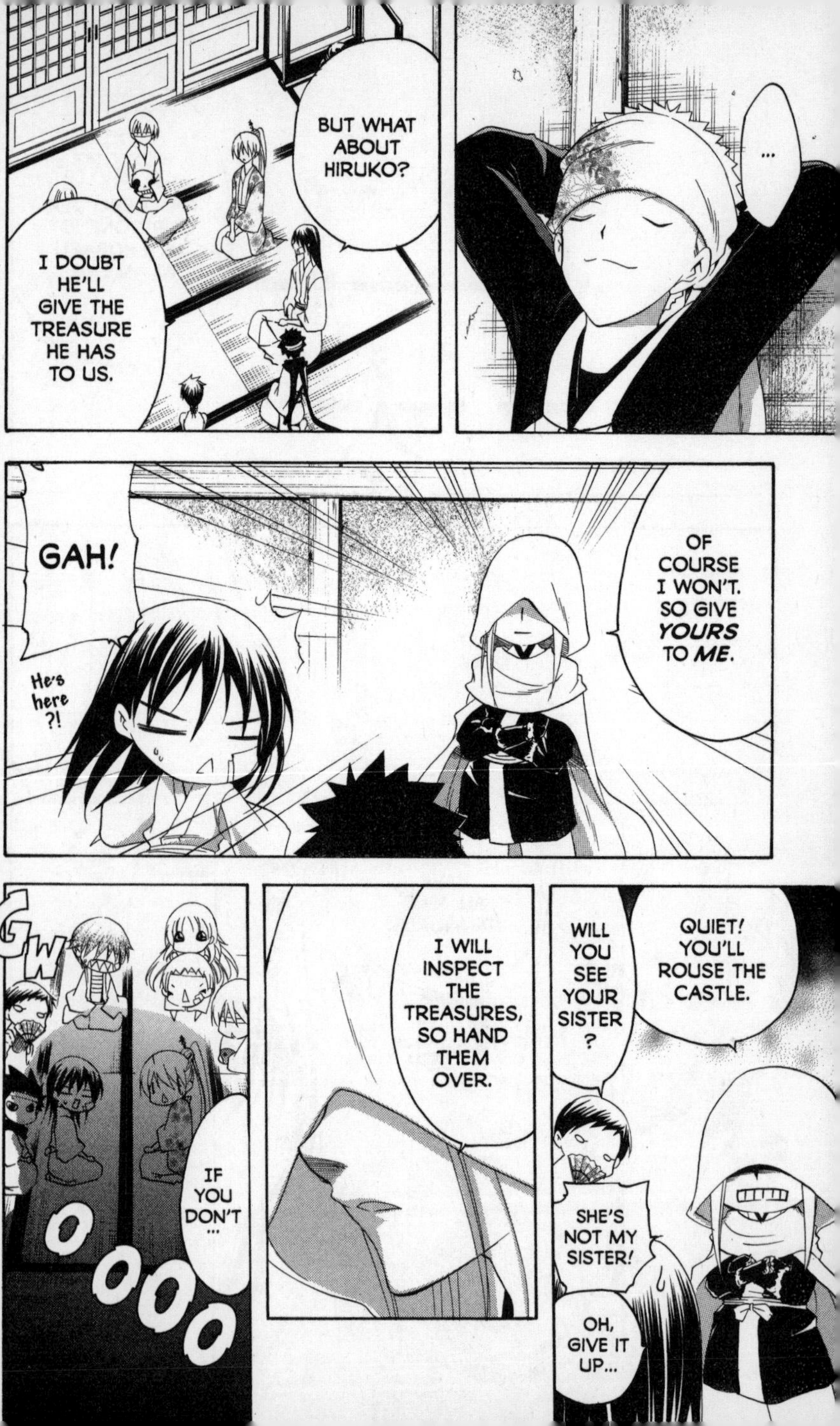
...
BUT WHAT ABOUT HIRUKO?
I DOUBT HE'LL GIVE THE TREASURE HE HAS TO US.
OF COURSE I WON'T. SO GIVE *YOURS* TO *ME*.
GAH!
He's here?!
QUIET! YOU'LL ROUSE THE CASTLE.
WILL YOU SEE YOUR SISTER?
SHE'S NOT MY SISTER!
OH, GIVE IT UP...
I WILL INSPECT THE TREASURES, SO HAND THEM OVER.
GWOOOO
IF YOU DON'T...

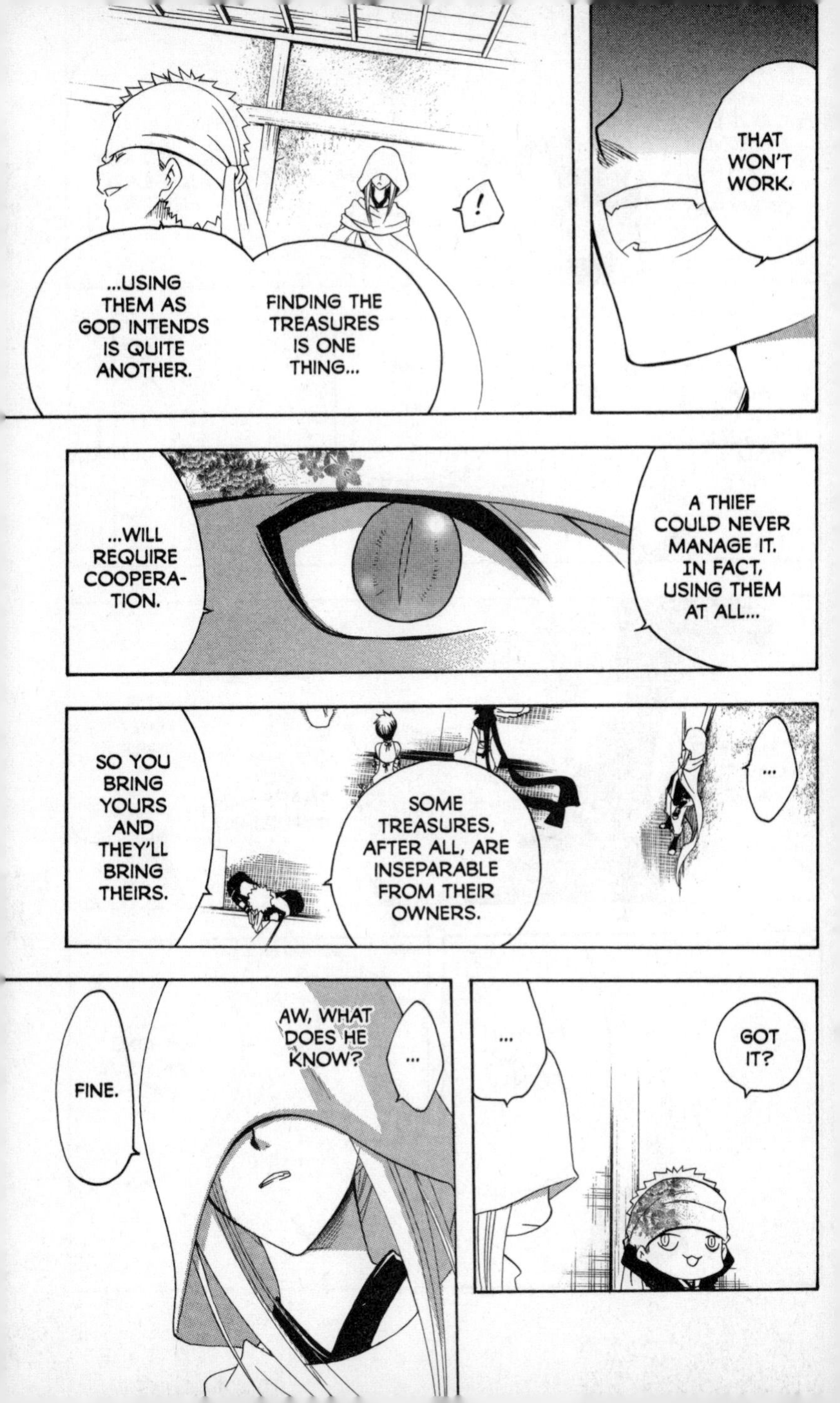
THAT WON'T WORK.
!
FINDING THE TREASURES IS ONE THING...
...USING THEM AS GOD INTENDS IS QUITE ANOTHER.
A THIEF COULD NEVER MANAGE IT. IN FACT, USING THEM AT ALL...
...WILL REQUIRE COOPERATION.
...
SOME TREASURES, AFTER ALL, ARE INSEPARABLE FROM THEIR OWNERS.
SO YOU BRING YOURS AND THEY'LL BRING THEIRS.
GOT IT?
...
...
AW, WHAT DOES HE KNOW?
FINE.

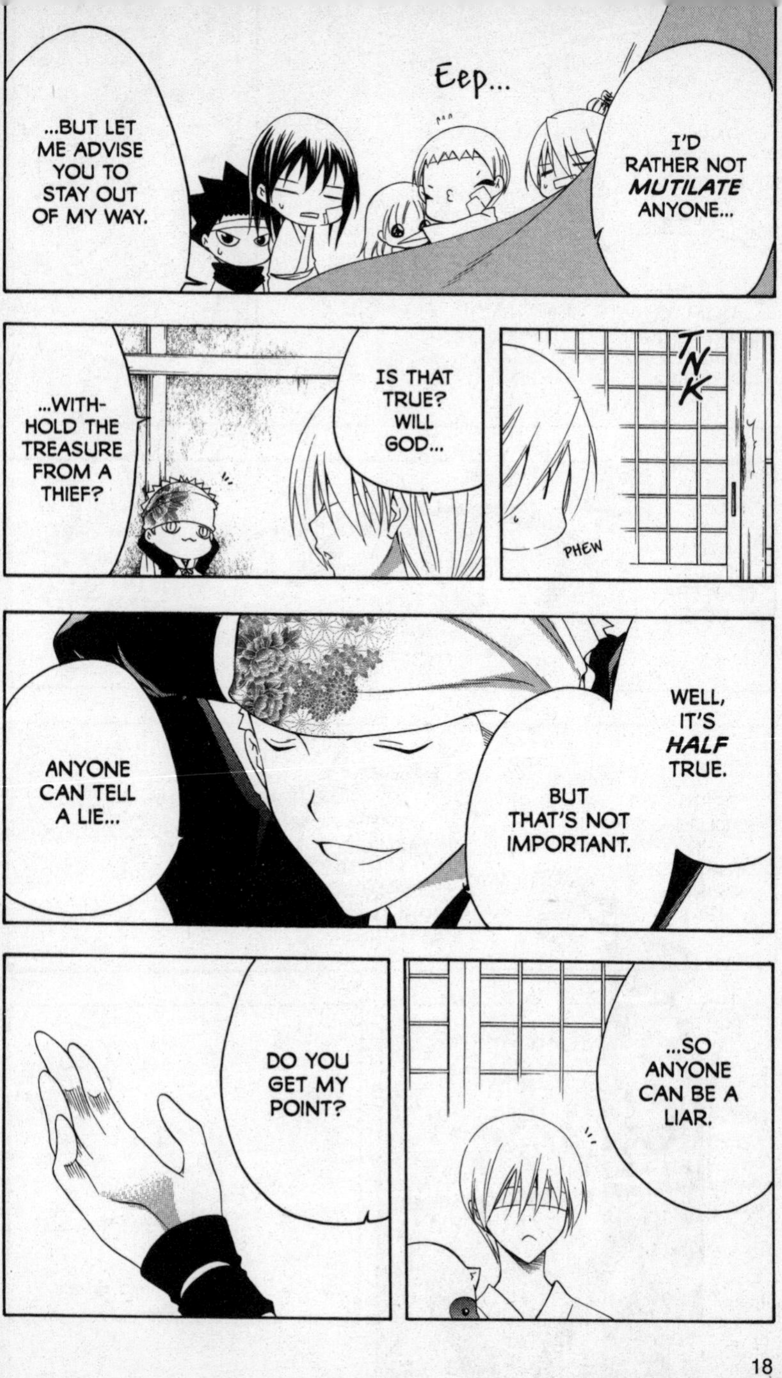
I'D RATHER NOT MUTILATE ANYONE...
Eep...
...BUT LET ME ADVISE YOU TO STAY OUT OF MY WAY.
TNK
PHEW
IS THAT TRUE? WILL GOD...
...WITH-HOLD THE TREASURE FROM A THIEF?
WELL, IT'S HALF TRUE.
BUT THAT'S NOT IMPORTANT.
ANYONE CAN TELL A LIE...
...SO ANYONE CAN BE A LIAR.
DO YOU GET MY POINT?

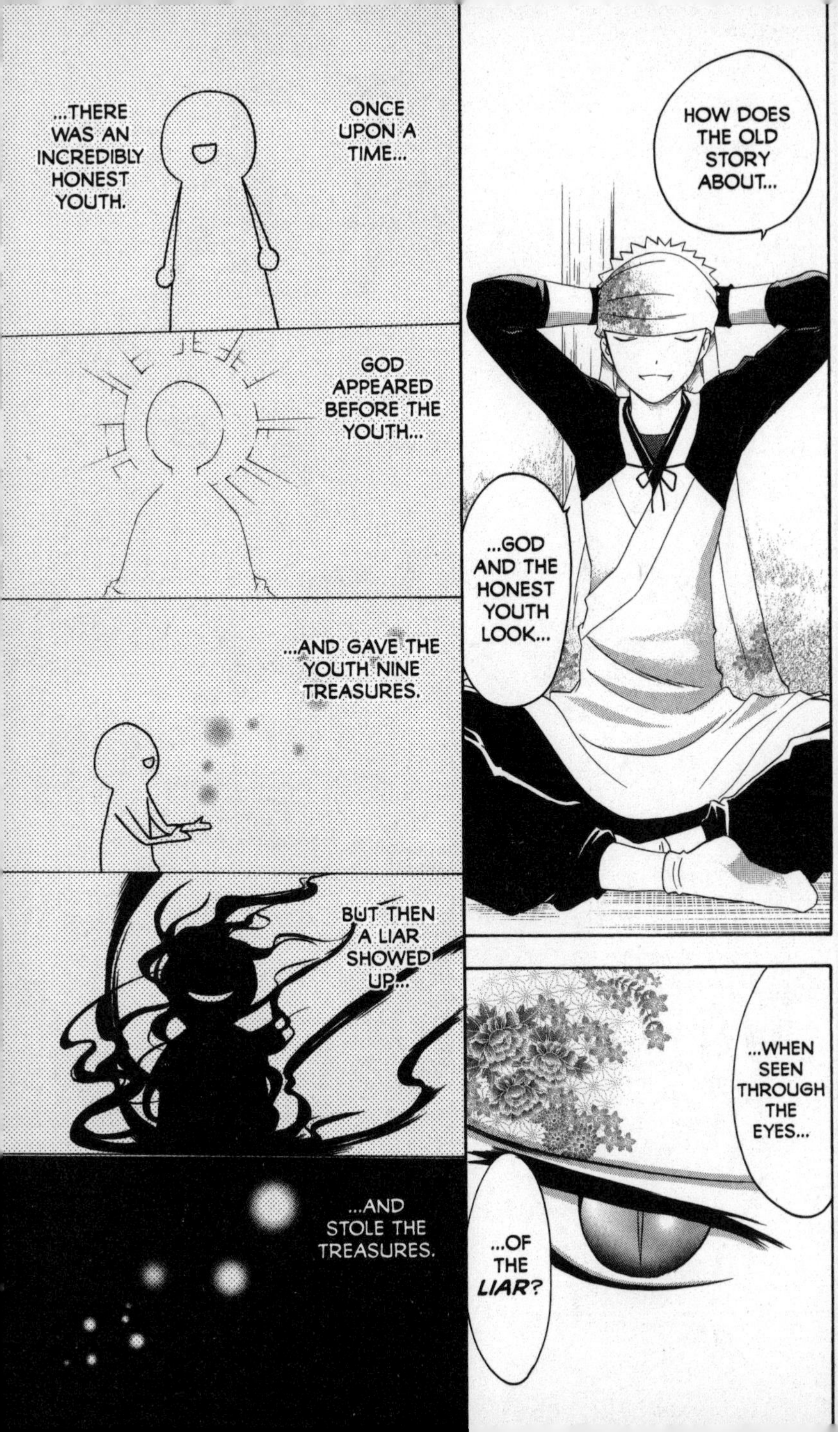
HOW DOES THE OLD STORY ABOUT...
...GOD AND THE HONEST YOUTH LOOK...
...WHEN SEEN THROUGH THE EYES...
...OF THE *LIAR*?
ONCE UPON A TIME...
...THERE WAS AN INCREDIBLY HONEST YOUTH.
GOD APPEARED BEFORE THE YOUTH...
...AND GAVE THE YOUTH NINE TREASURES.
BUT THEN A LIAR SHOWED UP...
...AND STOLE THE TREASURES.

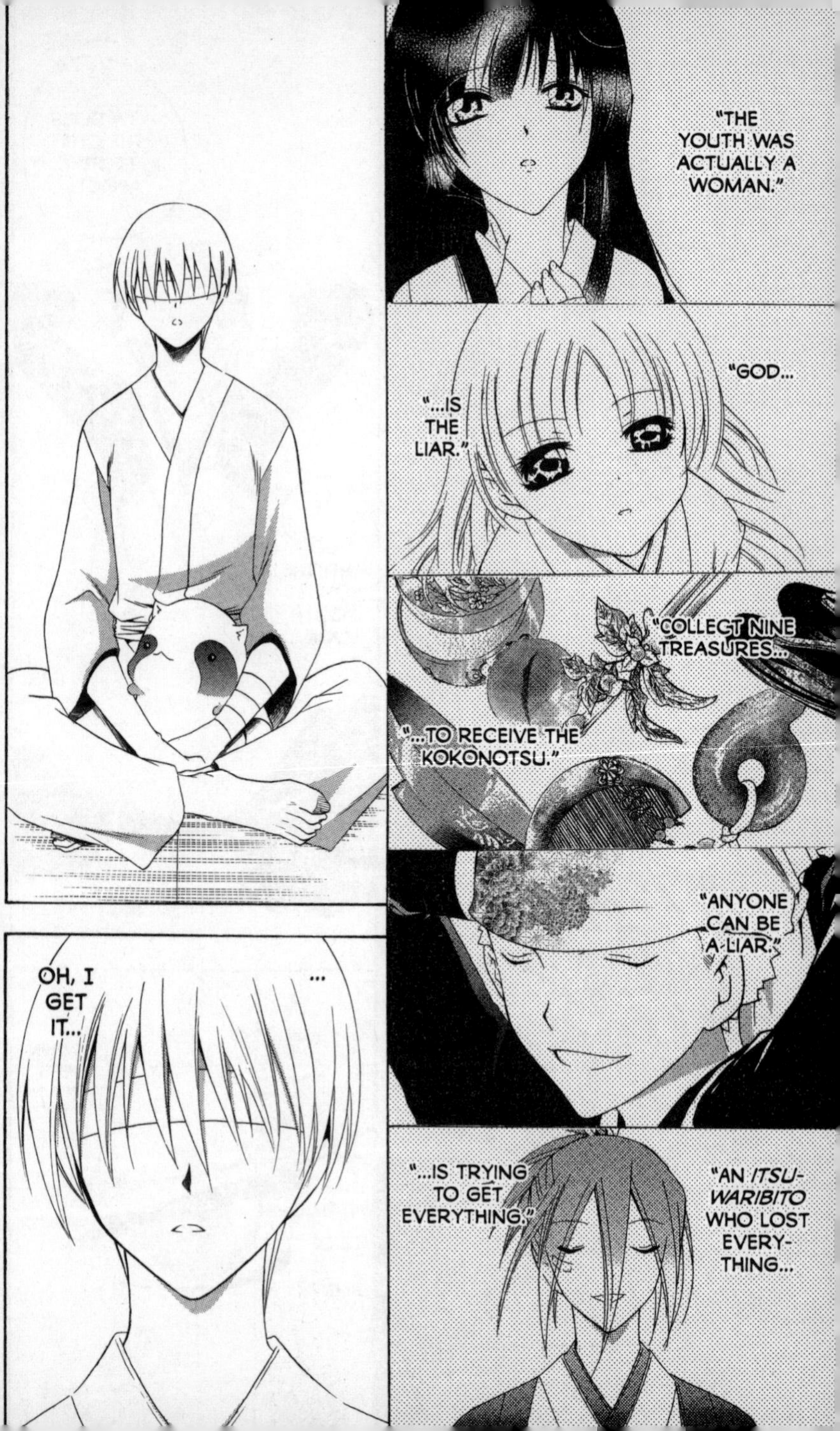
"THE YOUTH WAS ACTUALLY A WOMAN."
"GOD...
"...IS THE LIAR."
"COLLECT NINE TREASURES...
"...TO RECEIVE THE KOKONOTSU."
"ANYONE CAN BE A LIAR."
"AN *ITSU-WARIBITO* WHO LOST EVERY-THING...
"...IS TRYING TO GET EVERYTHING."
...
OH, I GET IT...

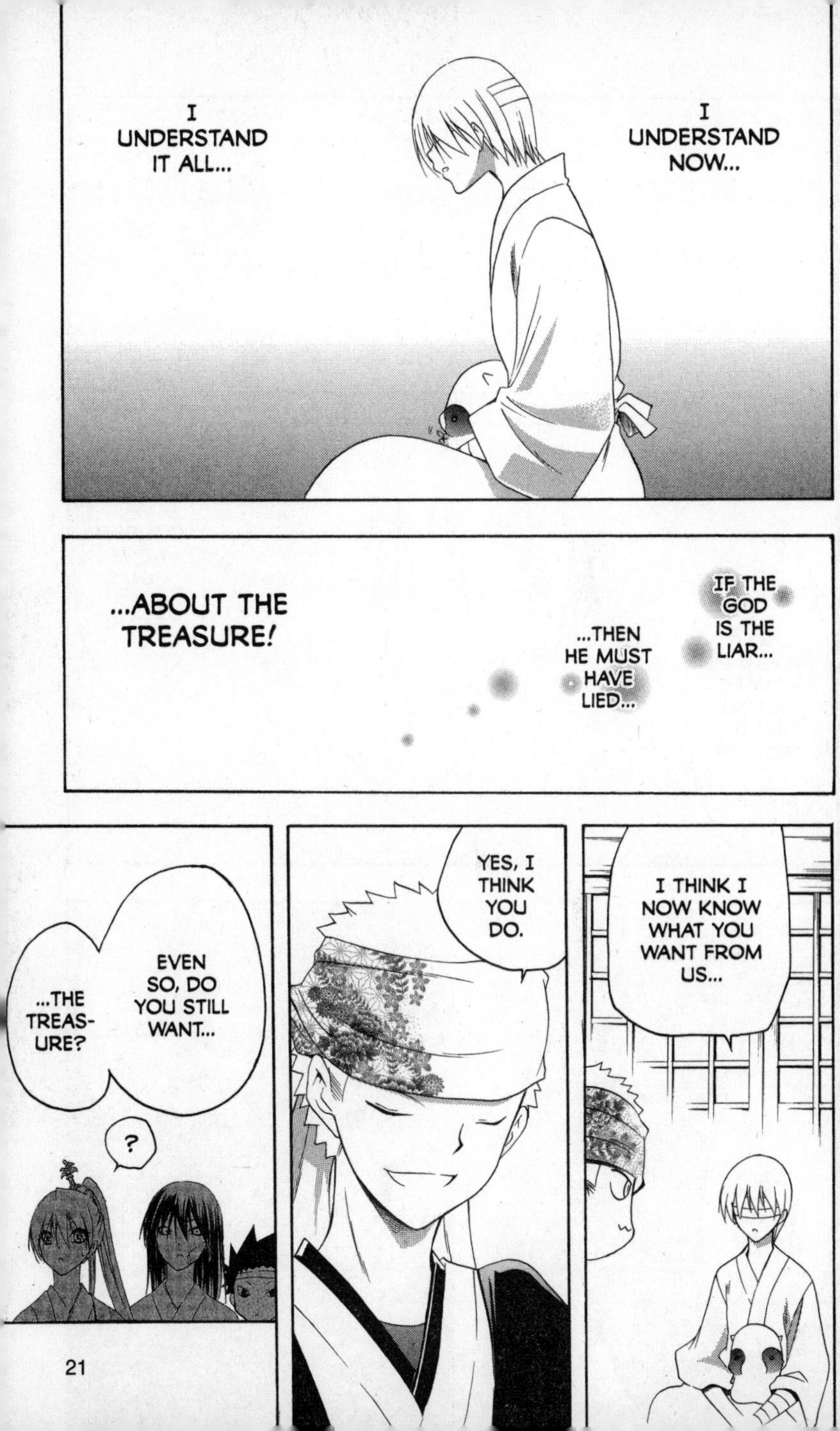
I UNDERSTAND NOW...
I UNDERSTAND IT ALL...
IF THE GOD IS THE LIAR...
...THEN HE MUST HAVE LIED...
...ABOUT THE TREASURE!
I THINK I NOW KNOW WHAT YOU WANT FROM US...
YES, I THINK YOU DO.
EVEN SO, DO YOU STILL WANT...
...THE TREAS-URE?
?

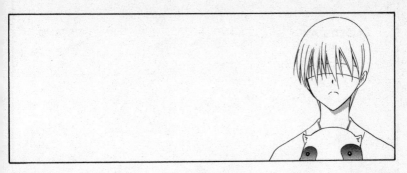

OF COURSE! WE'VE COME THIS FAR...

...SO IT WOULD BE A SHAME NOT TO SEE IT THROUGH!

SO LET'S...

...GO FIND GOD!

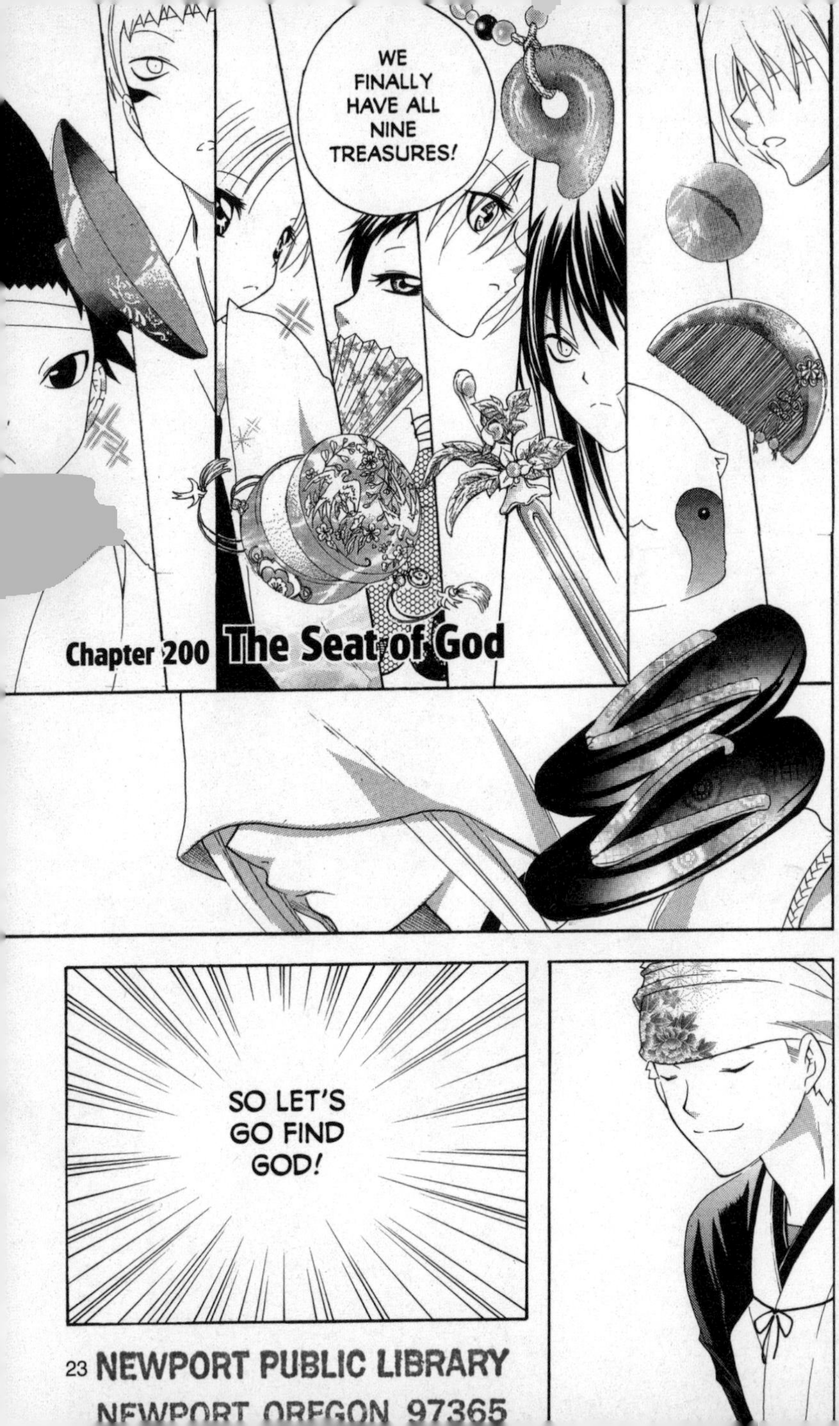
WE FINALLY HAVE ALL NINE TREASURES!
Chapter 200 The Seat of God
SO LET'S GO FIND GOD!

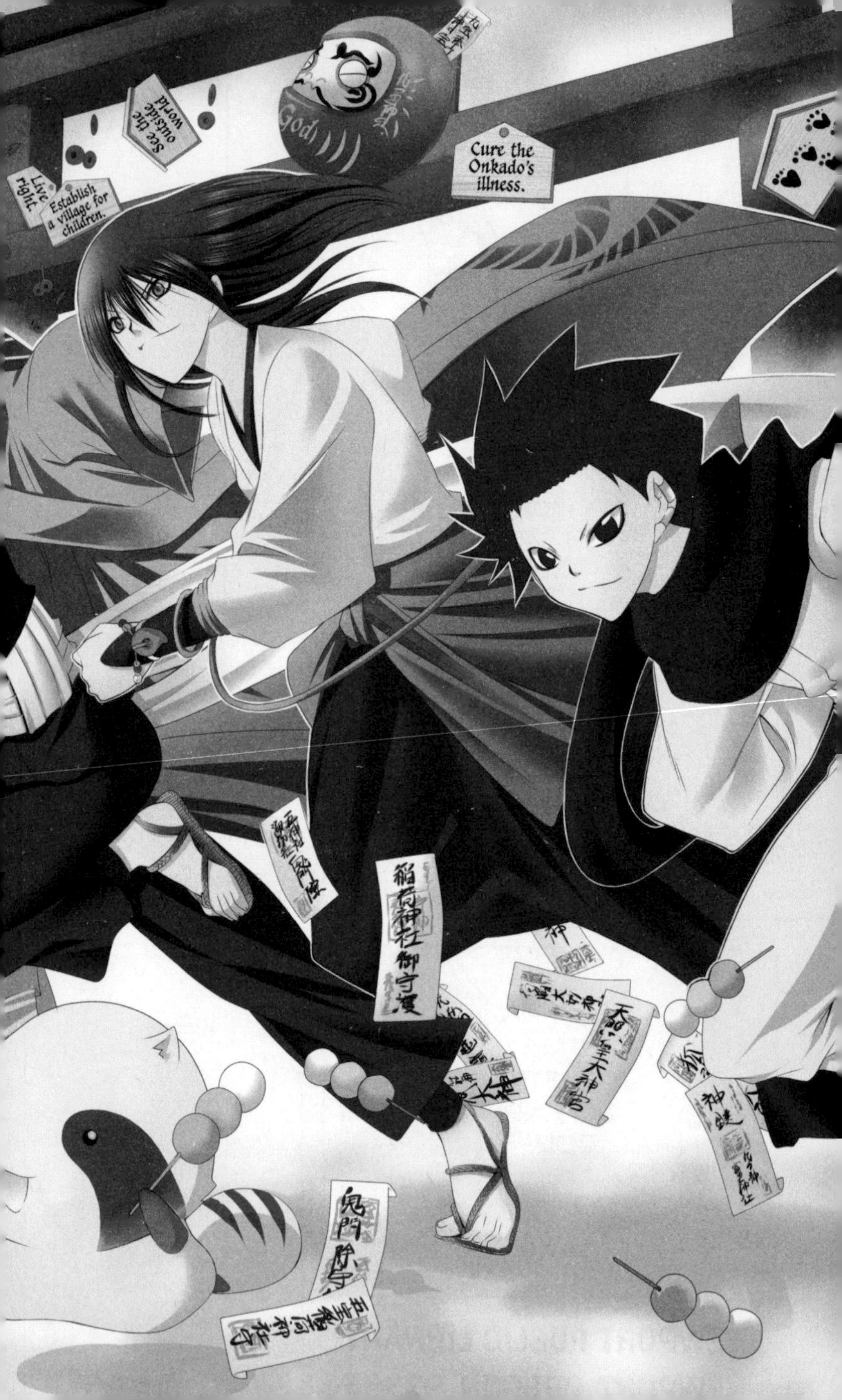
God
See the outside world
Cure the Onkado's illness.
Live right.
Establish a village for children.
稲荷神社御守護

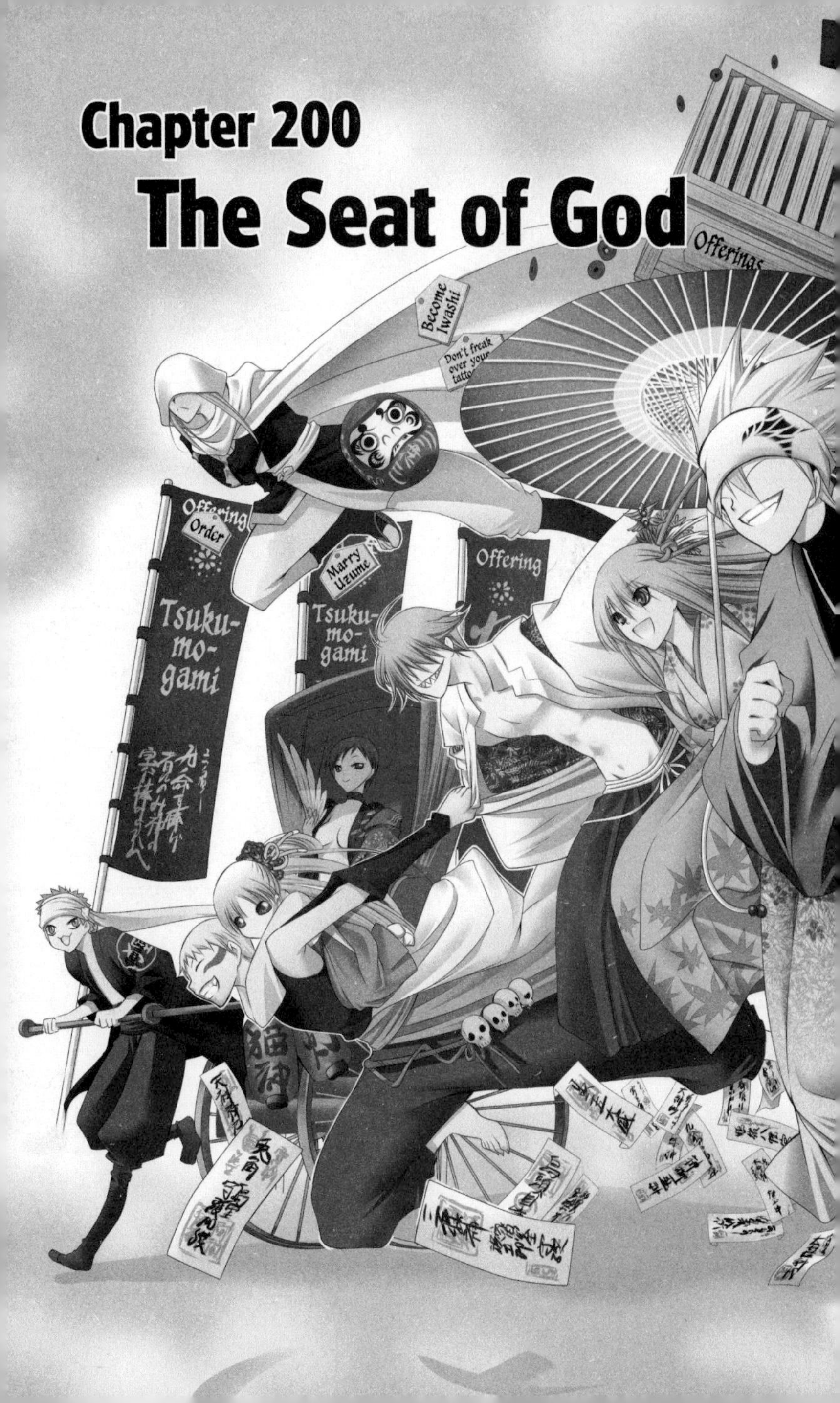
Chapter 200
The Seat of God
Offerings
Become Iwashi
Don't freak over your tatto
Offering
Order
Tsuku-mo-gami
Marry Uzume
Tsuku-mo-gami
Offering

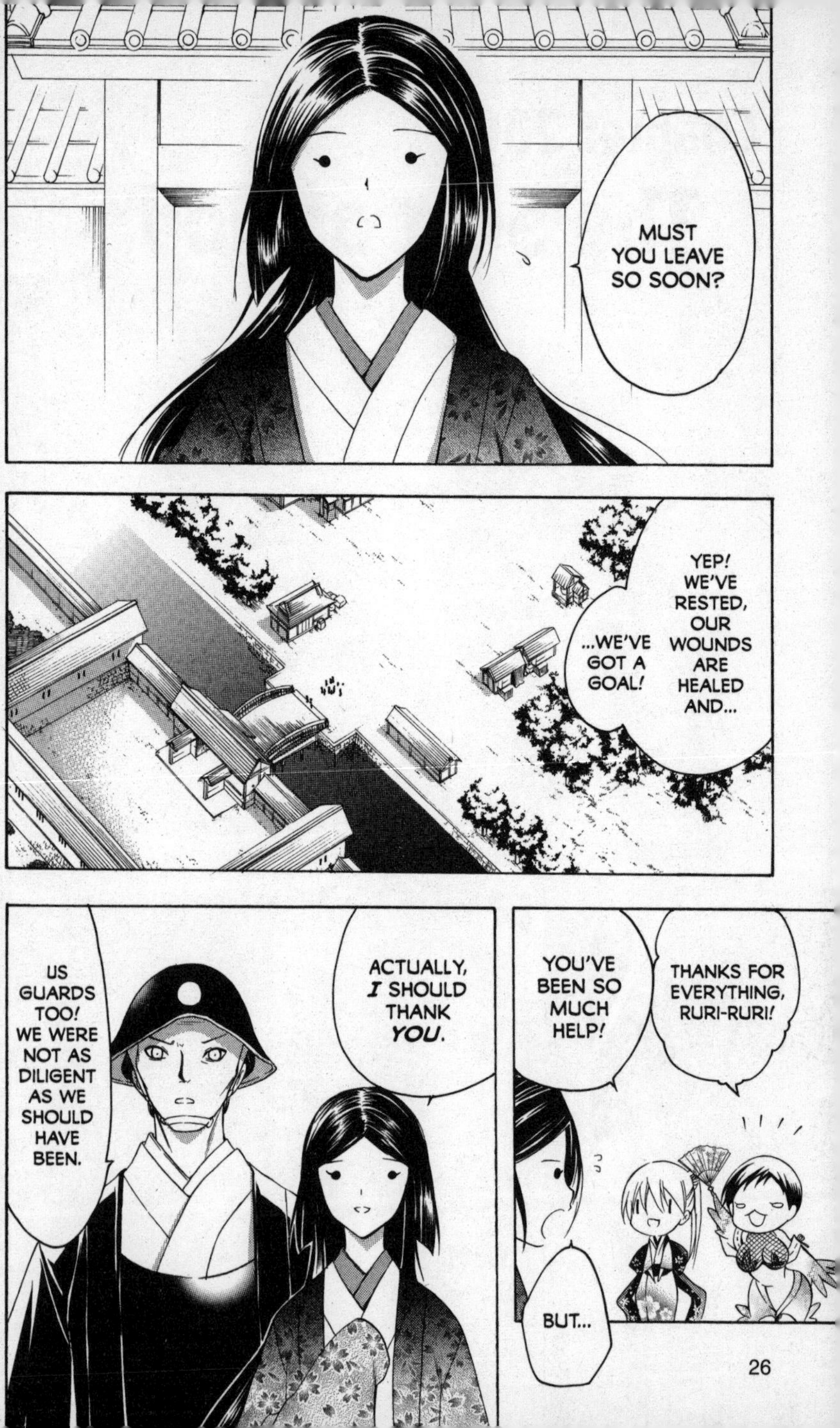

MUST YOU LEAVE SO SOON?
YEP! WE'VE RESTED, OUR WOUNDS ARE HEALED AND...
...WE'VE GOT A GOAL!
THANKS FOR EVERYTHING, RURI-RURI!
YOU'VE BEEN SO MUCH HELP!
BUT...
ACTUALLY, *I* SHOULD THANK ***YOU***.
US GUARDS TOO! WE WERE NOT AS DILIGENT AS WE SHOULD HAVE BEEN.

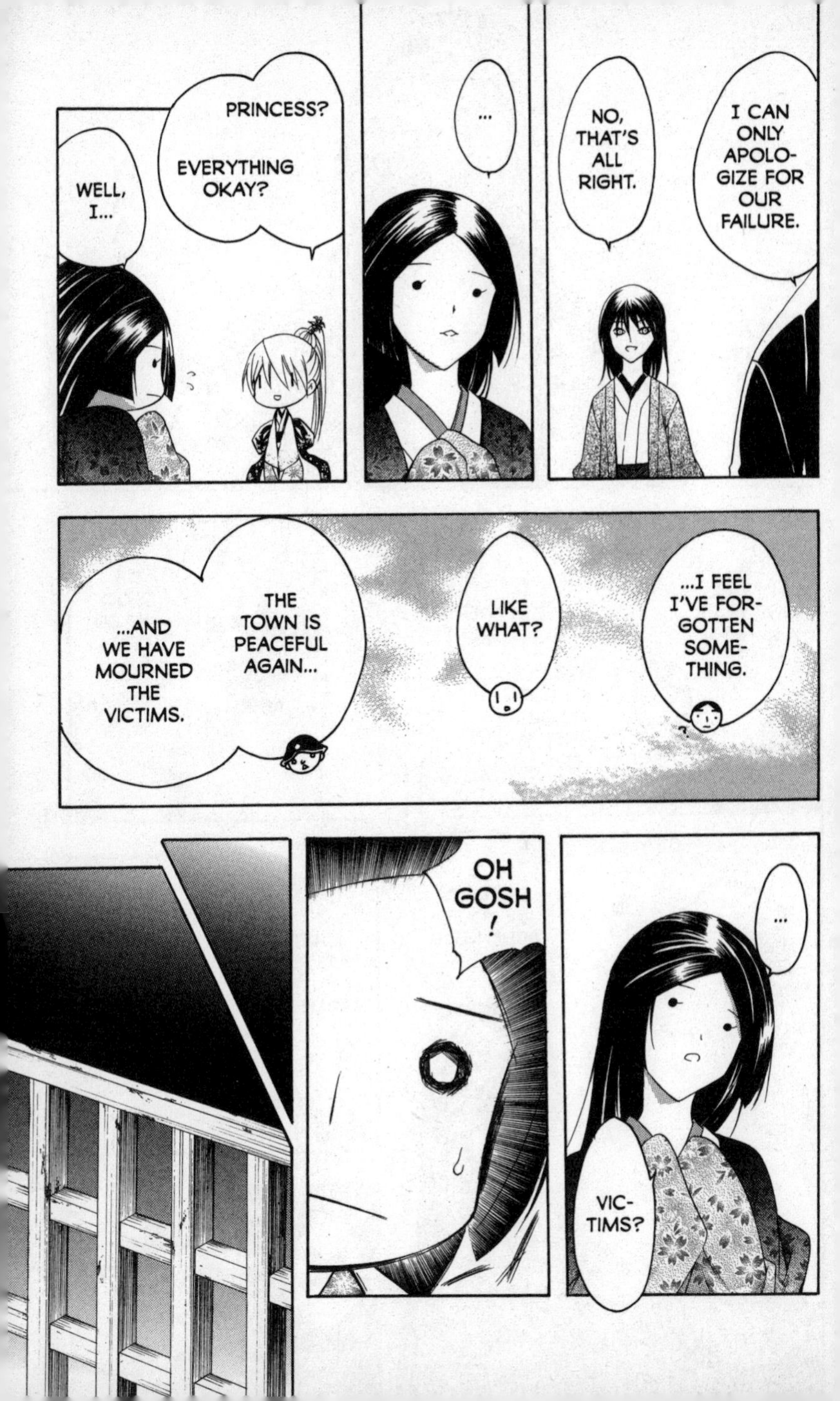
I CAN ONLY APOLOGIZE FOR OUR FAILURE.
NO, THAT'S ALL RIGHT.
...
PRINCESS?
EVERYTHING OKAY?
WELL, I...
...I FEEL I'VE FORGOTTEN SOMETHING.
LIKE WHAT?
THE TOWN IS PEACEFUL AGAIN...
...AND WE HAVE MOURNED THE VICTIMS.
...
VICTIMS?
OH GOSH!

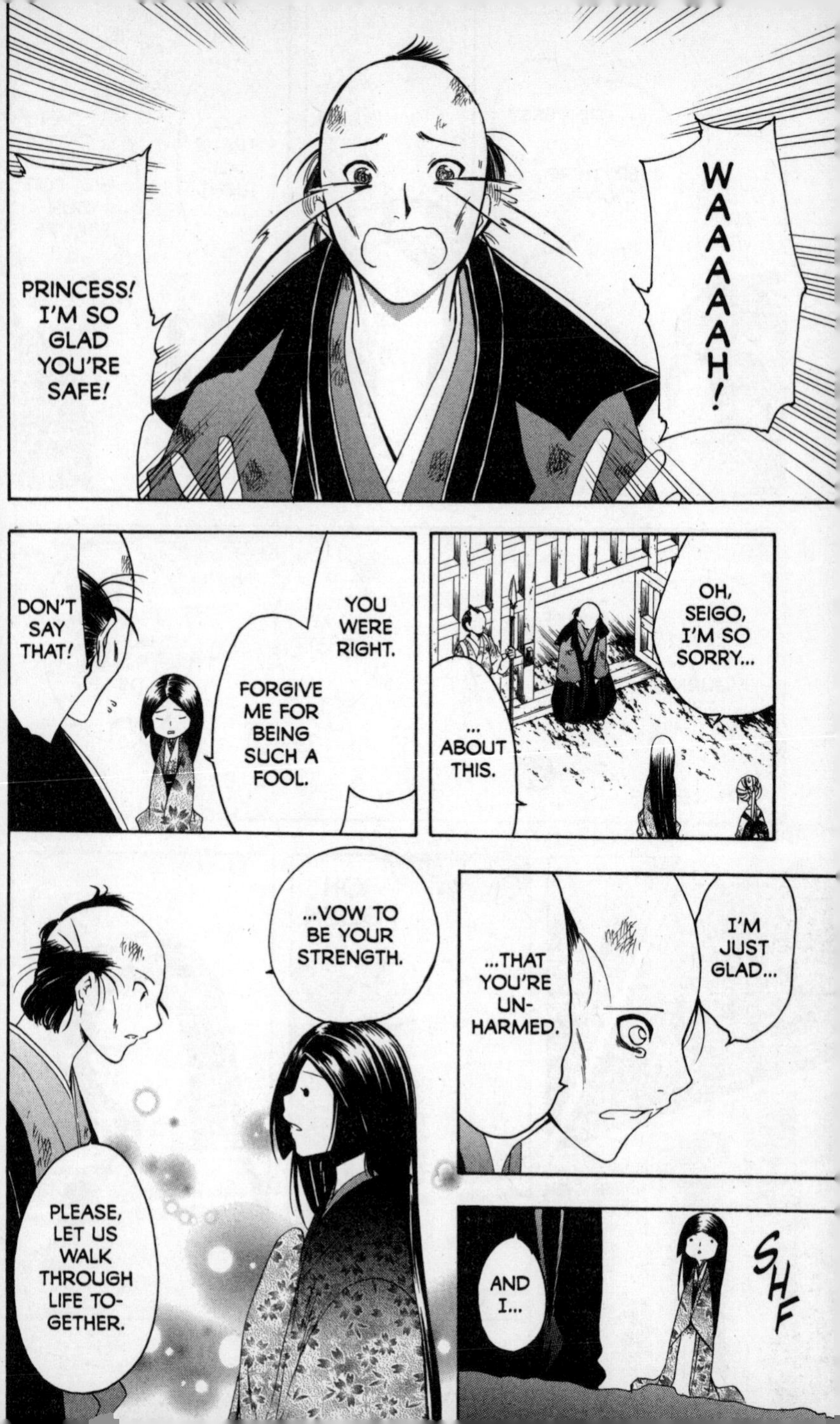
WAAAAAH!
PRINCESS! I'M SO GLAD YOU'RE SAFE!
OH, SEIGO, I'M SO SORRY...
...ABOUT THIS.
YOU WERE RIGHT.
FORGIVE ME FOR BEING SUCH A FOOL.
DON'T SAY THAT!
I'M JUST GLAD...
...THAT YOU'RE UN-HARMED.
SHF
AND I...
...VOW TO BE YOUR STRENGTH.
PLEASE, LET US WALK THROUGH LIFE TO-GETHER.

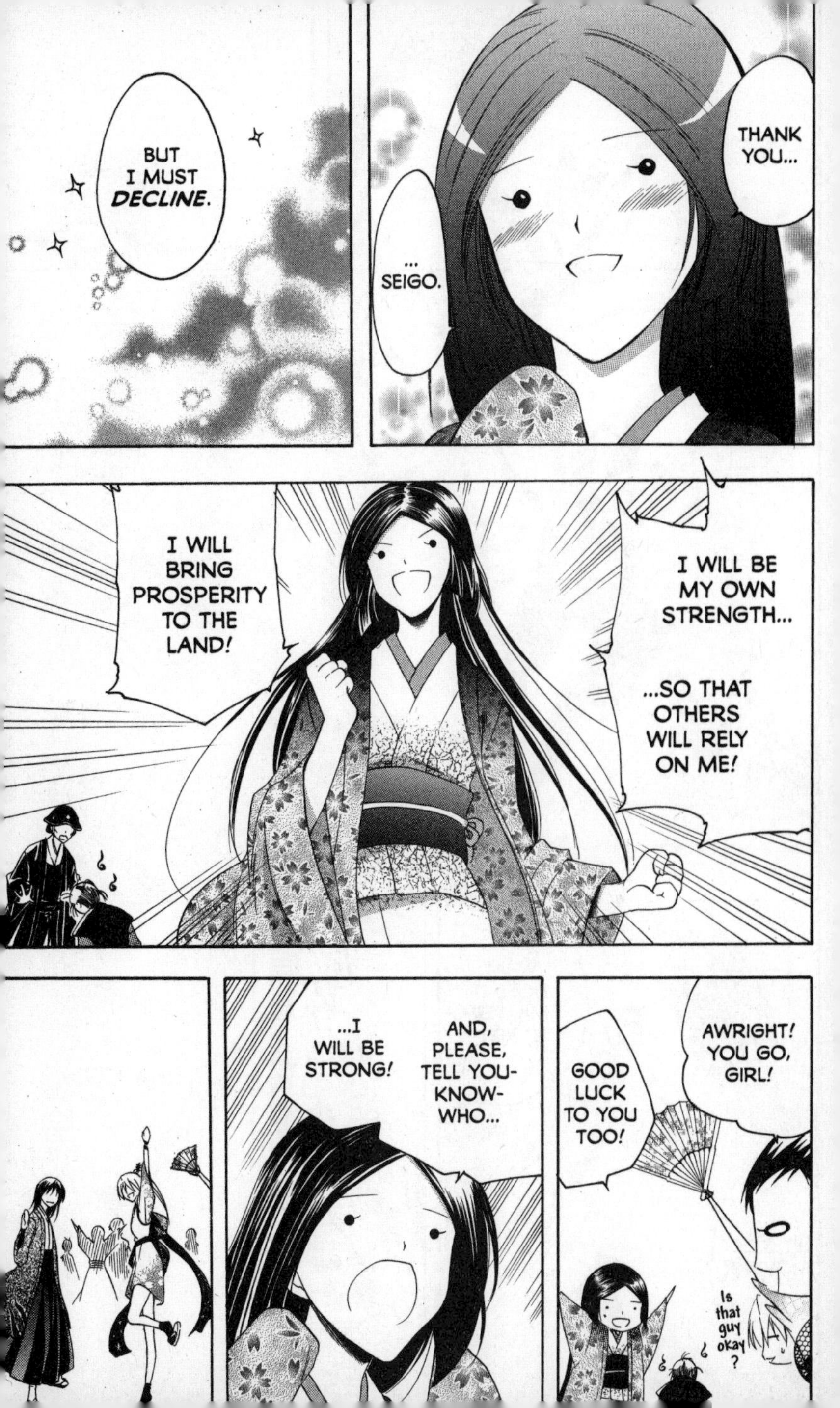
THANK YOU...
...SEIGO.
BUT I MUST *DECLINE*.
I WILL BE MY OWN STRENGTH...
...SO THAT OTHERS WILL RELY ON ME!
I WILL BRING PROSPERITY TO THE LAND!
AWRIGHT! YOU GO, GIRL!
GOOD LUCK TO YOU TOO!
Is that guy okay?
AND, PLEASE, TELL YOU-KNOW-WHO...
...I WILL BE STRONG!

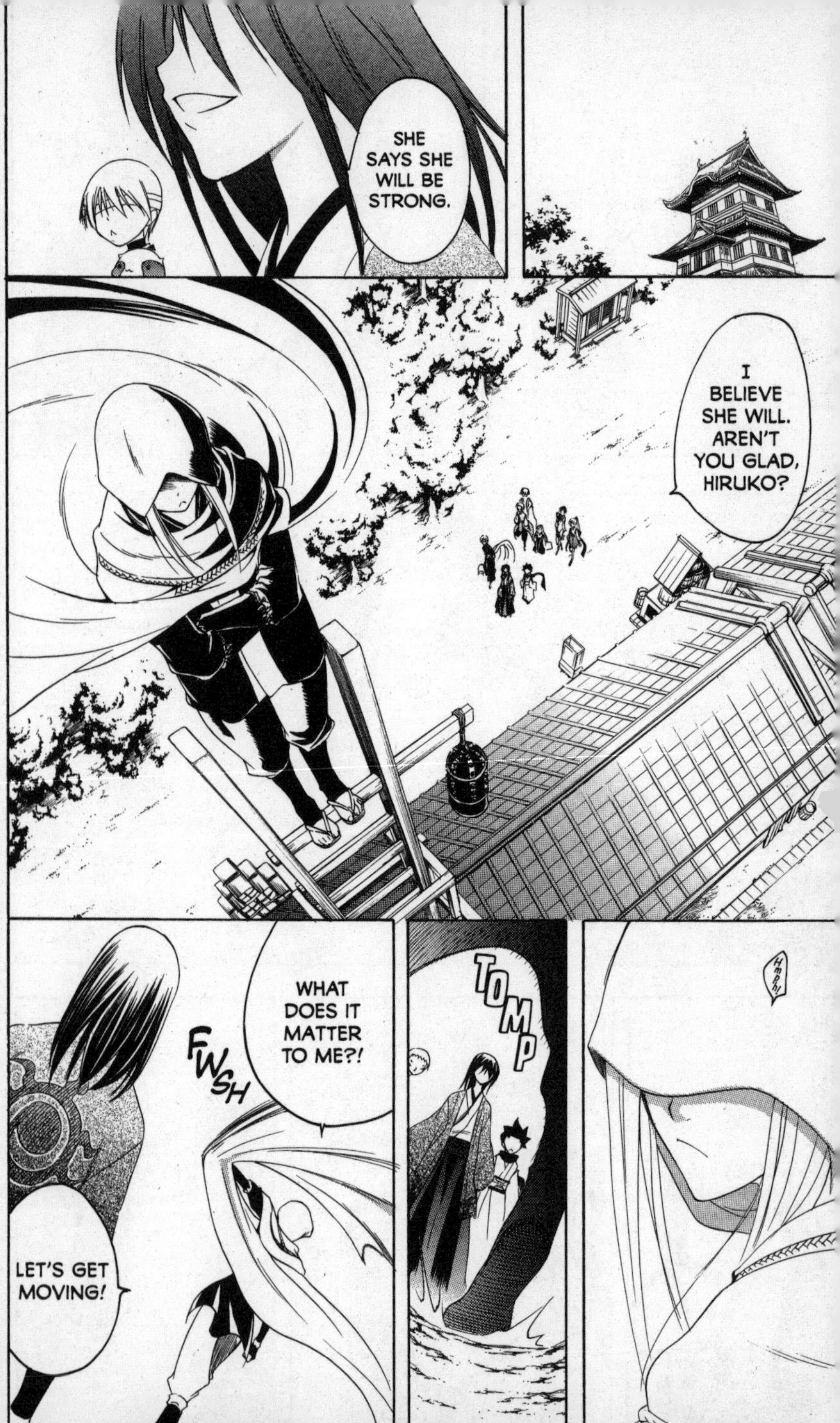
SHE SAYS SHE WILL BE STRONG.
I BELIEVE SHE WILL. AREN'T YOU GLAD, HIRUKO?
Hmph!
TOMP
WHAT DOES IT MATTER TO ME?!
FWSH
LET'S GET MOVING!

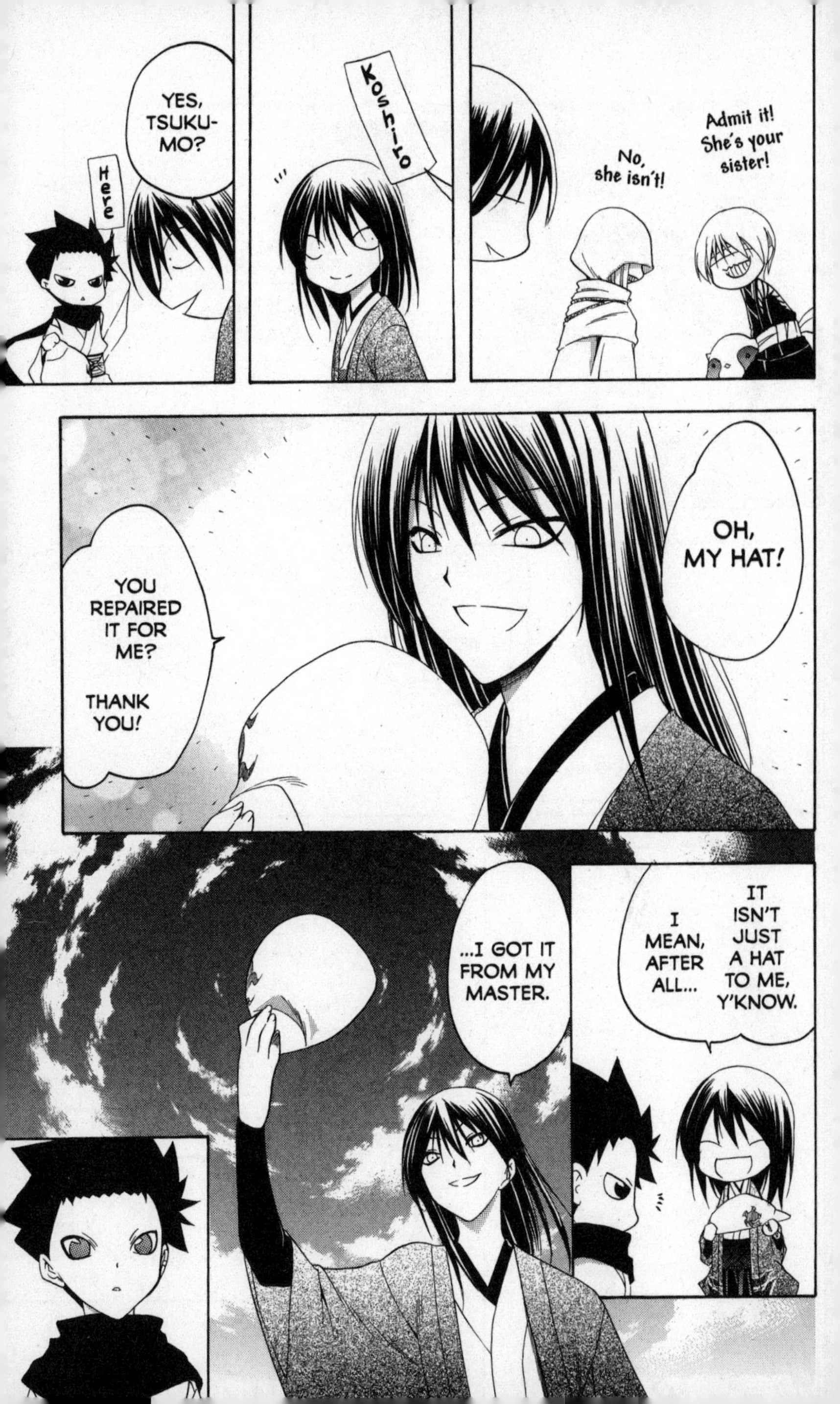
Admit it! She's your sister!
No, she isn't!
Koshiro
YES, TSUKU-MO?
Here
OH, MY HAT!
YOU REPAIRED IT FOR ME?
THANK YOU!
IT ISN'T JUST A HAT TO ME, Y'KNOW.
I MEAN, AFTER ALL...
...I GOT IT FROM MY MASTER.

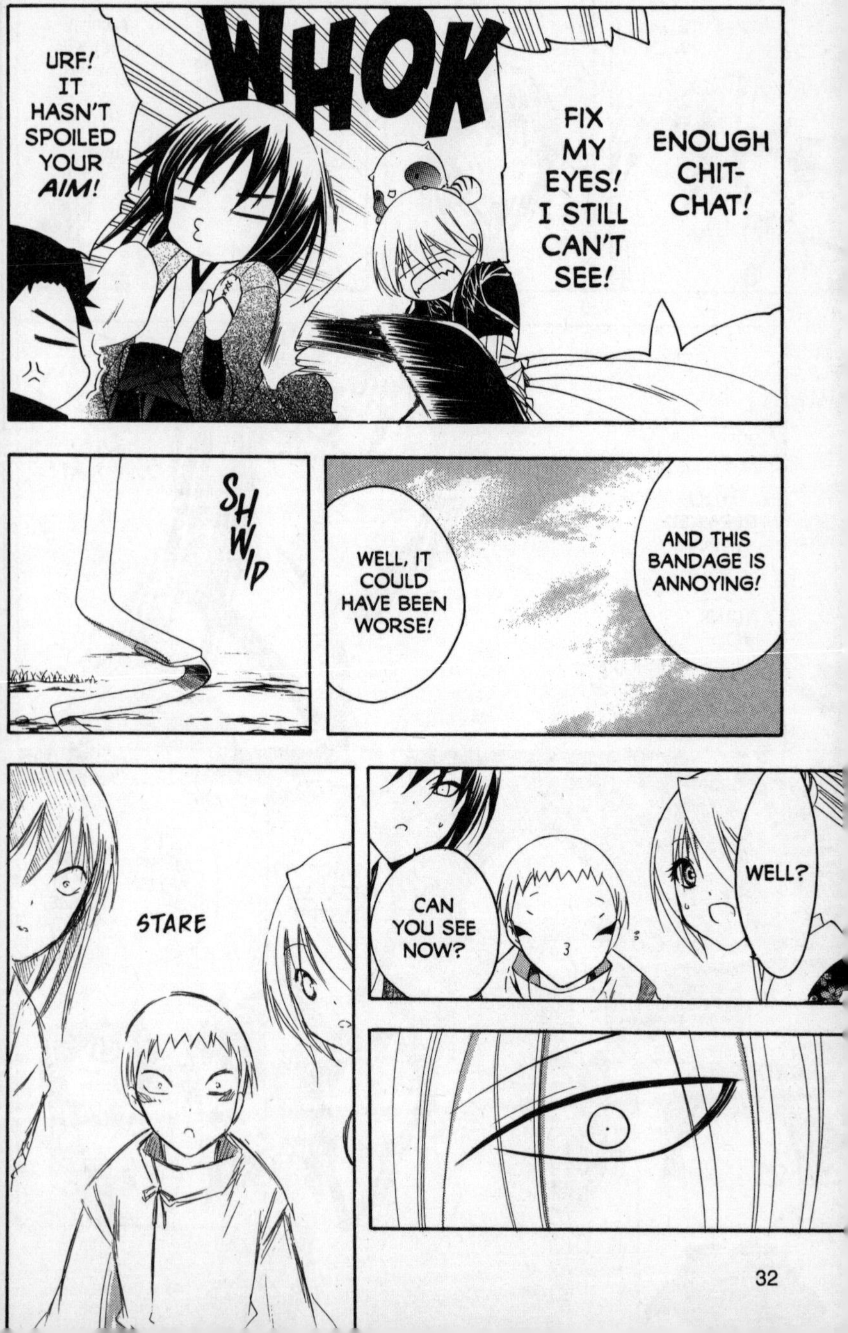
ENOUGH CHIT-CHAT!
FIX MY EYES! I STILL CAN'T SEE!
WHOK
URF! IT HASN'T SPOILED YOUR *AIM!*
AND THIS BANDAGE IS ANNOYING!
WELL, IT COULD HAVE BEEN WORSE!
SHWIP
WELL?
CAN YOU SEE NOW?
STARE

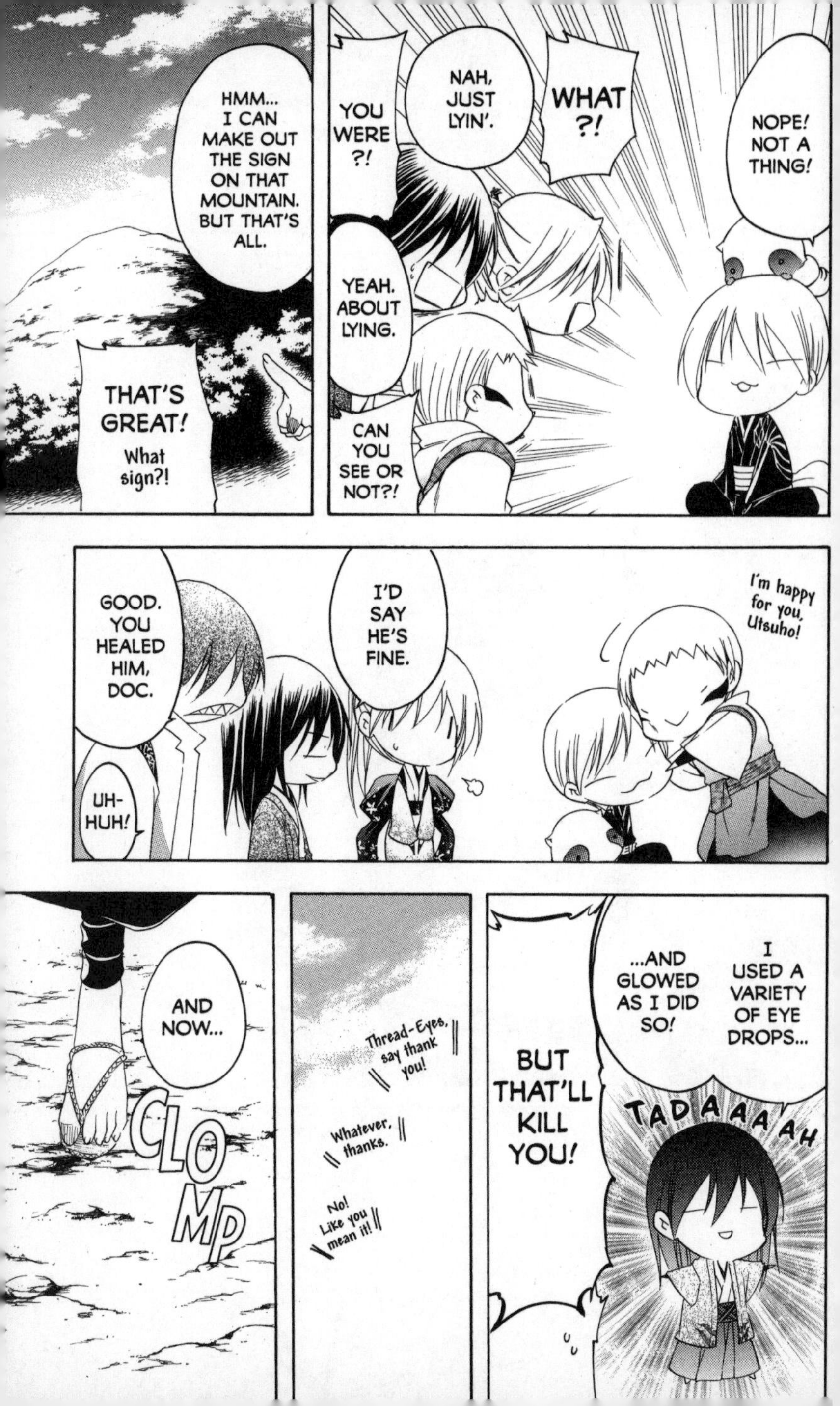
NOPE! NOT A THING!
WHAT?!
NAH, JUST LYIN'.
YOU WERE?!
YEAH. ABOUT LYING.
CAN YOU SEE OR NOT?!
HMM... I CAN MAKE OUT THE SIGN ON THAT MOUNTAIN. BUT THAT'S ALL.
THAT'S GREAT!
What sign?!
I'm happy for you, Utsuho!
I'D SAY HE'S FINE.
GOOD. YOU HEALED HIM, DOC.
UH-HUH!
I USED A VARIETY OF EYE DROPS...
...AND GLOWED AS I DID SO!
TADAAAAAH
BUT THAT'LL KILL YOU!
Thread-Eyes, say thank you!
Whatever, thanks.
No! Like you mean it!
AND NOW...
CLOMP

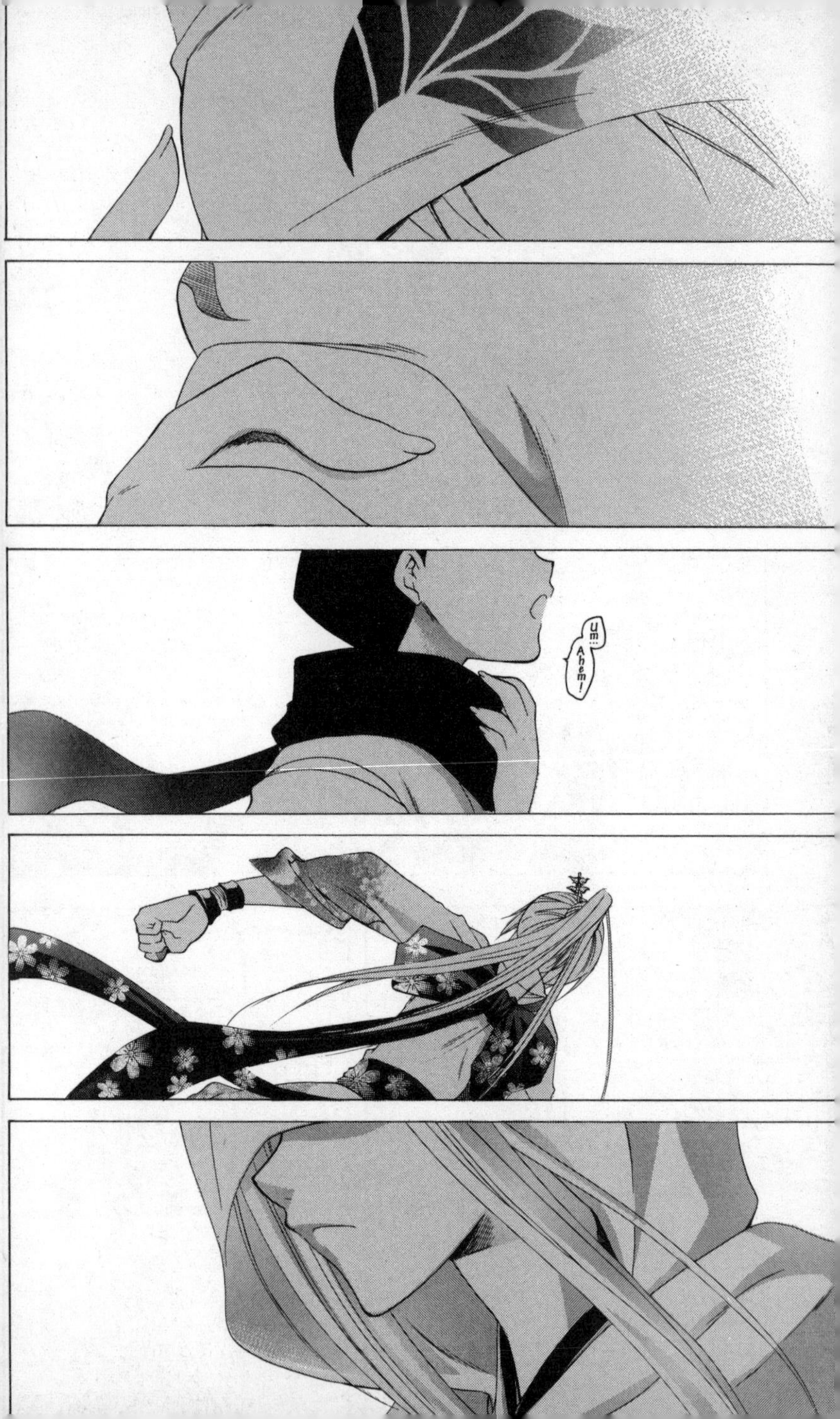
Um... Ahem!

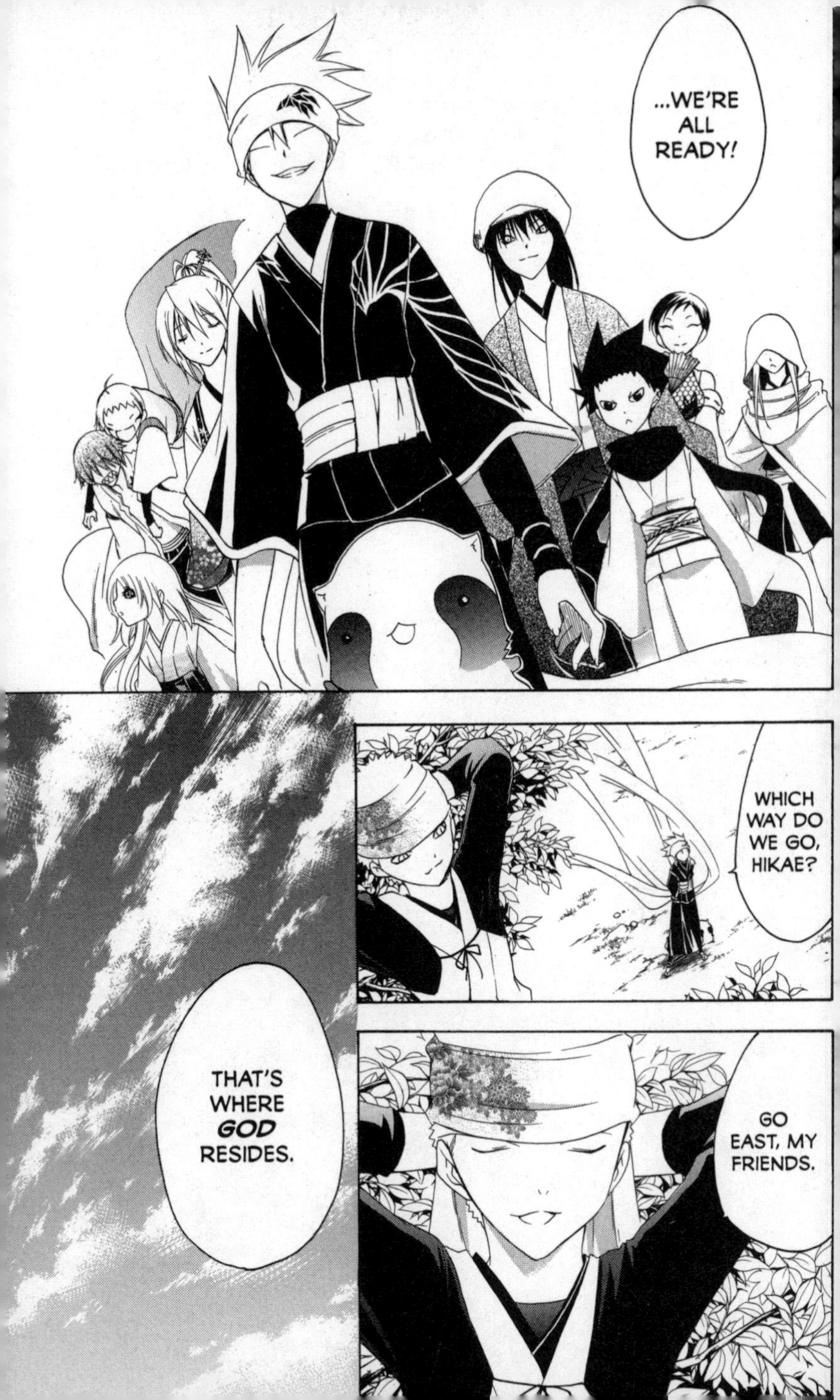
...WE'RE ALL READY!
WHICH WAY DO WE GO, HIKAE?
GO EAST, MY FRIENDS.
THAT'S WHERE *GOD* RESIDES.

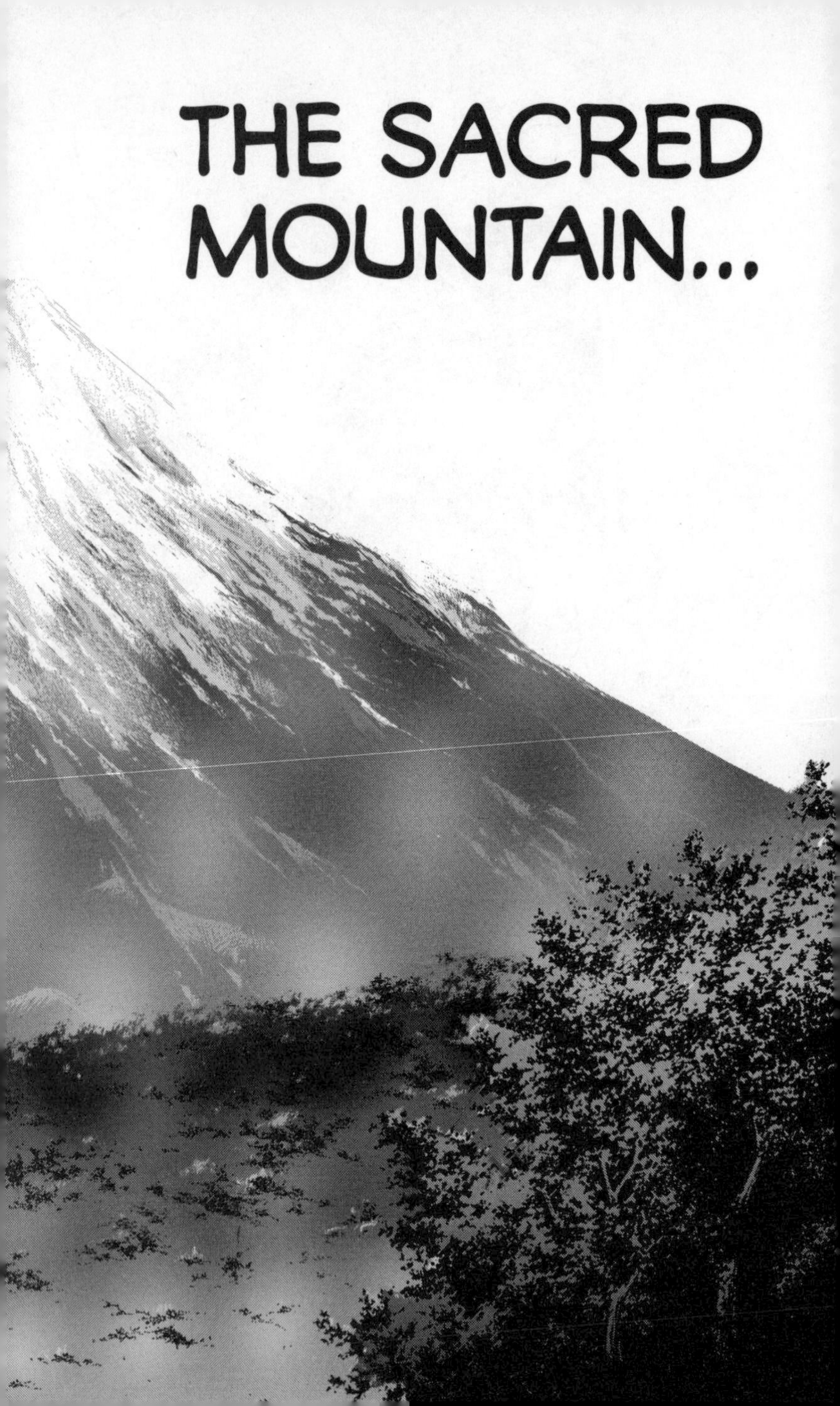
THE SACRED MOUNTAIN...

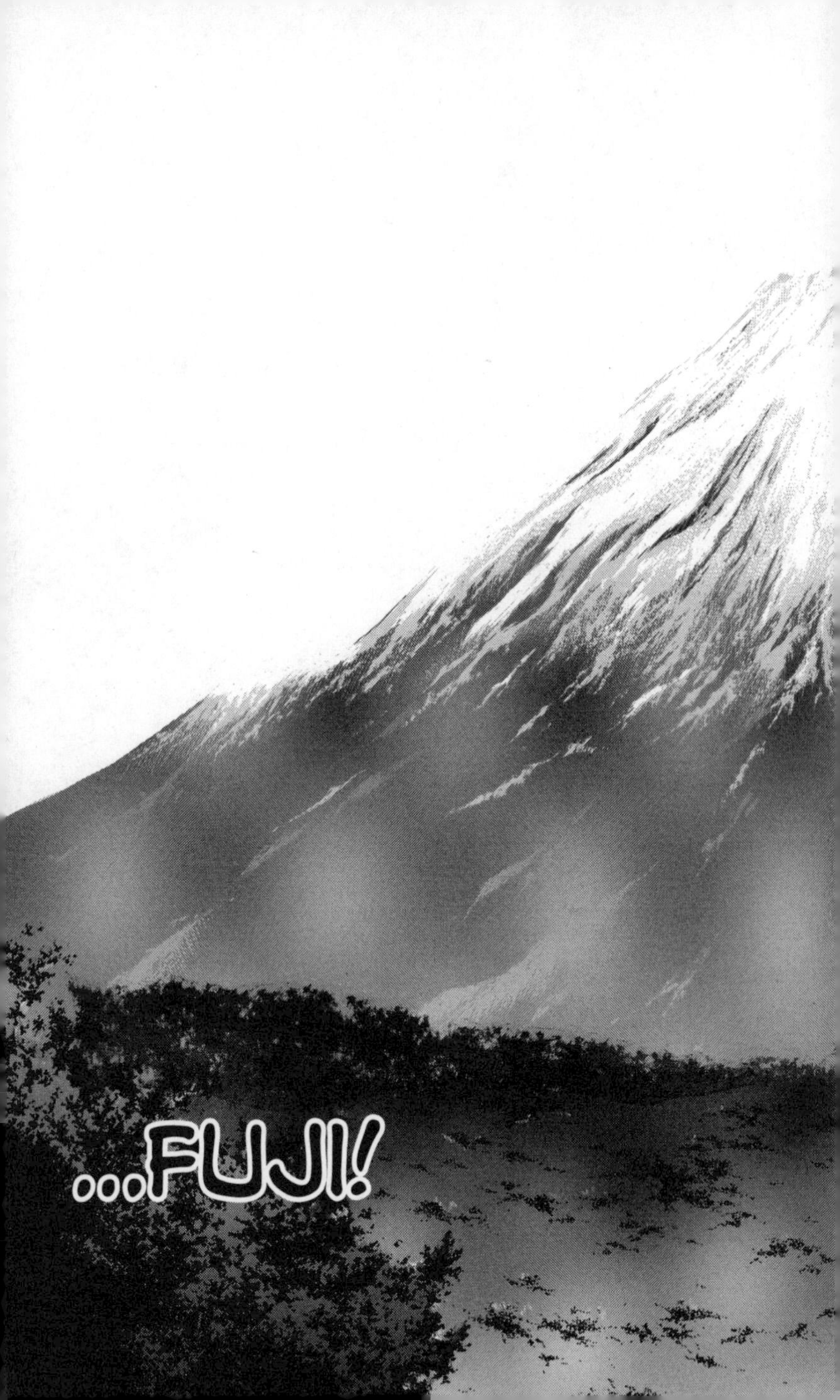
...FUJI!

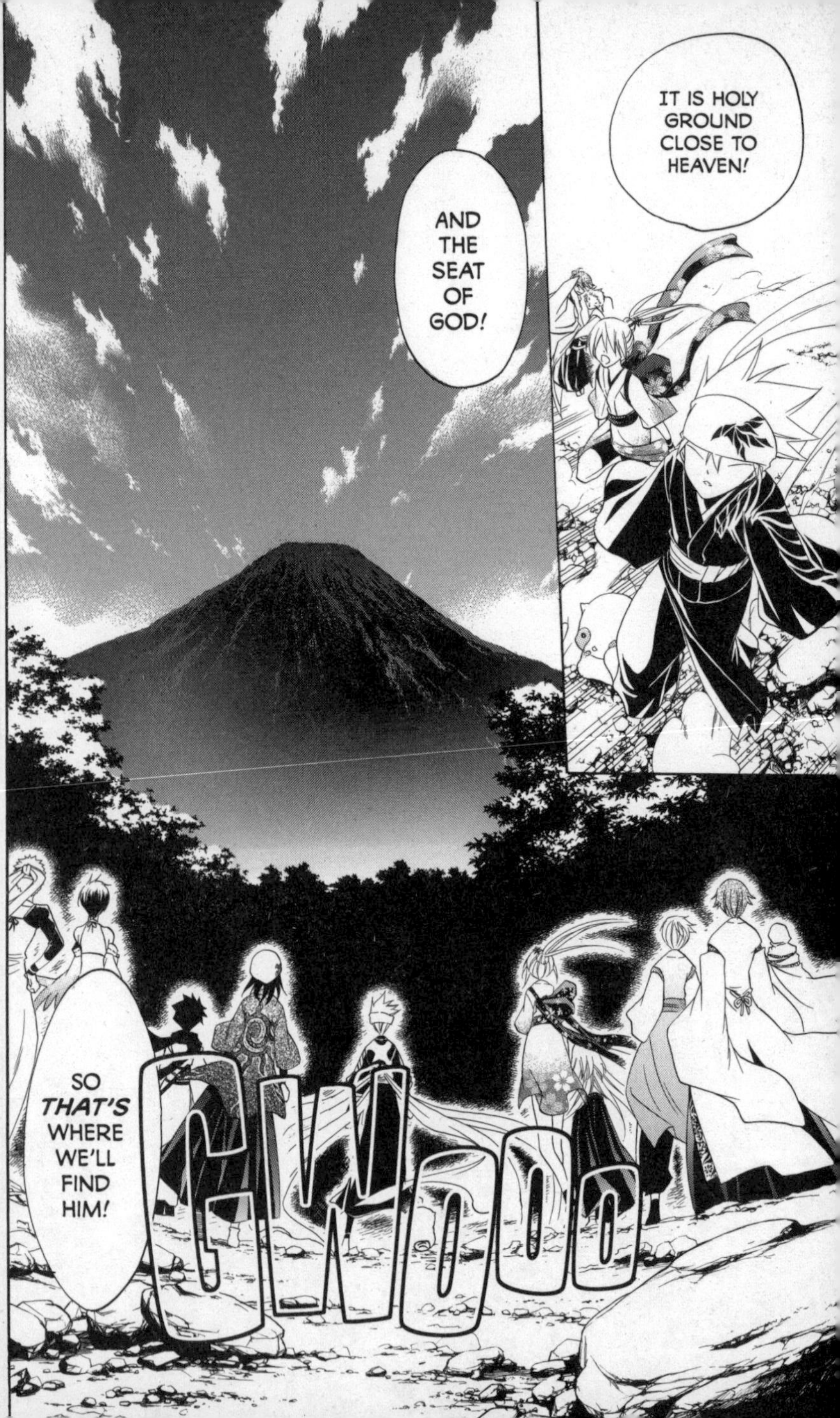
IT IS HOLY GROUND CLOSE TO HEAVEN!
AND THE SEAT OF GOD!
SO *THAT'S* WHERE WE'LL FIND HIM!
GWOOOO

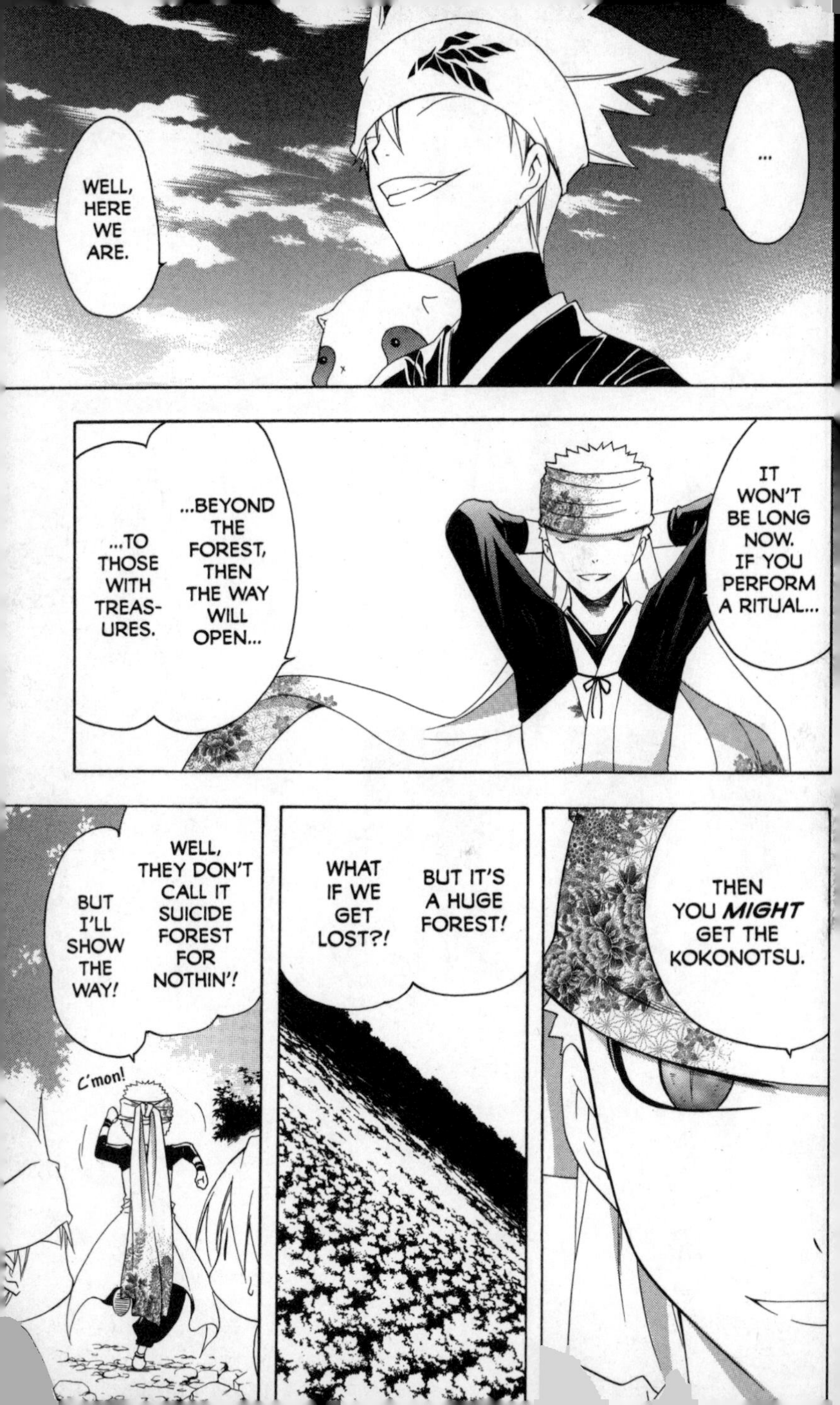
...
WELL, HERE WE ARE.
IT WON'T BE LONG NOW. IF YOU PERFORM A RITUAL...
...BEYOND THE FOREST, THEN THE WAY WILL OPEN...
...TO THOSE WITH TREAS-URES.
THEN YOU *MIGHT* GET THE KOKONOTSU.
BUT IT'S A HUGE FOREST!
WHAT IF WE GET LOST?!
WELL, THEY DON'T CALL IT SUICIDE FOREST FOR NOTHIN'!
BUT I'LL SHOW THE WAY!
C'mon!

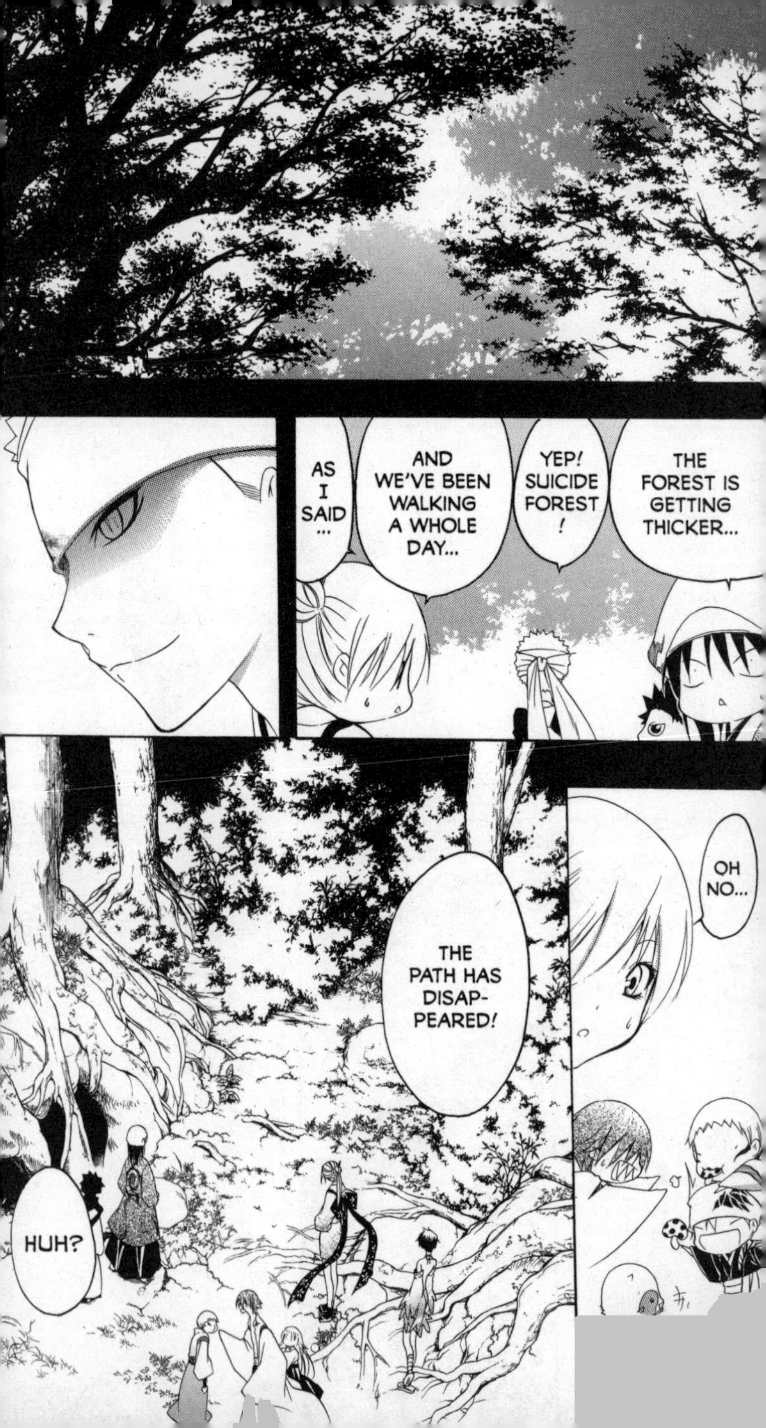
THE FOREST IS GETTING THICKER...
YEP! SUICIDE FOREST!
AND WE'VE BEEN WALKING A WHOLE DAY...
AS I SAID...
OH NO...
THE PATH HAS DISAP-PEARED!
HUH?

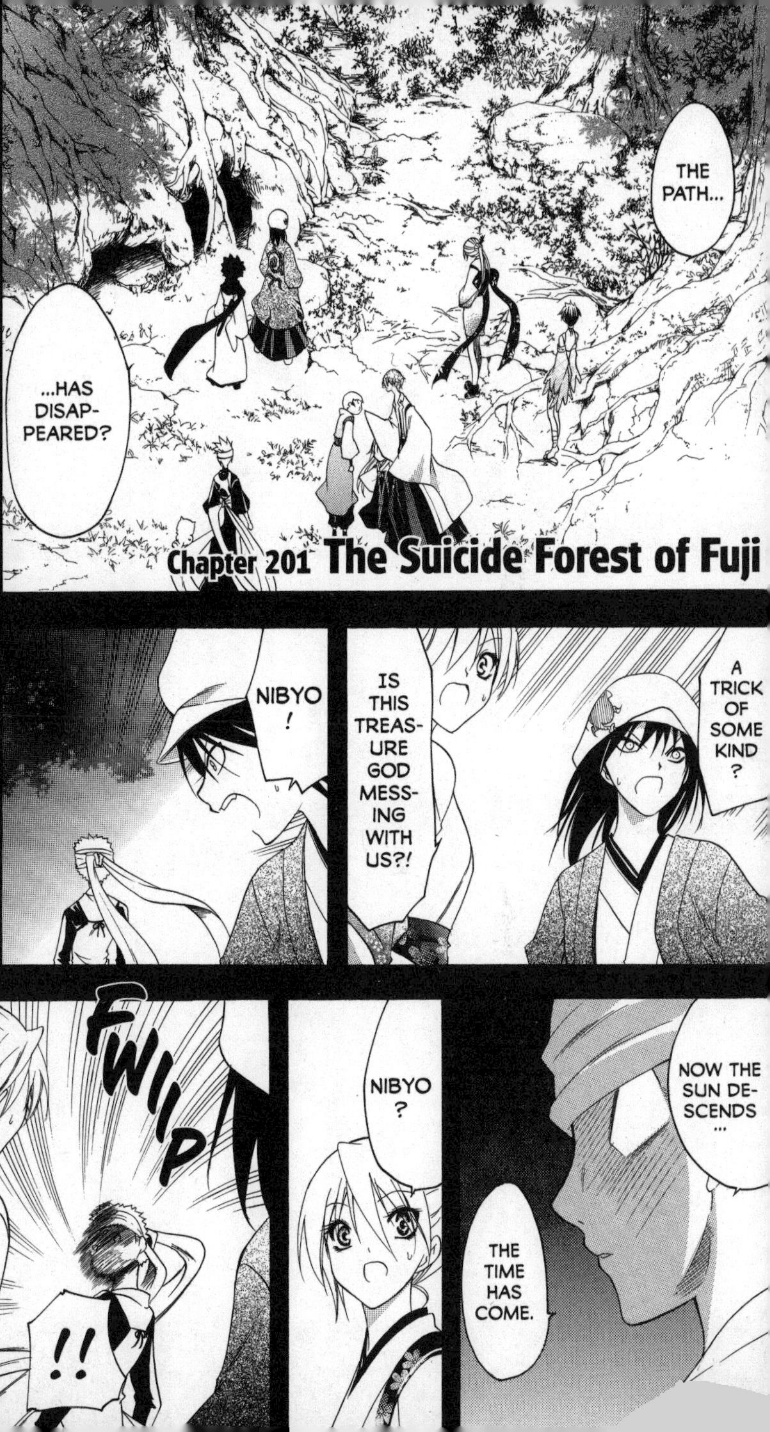
THE PATH...
...HAS DISAP-PEARED?
Chapter 201 The Suicide Forest of Fuji
A TRICK OF SOME KIND?
IS THIS TREAS-URE GOD MESS-ING WITH US?!
NIBYO!
NOW THE SUN DE-SCENDS...
THE TIME HAS COME.
NIBYO?
FWIIP
!!

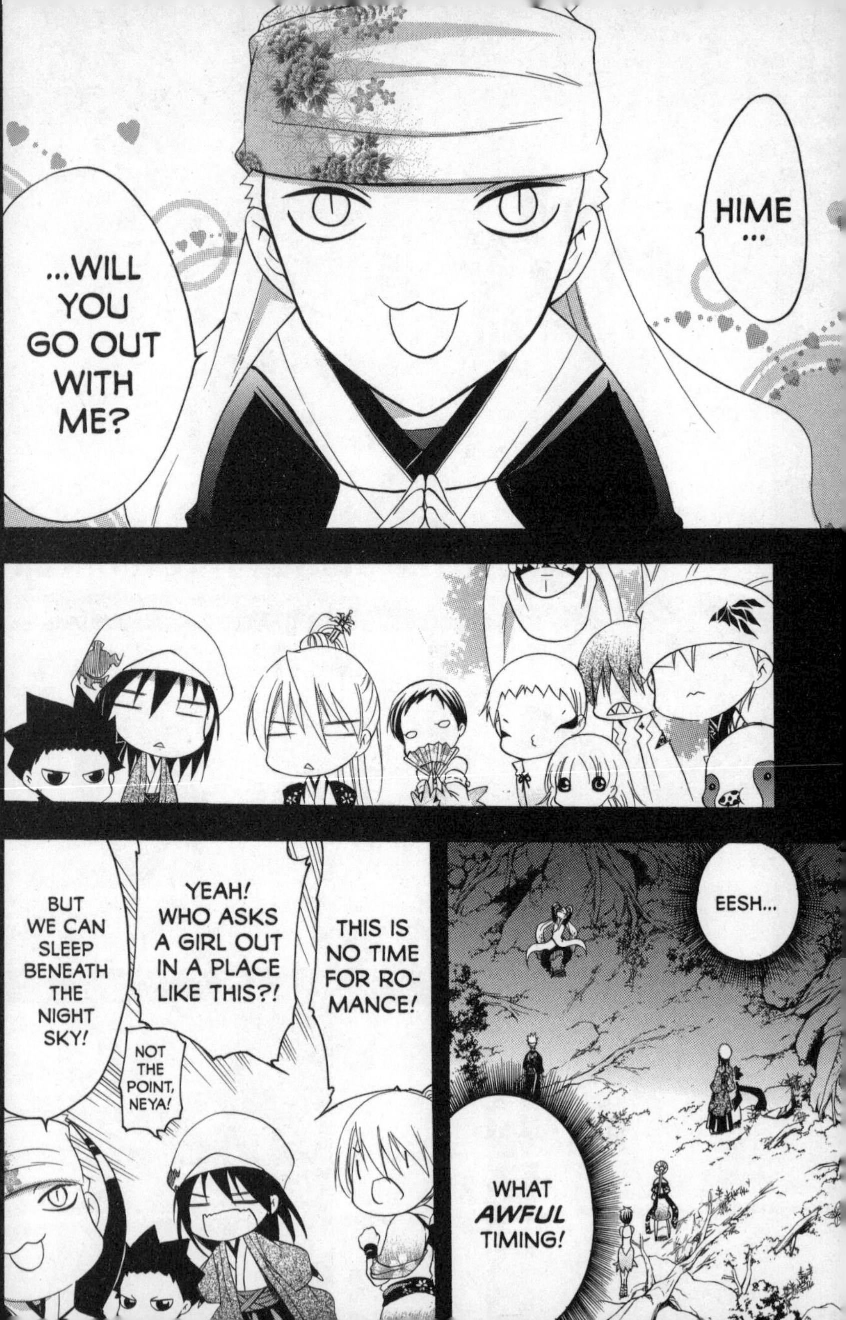
HIME...
...WILL YOU GO OUT WITH ME?
EESH...
WHAT *AWFUL* TIMING!
THIS IS NO TIME FOR RO-MANCE!
YEAH! WHO ASKS A GIRL OUT IN A PLACE LIKE THIS?!
BUT WE CAN SLEEP BENEATH THE NIGHT SKY!
NOT THE POINT, NEYA!

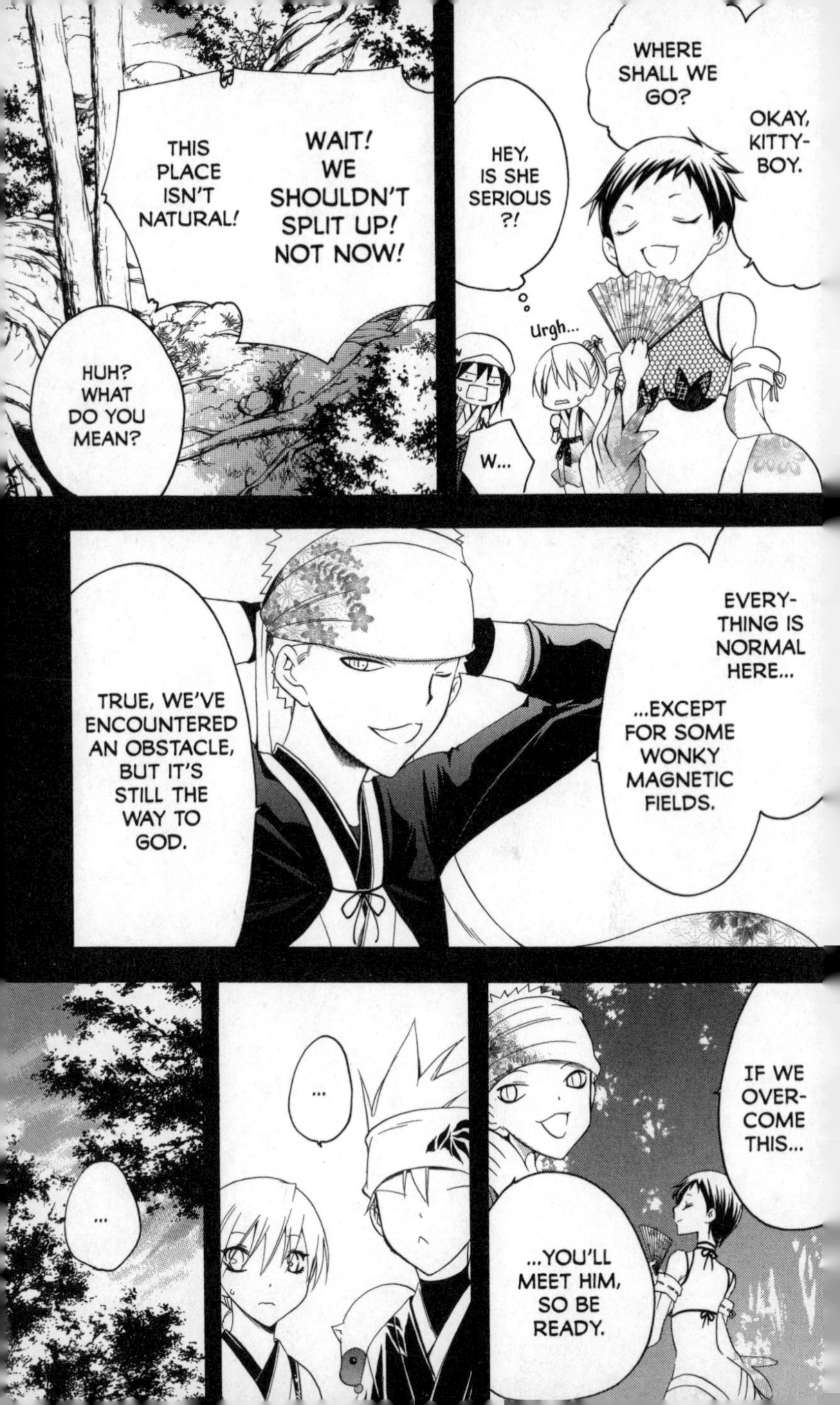

OKAY, KITTY-BOY.
WHERE SHALL WE GO?
HEY, IS SHE SERIOUS?!
Urgh...
W...
WAIT! WE SHOULDN'T SPLIT UP! NOT NOW!
THIS PLACE ISN'T NATURAL!
HUH? WHAT DO YOU MEAN?
EVERY-THING IS NORMAL HERE...
...EXCEPT FOR SOME WONKY MAGNETIC FIELDS.
TRUE, WE'VE ENCOUNTERED AN OBSTACLE, BUT IT'S STILL THE WAY TO GOD.
IF WE OVER-COME THIS...
...YOU'LL MEET HIM, SO BE READY.
...
...

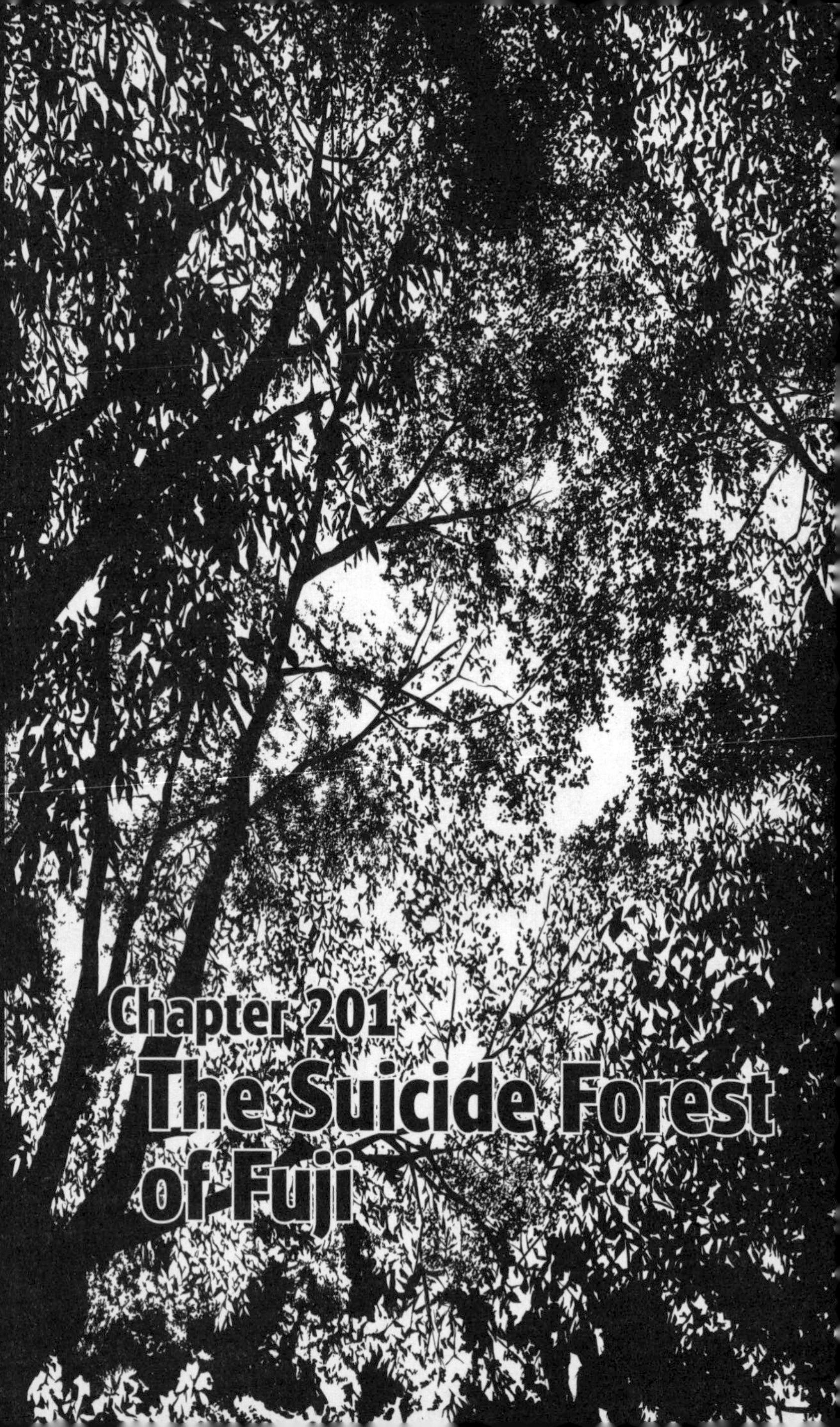
Chapter 201
The Suicide Forest of Fuji

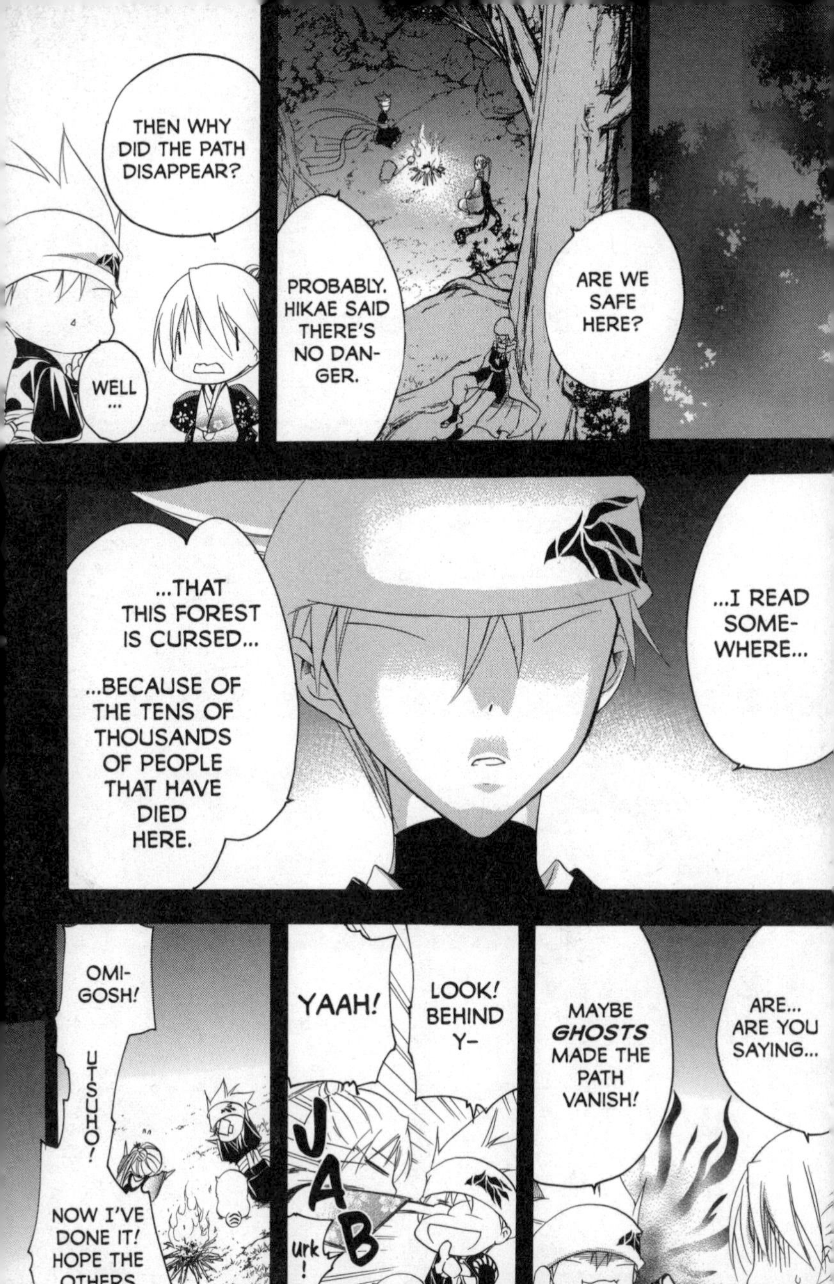
ARE WE SAFE HERE?
PROBABLY. HIKAE SAID THERE'S NO DAN-GER.
THEN WHY DID THE PATH DISAPPEAR?
WELL ...
...I READ SOME-WHERE...
...THAT THIS FOREST IS CURSED...
...BECAUSE OF THE TENS OF THOUSANDS OF PEOPLE THAT HAVE DIED HERE.
ARE... ARE YOU SAYING...
MAYBE *GHOSTS* MADE THE PATH VANISH!
LOOK! BEHIND Y-
YAAH!
JAB
urk!
OMI-GOSH!
UTSUHO!
NOW I'VE DONE IT! HOPE THE OTHERS ARE

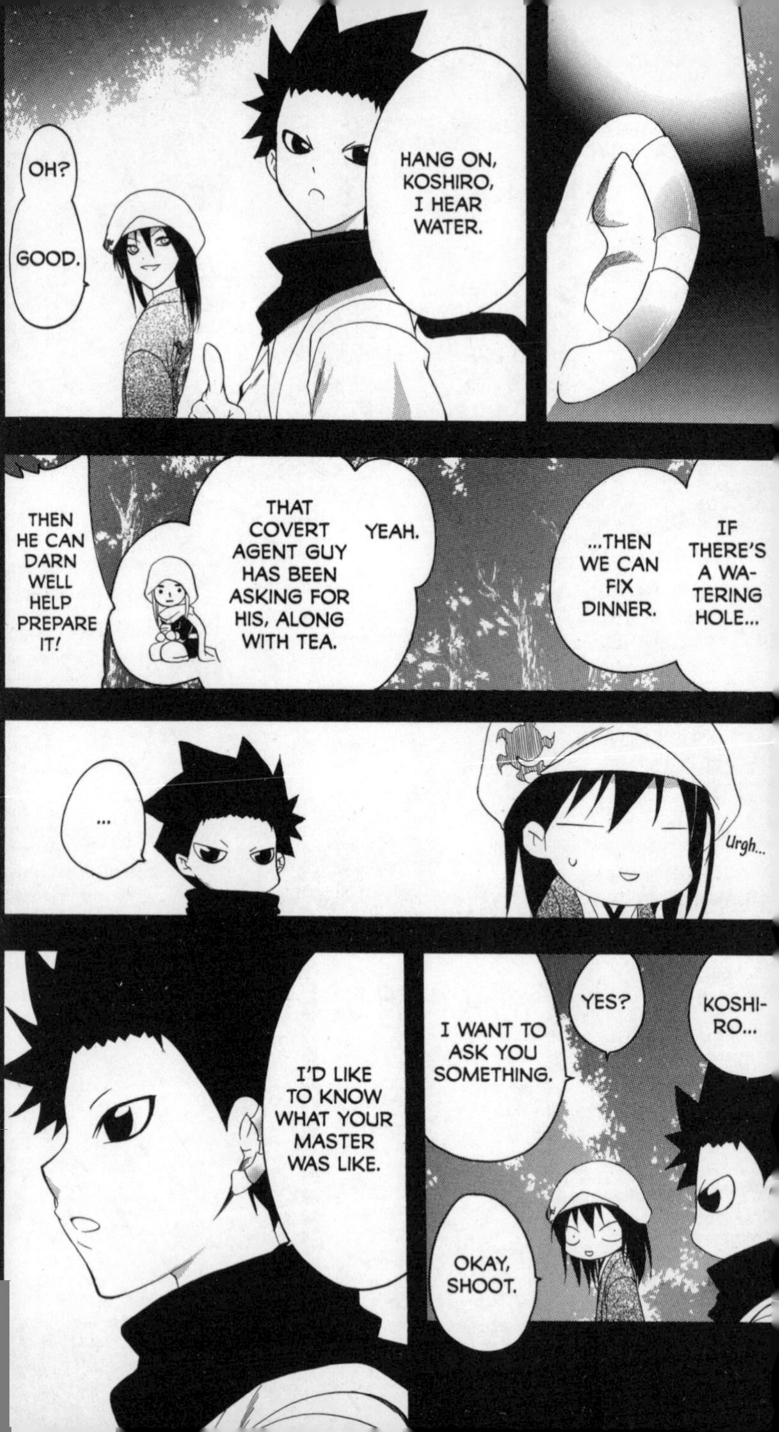
HANG ON, KOSHIRO, I HEAR WATER.
OH?
GOOD.
IF THERE'S A WA-TERING HOLE...
...THEN WE CAN FIX DINNER.
YEAH.
THAT COVERT AGENT GUY HAS BEEN ASKING FOR HIS, ALONG WITH TEA.
THEN HE CAN DARN WELL HELP PREPARE IT!
Urgh...
...
KOSHI-RO...
YES?
I WANT TO ASK YOU SOMETHING.
OKAY, SHOOT.
I'D LIKE TO KNOW WHAT YOUR MASTER WAS LIKE.

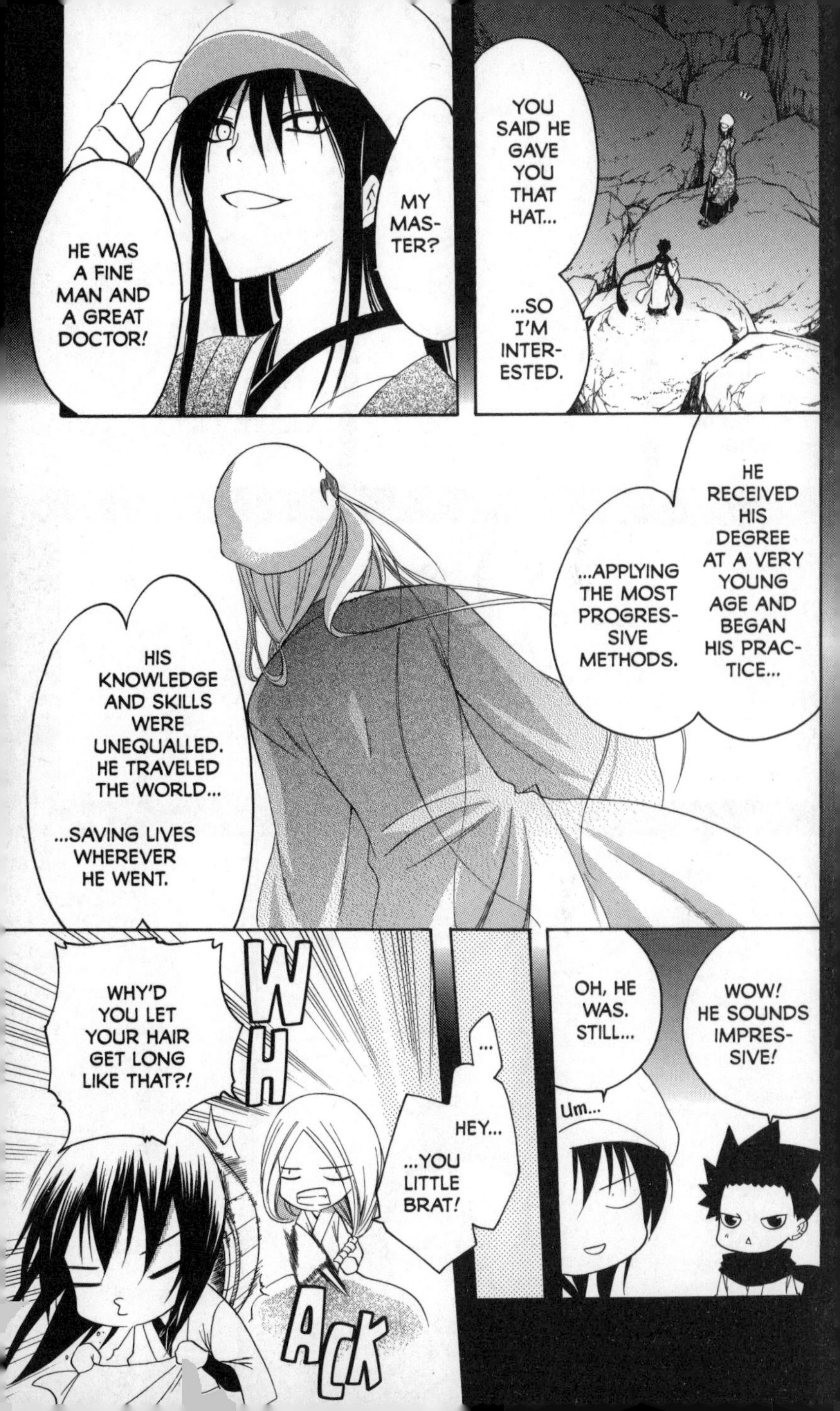
YOU SAID HE GAVE YOU THAT HAT...
...SO I'M INTERESTED.
MY MASTER?
HE WAS A FINE MAN AND A GREAT DOCTOR!
HE RECEIVED HIS DEGREE AT A VERY YOUNG AGE AND BEGAN HIS PRACTICE...
...APPLYING THE MOST PROGRESSIVE METHODS.
HIS KNOWLEDGE AND SKILLS WERE UNEQUALLED. HE TRAVELED THE WORLD...
...SAVING LIVES WHEREVER HE WENT.
WOW! HE SOUNDS IMPRESSIVE!
OH, HE WAS. STILL...
Um...
WHY'D YOU LET YOUR HAIR GET LONG LIKE THAT?!
WHACK
...
HEY...
...YOU LITTLE BRAT!

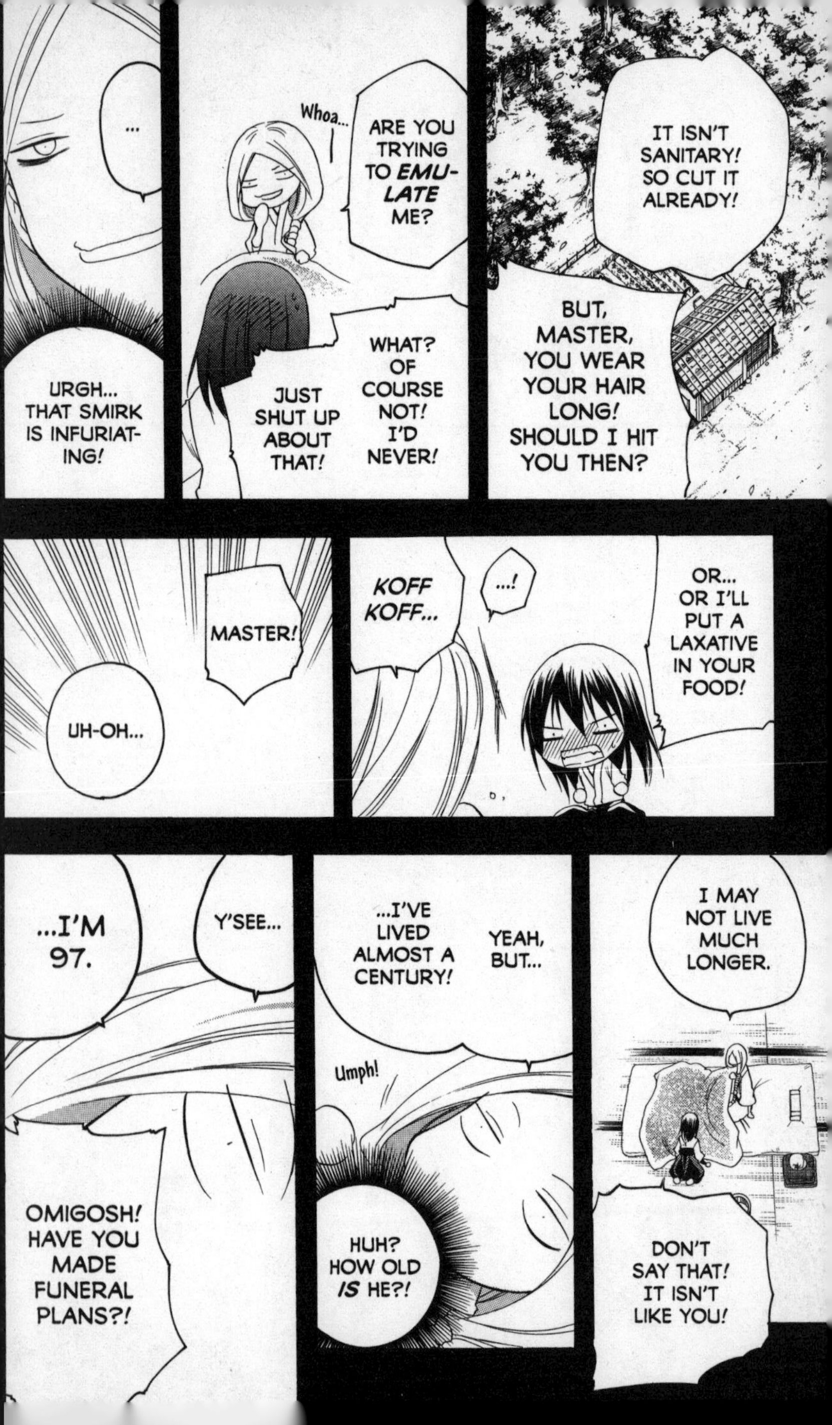
IT ISN'T SANITARY! SO CUT IT ALREADY!
BUT, MASTER, YOU WEAR YOUR HAIR LONG! SHOULD I HIT YOU THEN?
ARE YOU TRYING TO *EMULATE* ME?
Whoa...
WHAT? OF COURSE NOT! I'D NEVER!
JUST SHUT UP ABOUT THAT!
...
URGH... THAT SMIRK IS INFURIATING!
OR... OR I'LL PUT A LAXATIVE IN YOUR FOOD!
...!
KOFF KOFF...
MASTER!
UH-OH...
I MAY NOT LIVE MUCH LONGER.
DON'T SAY THAT! IT ISN'T LIKE YOU!
YEAH, BUT...
...I'VE LIVED ALMOST A CENTURY!
Umph!
HUH? HOW OLD *IS* HE?!
Y'SEE...
...I'M 97.
OMIGOSH! HAVE YOU MADE FUNERAL PLANS?!

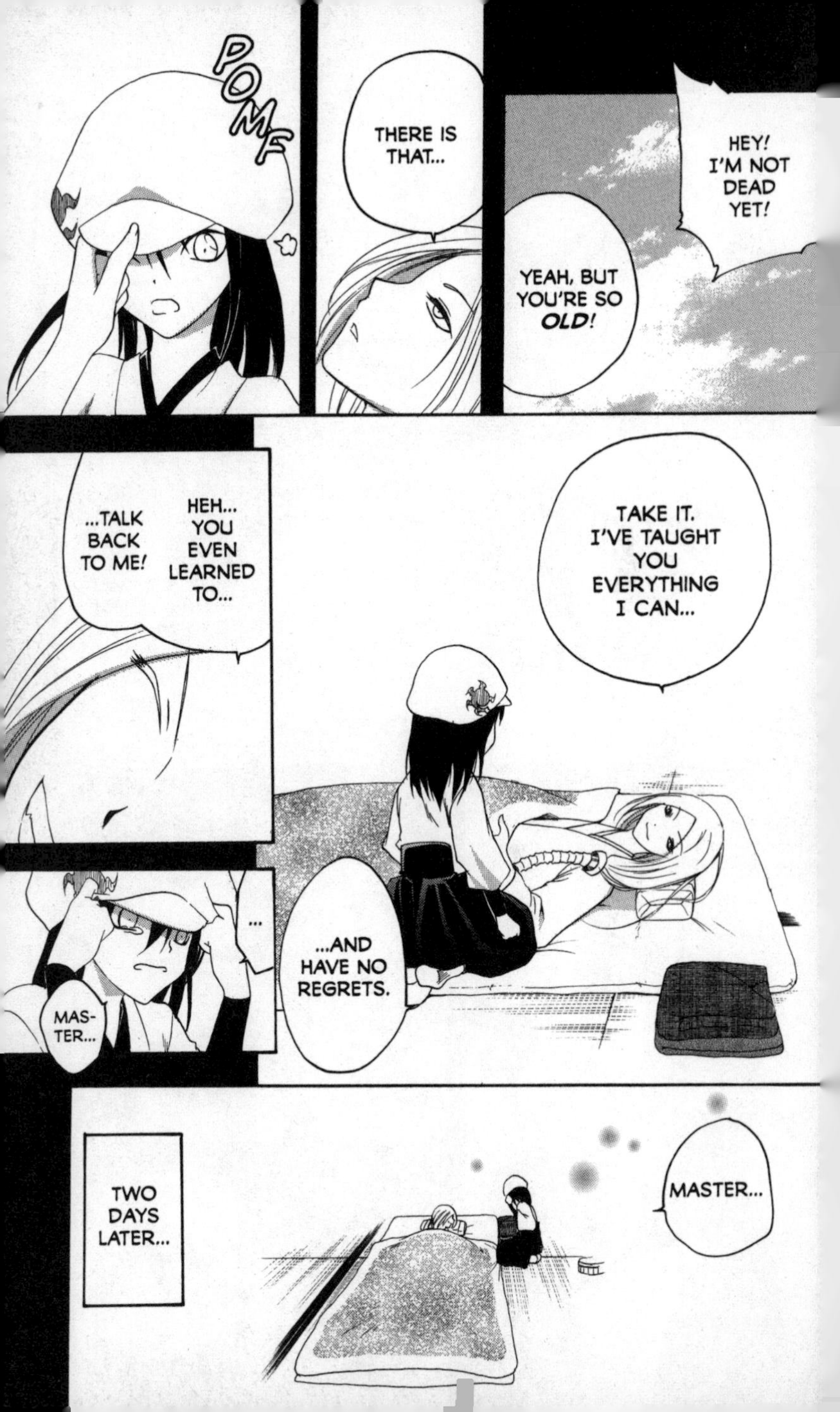
HEY! I'M NOT DEAD YET!
YEAH, BUT YOU'RE SO *OLD*!
THERE IS THAT...
POMF
TAKE IT. I'VE TAUGHT YOU EVERYTHING I CAN...
...AND HAVE NO REGRETS.
HEH... YOU EVEN LEARNED TO...
...TALK BACK TO ME!
...
MAS-TER...
MASTER...
TWO DAYS LATER...

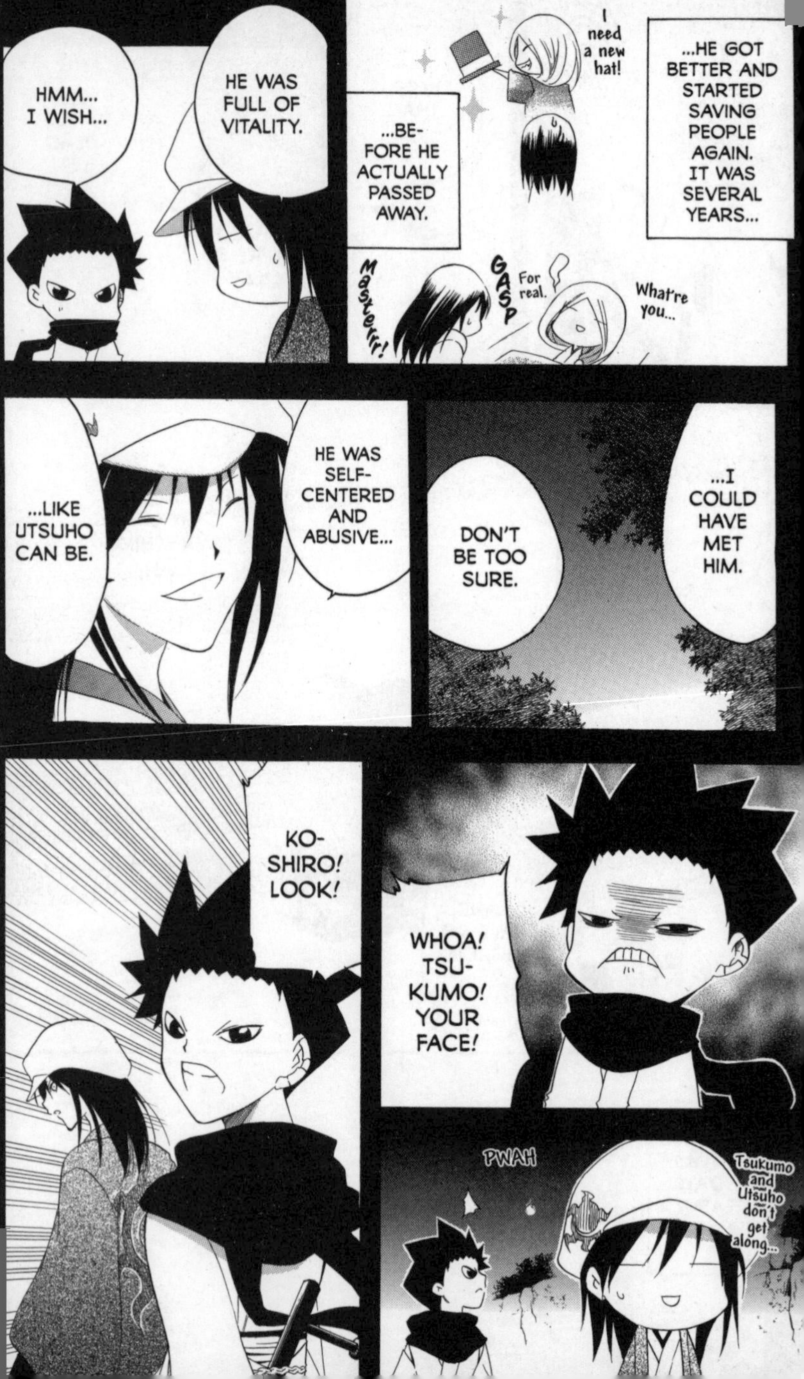
...HE GOT BETTER AND STARTED SAVING PEOPLE AGAIN. IT WAS SEVERAL YEARS...
I need a new hat!
...BE-FORE HE ACTUALLY PASSED AWAY.
What're you...
For real.
GASP
Masterrr!
HE WAS FULL OF VITALITY.
HMM... I WISH...
...I COULD HAVE MET HIM.
DON'T BE TOO SURE.
HE WAS SELF-CENTERED AND ABUSIVE...
...LIKE UTSUHO CAN BE.
WHOA! TSU-KUMO! YOUR FACE!
Tsukumo and Utsuho don't get along...
PWAH
KO-SHIRO! LOOK!

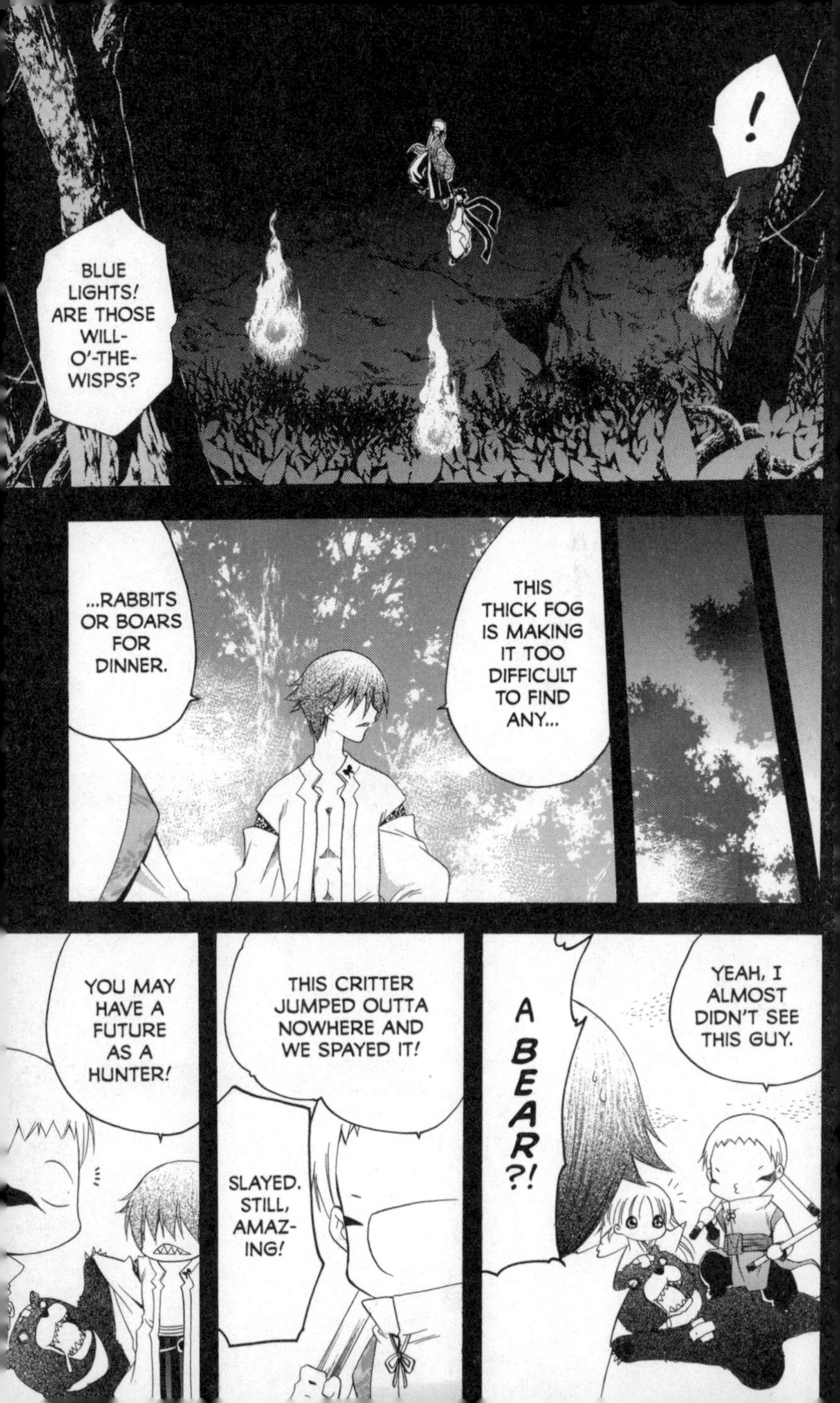
!
BLUE LIGHTS! ARE THOSE WILL-O'-THE-WISPS?
THIS THICK FOG IS MAKING IT TOO DIFFICULT TO FIND ANY...
...RABBITS OR BOARS FOR DINNER.
YEAH, I ALMOST DIDN'T SEE THIS GUY.
A BEAR?!
THIS CRITTER JUMPED OUTTA NOWHERE AND WE SPAYED IT!
SLAYED. STILL, AMAZING!
YOU MAY HAVE A FUTURE AS A HUNTER!

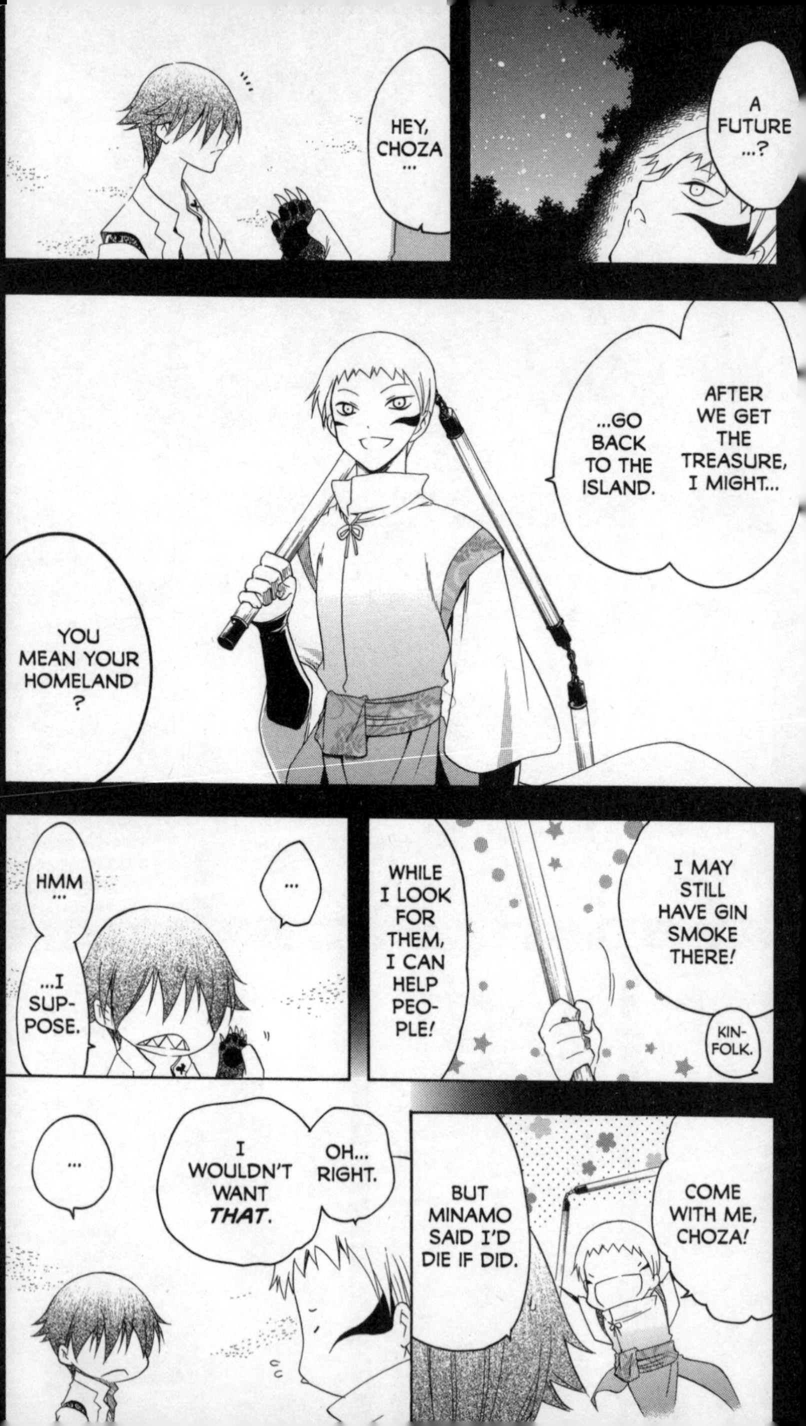
A FUTURE ...?
HEY, CHOZA ...
AFTER WE GET THE TREASURE, I MIGHT...
...GO BACK TO THE ISLAND.
YOU MEAN YOUR HOMELAND ?
I MAY STILL HAVE GIN SMOKE THERE!
KIN-FOLK.
WHILE I LOOK FOR THEM, I CAN HELP PEO-PLE!
...
HMM ...
...I SUP-POSE.
COME WITH ME, CHOZA!
BUT MINAMO SAID I'D DIE IF DID.
OH... RIGHT.
I WOULDN'T WANT *THAT*.
...

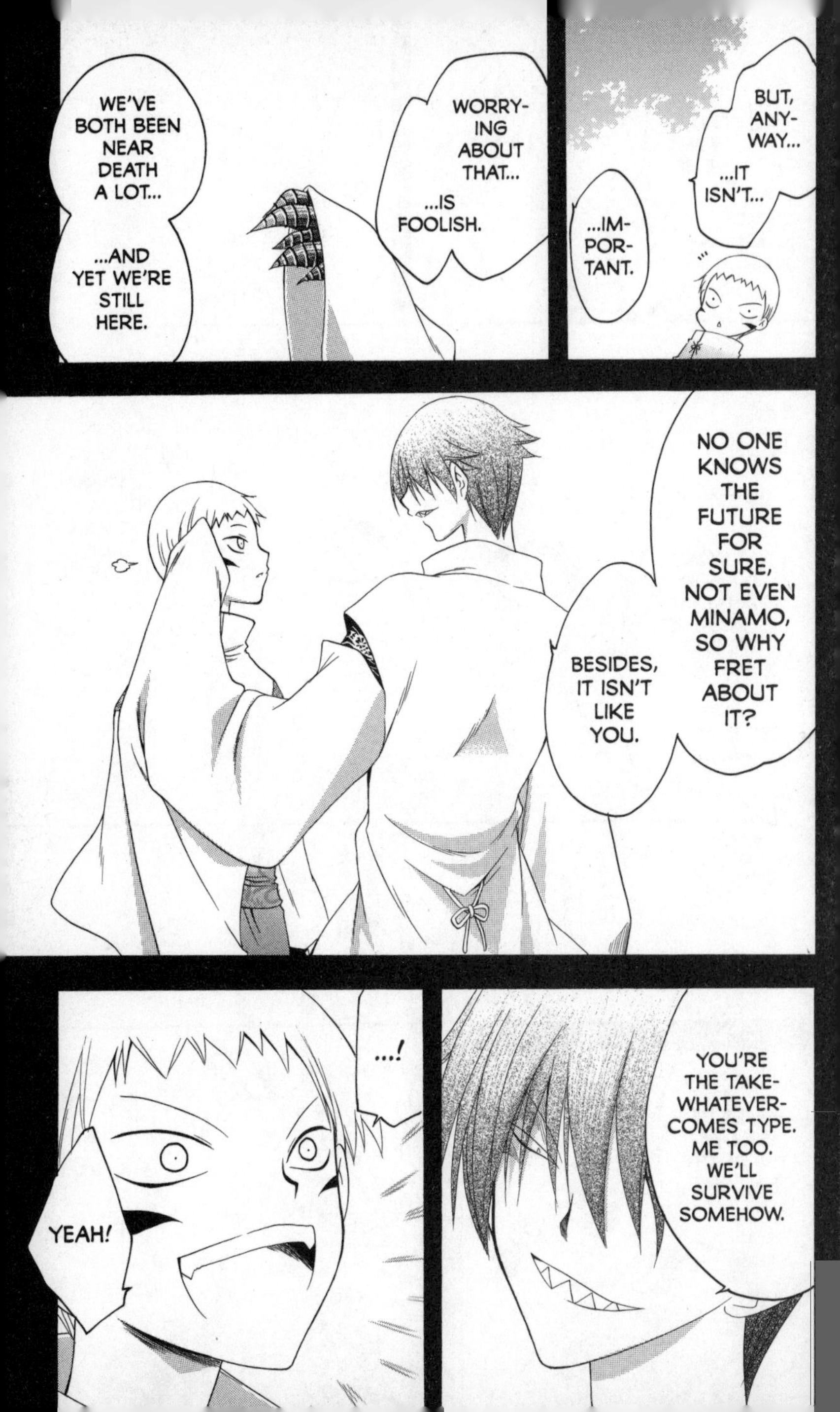
BUT, ANYWAY...
...IT ISN'T...
...IMPORTANT.
WORRYING ABOUT THAT...
...IS FOOLISH.
WE'VE BOTH BEEN NEAR DEATH A LOT...
...AND YET WE'RE STILL HERE.
NO ONE KNOWS THE FUTURE FOR SURE, NOT EVEN MINAMO, SO WHY FRET ABOUT IT?
BESIDES, IT ISN'T LIKE YOU.
YOU'RE THE TAKE-WHATEVER-COMES TYPE. ME TOO. WE'LL SURVIVE SOMEHOW.
...!
YEAH!

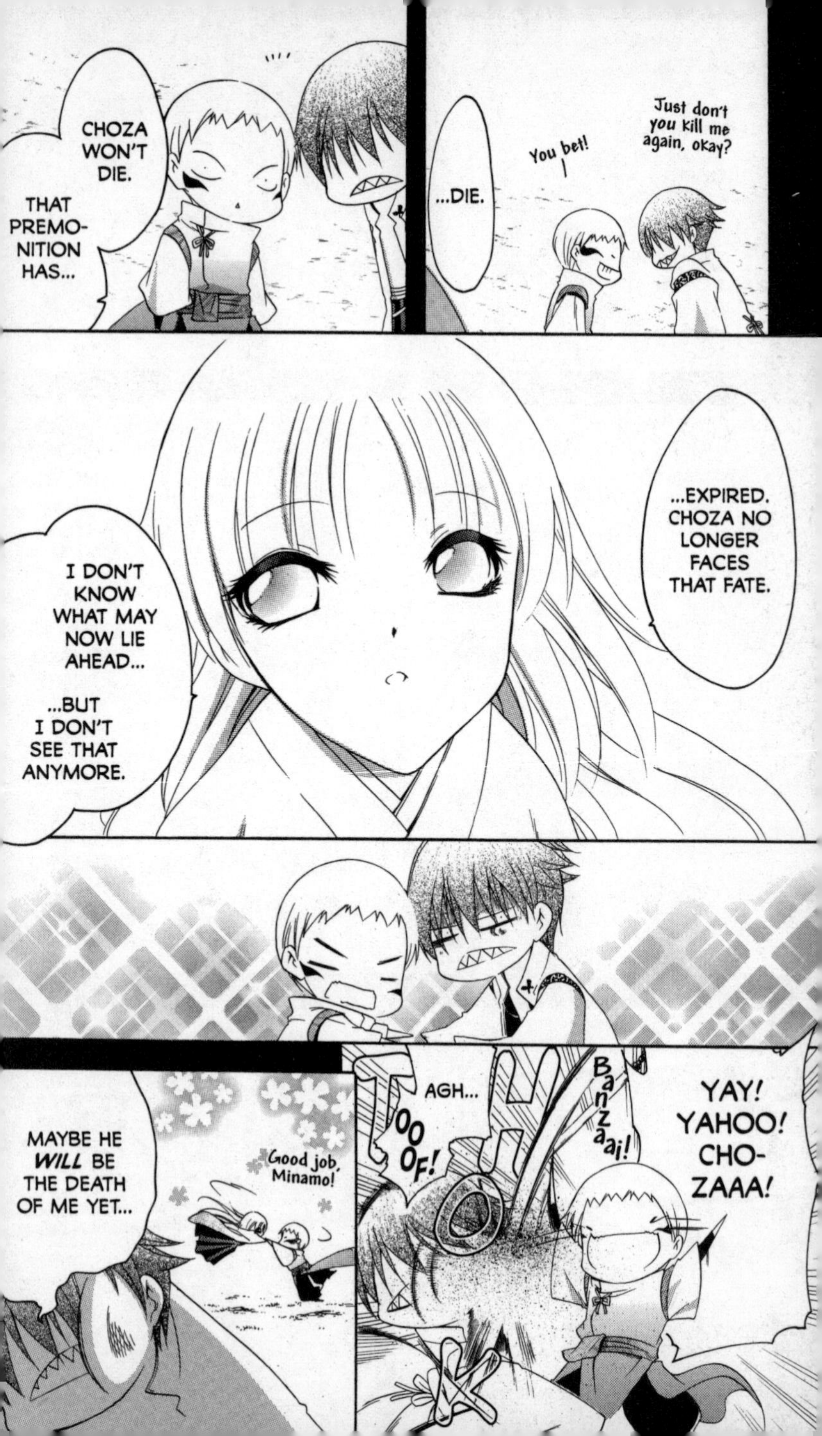

Just don't you kill me again, okay?
You bet!
...DIE.
CHOZA WON'T DIE.
THAT PREMONITION HAS...
...EXPIRED. CHOZA NO LONGER FACES THAT FATE.
I DON'T KNOW WHAT MAY NOW LIE AHEAD...
...BUT I DON'T SEE THAT ANYMORE.
YAY! YAHOO! CHO-ZAAA!
Banzaaai!
AGH...
OOOF!
Good job, Minamo!
MAYBE HE *WILL* BE THE DEATH OF ME YET...

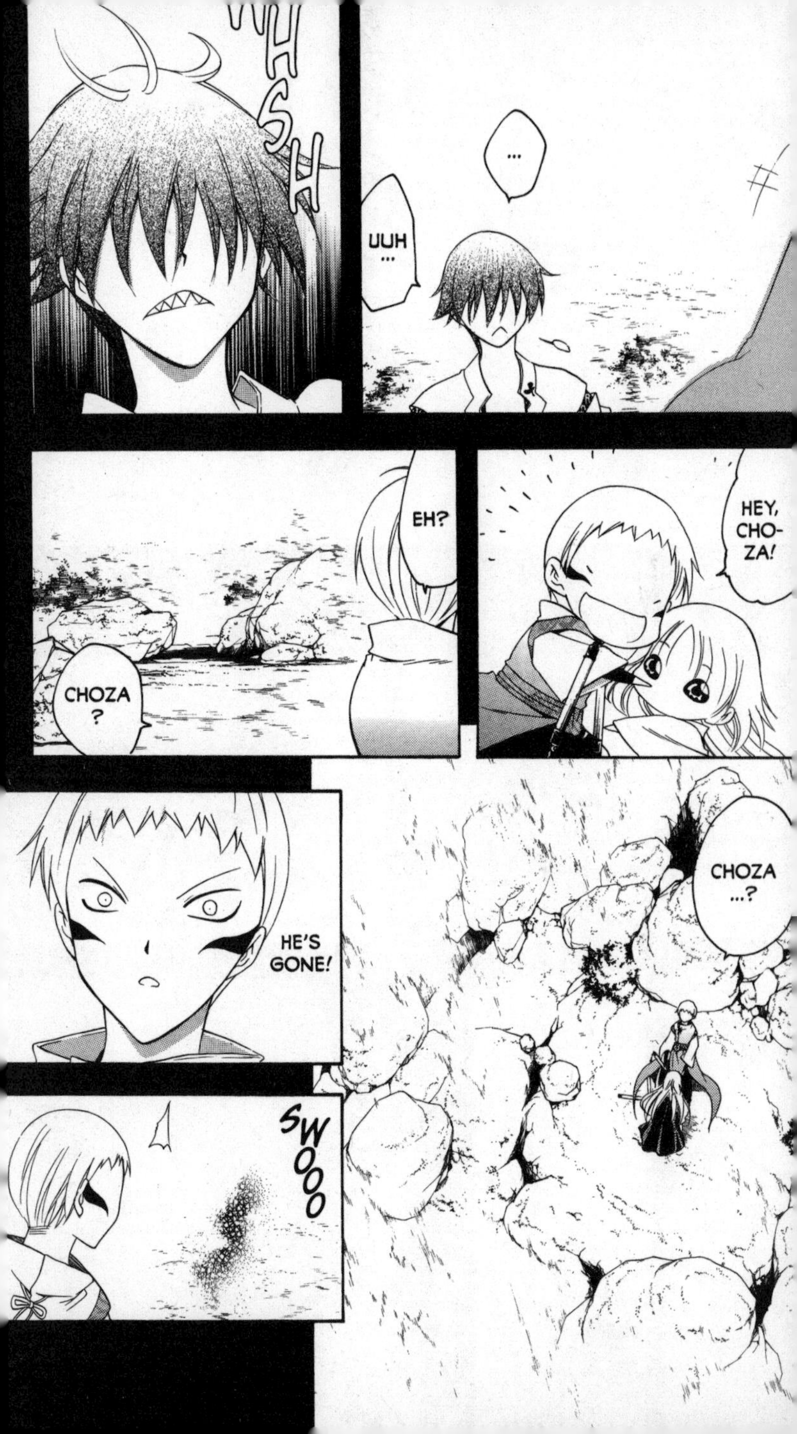
...
UUH ...
WHSH
HEY, CHO-ZA!
EH?
CHOZA ?
CHOZA ...?
HE'S GONE!
SWOOO

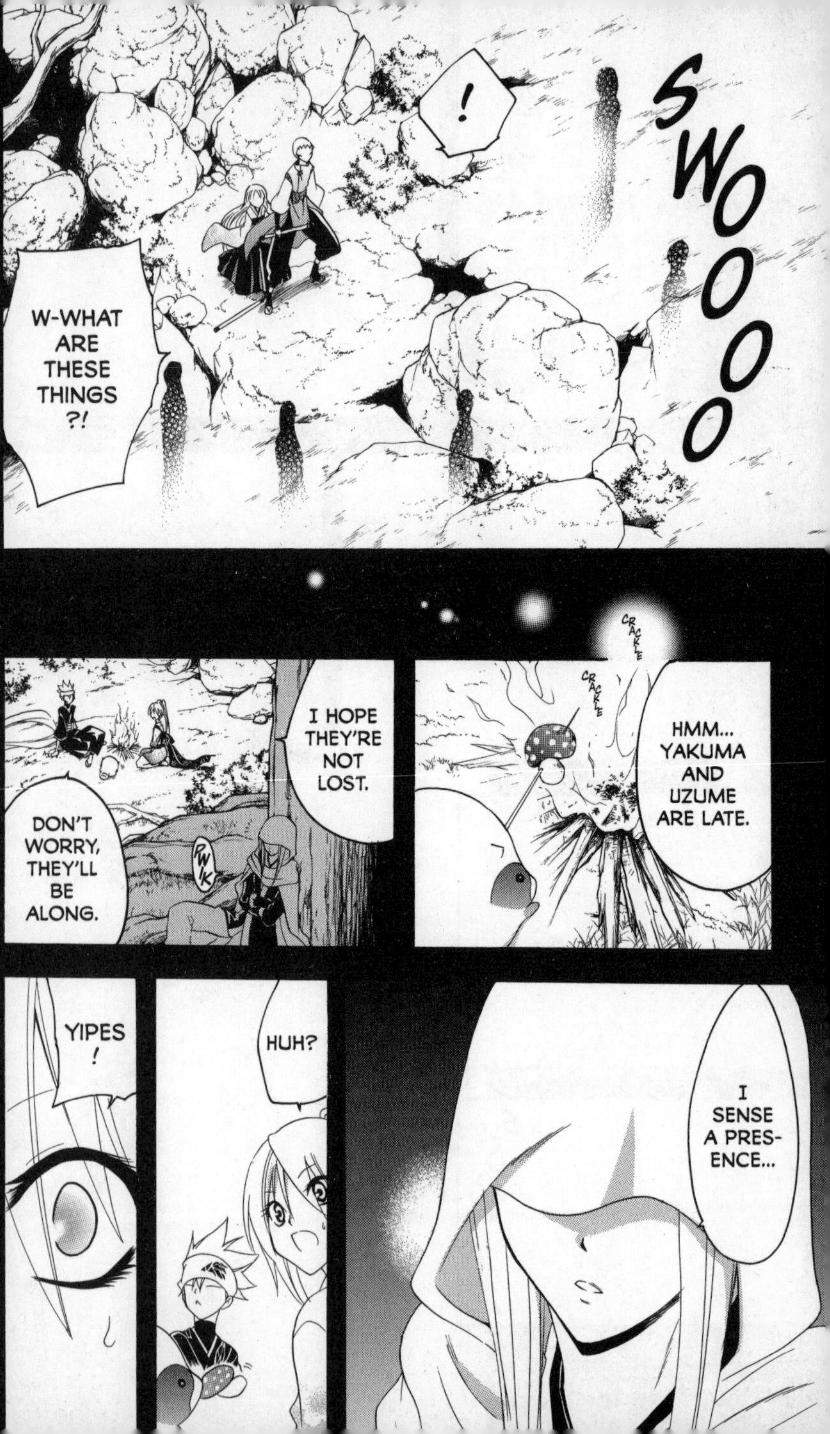
SWOOOO
!
W-WHAT ARE THESE THINGS?!
CRACKLE
CRACKLE
HMM... YAKUMA AND UZUME ARE LATE.
I HOPE THEY'RE NOT LOST.
PWIK
DON'T WORRY, THEY'LL BE ALONG.
I SENSE A PRESENCE...
HUH?
YIPES!

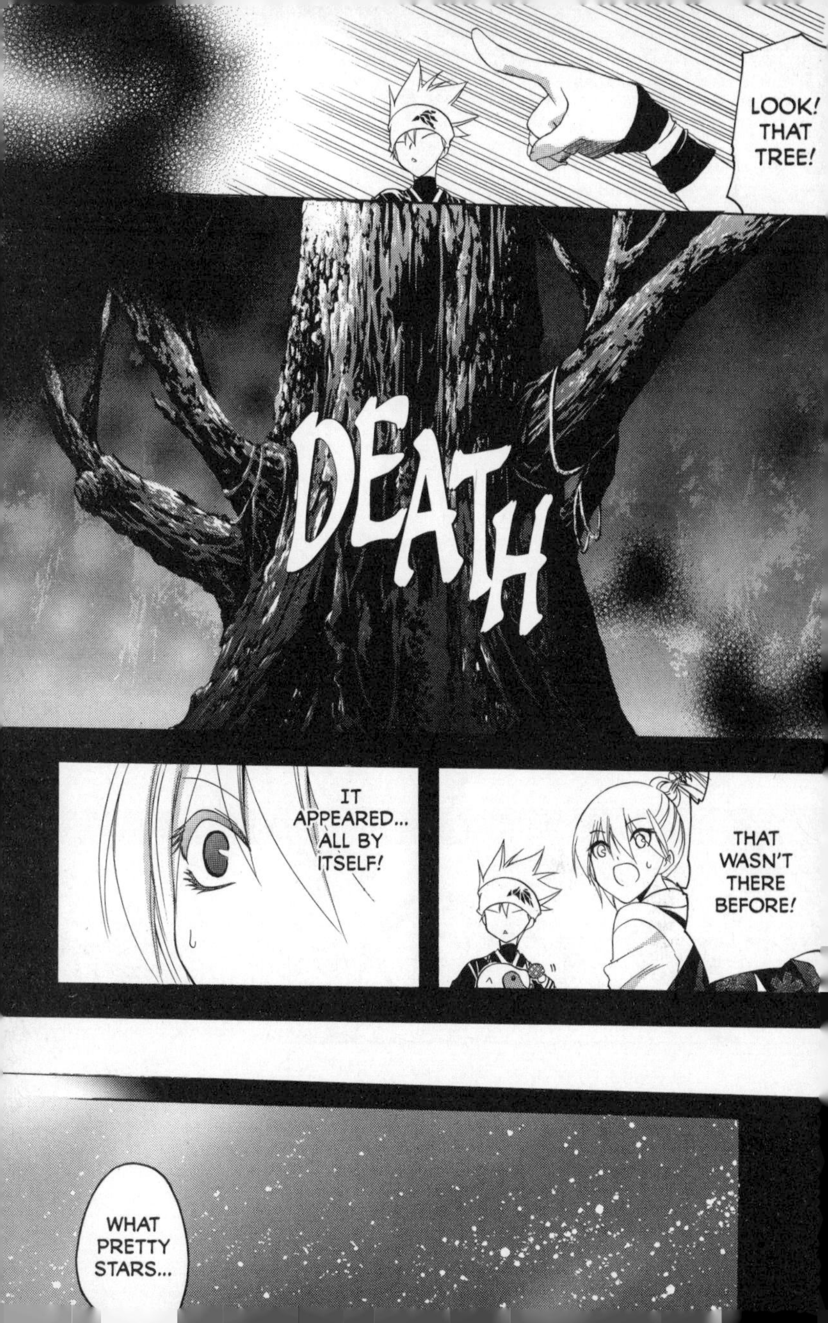
LOOK! THAT TREE!
DEATH
THAT WASN'T THERE BEFORE!
IT APPEARED... ALL BY ITSELF!
WHAT PRETTY STARS...

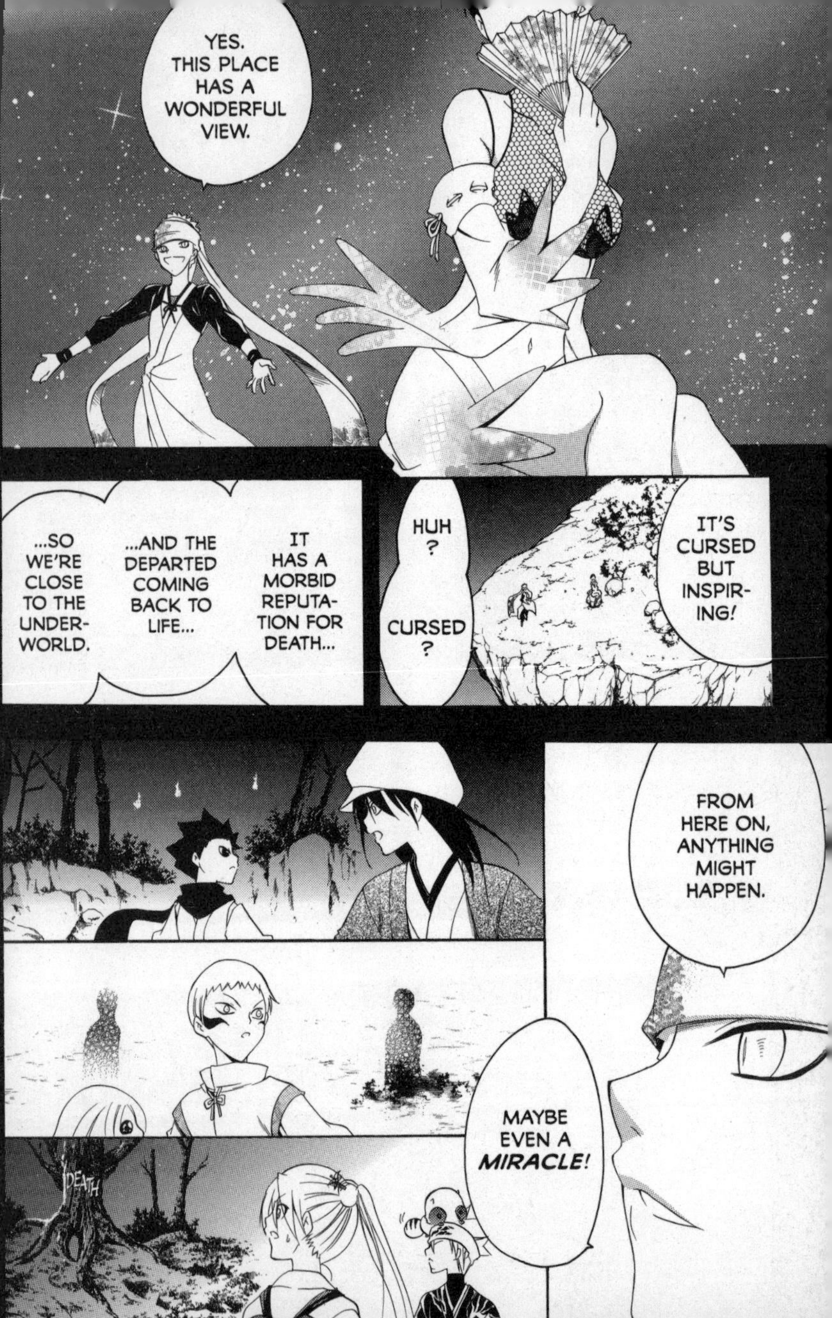
YES. THIS PLACE HAS A WONDERFUL VIEW.
IT'S CURSED BUT INSPIR-ING!
HUH? CURSED?
IT HAS A MORBID REPUTA-TION FOR DEATH...
...AND THE DEPARTED COMING BACK TO LIFE...
...SO WE'RE CLOSE TO THE UNDER-WORLD.
FROM HERE ON, ANYTHING MIGHT HAPPEN.
MAYBE EVEN A *MIRACLE*!
DEATH

Chapter 202 Anonymous Revenge

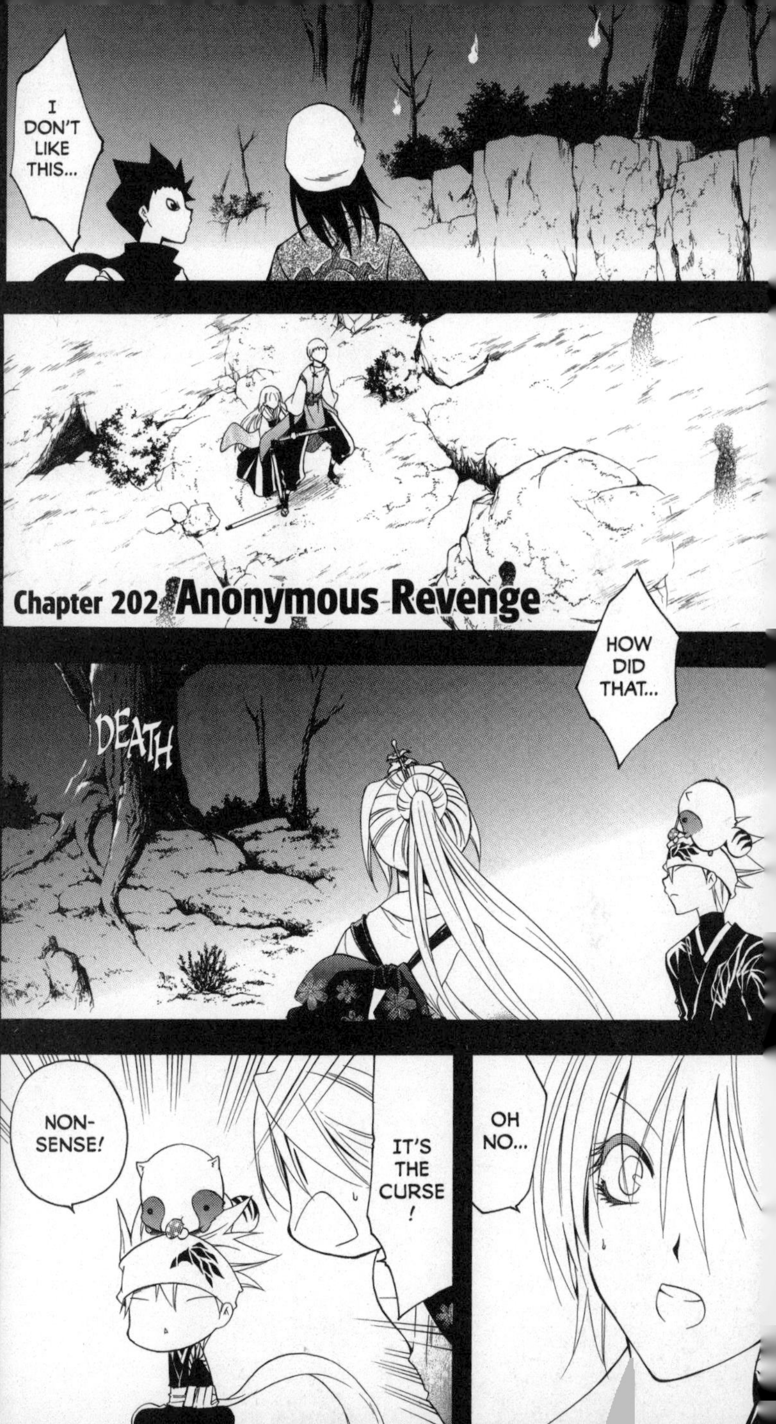

I DON'T LIKE THIS...
Chapter 202 Anonymous Revenge
HOW DID THAT...
DEATH
OH NO...
IT'S THE CURSE!
NON-SENSE!

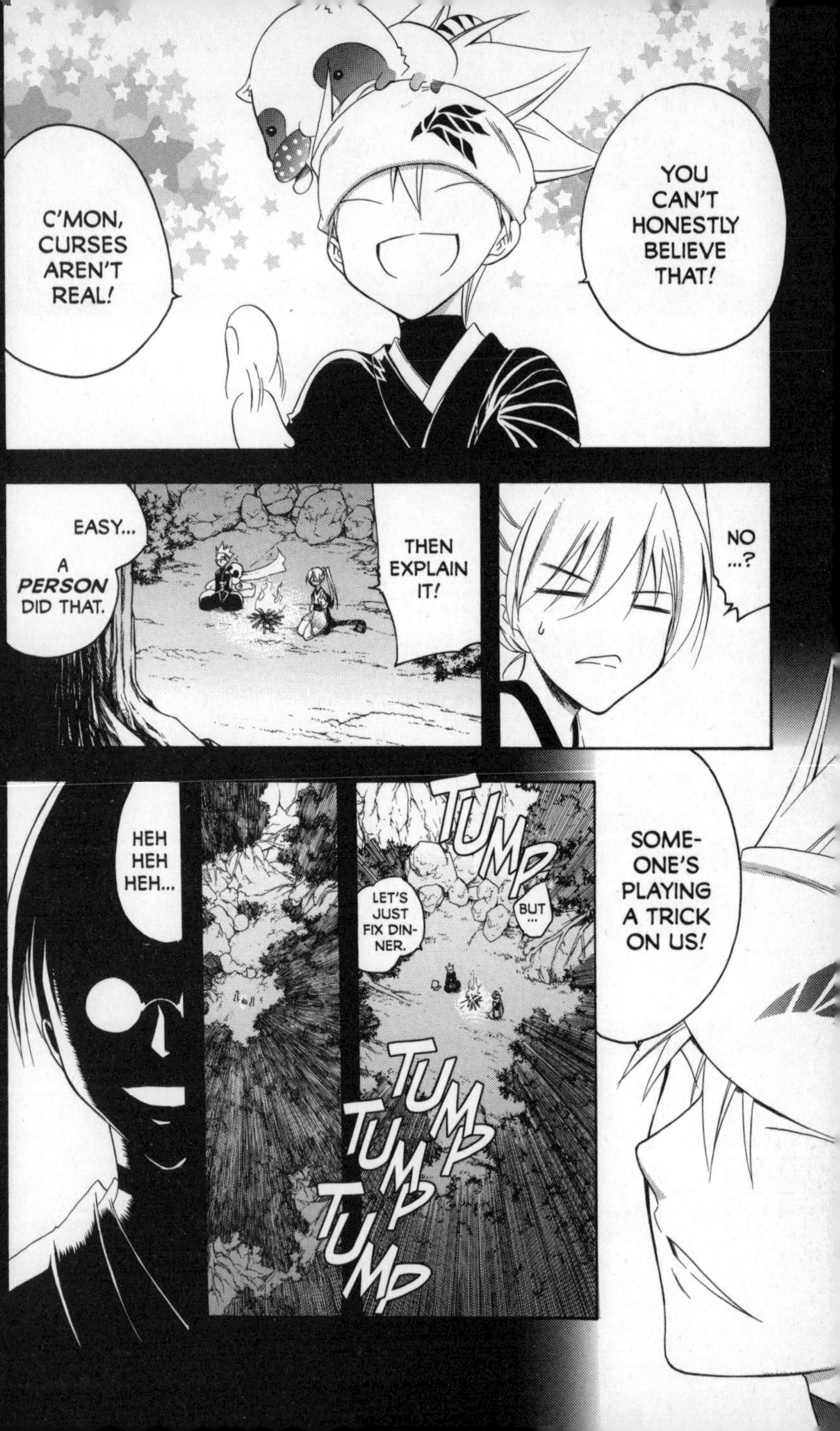
YOU CAN'T HONESTLY BELIEVE THAT!
C'MON, CURSES AREN'T REAL!
NO ...?
THEN EXPLAIN IT!
EASY... A *PERSON* DID THAT.
SOME-ONE'S PLAYING A TRICK ON US!
TUMP
BUT ...
LET'S JUST FIX DIN-NER.
TUMP
TUMP
TUMP
HEH HEH HEH...

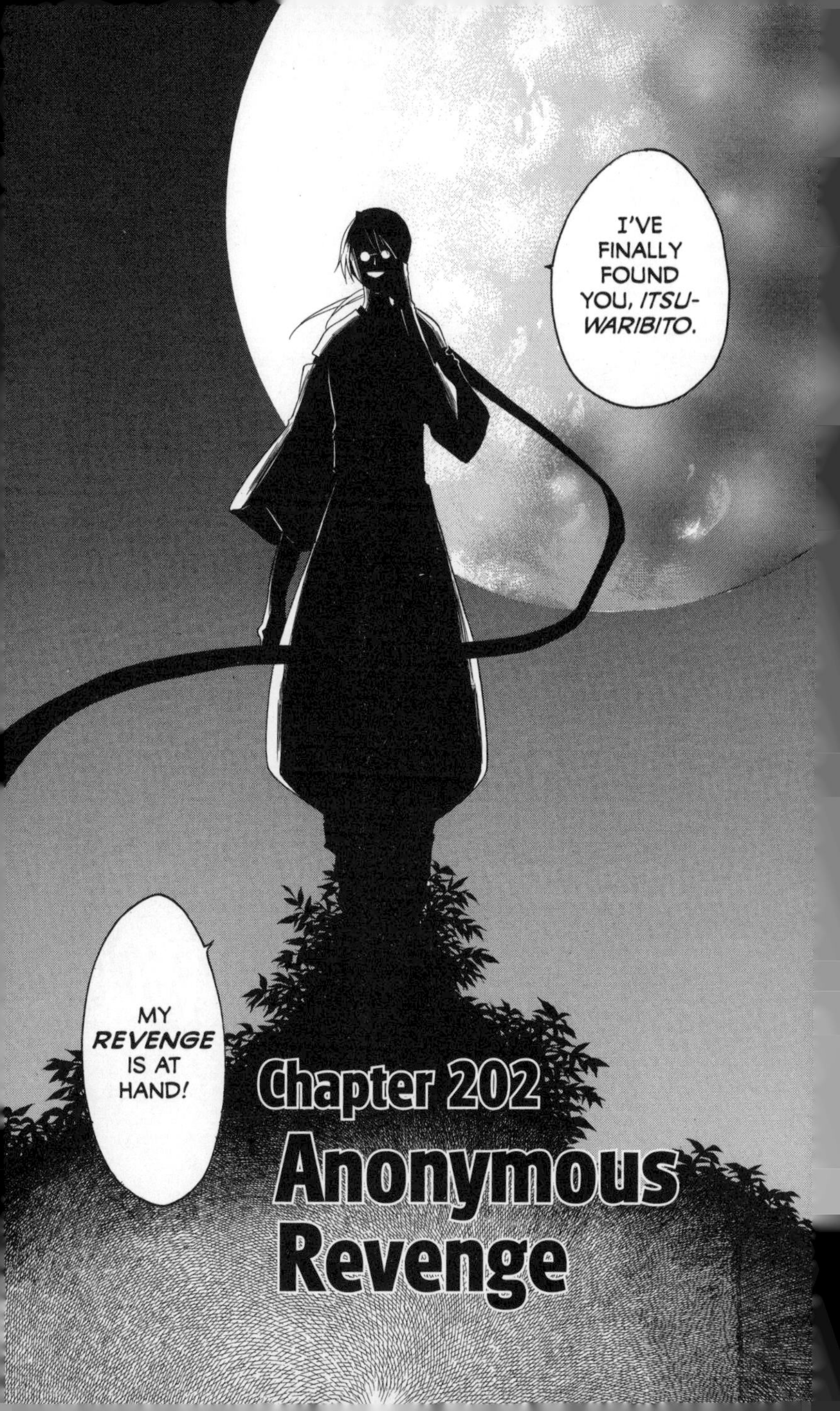
I'VE FINALLY FOUND YOU, *ITSU-WARIBITO.*
MY *REVENGE* IS AT HAND!
Chapter 202
Anonymous Revenge

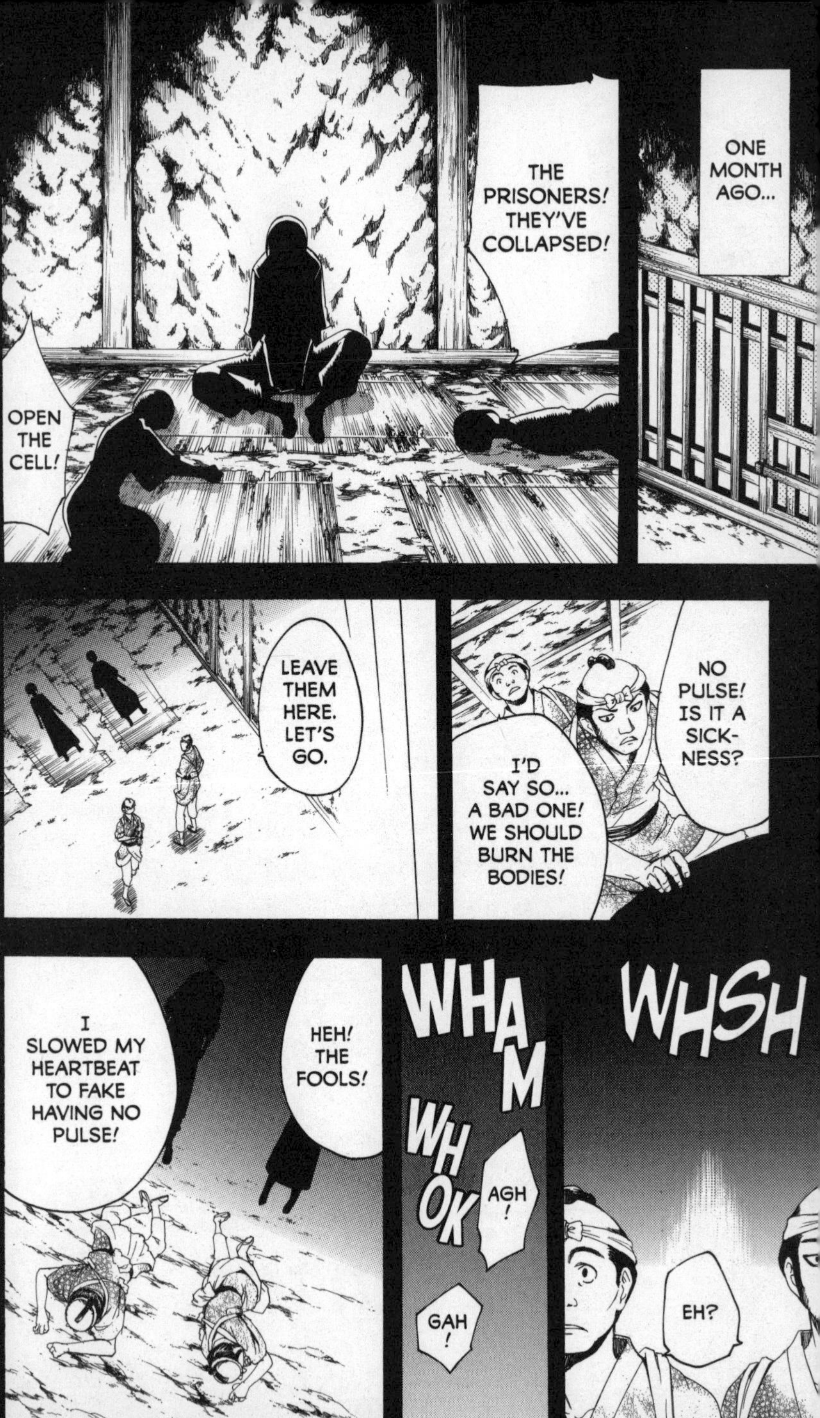
ONE MONTH AGO...
THE PRISONERS! THEY'VE COLLAPSED!
OPEN THE CELL!
NO PULSE! IS IT A SICKNESS?
I'D SAY SO... A BAD ONE! WE SHOULD BURN THE BODIES!
LEAVE THEM HERE. LET'S GO.
WHSH
EH?
WHAM
WHOK
AGH!
GAH!
HEH! THE FOOLS!
I SLOWED MY HEARTBEAT TO FAKE HAVING NO PULSE!

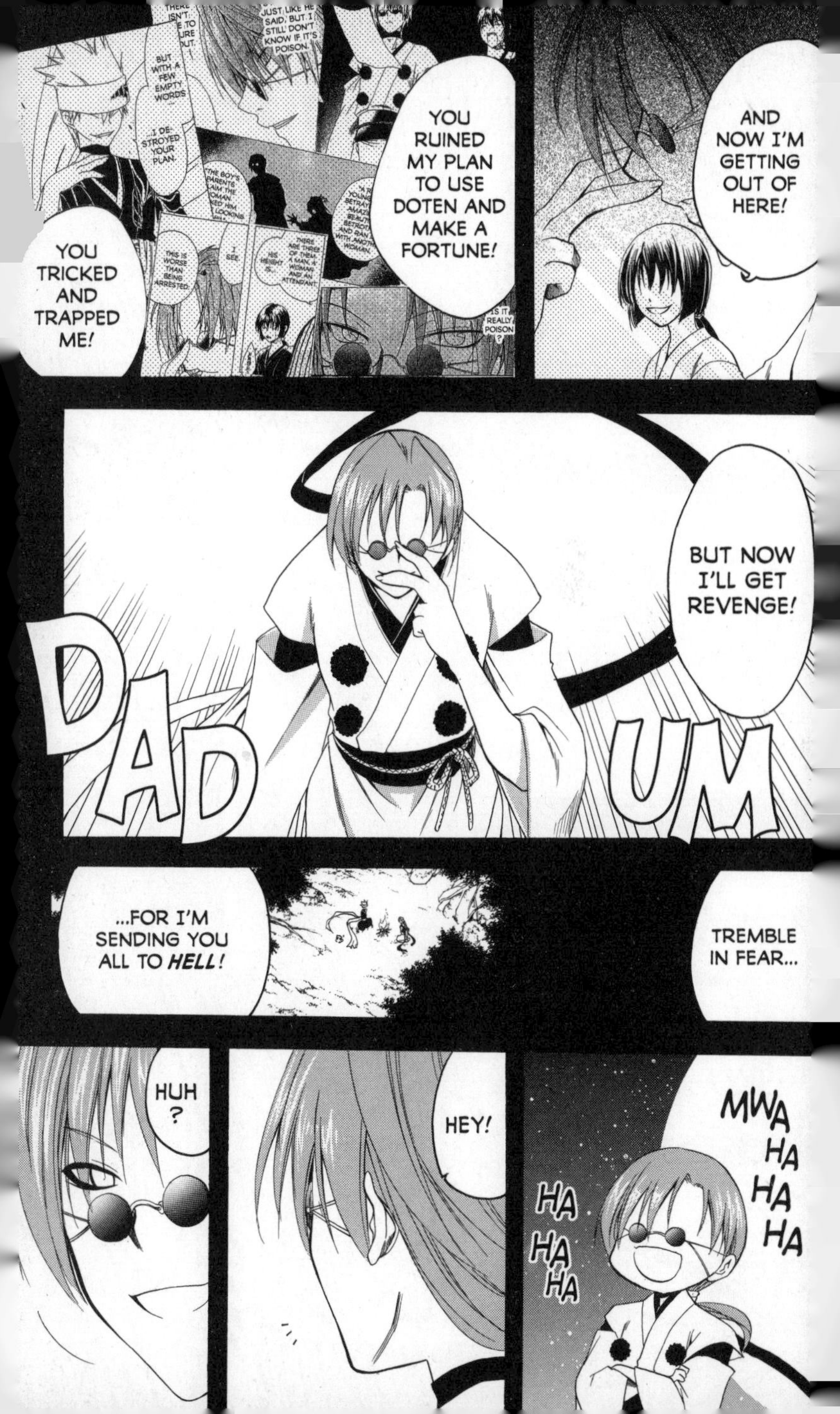
AND NOW I'M GETTING OUT OF HERE!
YOU RUINED MY PLAN TO USE DOTEN AND MAKE A FORTUNE!
JUST LIKE HE SAID, BUT I STILL DON'T KNOW IF IT'S POISON.
BUT WITH A FEW EMPTY WORDS...
I DE-STROYED YOUR PLAN.
THERE ARE THREE OF THEM. A MAN, A WOMAN AND AN ATTENDANT.
HIS HEIGHT IS...
I SEE.
THIS IS WORSE THAN BEING ARRESTED.
IS IT REALLY POISON?
YOU TRICKED AND TRAPPED ME!
BUT NOW I'LL GET REVENGE!
DADUM
TREMBLE IN FEAR...
...FOR I'M SENDING YOU ALL TO *HELL*!
MWAHAHAHAHA
HAHAHAHA
HEY!
HUH?

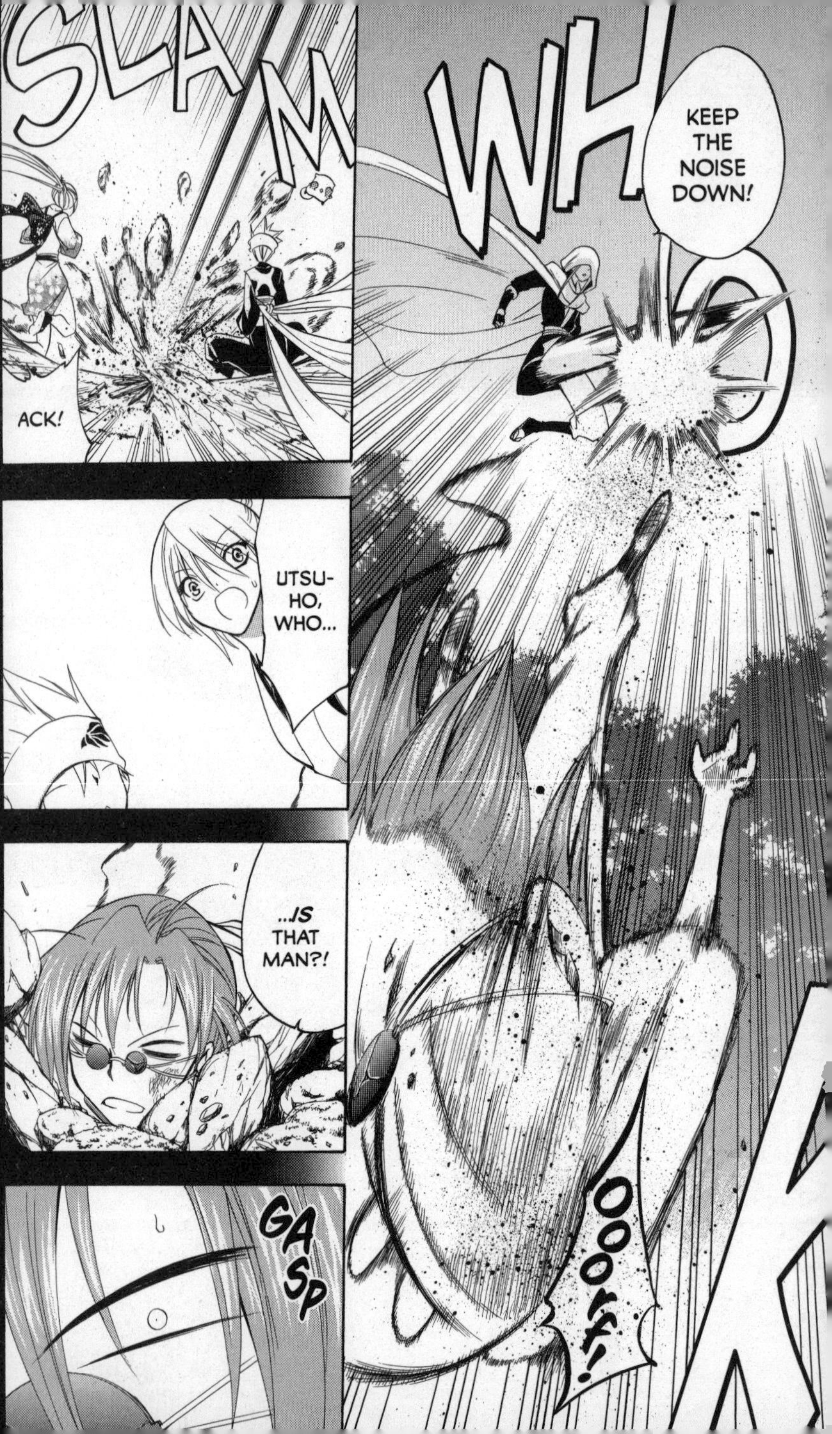
WHO
KEEP THE NOISE DOWN!
OOOOKK!!
K
SLAM
ACK!
UTSU-HO, WHO...
...IS THAT MAN?!
GASP

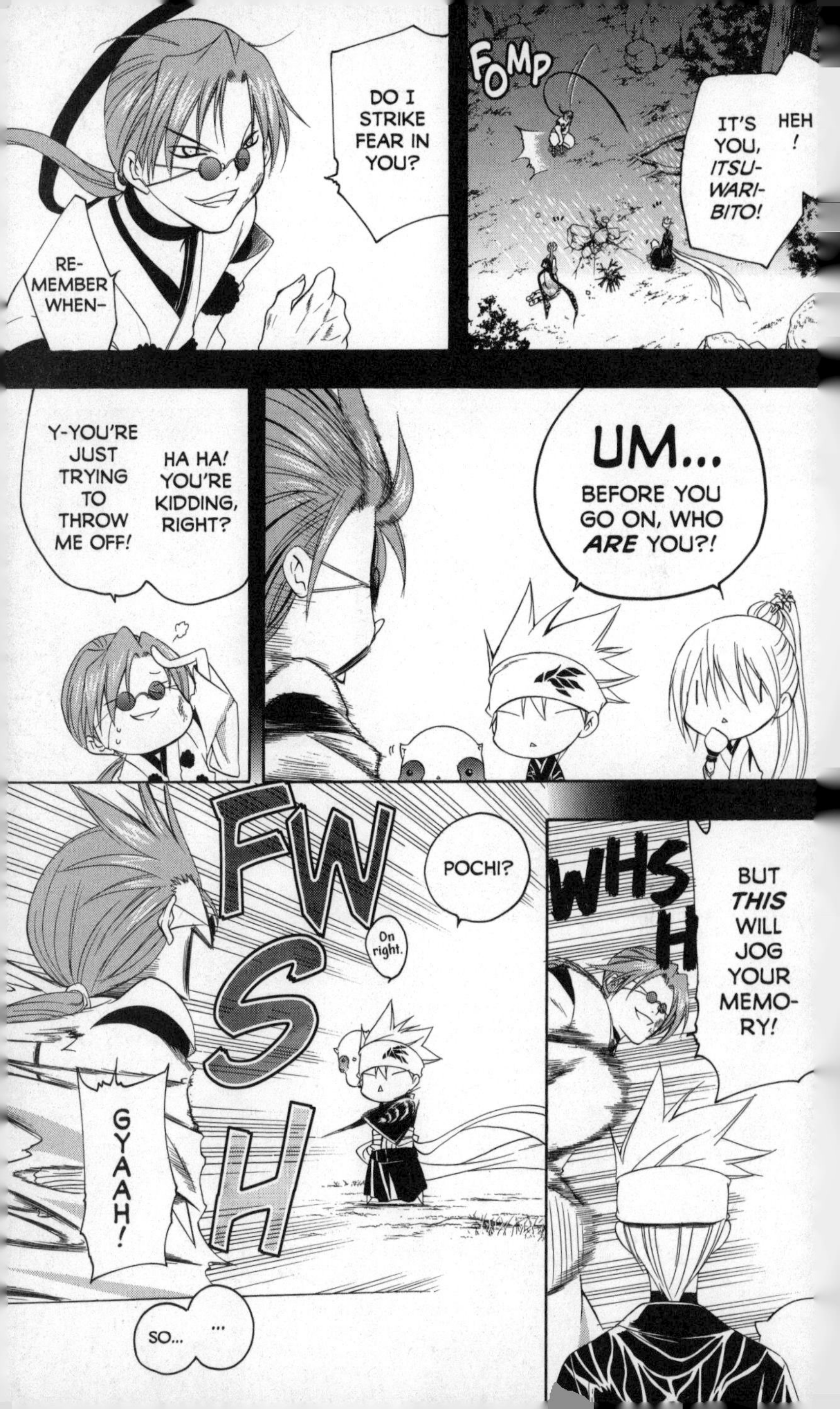
FOMP
HEH!
IT'S YOU, ITSUWARIBITO!
DO I STRIKE FEAR IN YOU?
REMEMBER WHEN–
UM... BEFORE YOU GO ON, WHO ARE YOU?!
HA HA! YOU'RE KIDDING, RIGHT?
Y-YOU'RE JUST TRYING TO THROW ME OFF!
WHSH
BUT THIS WILL JOG YOUR MEMORY!
FWSH
POCHI?
On right.
GYAAH!
...
SO...

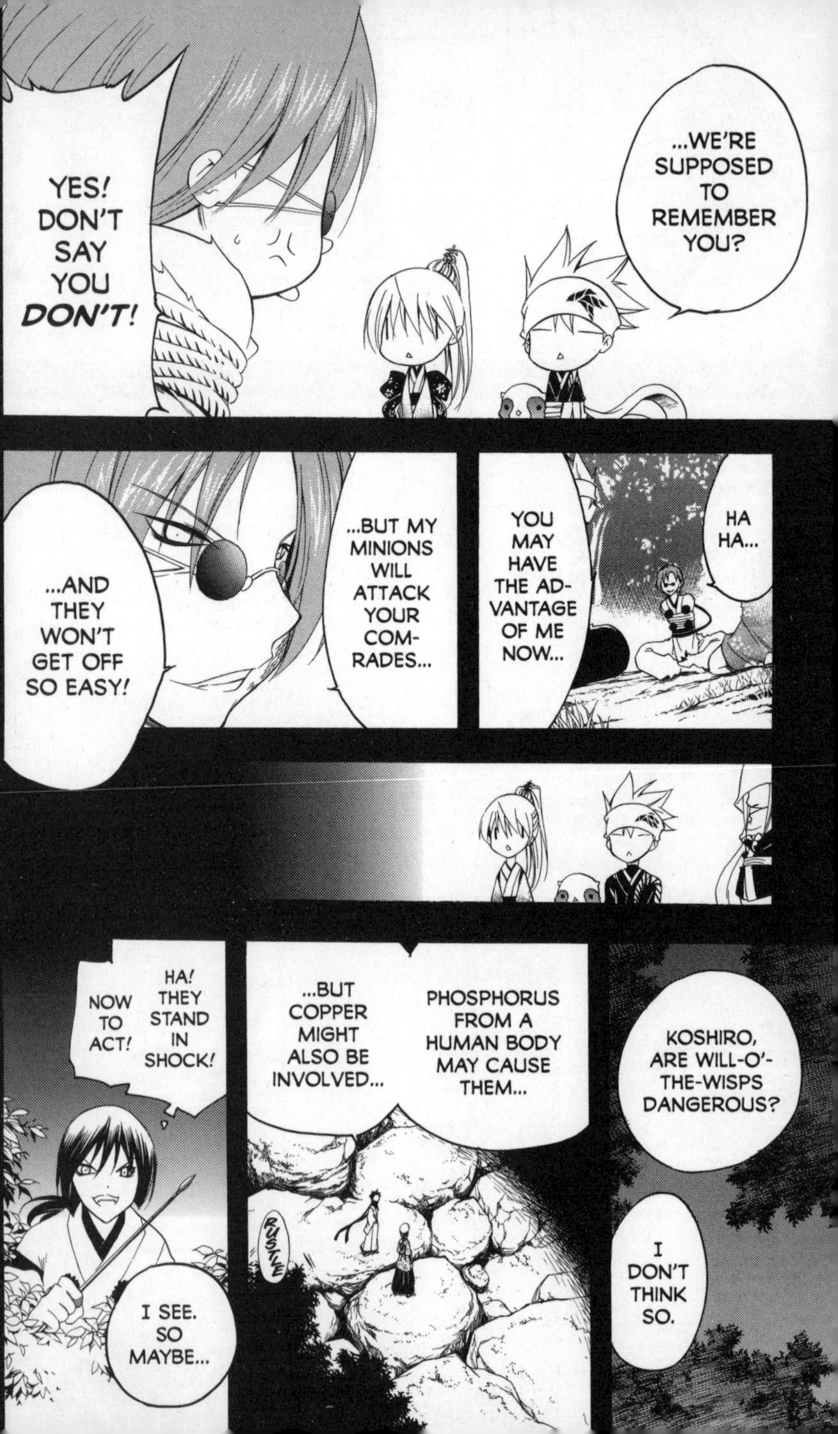
...WE'RE SUPPOSED TO REMEMBER YOU?
YES! DON'T SAY YOU *DON'T*!
HA HA...
YOU MAY HAVE THE AD-VANTAGE OF ME NOW...
...BUT MY MINIONS WILL ATTACK YOUR COM-RADES...
...AND THEY WON'T GET OFF SO EASY!
KOSHIRO, ARE WILL-O'-THE-WISPS DANGEROUS?
I DON'T THINK SO.
PHOSPHORUS FROM A HUMAN BODY MAY CAUSE THEM...
...BUT COPPER MIGHT ALSO BE INVOLVED...
RUSTLE
HA! THEY STAND IN SHOCK!
NOW TO ACT!
I SEE. SO MAYBE...

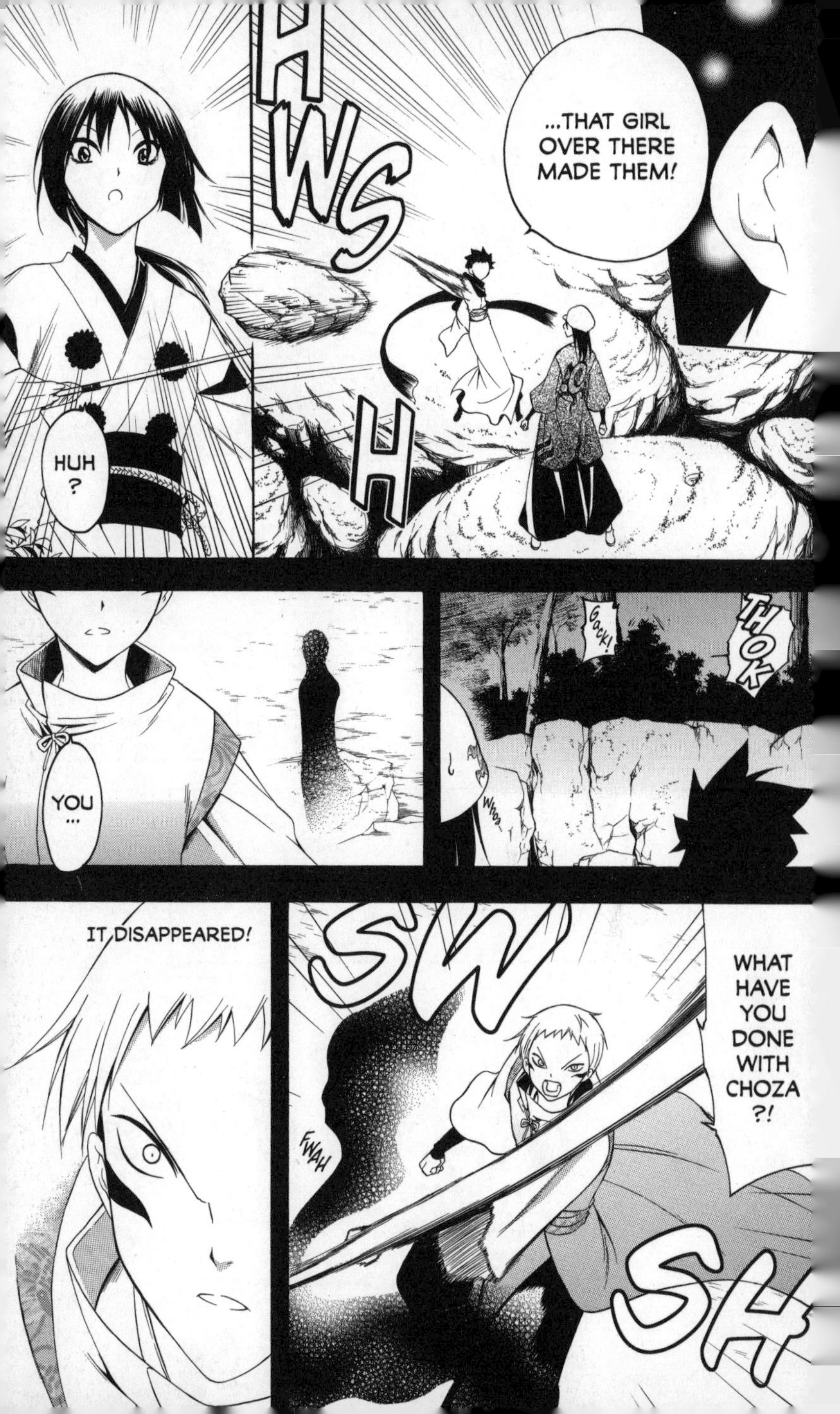

...THAT GIRL OVER THERE MADE THEM!
HWS
H
HUH ?
THOK
GACK!
WHOA...
YOU ...
SW
WHAT HAVE YOU DONE WITH CHOZA ?!
FWAH
SH
IT DISAPPEARED!

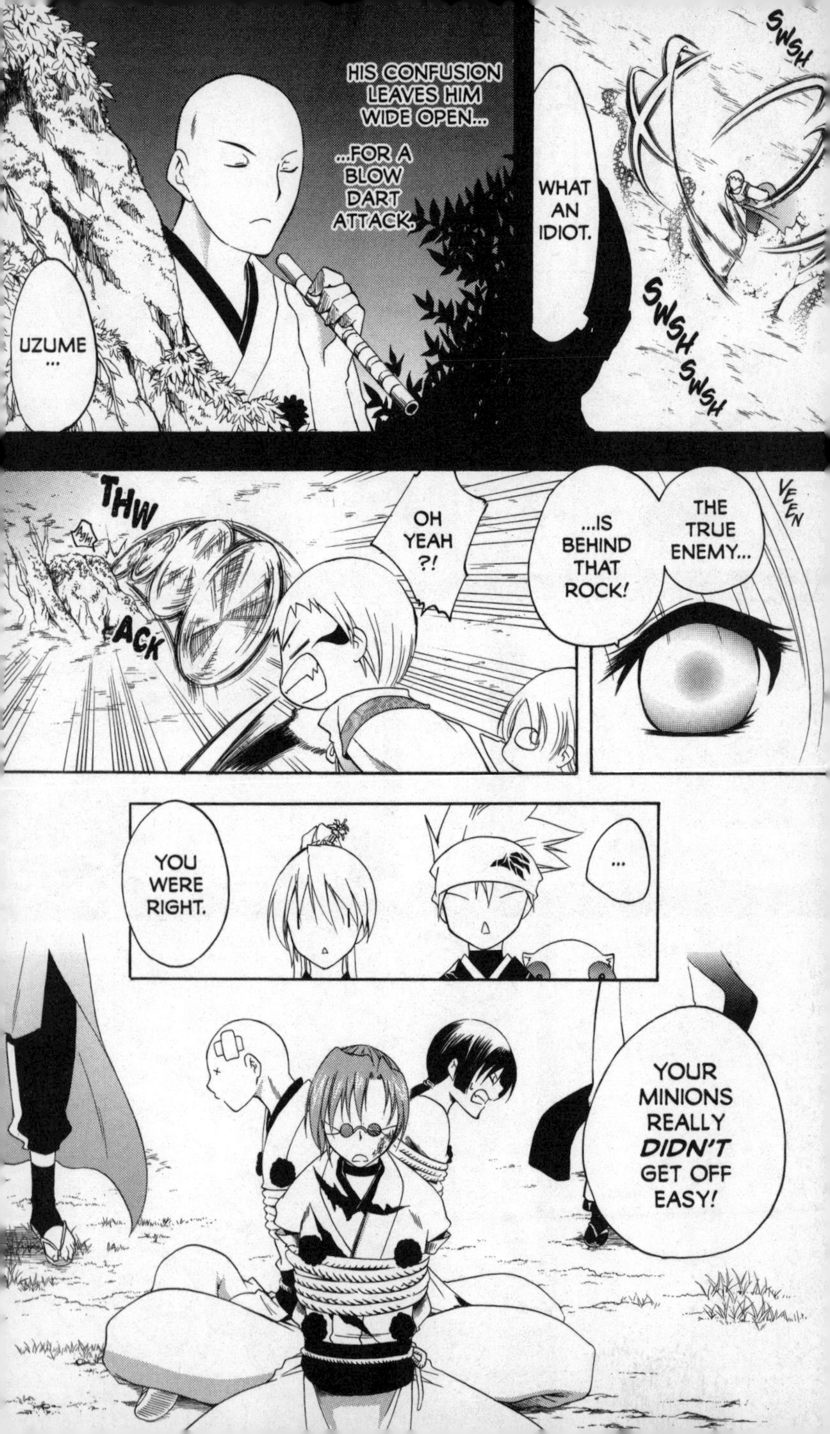
SWSH
WHAT AN IDIOT.
SWSH SWSH
HIS CONFUSION LEAVES HIM WIDE OPEN...
...FOR A BLOW DART ATTACK.
UZUME...
VEEN
THE TRUE ENEMY...
...IS BEHIND THAT ROCK!
OH YEAH?!
THWACK
...
YOU WERE RIGHT.
YOUR MINIONS REALLY *DIDN'T* GET OFF EASY!

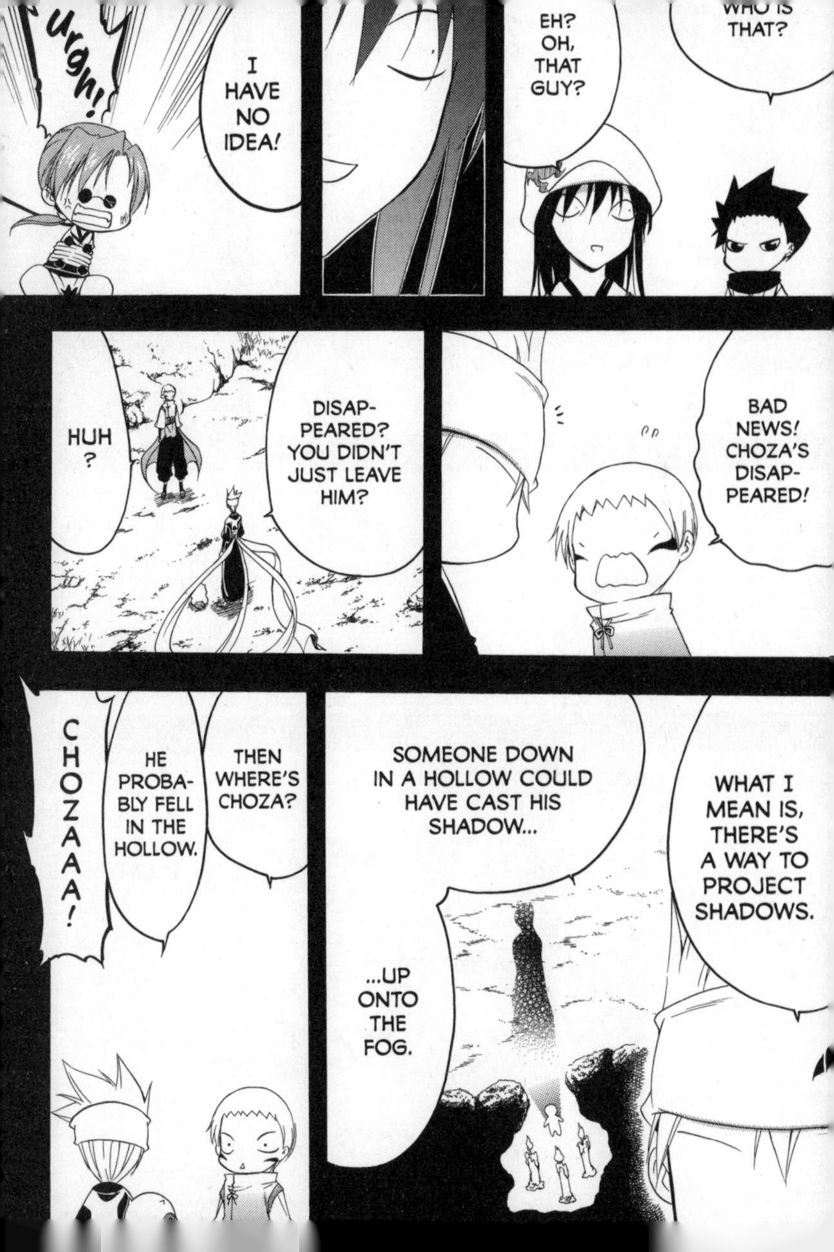
WHO IS THAT?
EH? OH, THAT GUY?
I HAVE NO IDEA!
urgh!
BAD NEWS! CHOZA'S DISAP-PEARED!
DISAP-PEARED? YOU DIDN'T JUST LEAVE HIM?
HUH ?
WHAT I MEAN IS, THERE'S A WAY TO PROJECT SHADOWS.
SOMEONE DOWN IN A HOLLOW COULD HAVE CAST HIS SHADOW...
...UP ONTO THE FOG.
THEN WHERE'S CHOZA?
HE PROBA-BLY FELL IN THE HOLLOW.
CHOZAAAA!

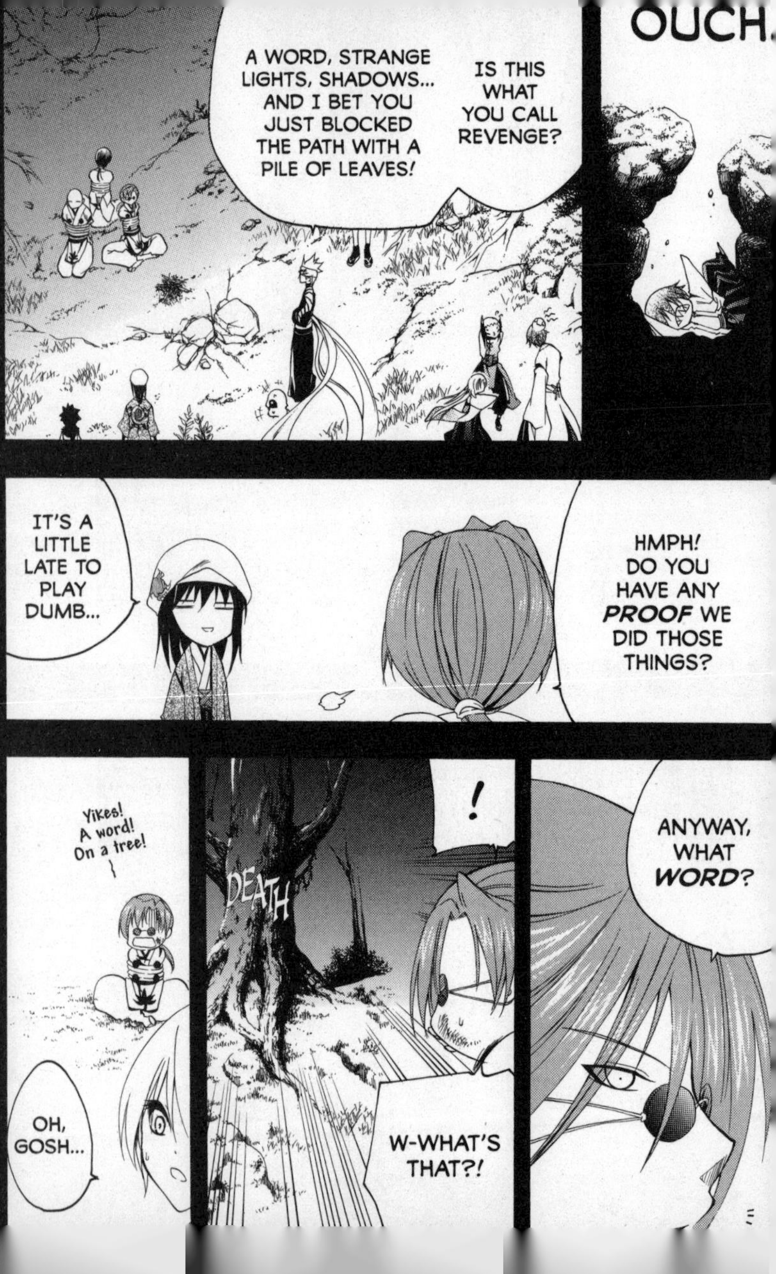
OUCH.
A WORD, STRANGE LIGHTS, SHADOWS... AND I BET YOU JUST BLOCKED THE PATH WITH A PILE OF LEAVES!
IS THIS WHAT YOU CALL REVENGE?
HMPH! DO YOU HAVE ANY ***PROOF*** WE DID THOSE THINGS?
IT'S A LITTLE LATE TO PLAY DUMB...
ANYWAY, WHAT ***WORD***?
!
DEATH
W-WHAT'S THAT?!
Yikes! A word! On a tree!
OH, GOSH...

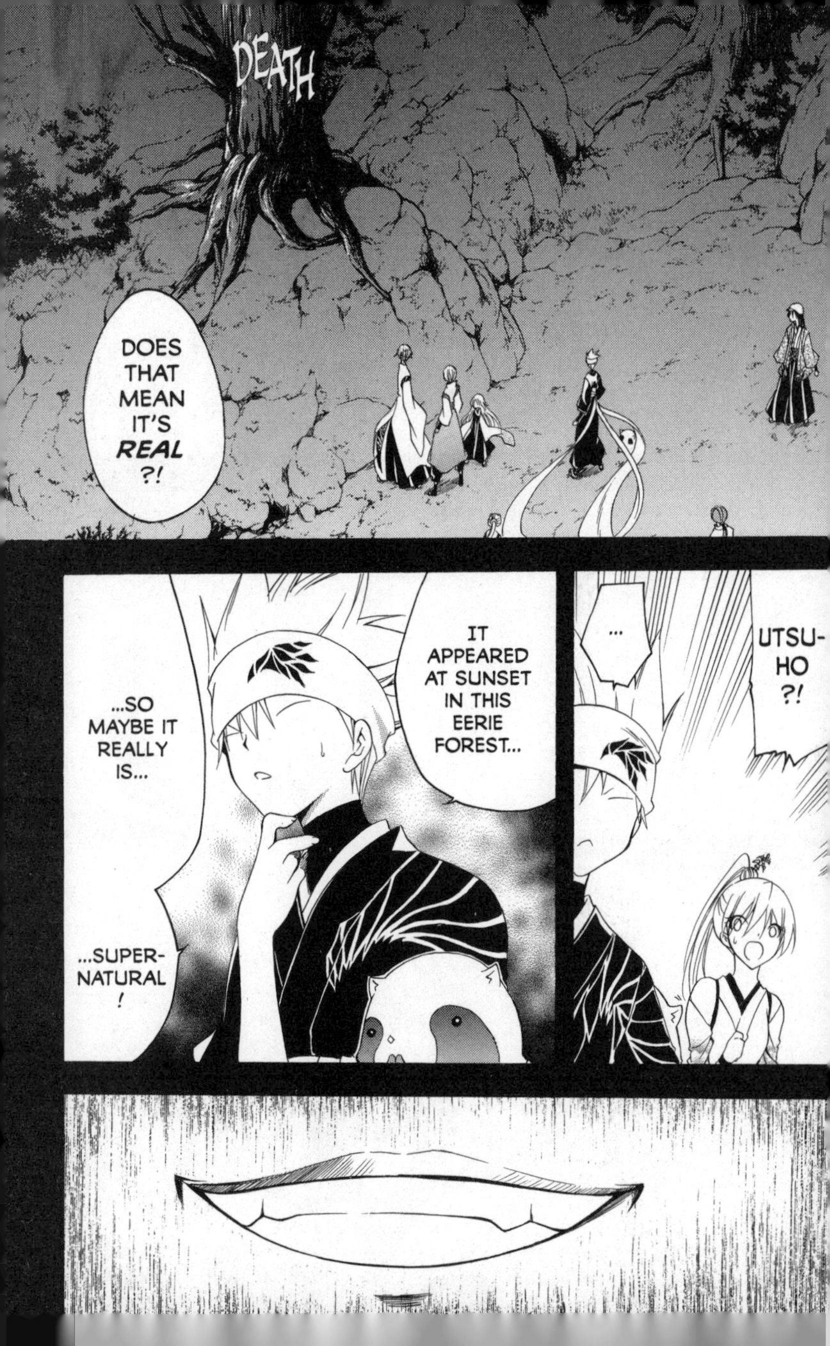
DEATH
DOES THAT MEAN IT'S *REAL*?!
UTSU-HO?!
...
IT APPEARED AT SUNSET IN THIS EERIE FOREST...
...SO MAYBE IT REALLY IS...
...SUPER-NATURAL!

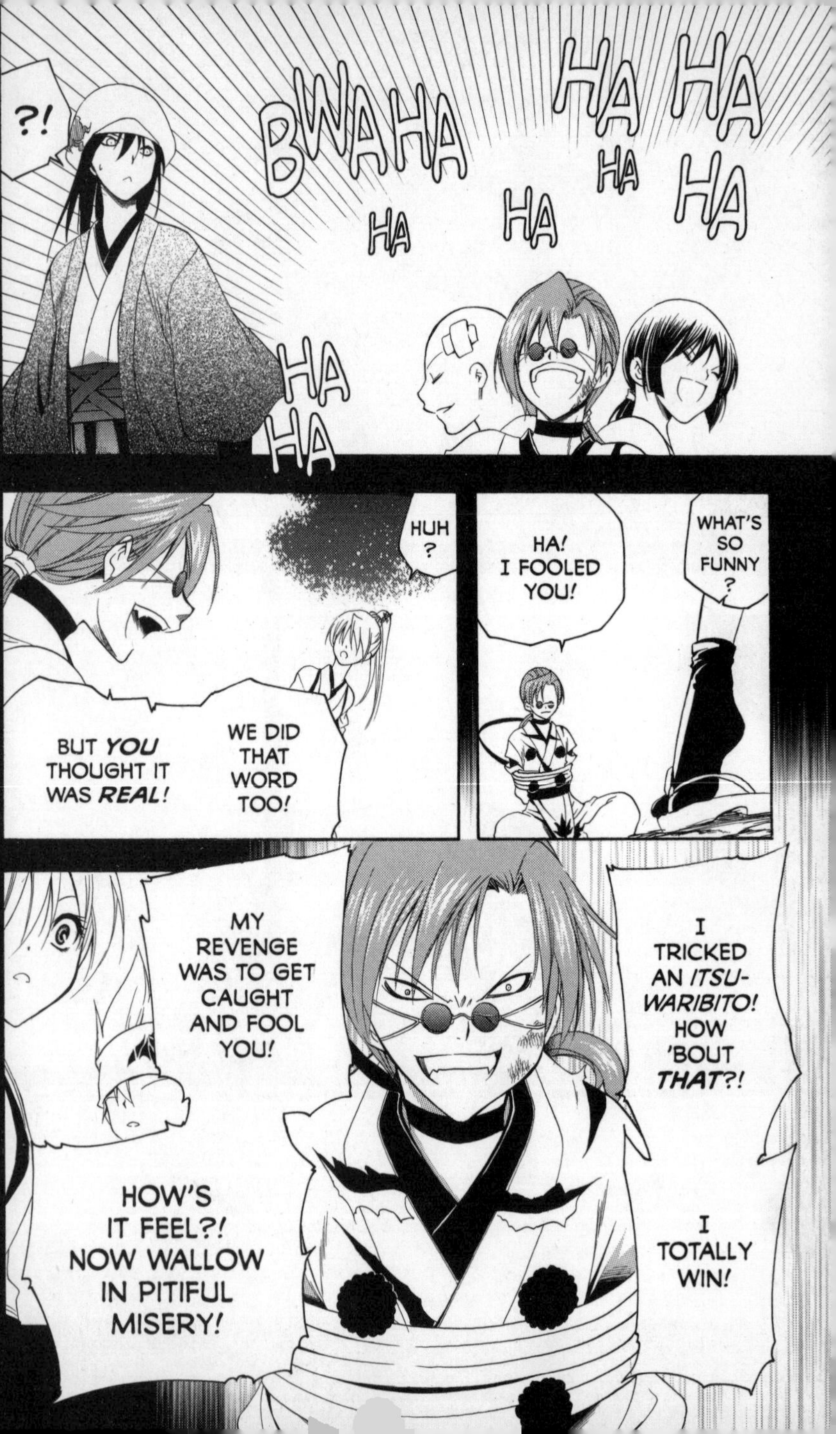
HA HA
HA
HA
BWAHAHA
HA
HA
?!
HA HA
WHAT'S SO FUNNY?
HA! I FOOLED YOU!
HUH?
WE DID THAT WORD TOO!
BUT YOU THOUGHT IT WAS REAL!
I TRICKED AN ITSU-WARIBITO! HOW 'BOUT THAT?!
MY REVENGE WAS TO GET CAUGHT AND FOOL YOU!
I TOTALLY WIN!
HOW'S IT FEEL?! NOW WALLOW IN PITIFUL MISERY!

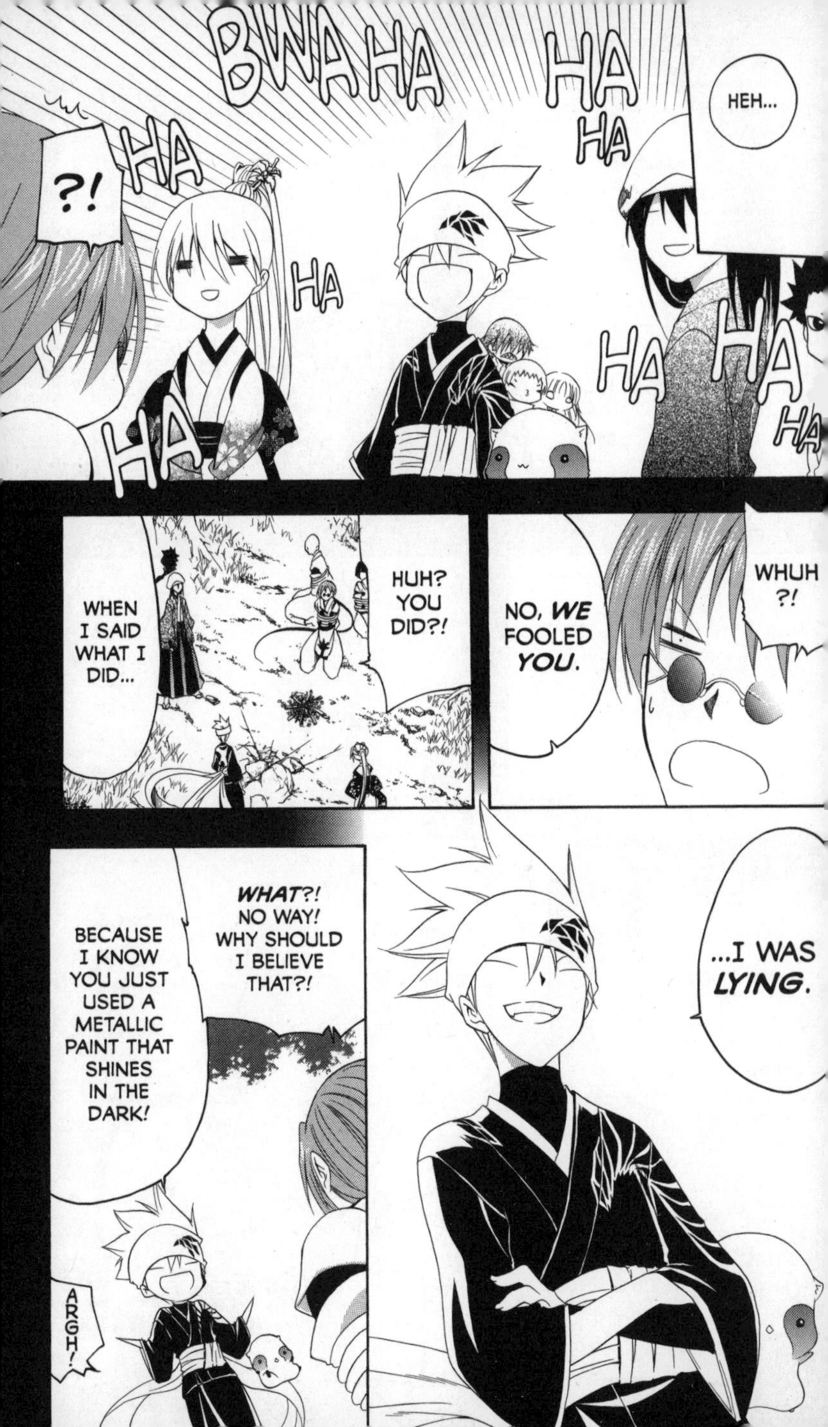
HEH...
BWAHA HA
HA
HA
HA
HA
HA HA
HA
?!
WHUH ?!
NO, *WE* FOOLED *YOU*.
HUH? YOU DID?!
WHEN I SAID WHAT I DID...
...I WAS *LYING*.
WHAT?! NO WAY! WHY SHOULD I BELIEVE THAT?!
BECAUSE I KNOW YOU JUST USED A METALLIC PAINT THAT SHINES IN THE DARK!
ARGH!

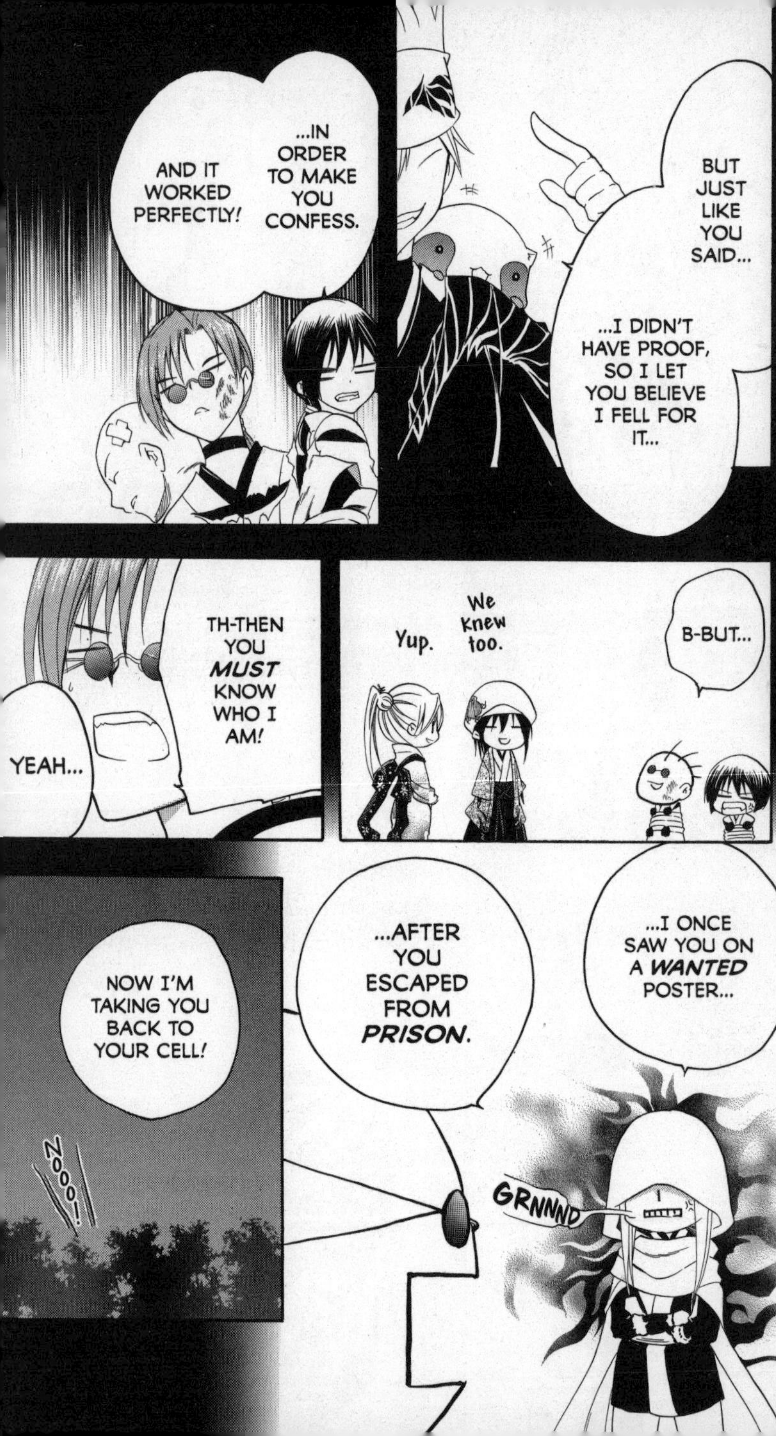
BUT JUST LIKE YOU SAID...
...I DIDN'T HAVE PROOF, SO I LET YOU BELIEVE I FELL FOR IT...
...IN ORDER TO MAKE YOU CONFESS.
AND IT WORKED PERFECTLY!
B-BUT...
We knew too.
Yup.
TH-THEN YOU MUST KNOW WHO I AM!
YEAH...
...I ONCE SAW YOU ON A WANTED POSTER...
...AFTER YOU ESCAPED FROM PRISON.
GRNNND
NOW I'M TAKING YOU BACK TO YOUR CELL!
NOOOO!

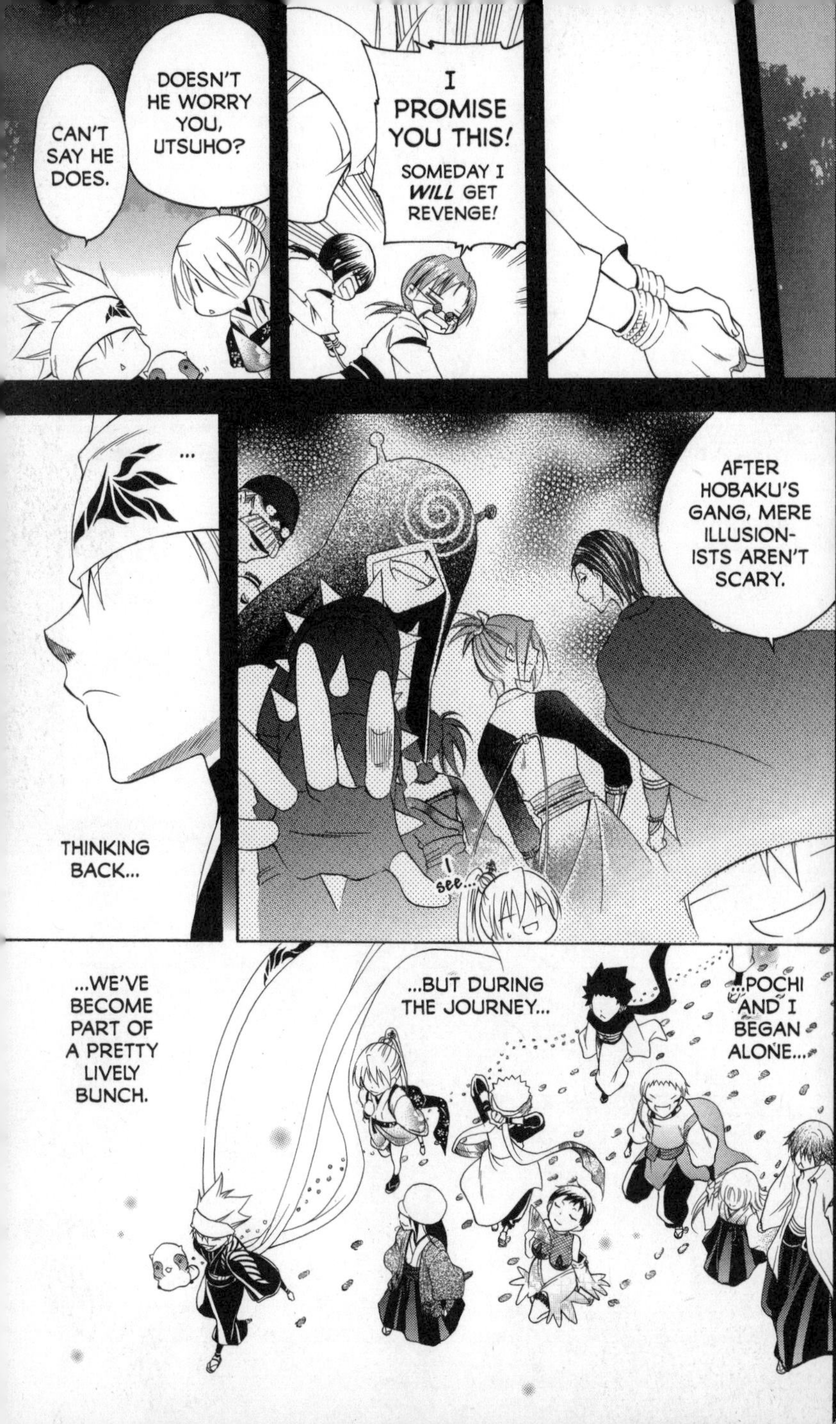
I PROMISE YOU THIS!
SOMEDAY I *WILL* GET REVENGE!
DOESN'T HE WORRY YOU, UTSUHO?
CAN'T SAY HE DOES.
AFTER HOBAKU'S GANG, MERE ILLUSION-ISTS AREN'T SCARY.
I see...
...
THINKING BACK...
...POCHI AND I BEGAN ALONE...
...BUT DURING THE JOURNEY...
...WE'VE BECOME PART OF A PRETTY LIVELY BUNCH.

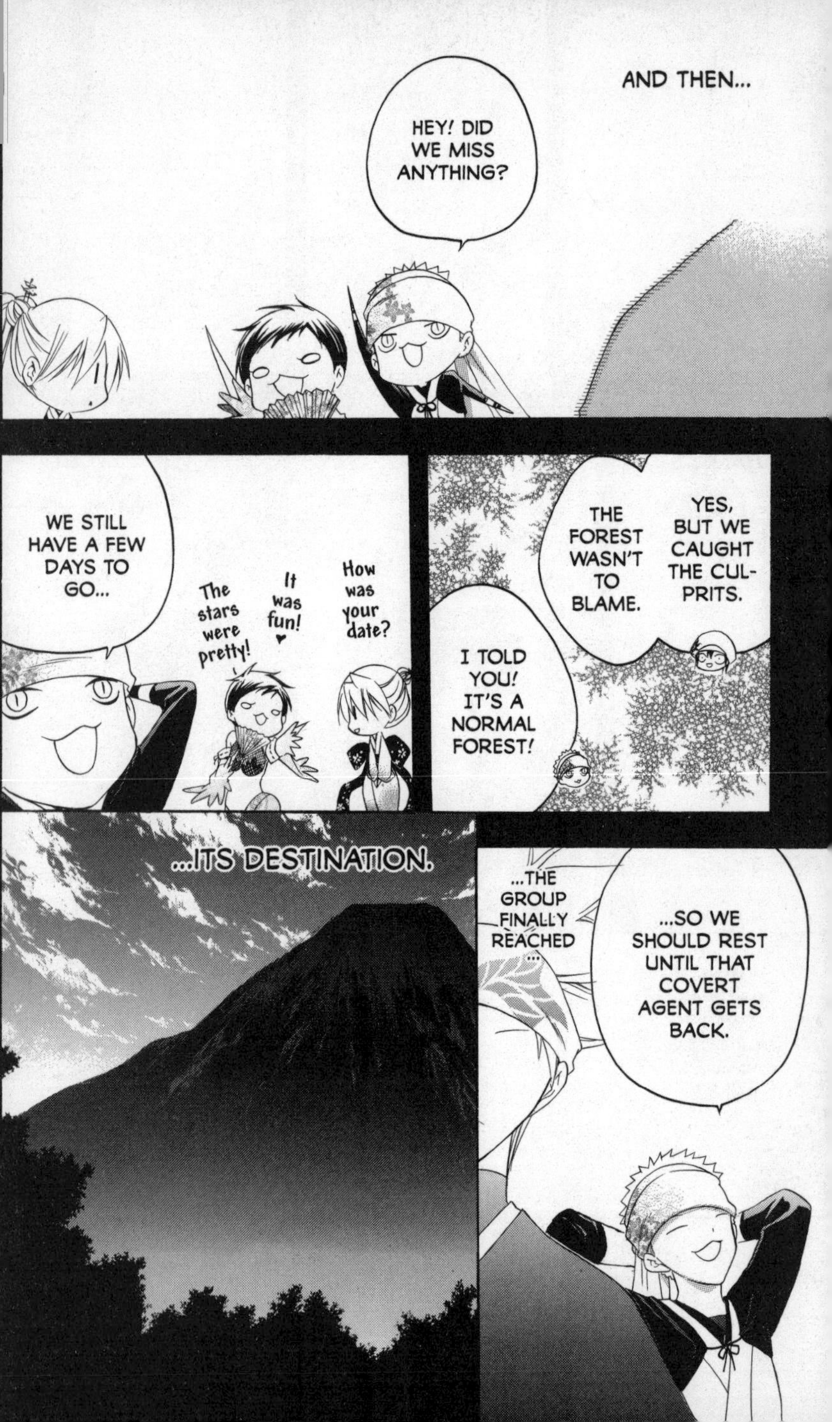
AND THEN...
HEY! DID WE MISS ANYTHING?
YES, BUT WE CAUGHT THE CUL-PRITS.
THE FOREST WASN'T TO BLAME.
I TOLD YOU! IT'S A NORMAL FOREST!
How was your date?
It was fun! ♥
The stars were pretty!
WE STILL HAVE A FEW DAYS TO GO...
...SO WE SHOULD REST UNTIL THAT COVERT AGENT GETS BACK.
...THE GROUP FINALLY REACHED...
...ITS DESTINATION.

Chapter 203 The Real Treasure

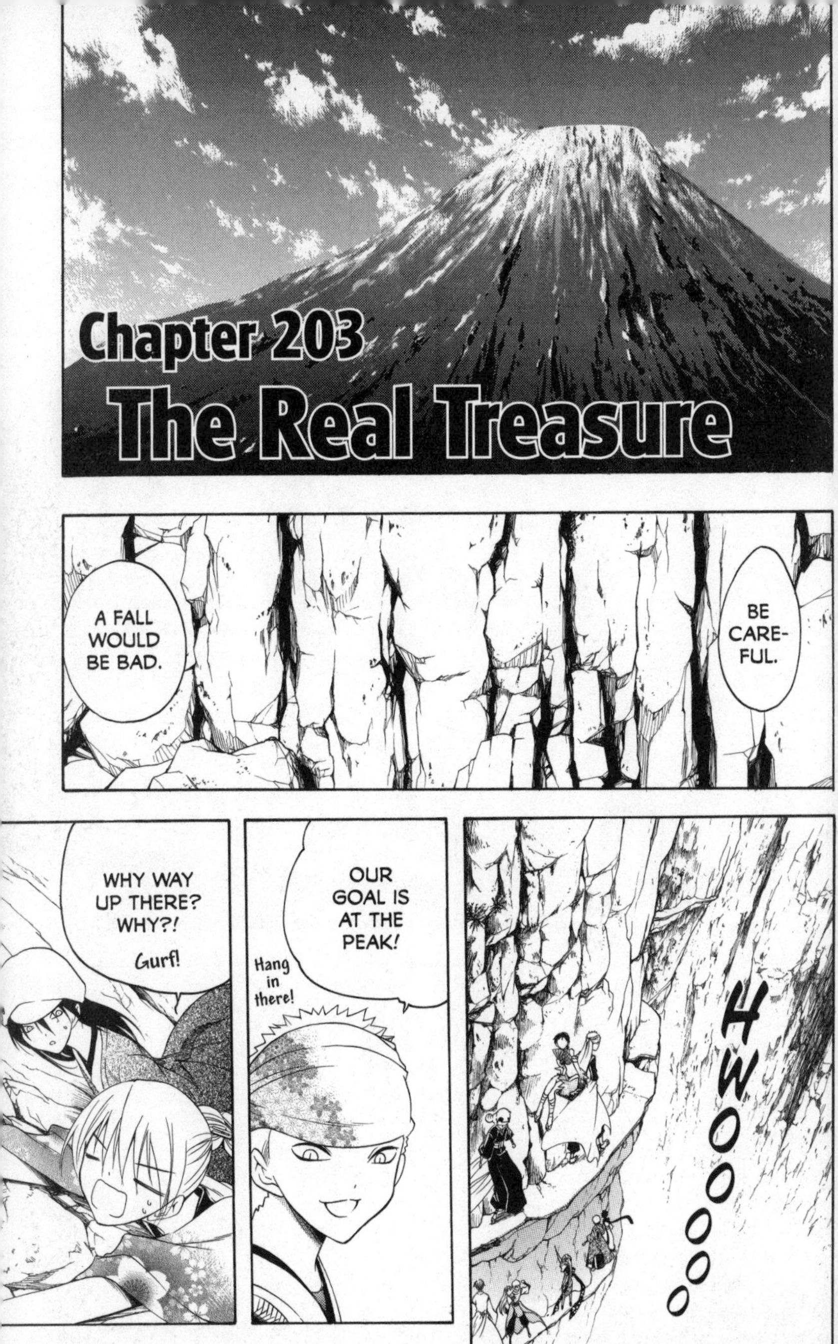

Chapter 203
The Real Treasure
BE CAREFUL.
A FALL WOULD BE BAD.
HWOOOOOOO
OUR GOAL IS AT THE PEAK!
Hang in there!
WHY WAY UP THERE? WHY?!
Gurf!

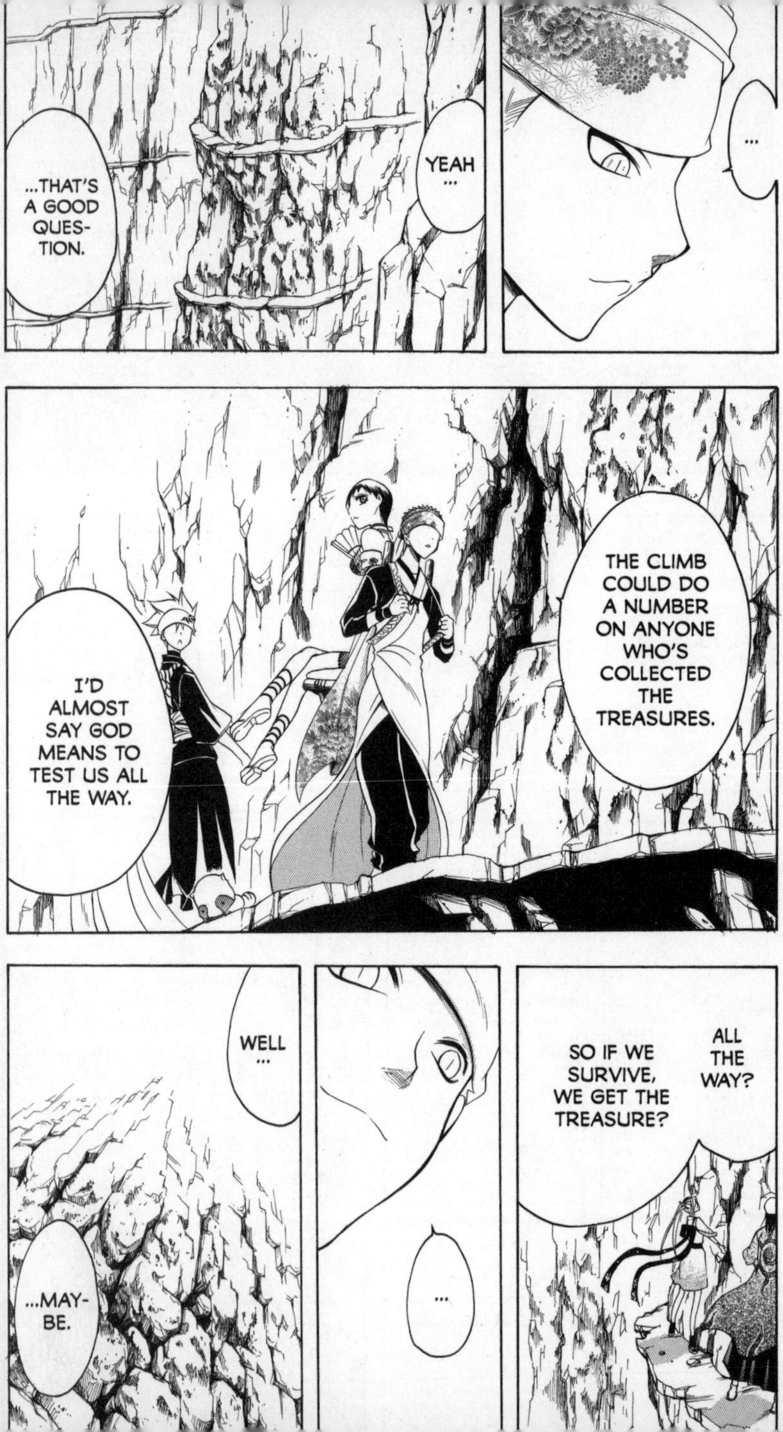
...
YEAH...
...THAT'S A GOOD QUES-TION.
THE CLIMB COULD DO A NUMBER ON ANYONE WHO'S COLLECTED THE TREASURES.
I'D ALMOST SAY GOD MEANS TO TEST US ALL THE WAY.
ALL THE WAY?
SO IF WE SURVIVE, WE GET THE TREASURE?
...
WELL...
...MAY-BE.

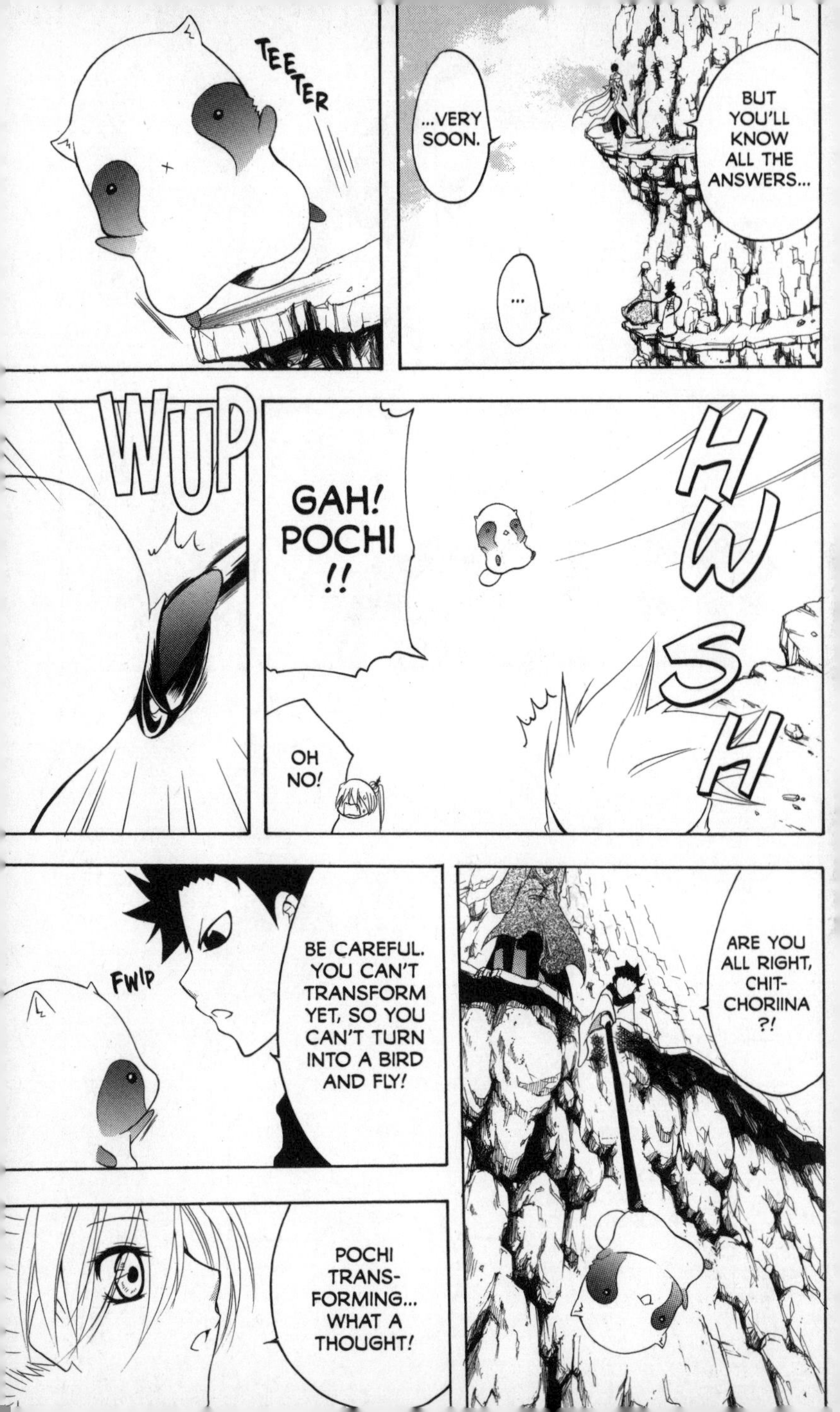

BUT YOU'LL KNOW ALL THE ANSWERS...
...VERY SOON.
...
TEETER
HWSH
GAH! POCHI!!
OH NO!
WUP
ARE YOU ALL RIGHT, CHIT-CHORIINA?!
BE CAREFUL. YOU CAN'T TRANSFORM YET, SO YOU CAN'T TURN INTO A BIRD AND FLY!
FWIP
POCHI TRANS-FORMING... WHAT A THOUGHT!

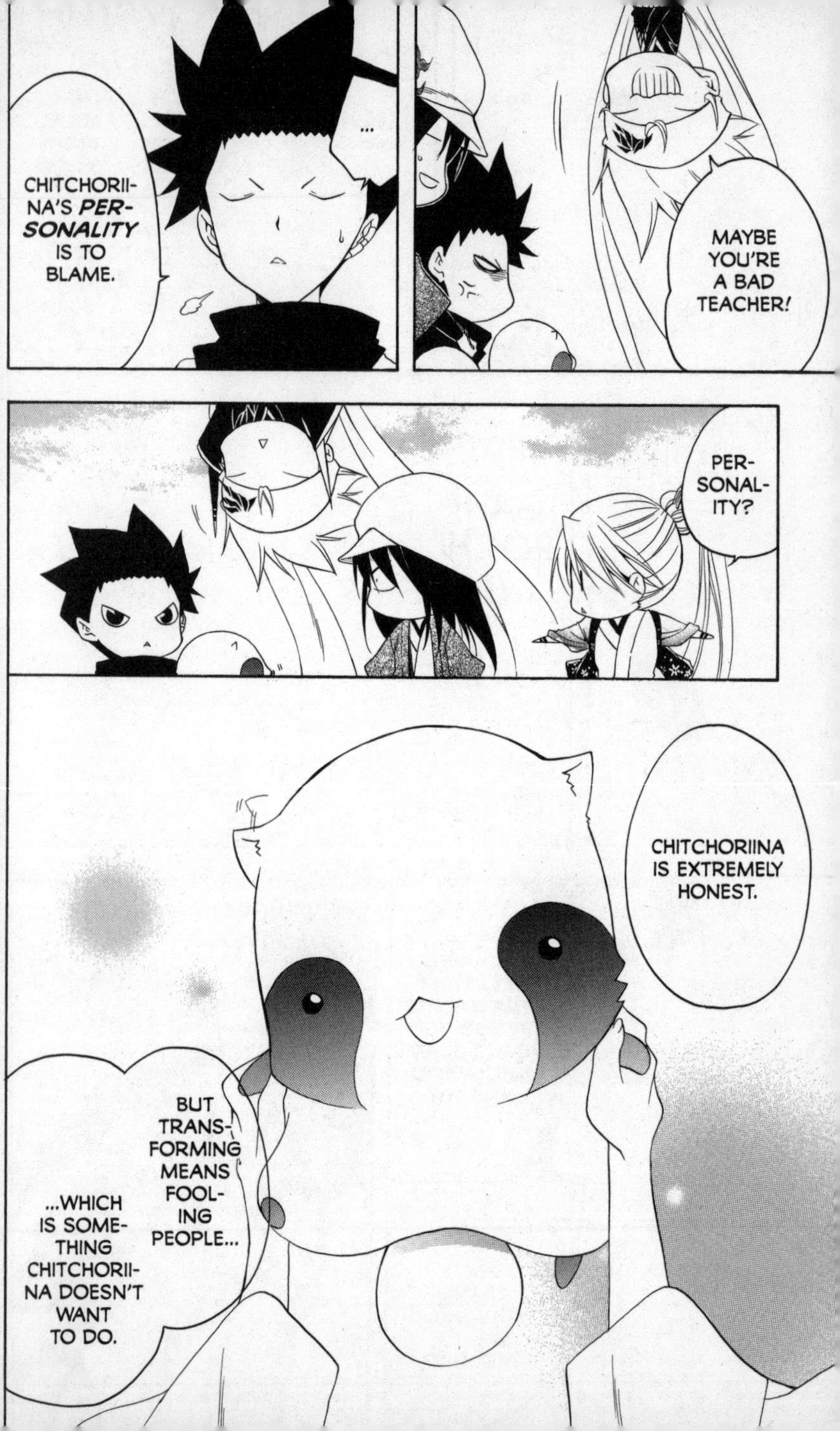
MAYBE YOU'RE A BAD TEACHER!
...
CHITCHORII-NA'S ***PER-SONALITY*** IS TO BLAME.
PER-SONAL-ITY?
CHITCHORIINA IS EXTREMELY HONEST.
BUT TRANS-FORMING MEANS FOOL-ING PEOPLE...
...WHICH IS SOME-THING CHITCHORII-NA DOESN'T WANT TO DO.

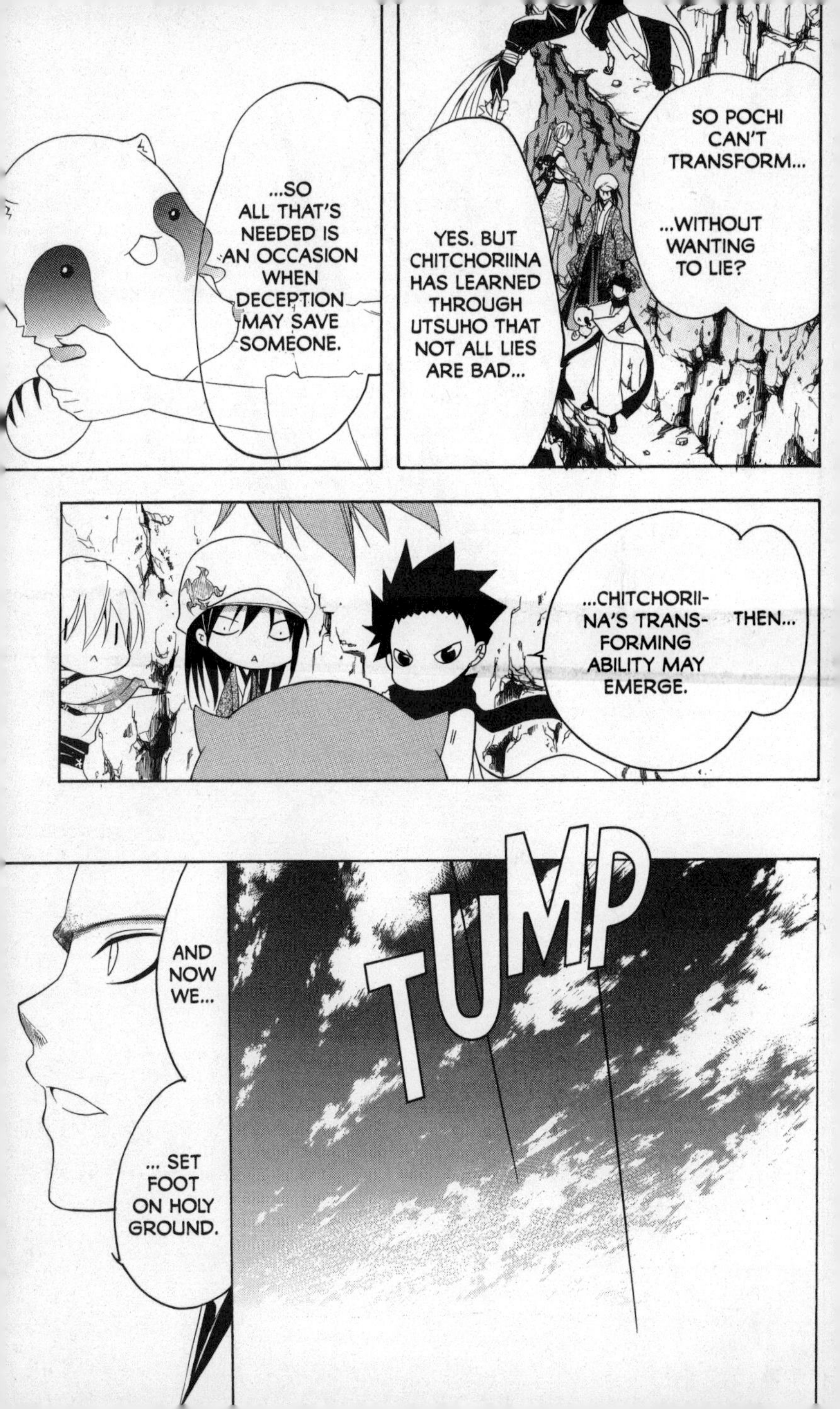
SO POCHI CAN'T TRANSFORM...
...WITHOUT WANTING TO LIE?
YES. BUT CHITCHORIINA HAS LEARNED THROUGH UTSUHO THAT NOT ALL LIES ARE BAD...
...SO ALL THAT'S NEEDED IS AN OCCASION WHEN DECEPTION MAY SAVE SOMEONE.
THEN...
...CHITCHORII-NA'S TRANS-FORMING ABILITY MAY EMERGE.
TUMP
AND NOW WE...
... SET FOOT ON HOLY GROUND.

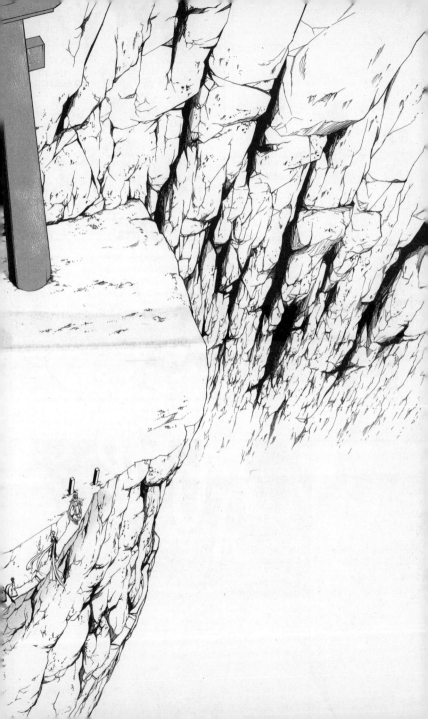

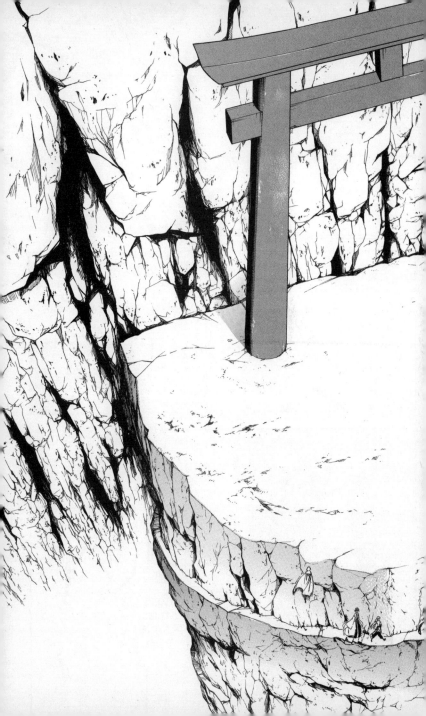

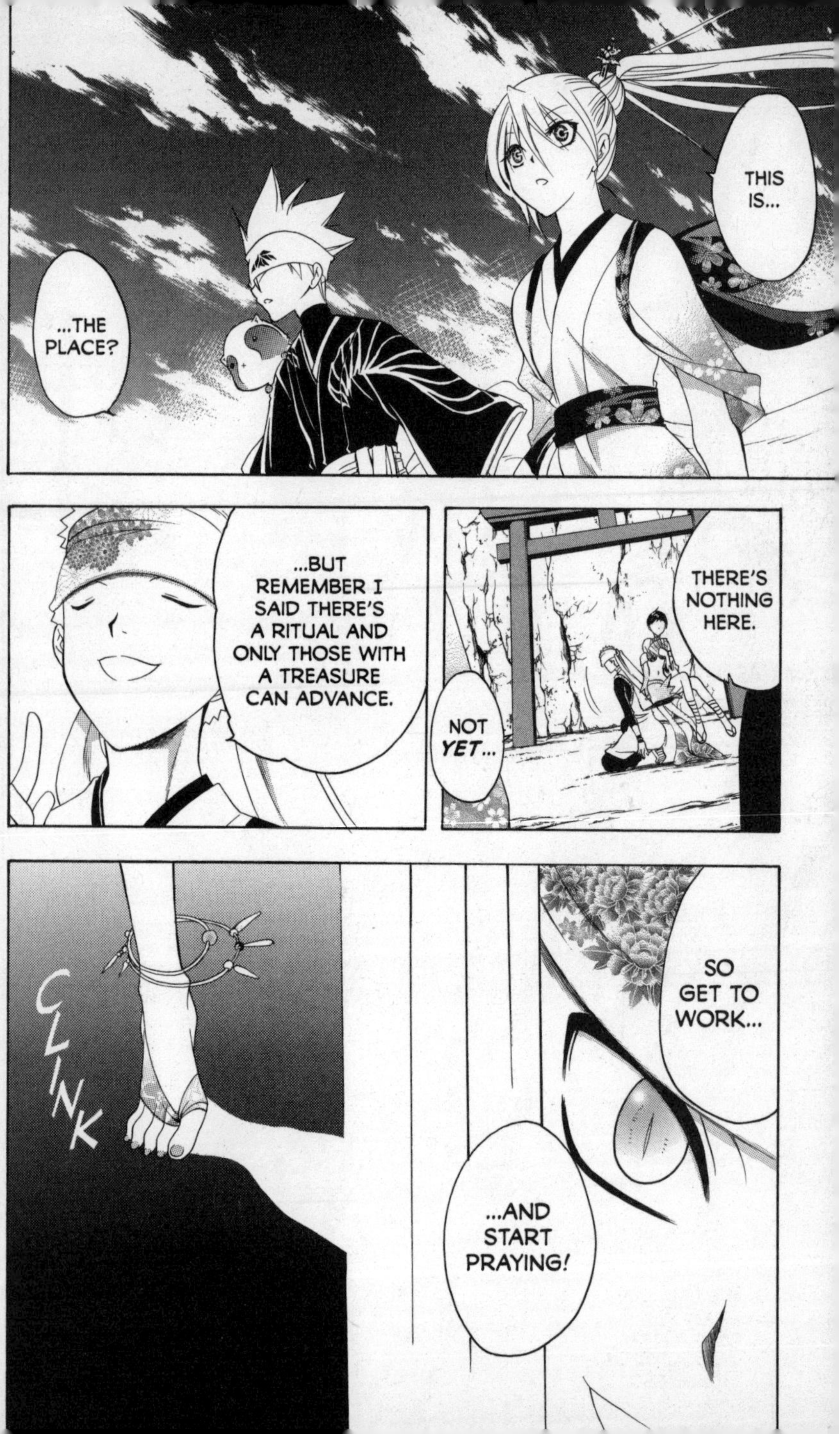
THIS IS...
...THE PLACE?
THERE'S NOTHING HERE.
NOT *YET*...
...BUT REMEMBER I SAID THERE'S A RITUAL AND ONLY THOSE WITH A TREASURE CAN ADVANCE.
SO GET TO WORK...
...AND START PRAYING!
CLINK

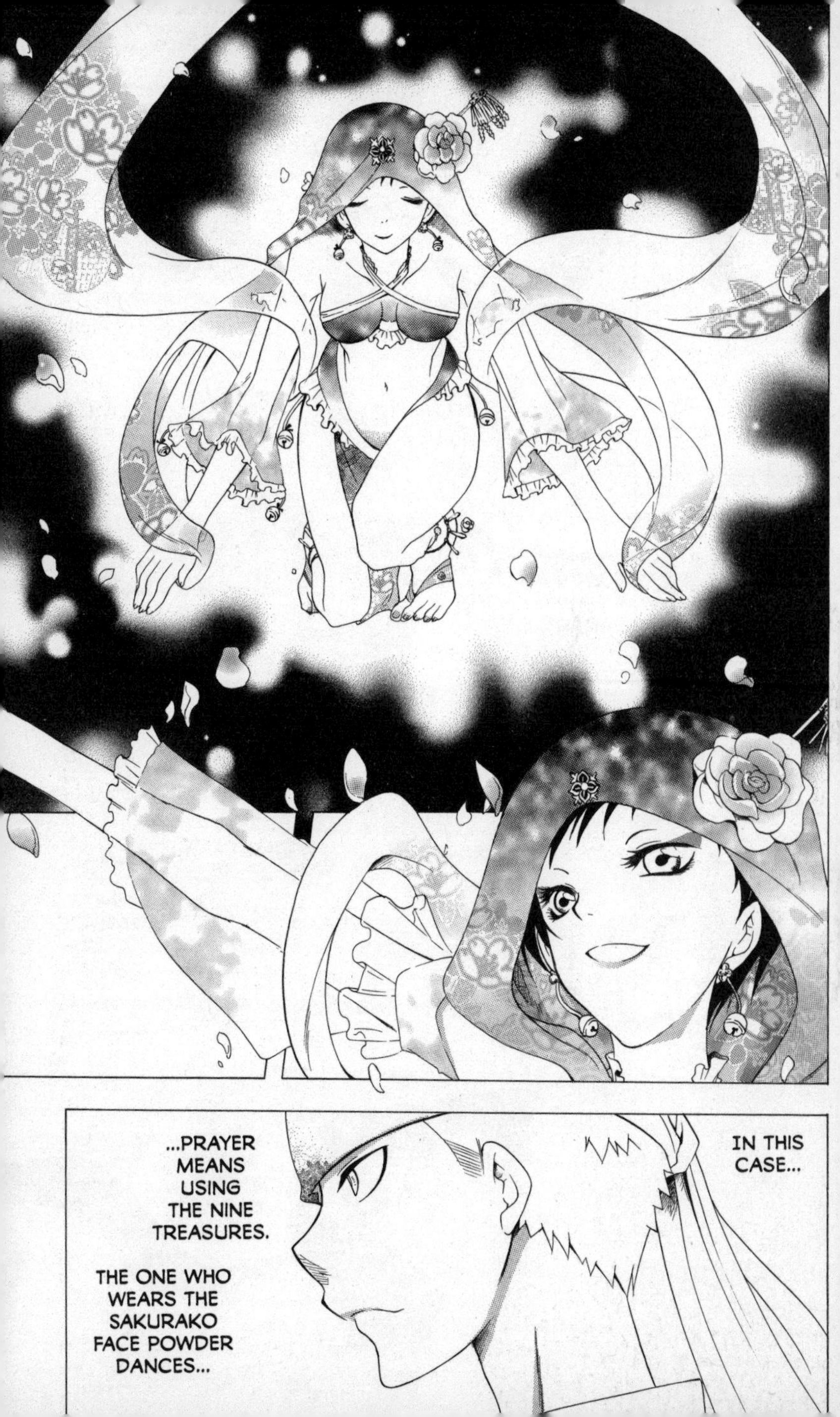
IN THIS CASE...
...PRAYER MEANS USING THE NINE TREASURES.
THE ONE WHO WEARS THE SAKURAKO FACE POWDER DANCES...

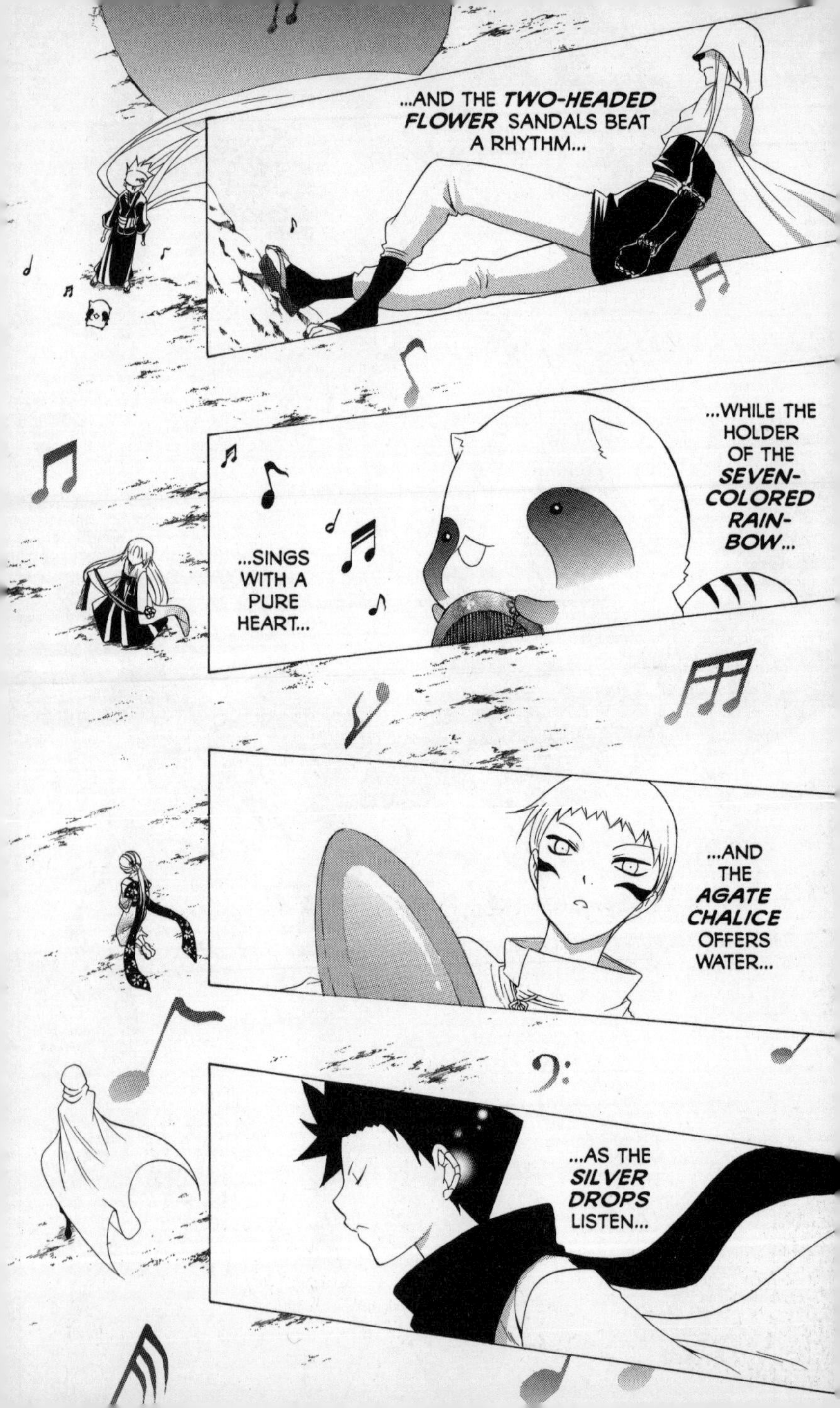
...AND THE TWO-HEADED FLOWER SANDALS BEAT A RHYTHM...
...WHILE THE HOLDER OF THE SEVEN-COLORED RAINBOW...
...SINGS WITH A PURE HEART...
...AND THE AGATE CHALICE OFFERS WATER...
...AS THE SILVER DROPS LISTEN...

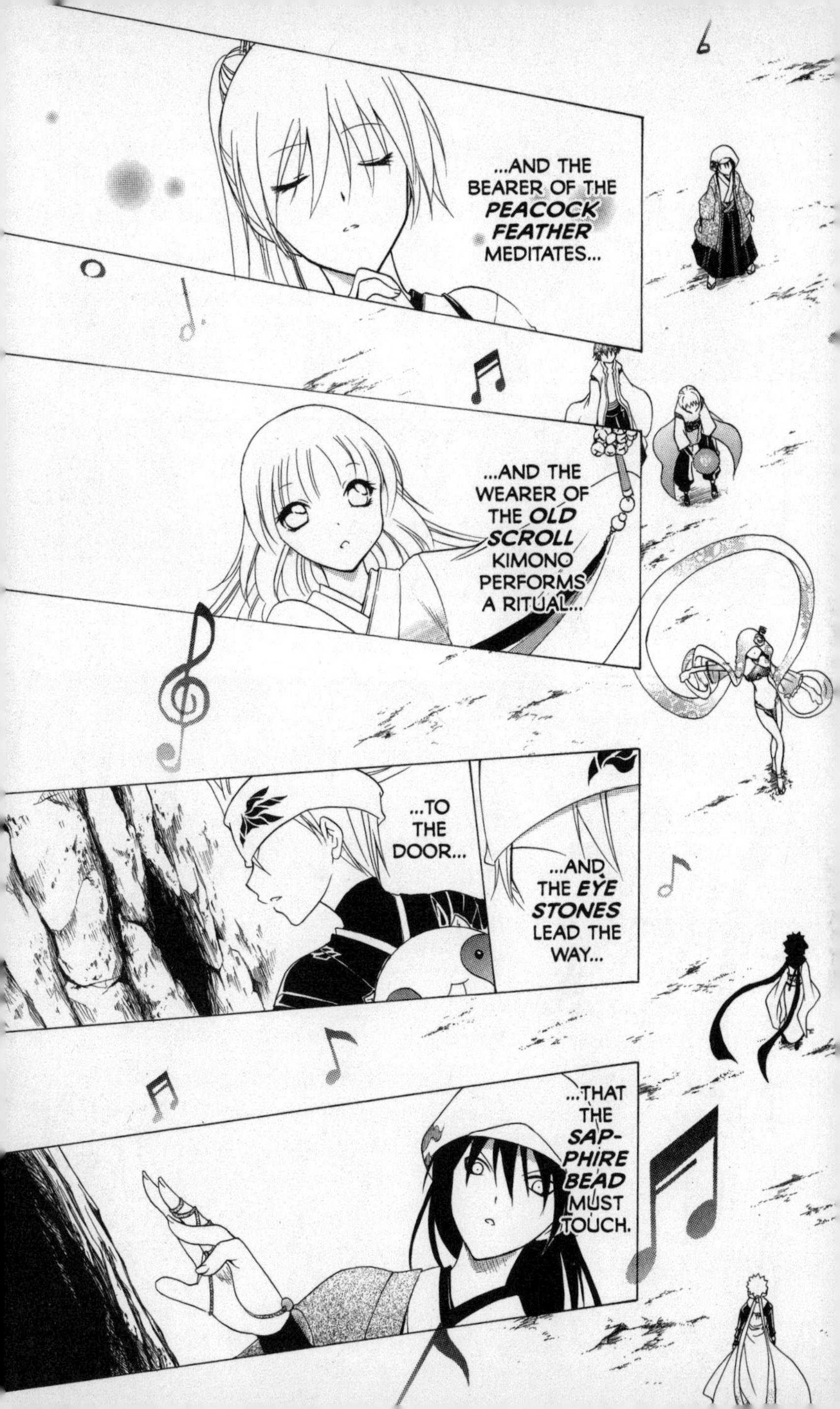

...AND THE BEARER OF THE PEACOCK FEATHER MEDITATES...
...AND THE WEARER OF THE OLD SCROLL KIMONO PERFORMS A RITUAL...
...AND THE EYE STONES LEAD THE WAY...
...TO THE DOOR...
...THAT THE SAPPHIRE BEAD MUST TOUCH.

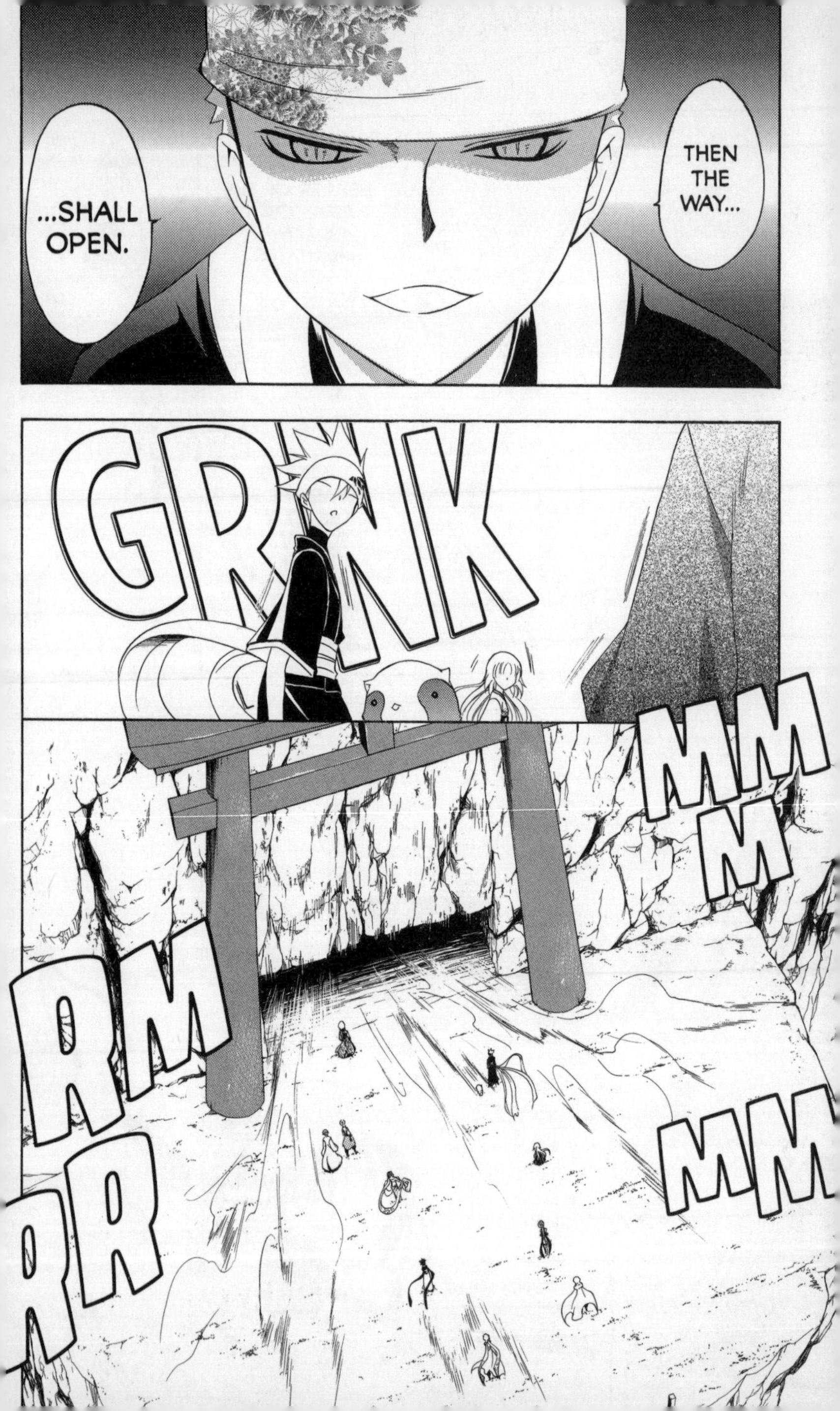
THEN THE WAY...
...SHALL OPEN.
GRNK
MM
M
MM
RM
RR

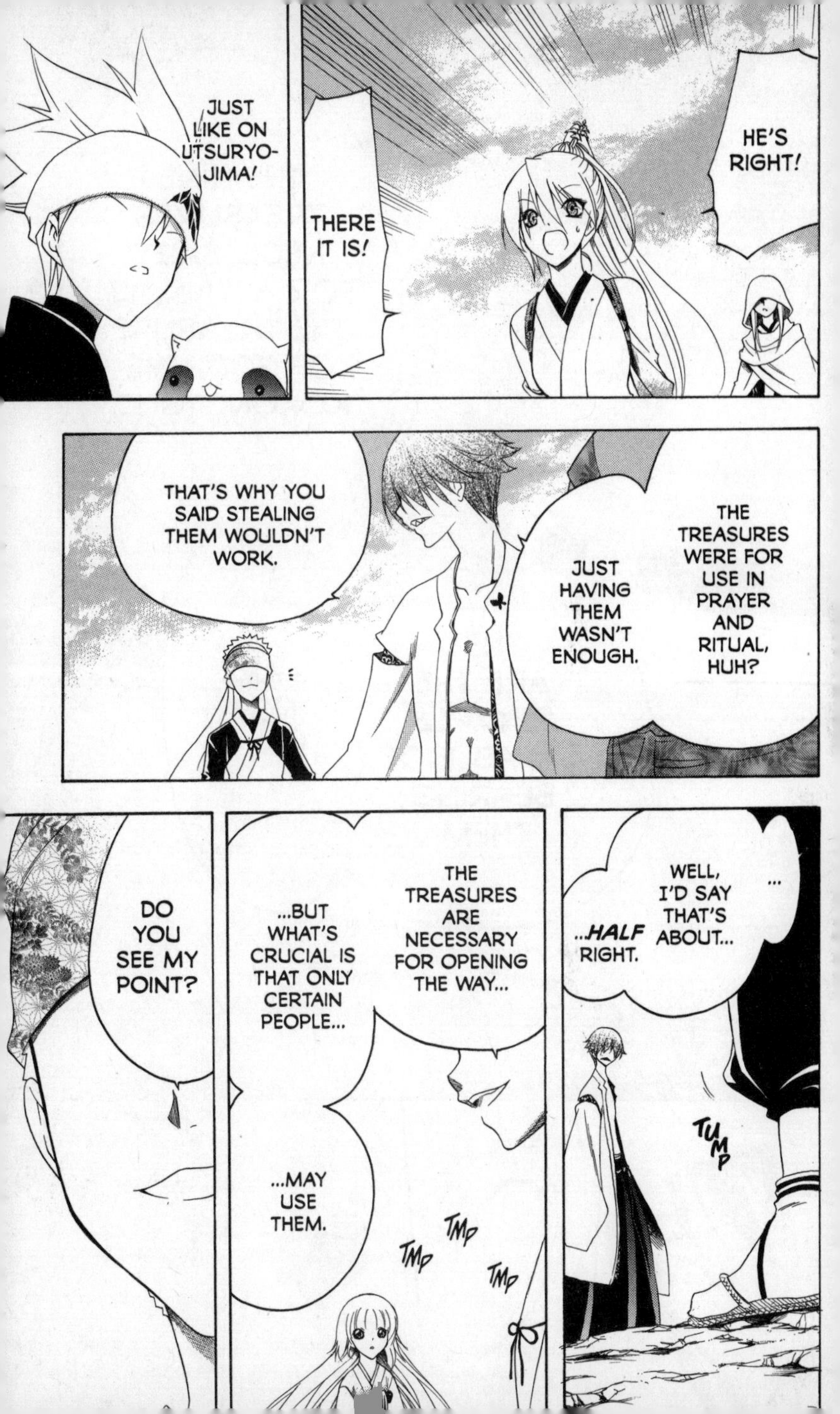
HE'S RIGHT!
THERE IT IS!
JUST LIKE ON UTSURYO-JIMA!
THE TREASURES WERE FOR USE IN PRAYER AND RITUAL, HUH?
JUST HAVING THEM WASN'T ENOUGH.
THAT'S WHY YOU SAID STEALING THEM WOULDN'T WORK.
...
WELL, I'D SAY THAT'S ABOUT...
...*HALF* RIGHT.
TUMP
THE TREASURES ARE NECESSARY FOR OPENING THE WAY...
...BUT WHAT'S CRUCIAL IS THAT ONLY CERTAIN PEOPLE...
...MAY USE THEM.
TMP
TMP
TMP
DO YOU SEE MY POINT?

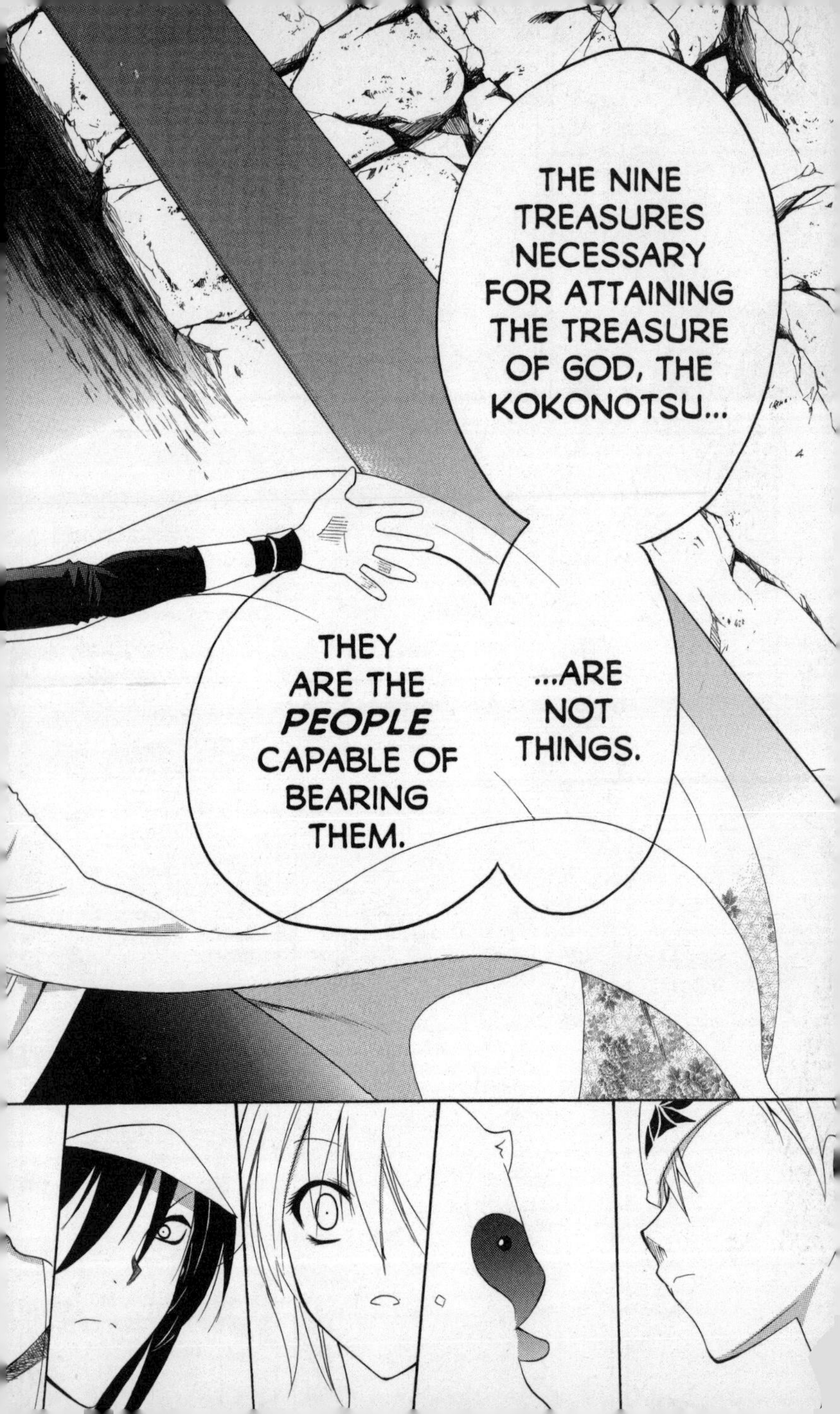
THE NINE TREASURES NECESSARY FOR ATTAINING THE TREASURE OF GOD, THE KOKONOTSU...
...ARE NOT THINGS.
THEY ARE THE *PEOPLE* CAPABLE OF BEARING THEM.

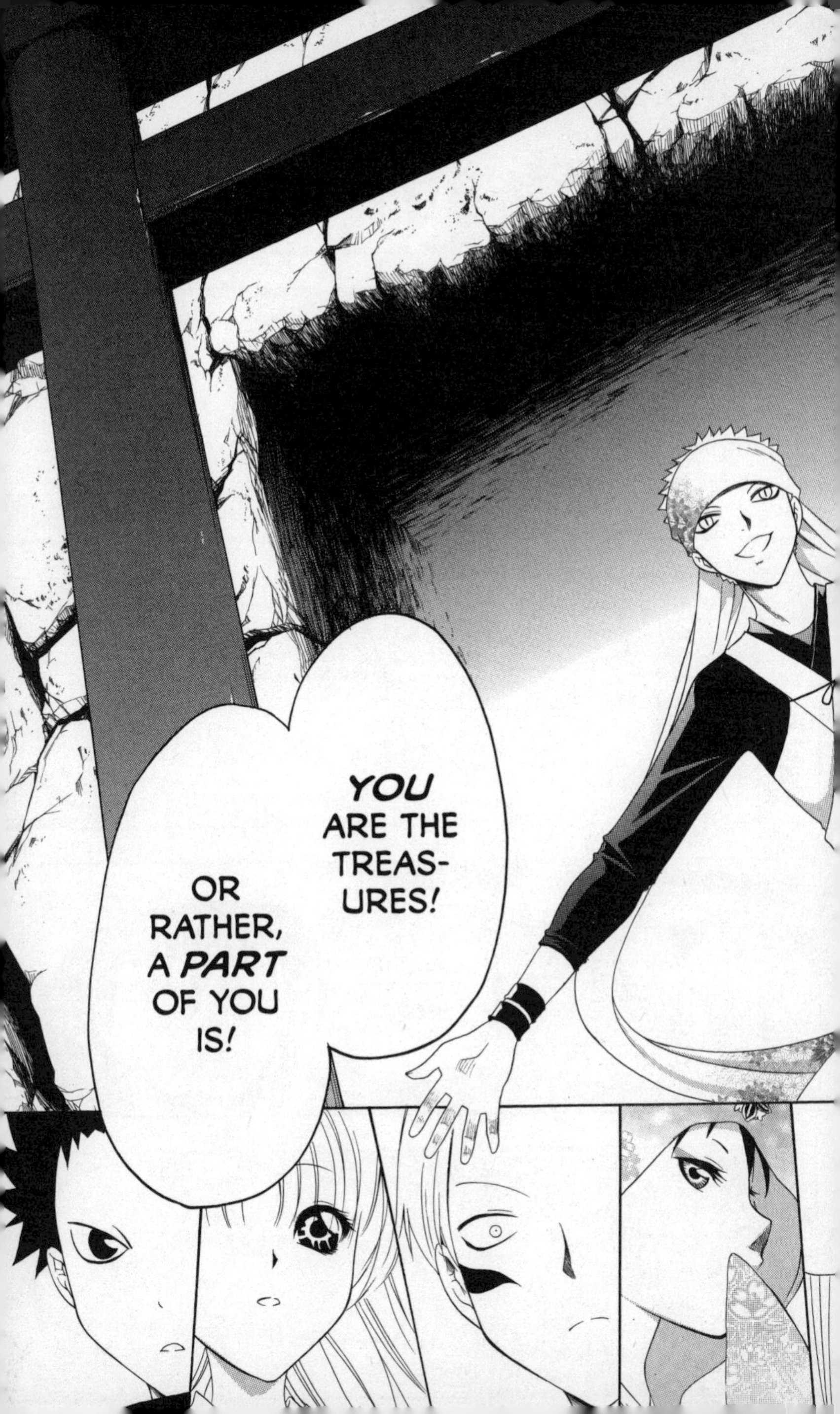
YOU ARE THE TREAS- URES!
OR RATHER, A *PART* OF YOU IS!

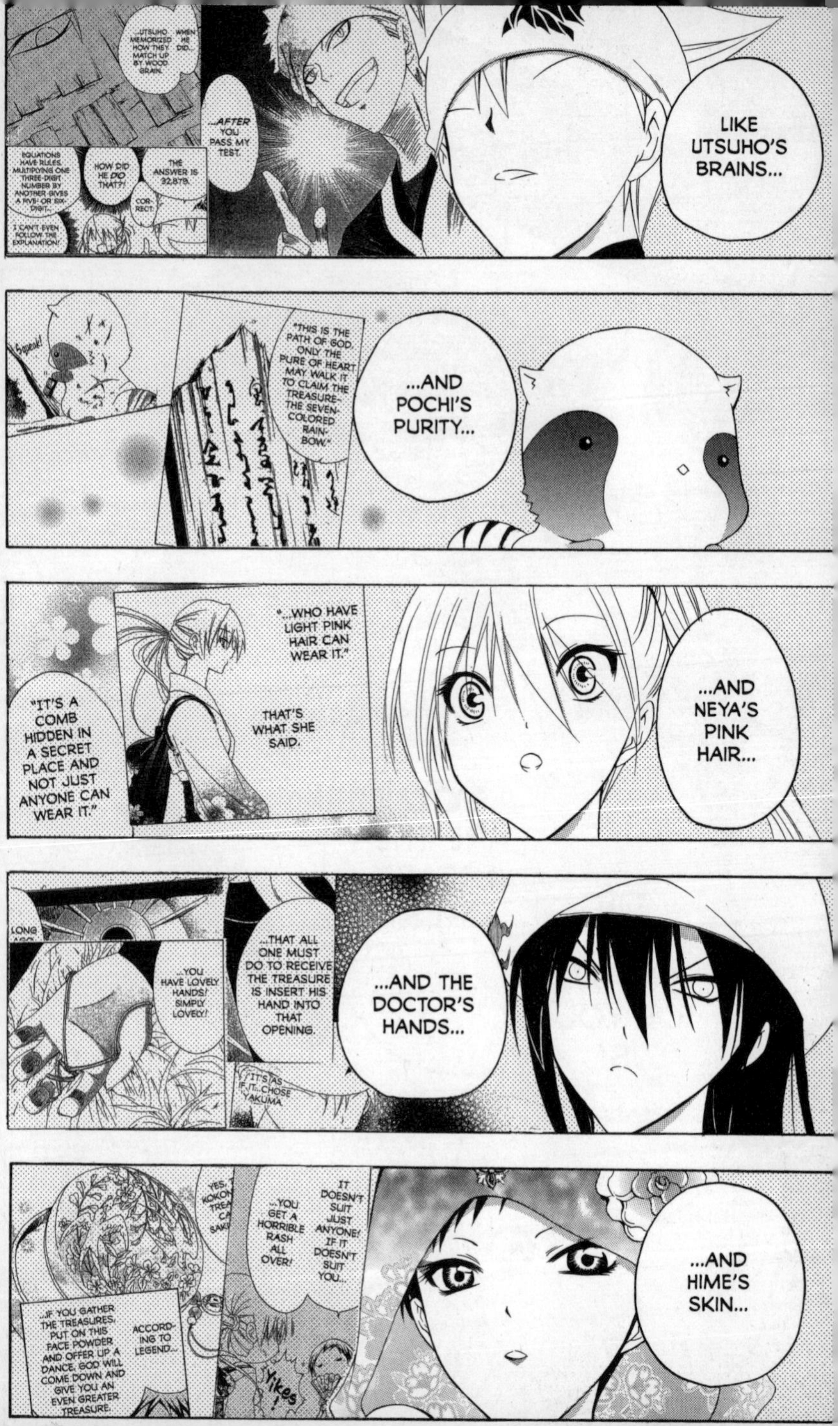
LIKE UTSUHO'S BRAINS...
...AFTER YOU PASS MY TEST.
WHEN HE DID...
...UTSUHO MEMORIZED HOW THEY MATCH UP BY WOOD GRAIN.
THE ANSWER IS 32,879.
CORRECT.
HOW DID HE DO THAT?!
EQUATIONS HAVE RULES. MULTIPLYING ONE THREE-DIGIT NUMBER BY ANOTHER GIVES A FIVE- OR SIX-DIGIT...
I CAN'T EVEN FOLLOW THE EXPLANATION!
...AND POCHI'S PURITY...
"THIS IS THE PATH OF GOD. ONLY THE PURE OF HEART MAY WALK IT TO CLAIM THE TREASURE-THE SEVEN-COLORED RAINBOW."
Squeak!
...AND NEYA'S PINK HAIR...
"...WHO HAVE LIGHT PINK HAIR CAN WEAR IT."
THAT'S WHAT SHE SAID.
"IT'S A COMB HIDDEN IN A SECRET PLACE AND NOT JUST ANYONE CAN WEAR IT."
...AND THE DOCTOR'S HANDS...
...THAT ALL ONE MUST DO TO RECEIVE THE TREASURE IS INSERT HIS HAND INTO THAT OPENING.
"IT'S AS IF IT...CHOSE YAKUMA.
LONG
...YOU HAVE LOVELY HANDS! SIMPLY LOVELY!
...AND HIME'S SKIN...
IT DOESN'T SUIT JUST ANYONE! IF IT DOESN'T SUIT YOU...
...YOU GET A HORRIBLE RASH ALL OVER!
Yikes!
ACCORDING TO LEGEND...
...IF YOU GATHER THE TREASURES, PUT ON THIS FACE POWDER AND OFFER UP A DANCE, GOD WILL COME DOWN AND GIVE YOU AN EVEN GREATER TREASURE.

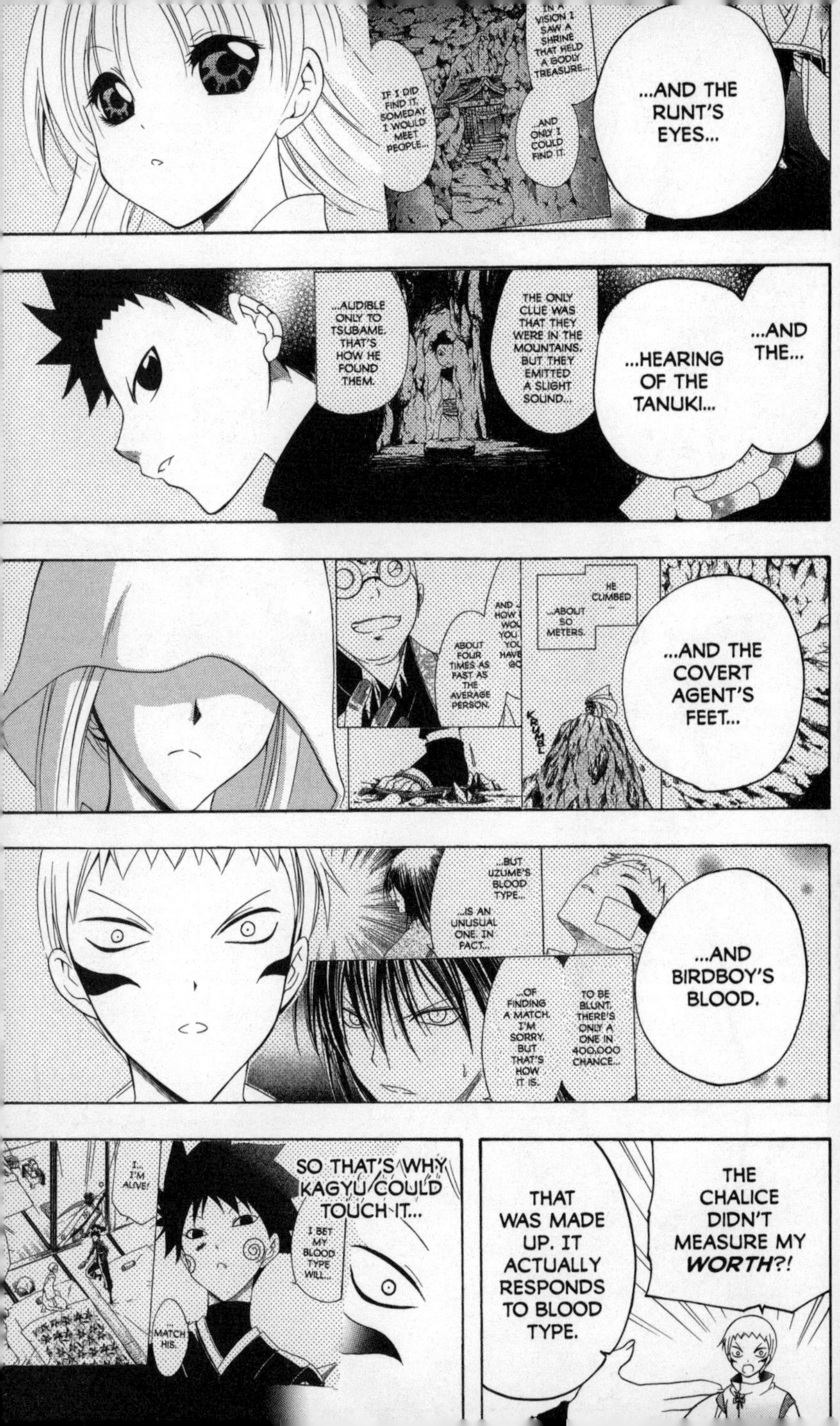
...AND THE RUNT'S EYES...
IN A VISION I SAW A SHRINE THAT HELD A GODLY TREASURE...
...AND ONLY I COULD FIND IT.
IF I DID FIND IT, SOMEDAY I WOULD MEET PEOPLE...
...AND THE...
...HEARING OF THE TANUKI...
THE ONLY CLUE WAS THAT THEY WERE IN THE MOUNTAINS, BUT THEY EMITTED A SLIGHT SOUND...
...AUDIBLE ONLY TO TSUBAME. THAT'S HOW HE FOUND THEM.
...AND THE COVERT AGENT'S FEET...
KRUMBL
HE CLIMBED...
...ABOUT 50 METERS.
ABOUT FOUR TIMES AS FAST AS THE AVERAGE PERSON.
...AND BIRDBOY'S BLOOD.
...BUT UZUME'S BLOOD TYPE...
...IS AN UNUSUAL ONE. IN FACT...
TO BE BLUNT, THERE'S ONLY A ONE IN 400,000 CHANCE...
...OF FINDING A MATCH. I'M SORRY, BUT THAT'S HOW IT IS.
THE CHALICE DIDN'T MEASURE MY *WORTH*?!
THAT WAS MADE UP. IT ACTUALLY RESPONDS TO BLOOD TYPE.
SO THAT'S WHY KAGYU COULD TOUCH IT...
I BET MY BLOOD TYPE WILL...
...MATCH HIS.
I... I'M ALIVE!

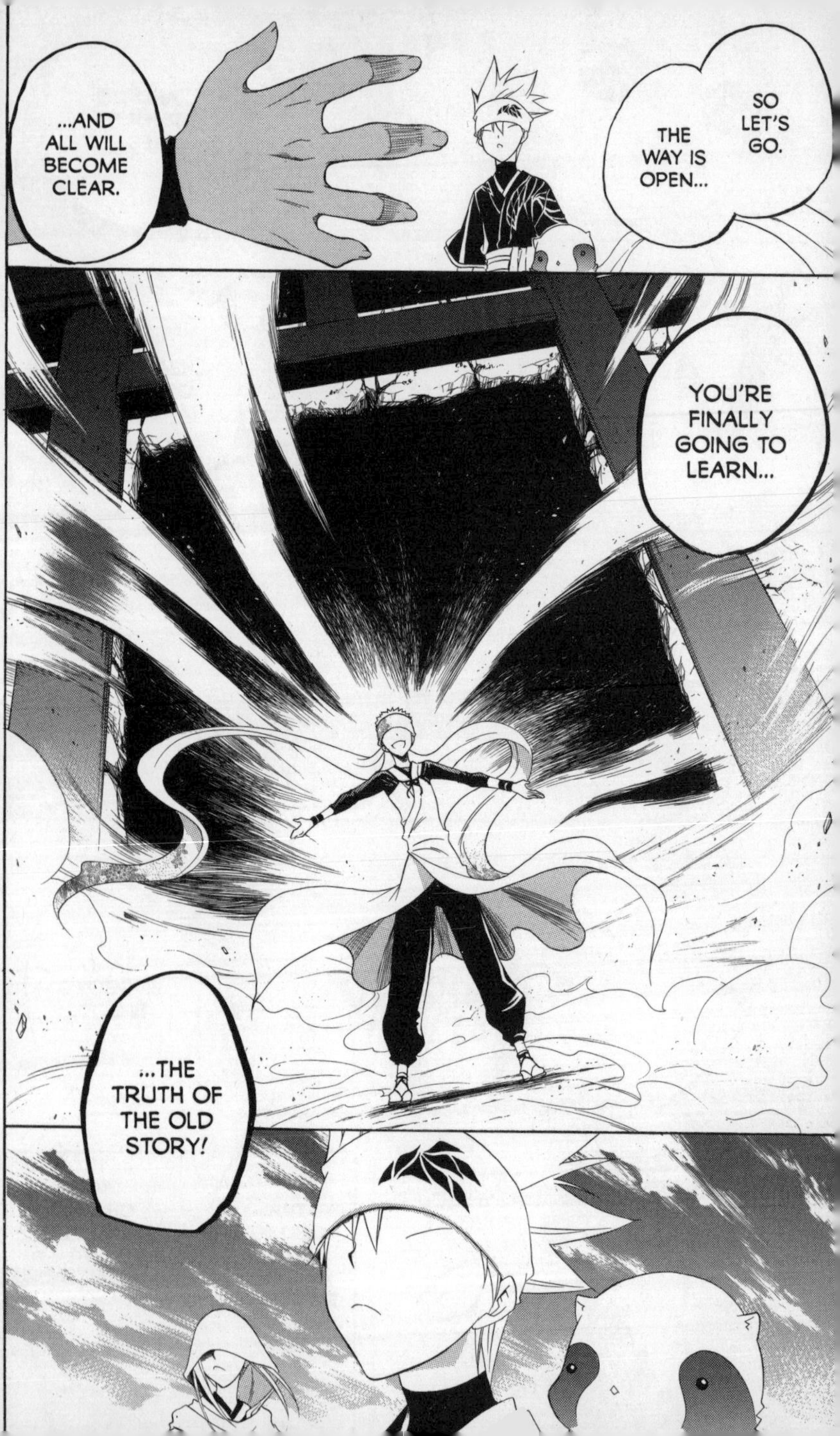
THE WAY IS OPEN...
SO LET'S GO.
...AND ALL WILL BECOME CLEAR.
YOU'RE FINALLY GOING TO LEARN...
...THE TRUTH OF THE OLD STORY!

Chapter 204 The Story in the Cave

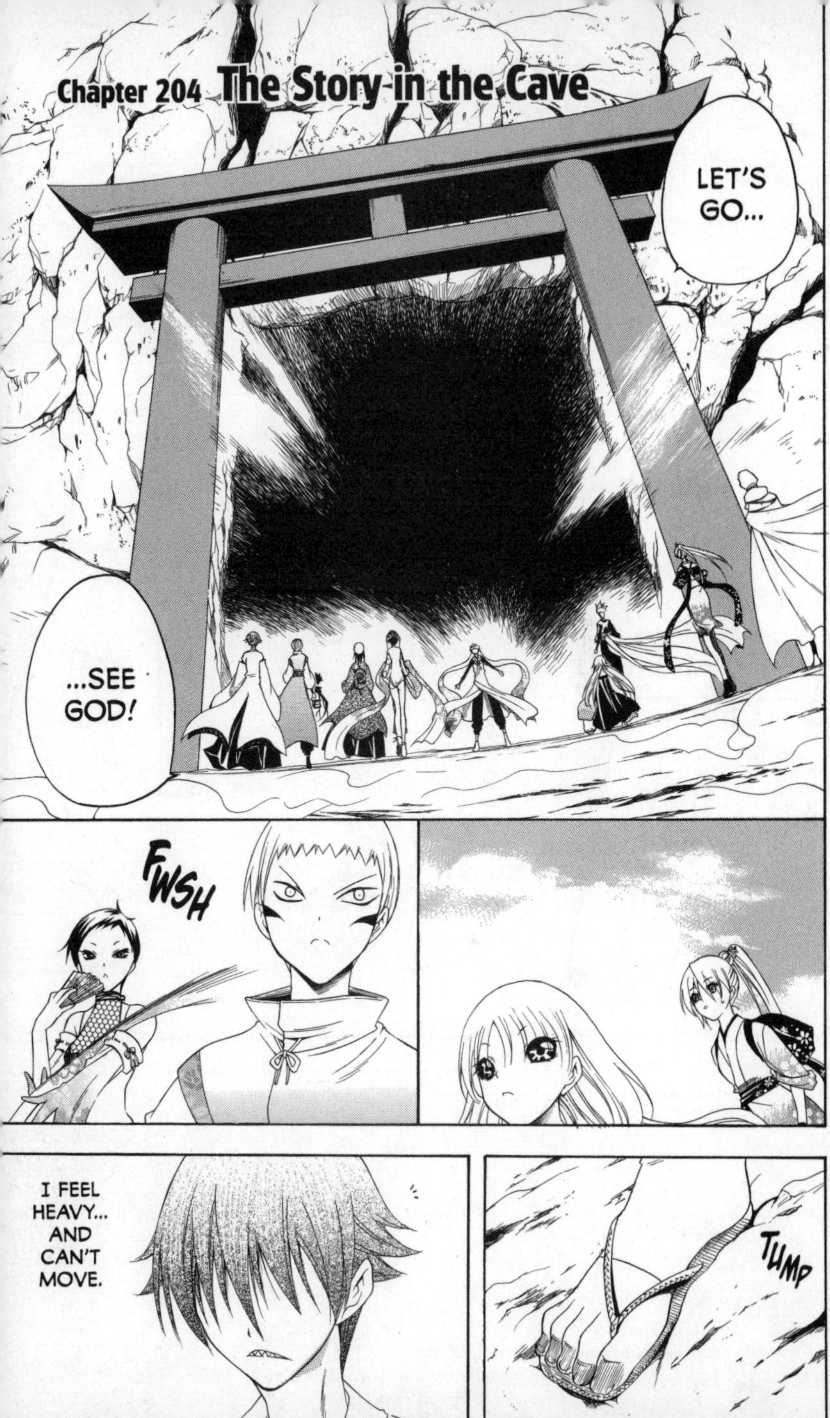
LET'S GO...
...SEE GOD!
FWSH
TUMP
I FEEL HEAVY... AND CAN'T MOVE.

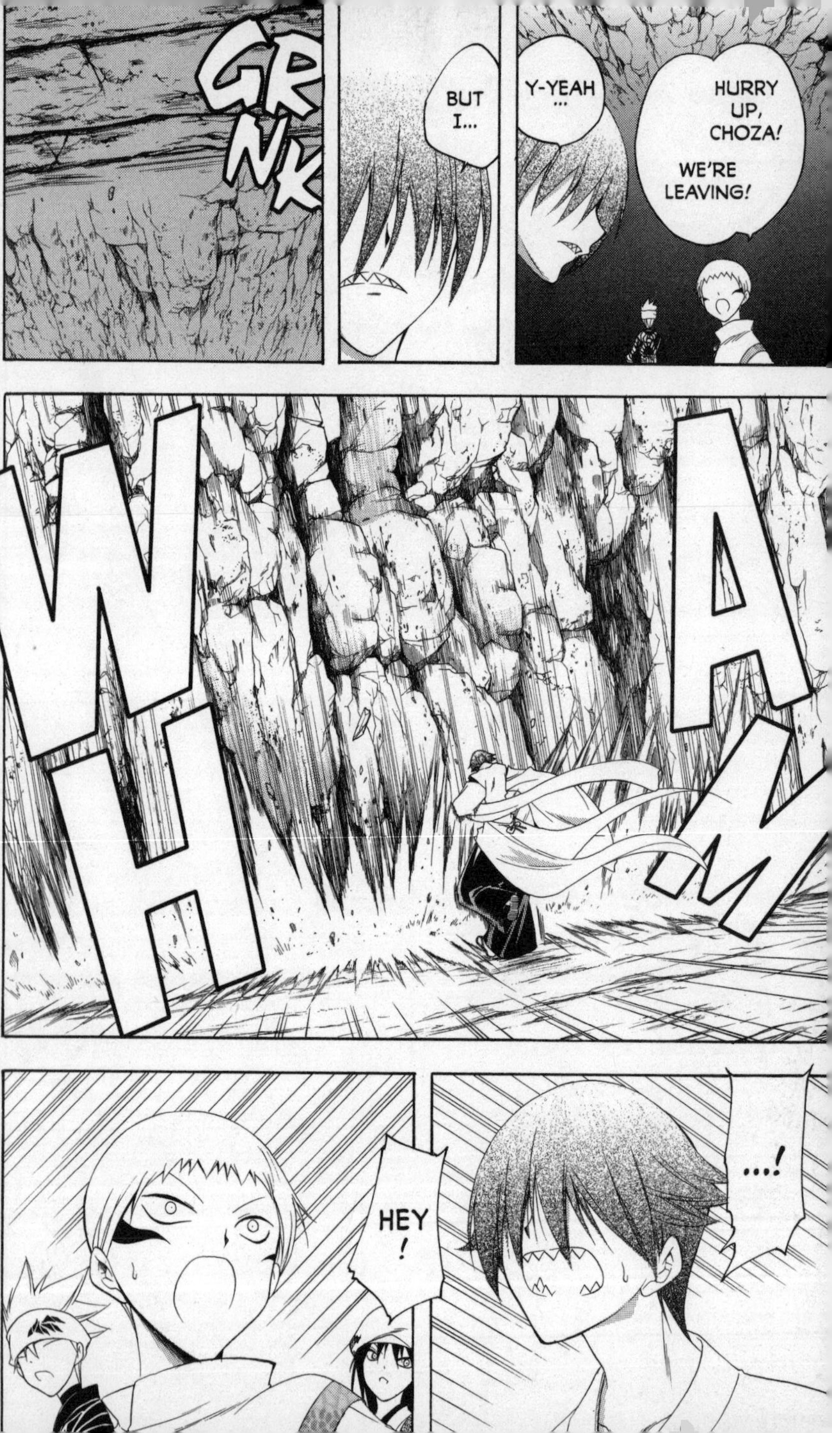
HURRY UP, CHOZA! WE'RE LEAVING!
Y-YEAH ...
BUT I...
GRNK
WHAM
...!
HEY!

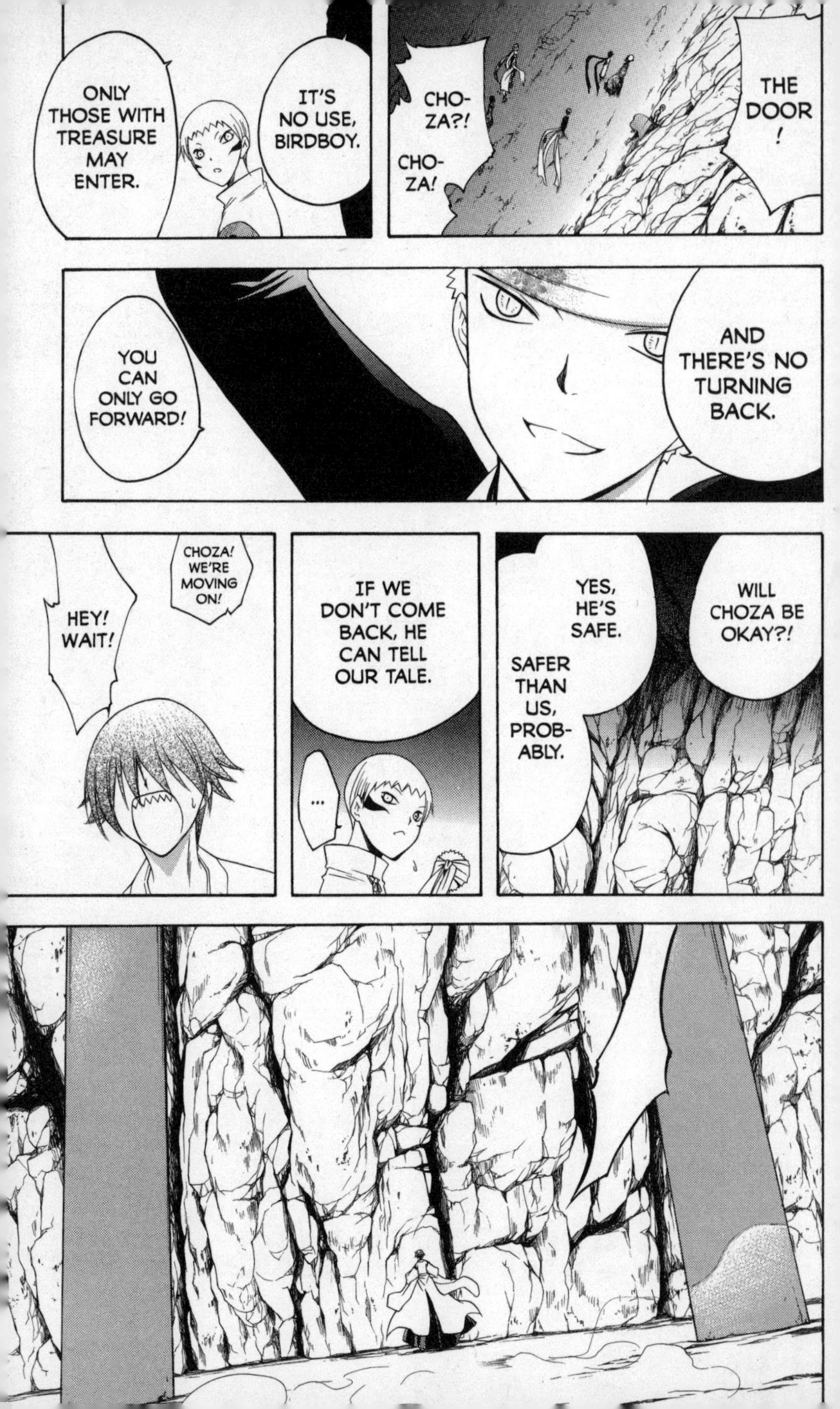
THE DOOR!
CHO-ZA?!
CHO-ZA!
IT'S NO USE, BIRDBOY.
ONLY THOSE WITH TREASURE MAY ENTER.
AND THERE'S NO TURNING BACK.
YOU CAN ONLY GO FORWARD!
WILL CHOZA BE OKAY?!
YES, HE'S SAFE.
SAFER THAN US, PROBABLY.
IF WE DON'T COME BACK, HE CAN TELL OUR TALE.
...
CHOZA! WE'RE MOVING ON!
HEY! WAIT!

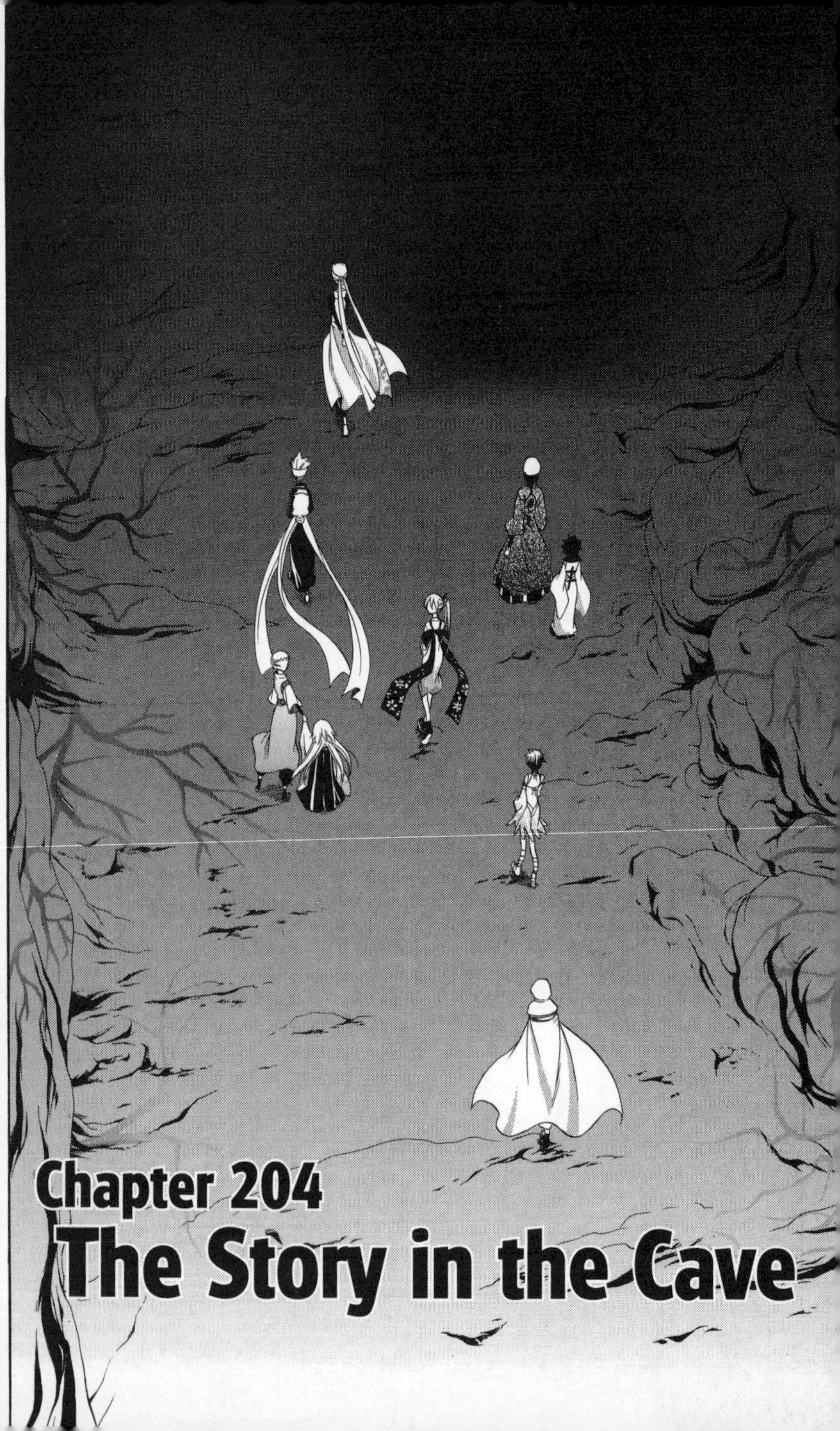
Chapter 204
The Story in the Cave

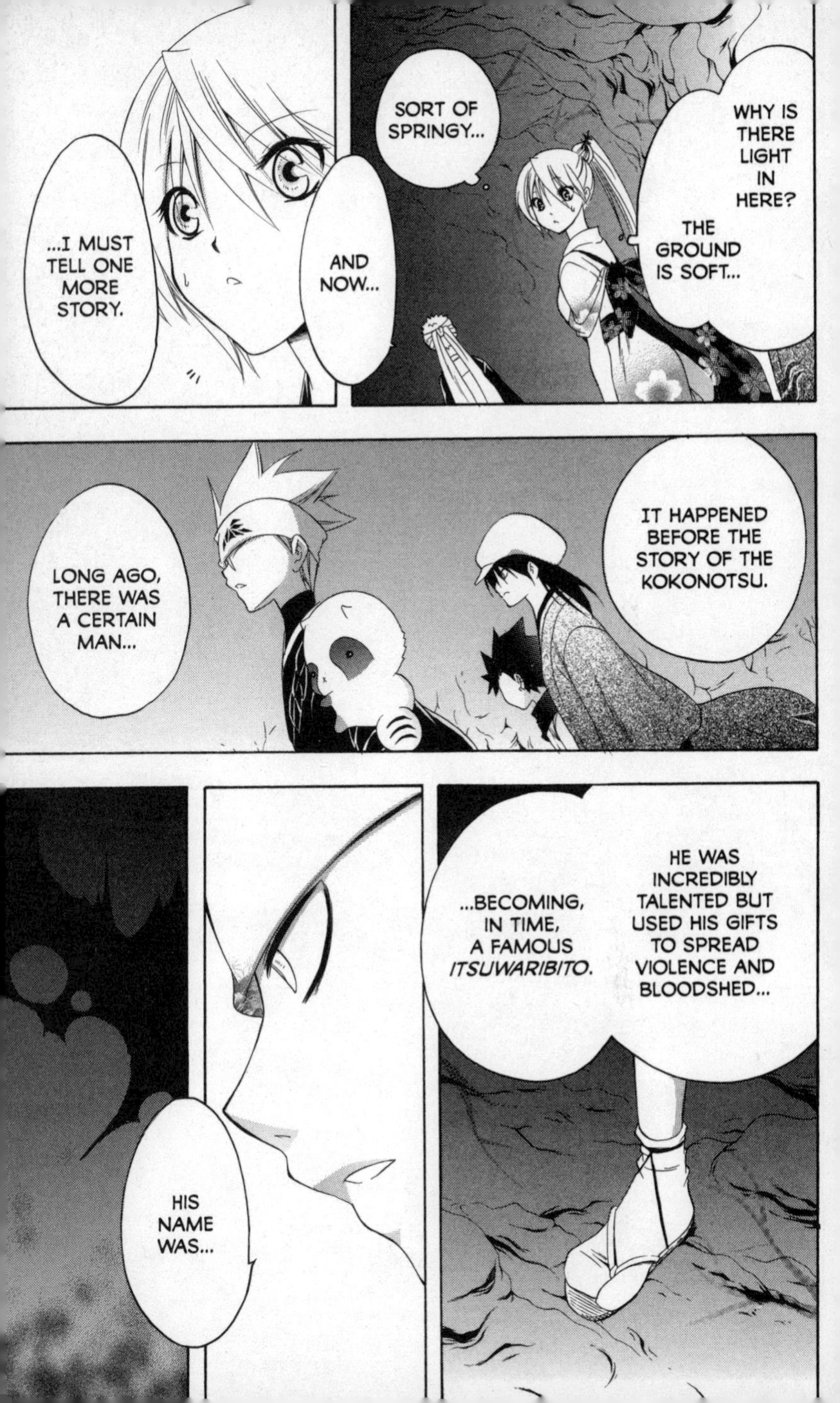
WHY IS THERE LIGHT IN HERE?
THE GROUND IS SOFT...
SORT OF SPRINGY...
AND NOW...
...I MUST TELL ONE MORE STORY.
IT HAPPENED BEFORE THE STORY OF THE KOKONOTSU.
LONG AGO, THERE WAS A CERTAIN MAN...
HE WAS INCREDIBLY TALENTED BUT USED HIS GIFTS TO SPREAD VIOLENCE AND BLOODSHED...
...BECOMING, IN TIME, A FAMOUS *ITSUWARIBITO*.
HIS NAME WAS...

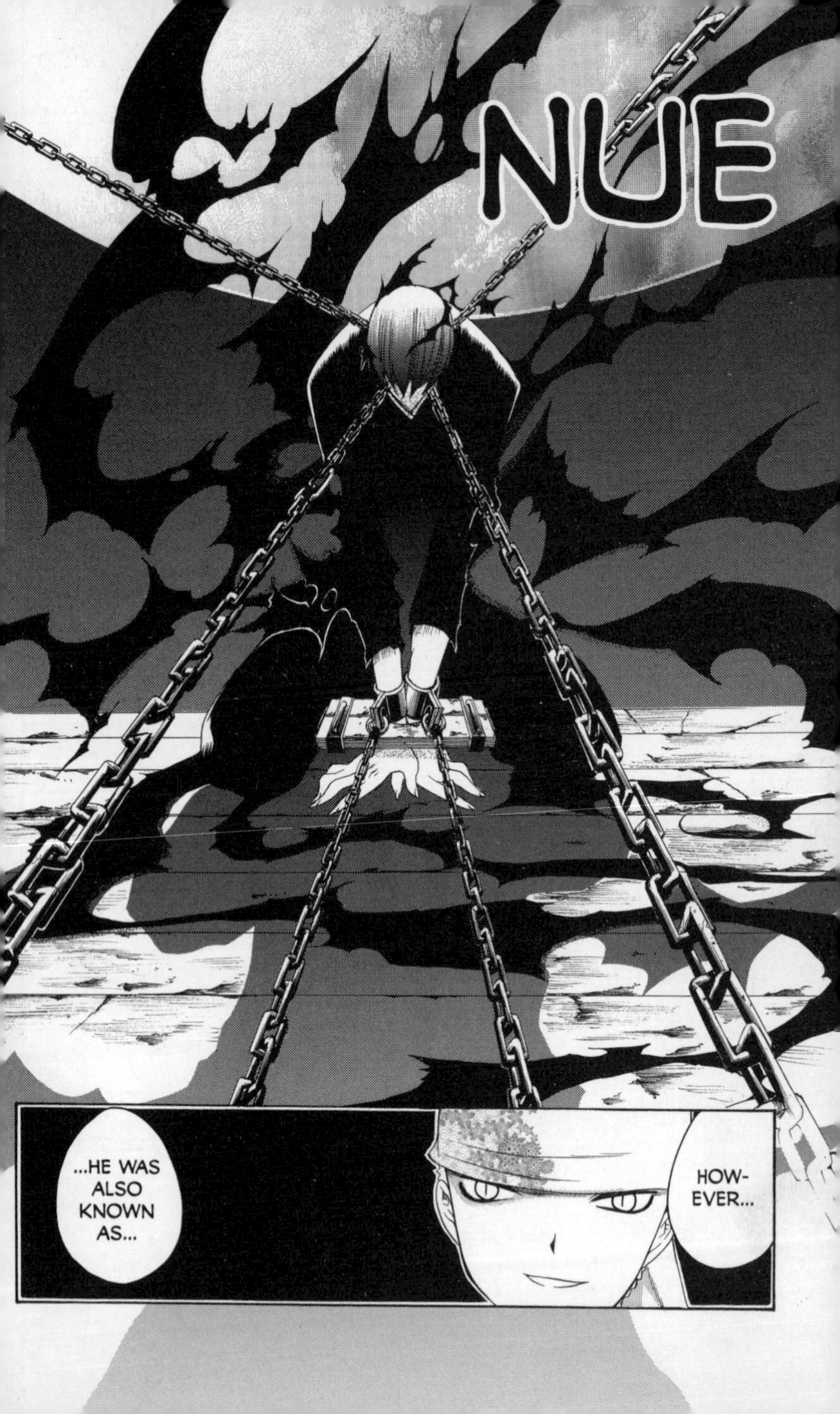
NUE
HOW-EVER...
...HE WAS ALSO KNOWN AS...

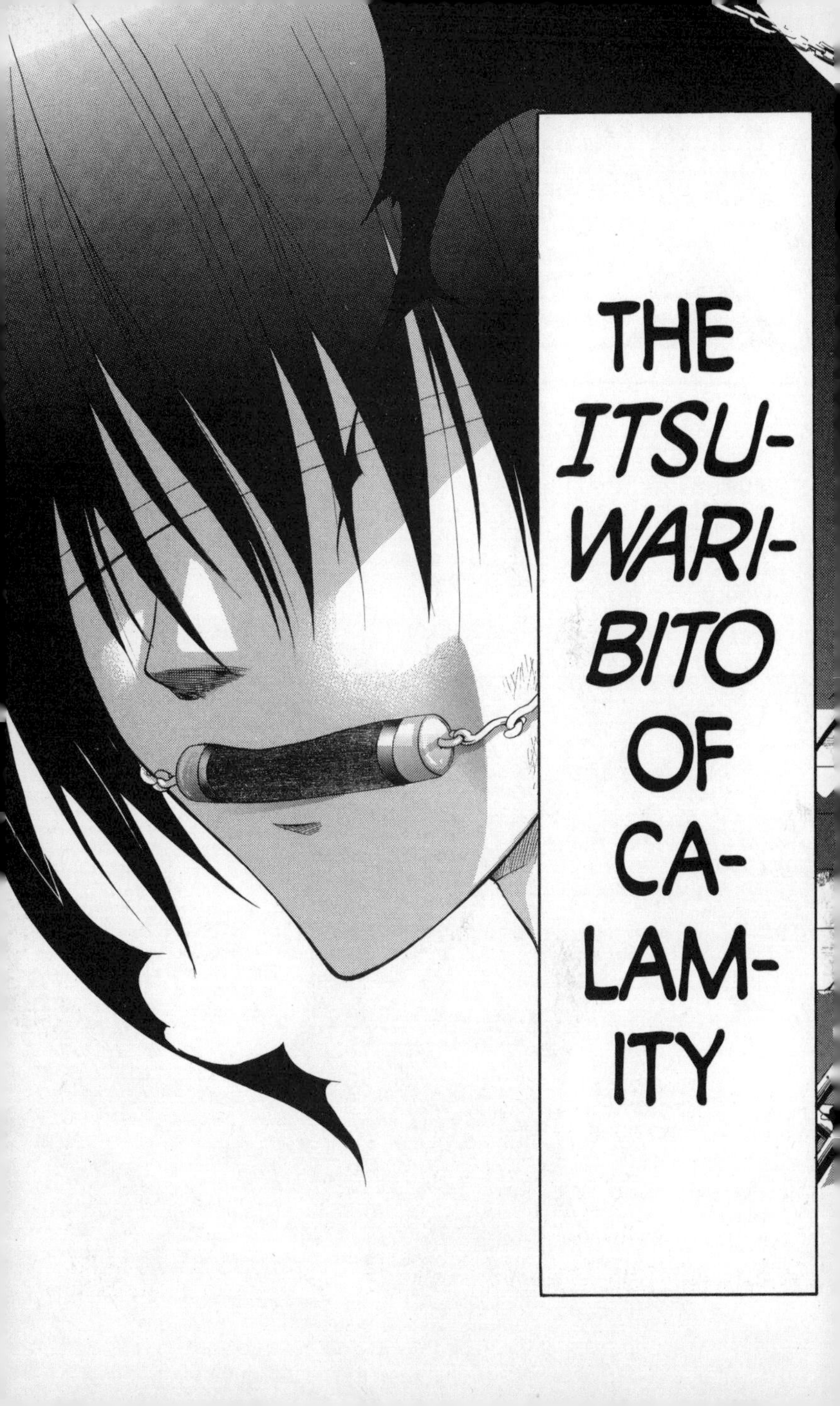
THE ITSU-WARI-BITO OF CA-LAM-ITY

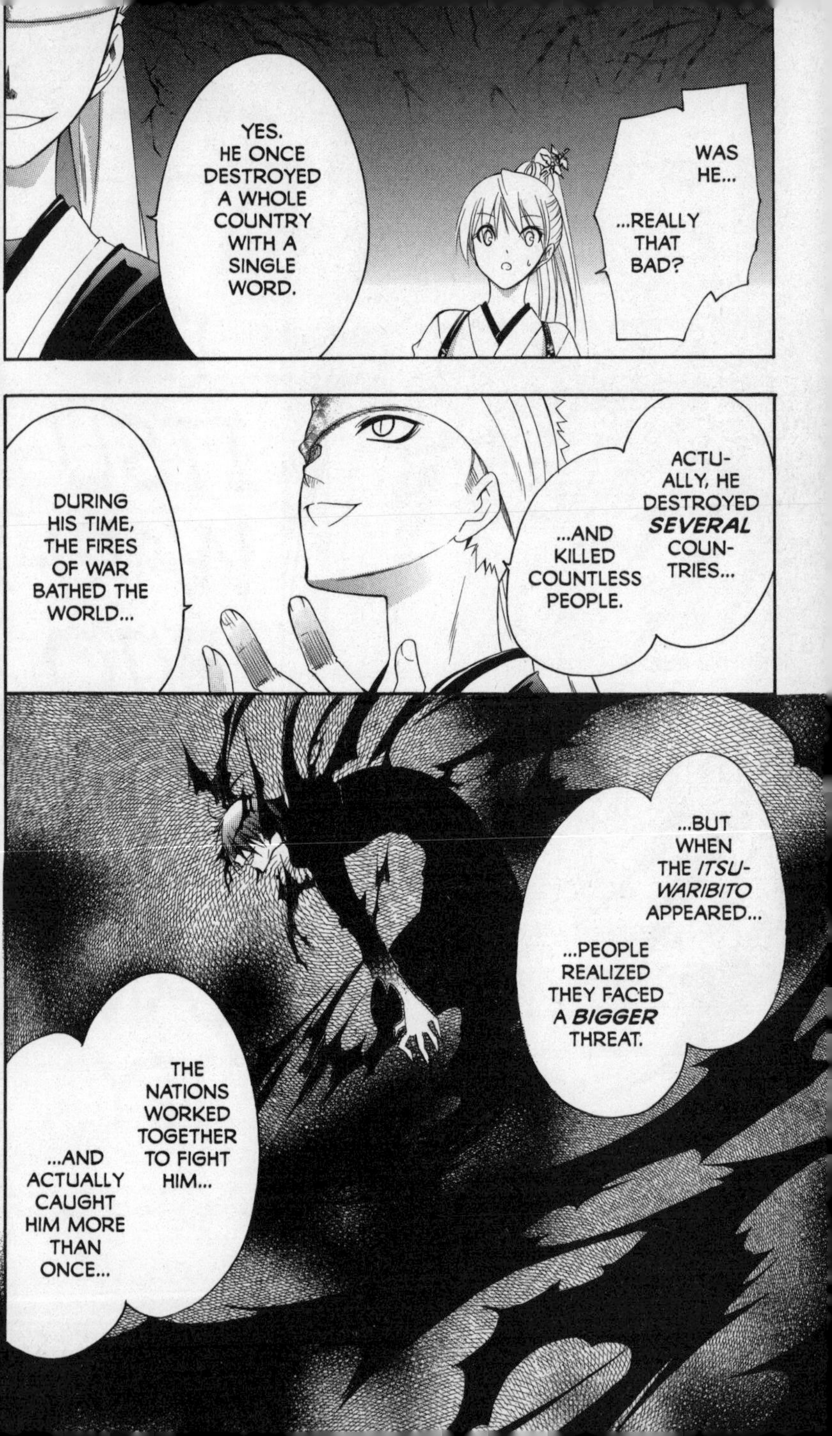
WAS HE...
...REALLY THAT BAD?
YES. HE ONCE DESTROYED A WHOLE COUNTRY WITH A SINGLE WORD.
ACTUALLY, HE DESTROYED *SEVERAL* COUNTRIES...
...AND KILLED COUNTLESS PEOPLE.
DURING HIS TIME, THE FIRES OF WAR BATHED THE WORLD...
...BUT WHEN THE *ITSUWARIBITO* APPEARED...
...PEOPLE REALIZED THEY FACED A *BIGGER* THREAT.
THE NATIONS WORKED TOGETHER TO FIGHT HIM...
...AND ACTUALLY CAUGHT HIM MORE THAN ONCE...

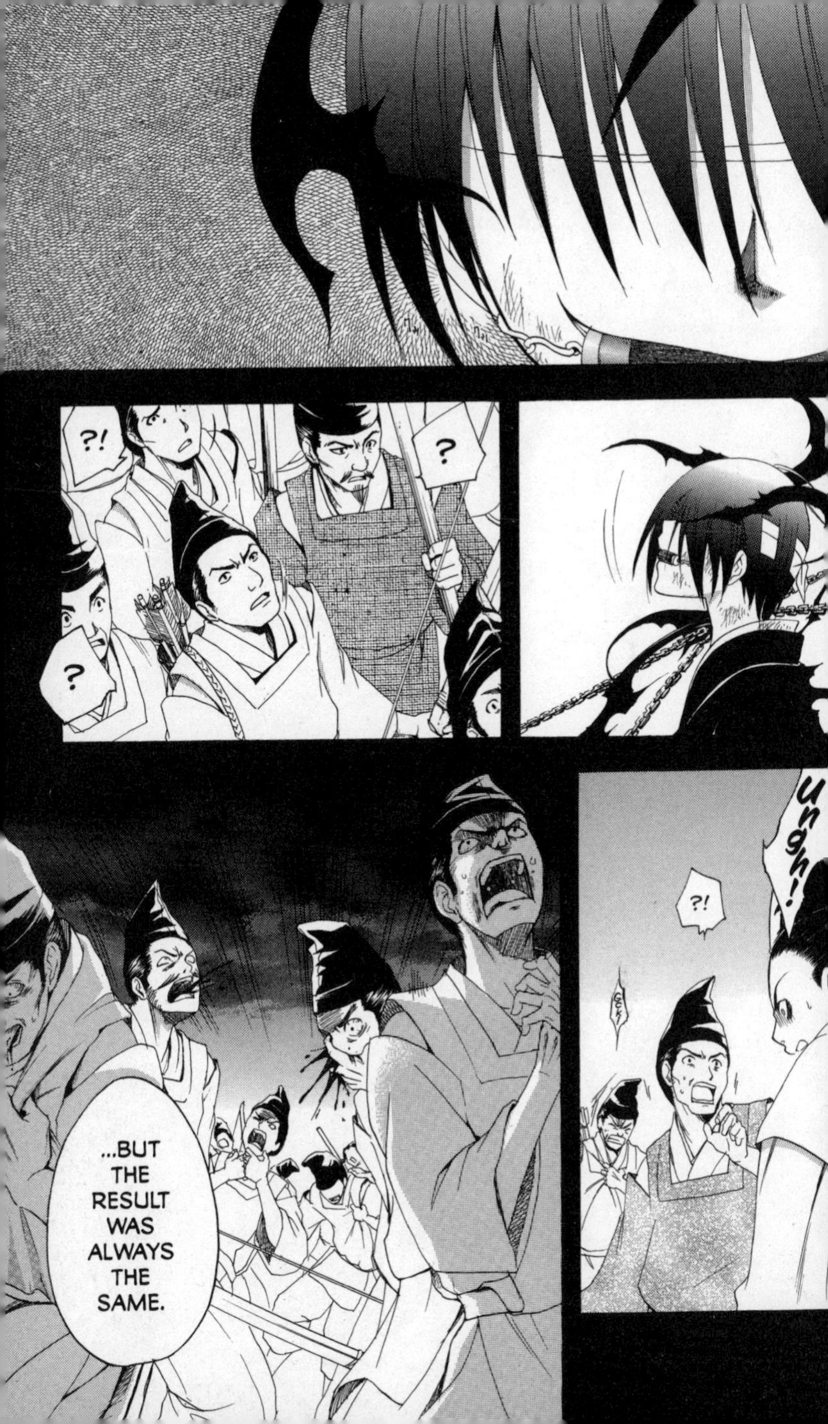

?
?!
?
Ungh!
?!
GCK!
...BUT THE RESULT WAS ALWAYS THE SAME.

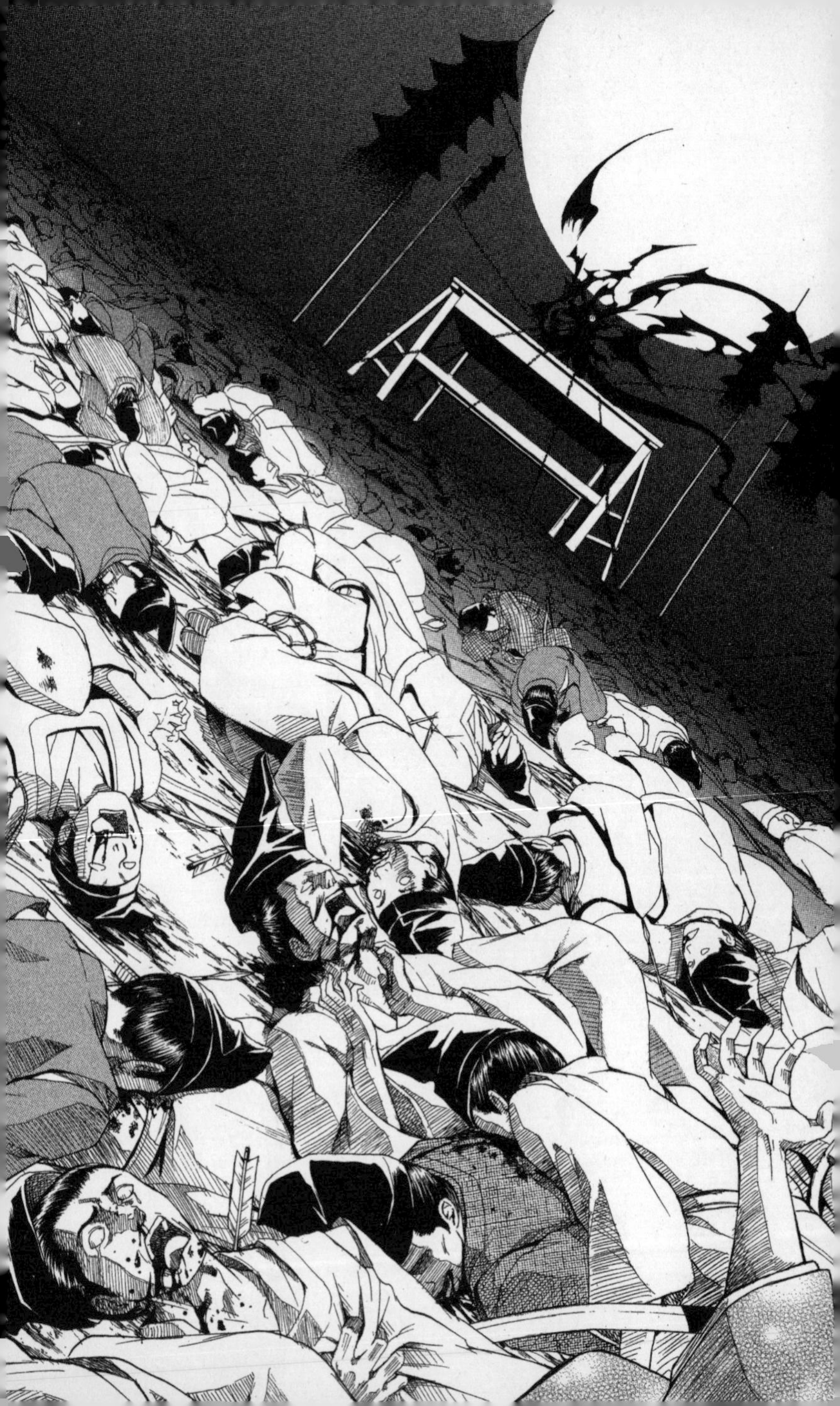

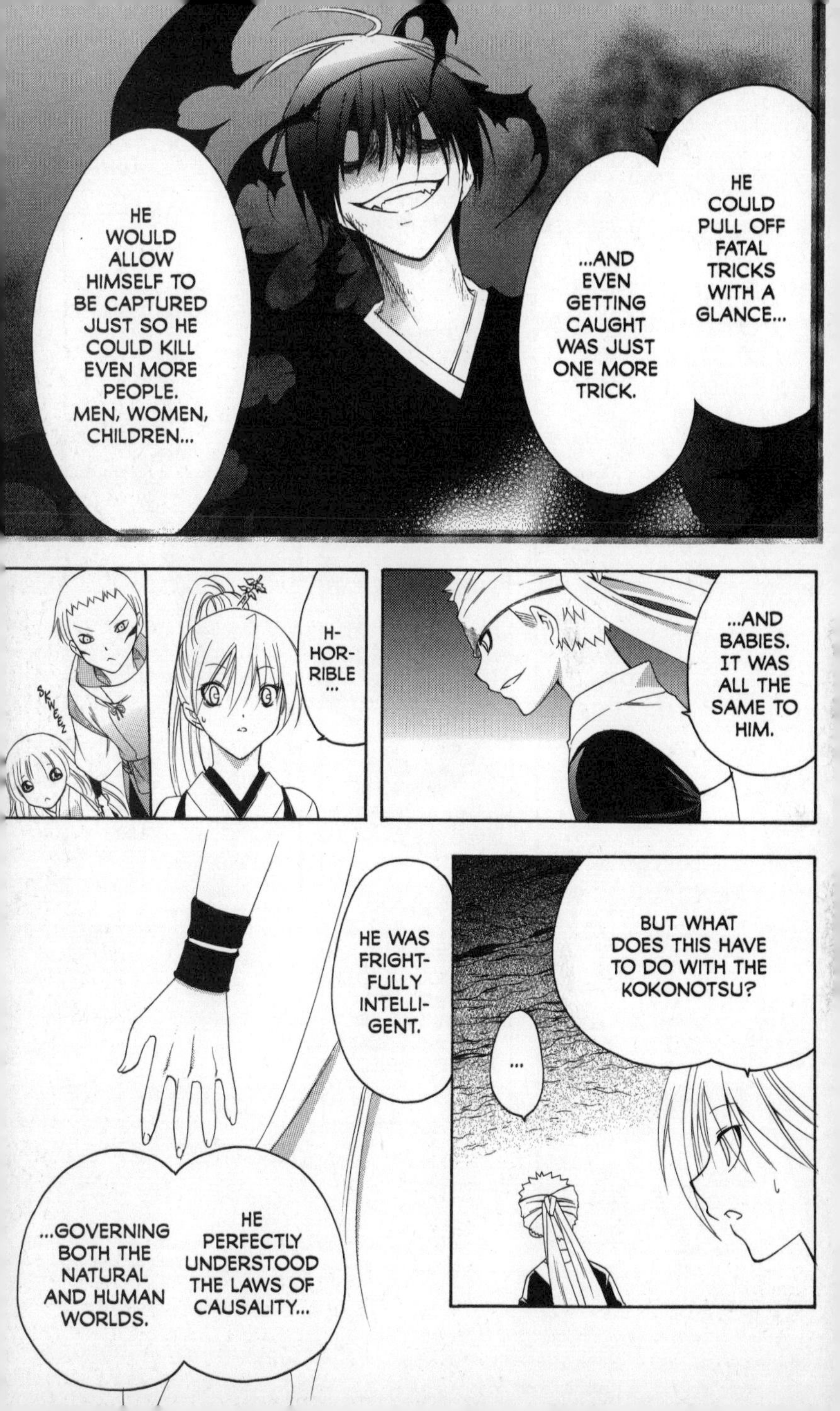
HE COULD PULL OFF FATAL TRICKS WITH A GLANCE...
...AND EVEN GETTING CAUGHT WAS JUST ONE MORE TRICK.
HE WOULD ALLOW HIMSELF TO BE CAPTURED JUST SO HE COULD KILL EVEN MORE PEOPLE. MEN, WOMEN, CHILDREN...
...AND BABIES. IT WAS ALL THE SAME TO HIM.
H-HOR-RIBLE...
BUT WHAT DOES THIS HAVE TO DO WITH THE KOKONOTSU?
...
HE WAS FRIGHT-FULLY INTELLI-GENT.
HE PERFECTLY UNDERSTOOD THE LAWS OF CAUSALITY...
...GOVERNING BOTH THE NATURAL AND HUMAN WORLDS.

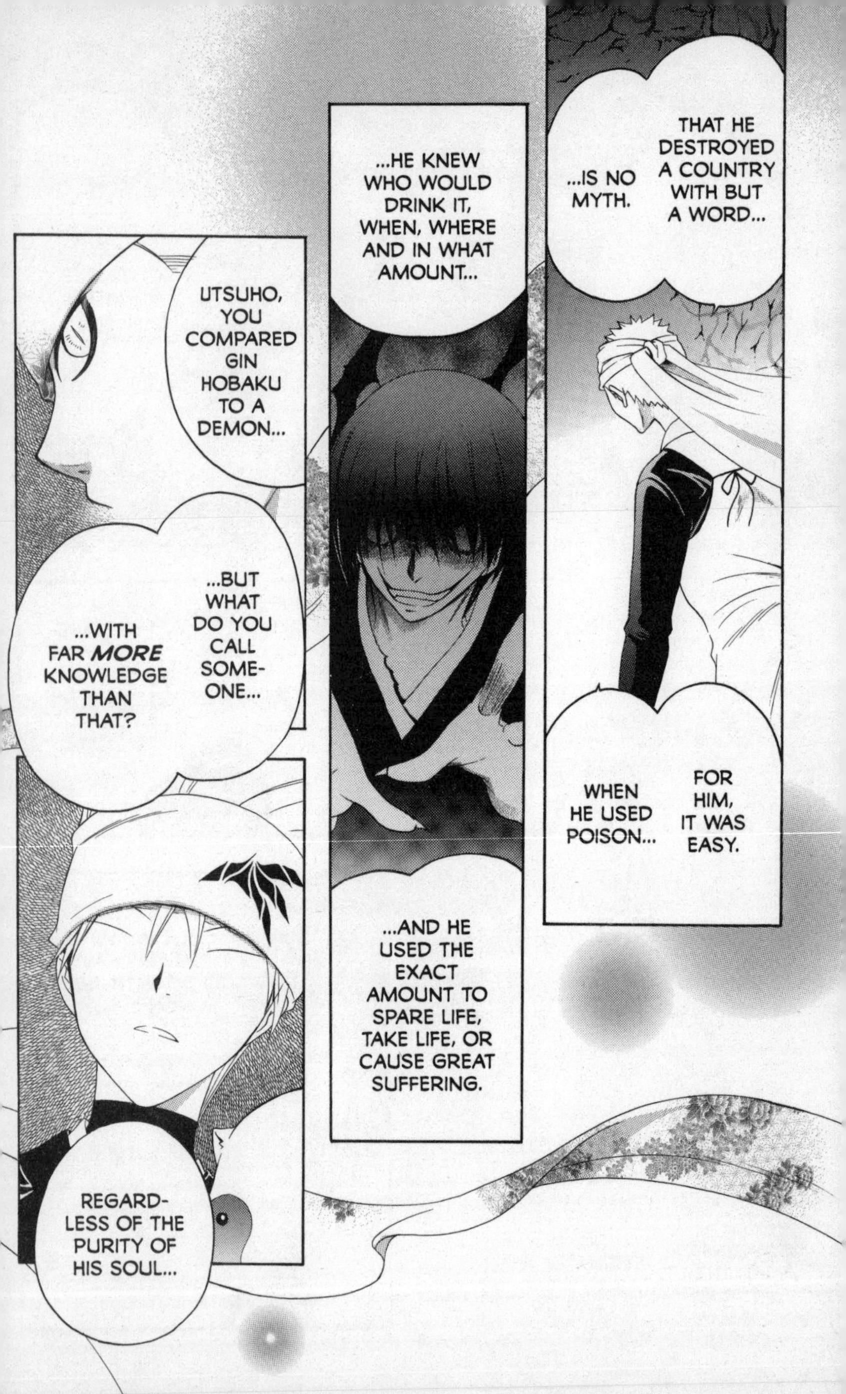
THAT HE DESTROYED A COUNTRY WITH BUT A WORD...
...IS NO MYTH.
FOR HIM, IT WAS EASY.
WHEN HE USED POISON...
...HE KNEW WHO WOULD DRINK IT, WHEN, WHERE AND IN WHAT AMOUNT...
...AND HE USED THE EXACT AMOUNT TO SPARE LIFE, TAKE LIFE, OR CAUSE GREAT SUFFERING.
UTSUHO, YOU COMPARED GIN HOBAKU TO A DEMON...
...BUT WHAT DO YOU CALL SOME-ONE...
...WITH FAR *MORE* KNOWLEDGE THAN THAT?
REGARD-LESS OF THE PURITY OF HIS SOUL...

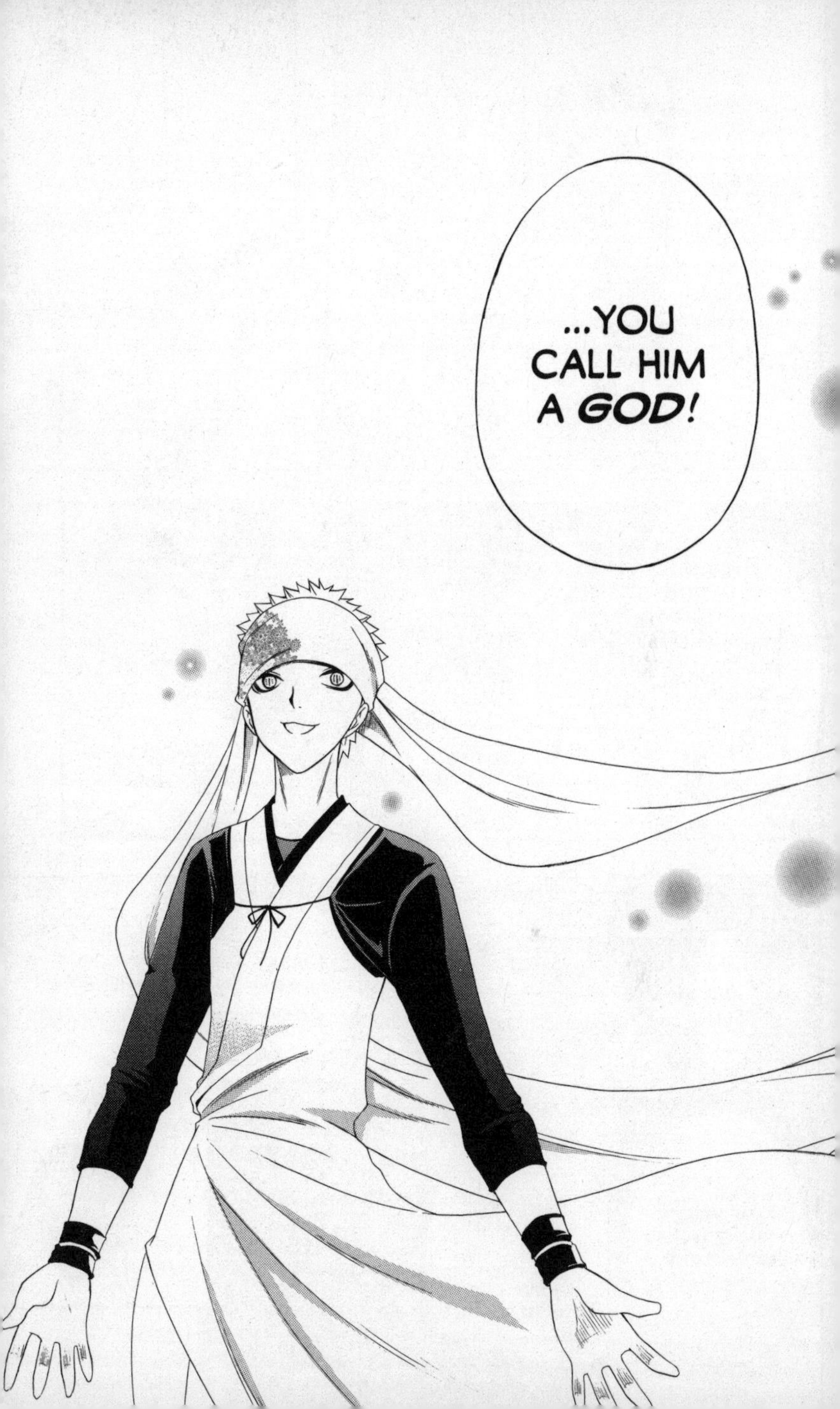
...YOU CALL HIM A *GOD*!

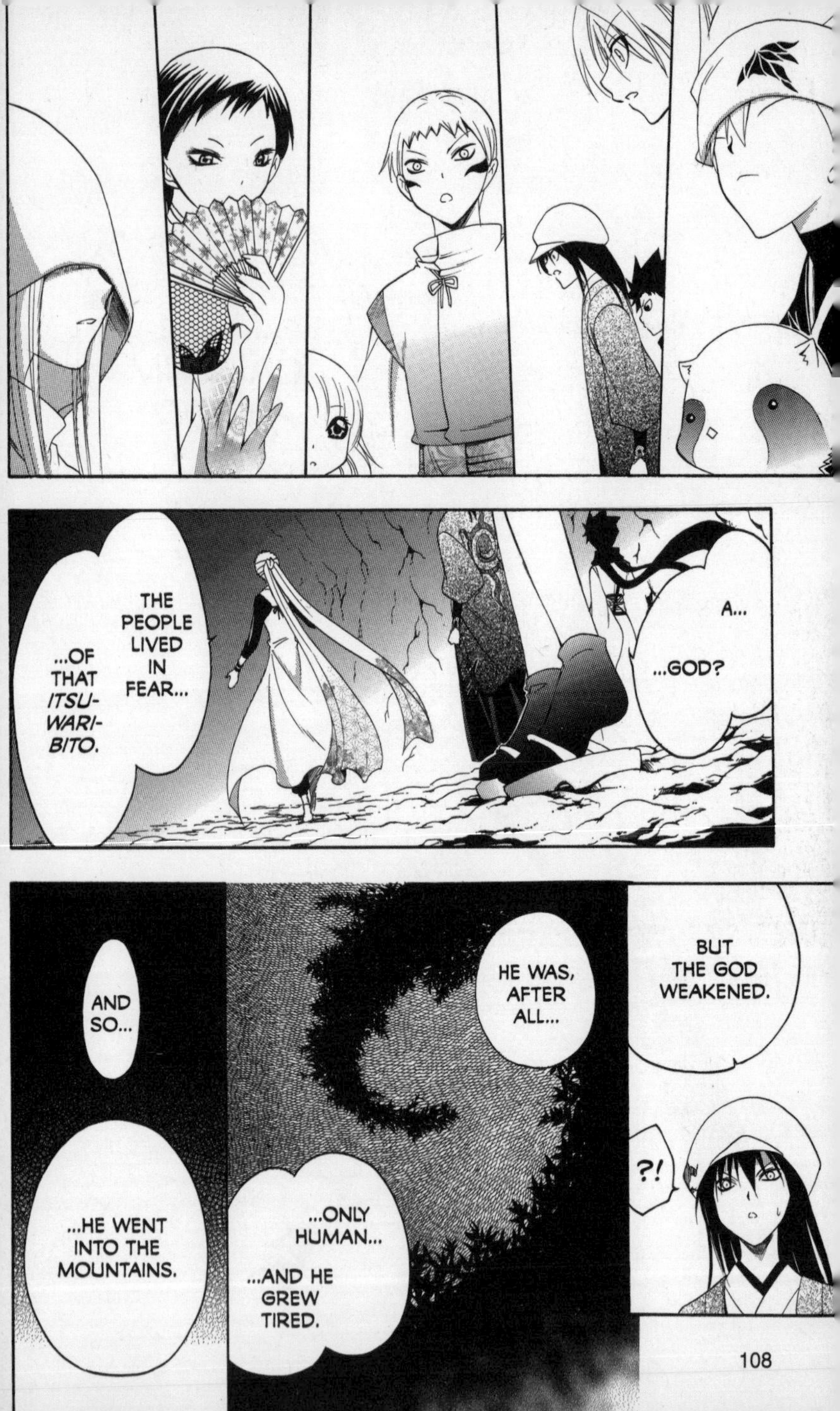
A...
...GOD?
THE PEOPLE LIVED IN FEAR...
...OF THAT *ITSUWARIBITO*.
BUT THE GOD WEAKENED.
?!
HE WAS, AFTER ALL...
...ONLY HUMAN...
...AND HE GREW TIRED.
AND SO...
...HE WENT INTO THE MOUNTAINS.

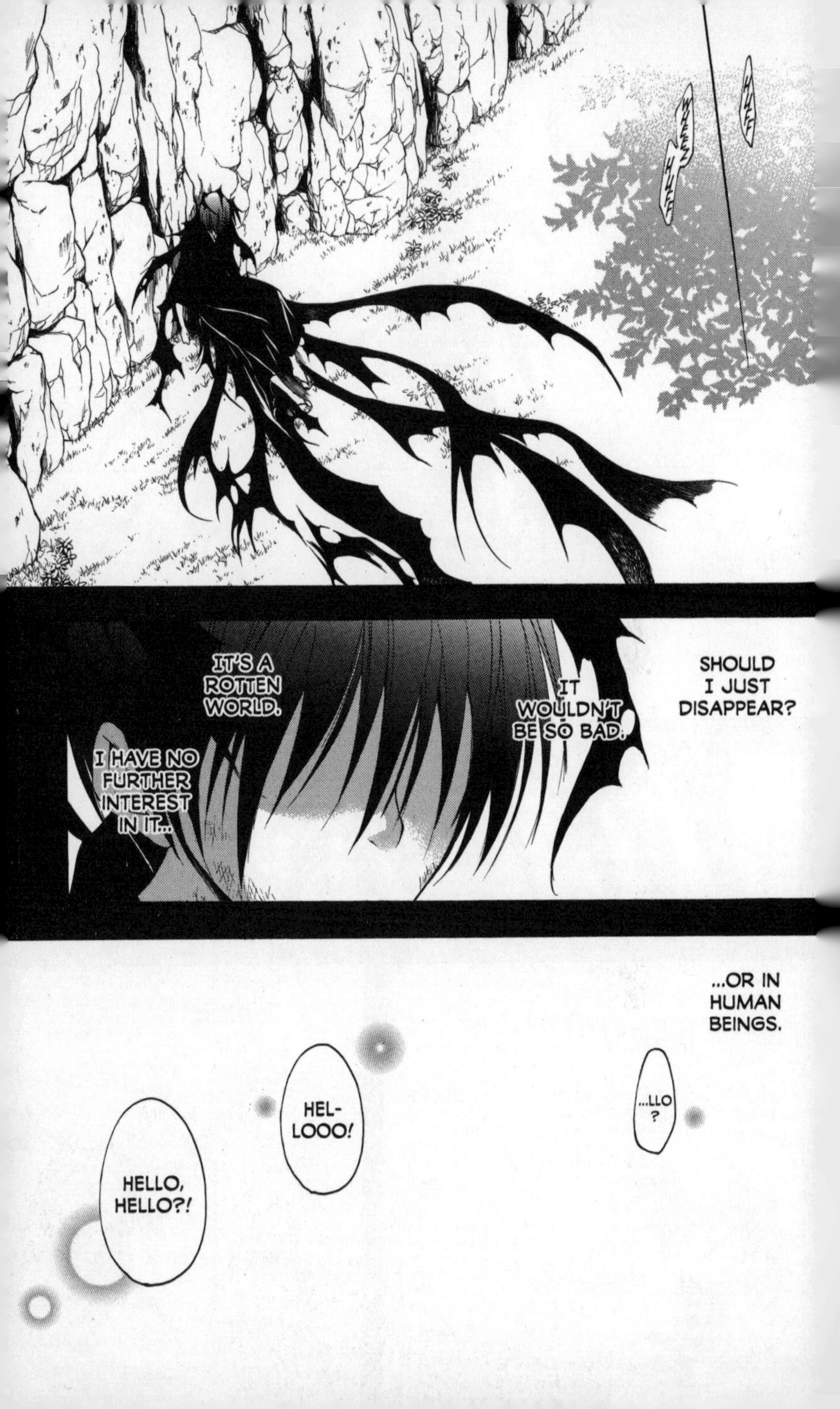
HUFF
WHEEZE
HUFF
SHOULD I JUST DISAPPEAR?
IT WOULDN'T BE SO BAD.
IT'S A ROTTEN WORLD.
I HAVE NO FURTHER INTEREST IN IT...
...OR IN HUMAN BEINGS.
...LLO?
HEL-LOOO!
HELLO, HELLO?!

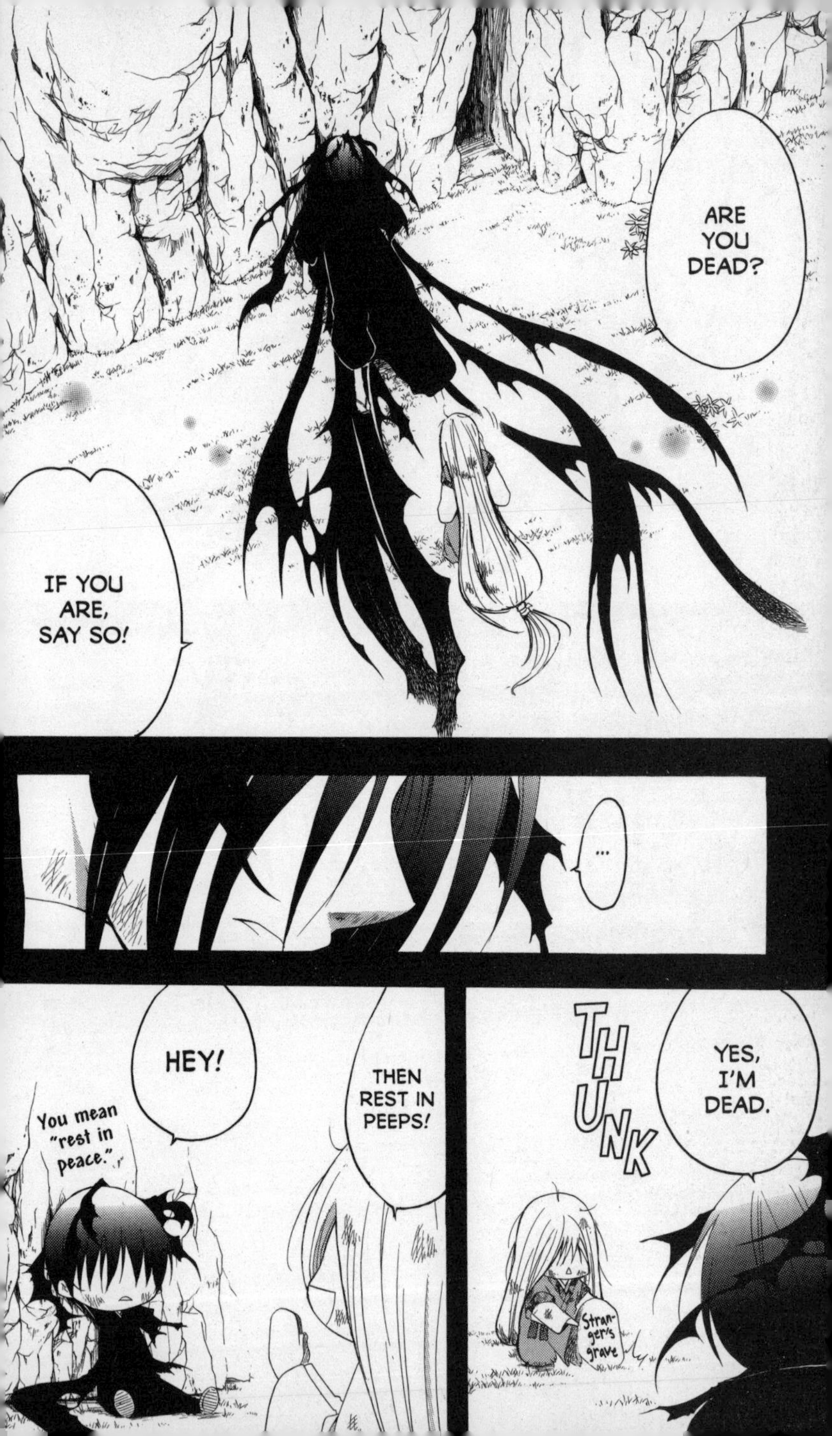
ARE YOU DEAD?
IF YOU ARE, SAY SO!
...
YES, I'M DEAD.
THUNK
Stranger's grave
THEN REST IN PEEPS!
HEY!
You mean "rest in peace."

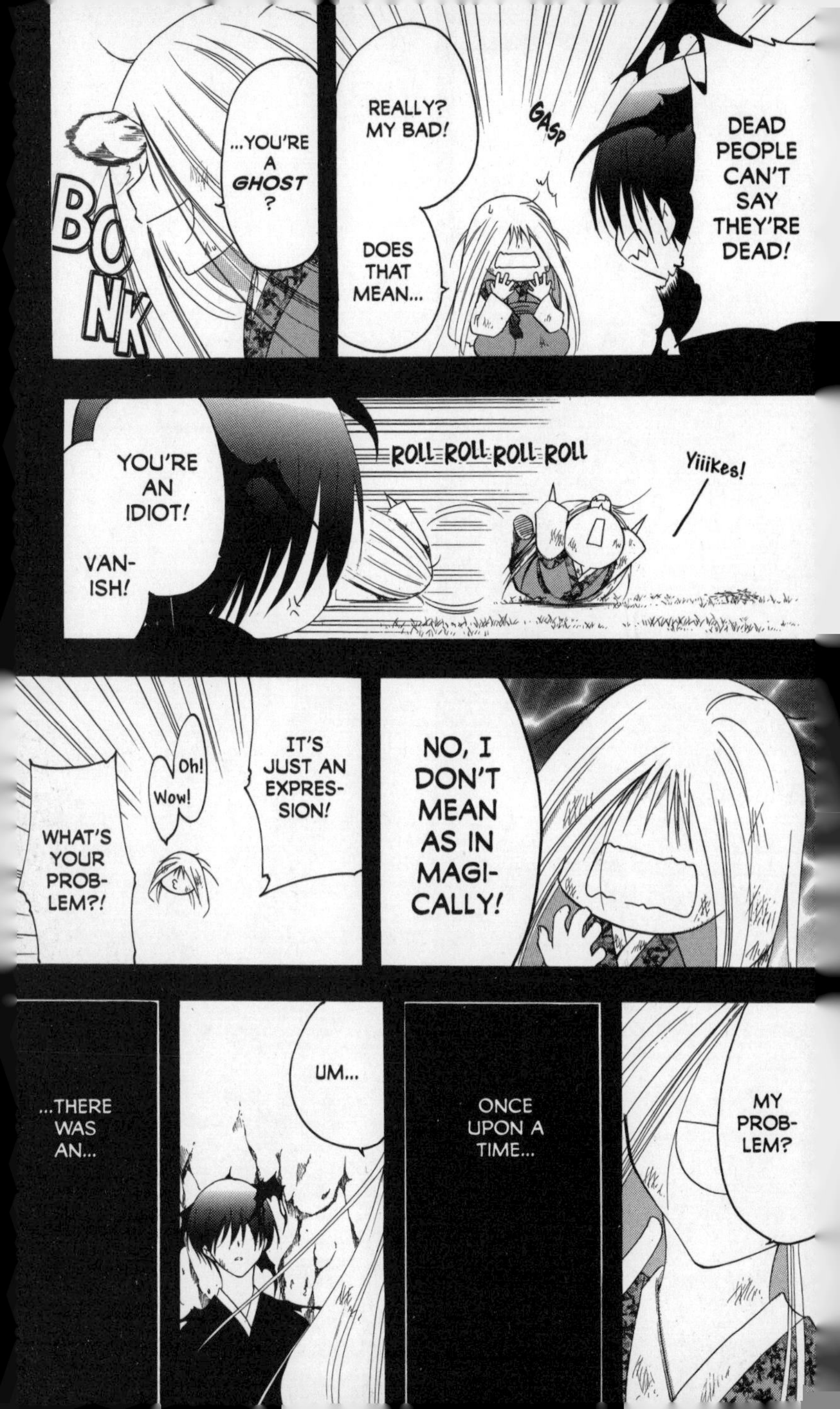

DEAD PEOPLE CAN'T SAY THEY'RE DEAD!
GASP
REALLY? MY BAD!
DOES THAT MEAN...
...YOU'RE A GHOST?
BONK
Yiiikes!
ROLL ROLL ROLL ROLL
YOU'RE AN IDIOT!
VAN-ISH!
NO, I DON'T MEAN AS IN MAGI-CALLY!
IT'S JUST AN EXPRES-SION!
Oh!
Wow!
WHAT'S YOUR PROB-LEM?!
MY PROB-LEM?
ONCE UPON A TIME...
UM...
...THERE WAS AN...

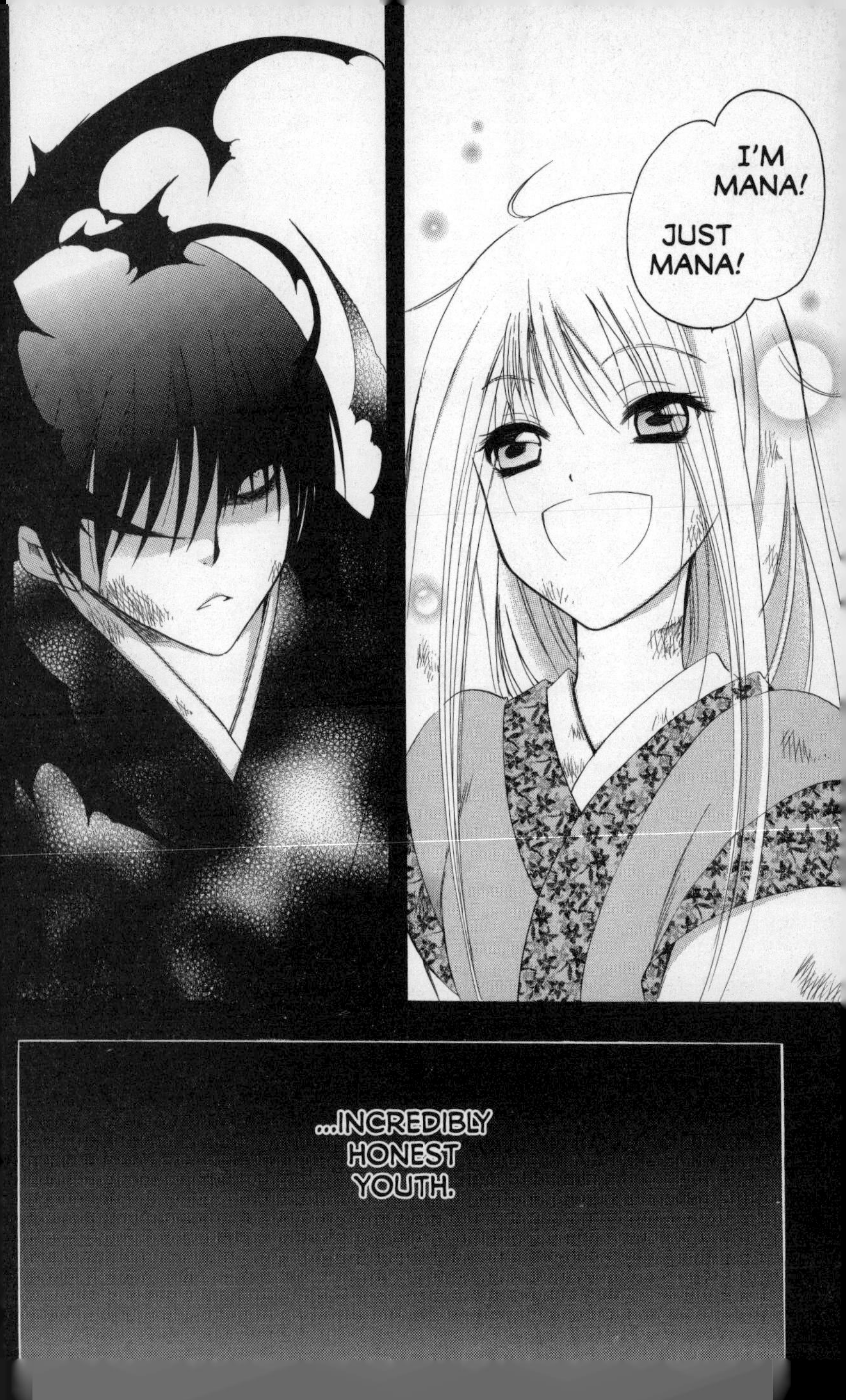
I'M MANA!
JUST MANA!
...INCREDIBLY HONEST YOUTH.

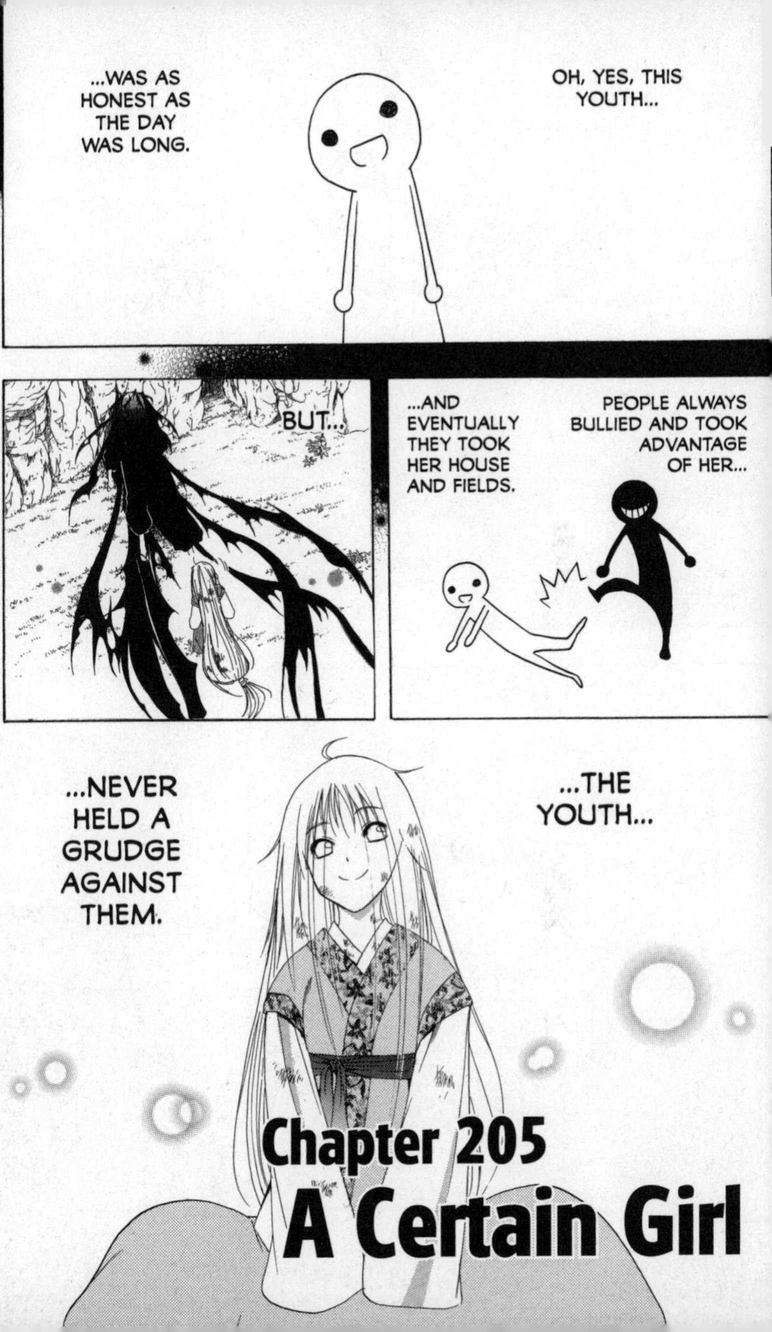
OH, YES, THIS YOUTH...
...WAS AS HONEST AS THE DAY WAS LONG.
PEOPLE ALWAYS BULLIED AND TOOK ADVANTAGE OF HER...
...AND EVENTUALLY THEY TOOK HER HOUSE AND FIELDS.
BUT...
...THE YOUTH...
...NEVER HELD A GRUDGE AGAINST THEM.
Chapter 205
A Certain Girl

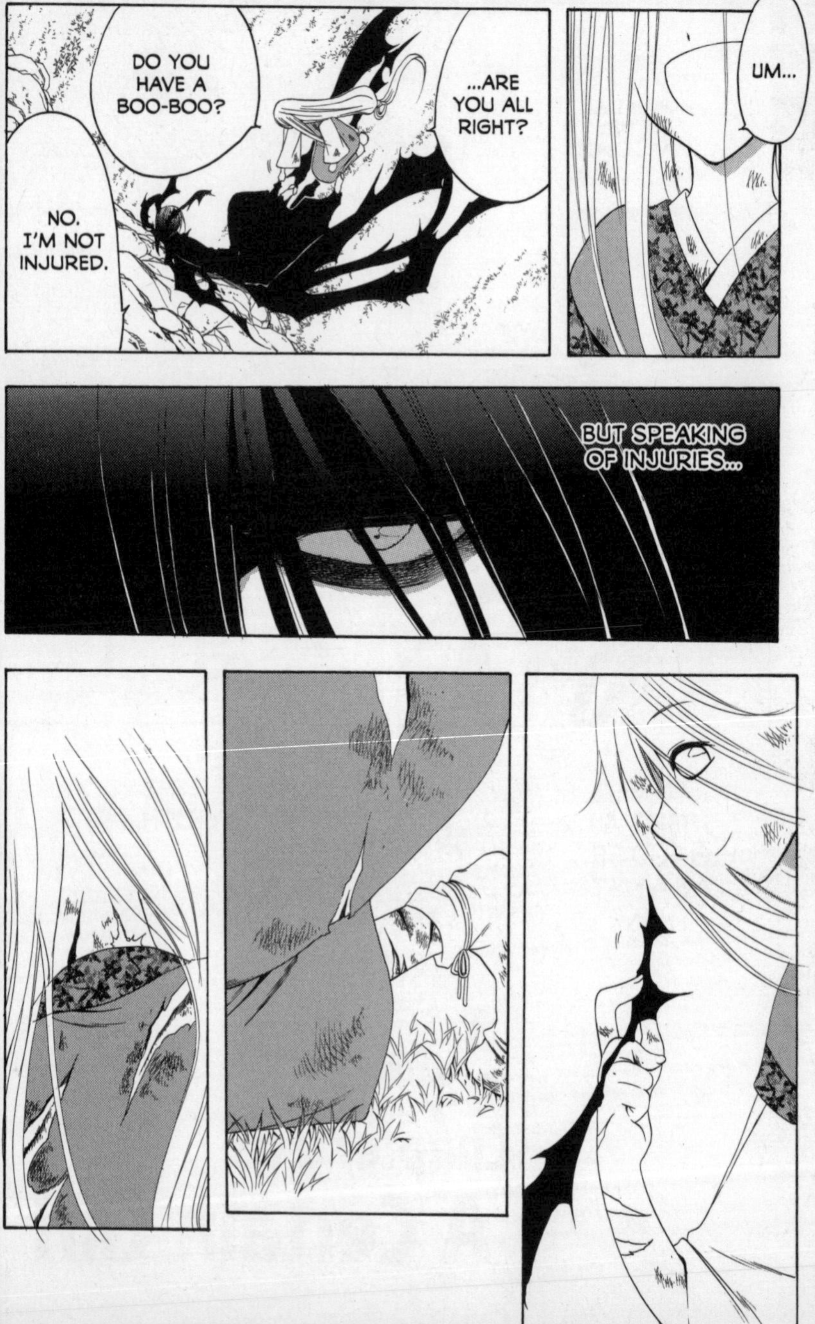
UM...
...ARE YOU ALL RIGHT?
DO YOU HAVE A BOO-BOO?
NO. I'M NOT INJURED.
BUT SPEAKING OF INJURIES...

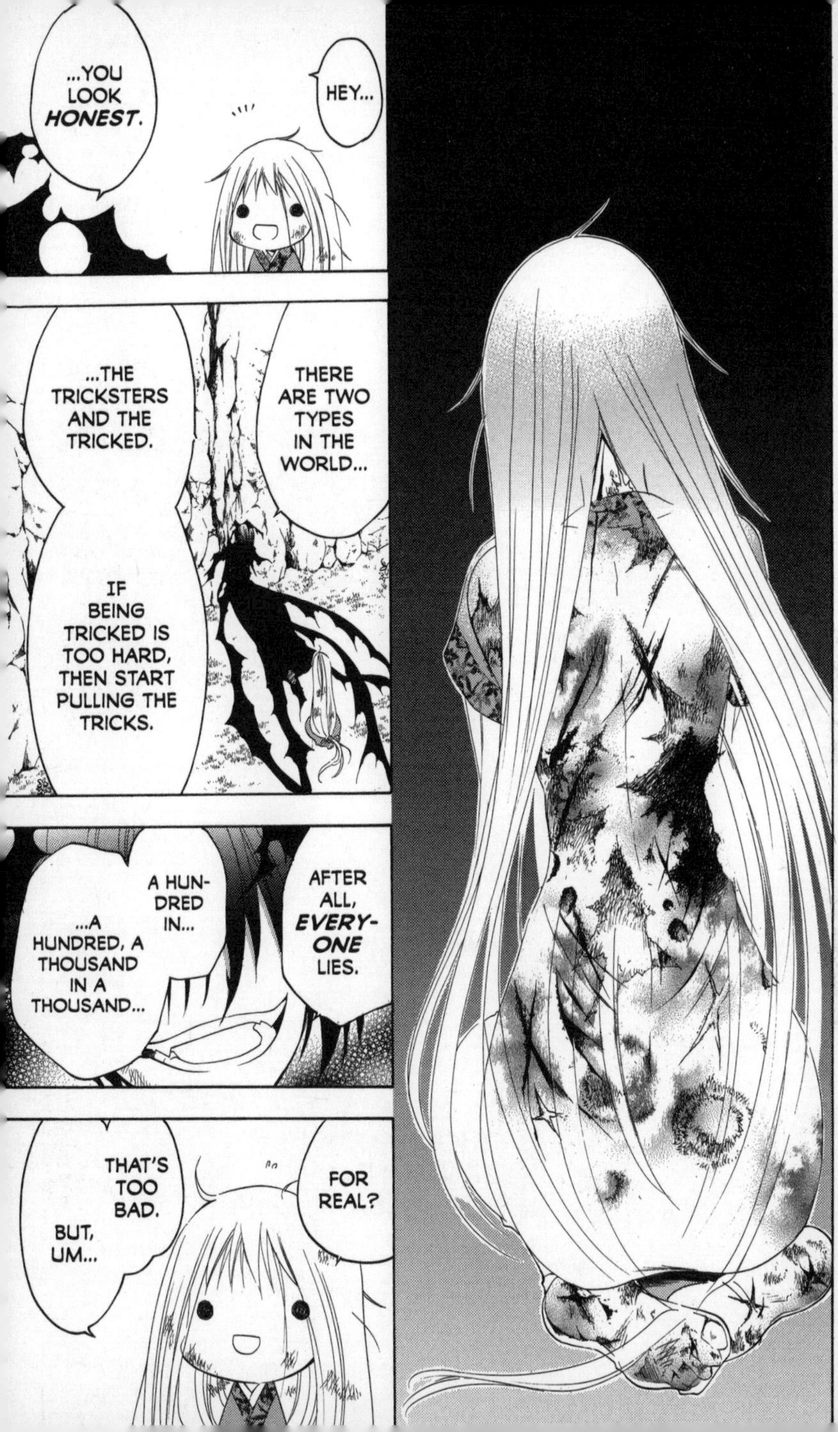
HEY...
...YOU LOOK HONEST.
THERE ARE TWO TYPES IN THE WORLD...
...THE TRICKSTERS AND THE TRICKED.
IF BEING TRICKED IS TOO HARD, THEN START PULLING THE TRICKS.
AFTER ALL, EVERYONE LIES.
A HUNDRED IN...
...A HUNDRED, A THOUSAND IN A THOUSAND...
FOR REAL?
THAT'S TOO BAD.
BUT, UM...

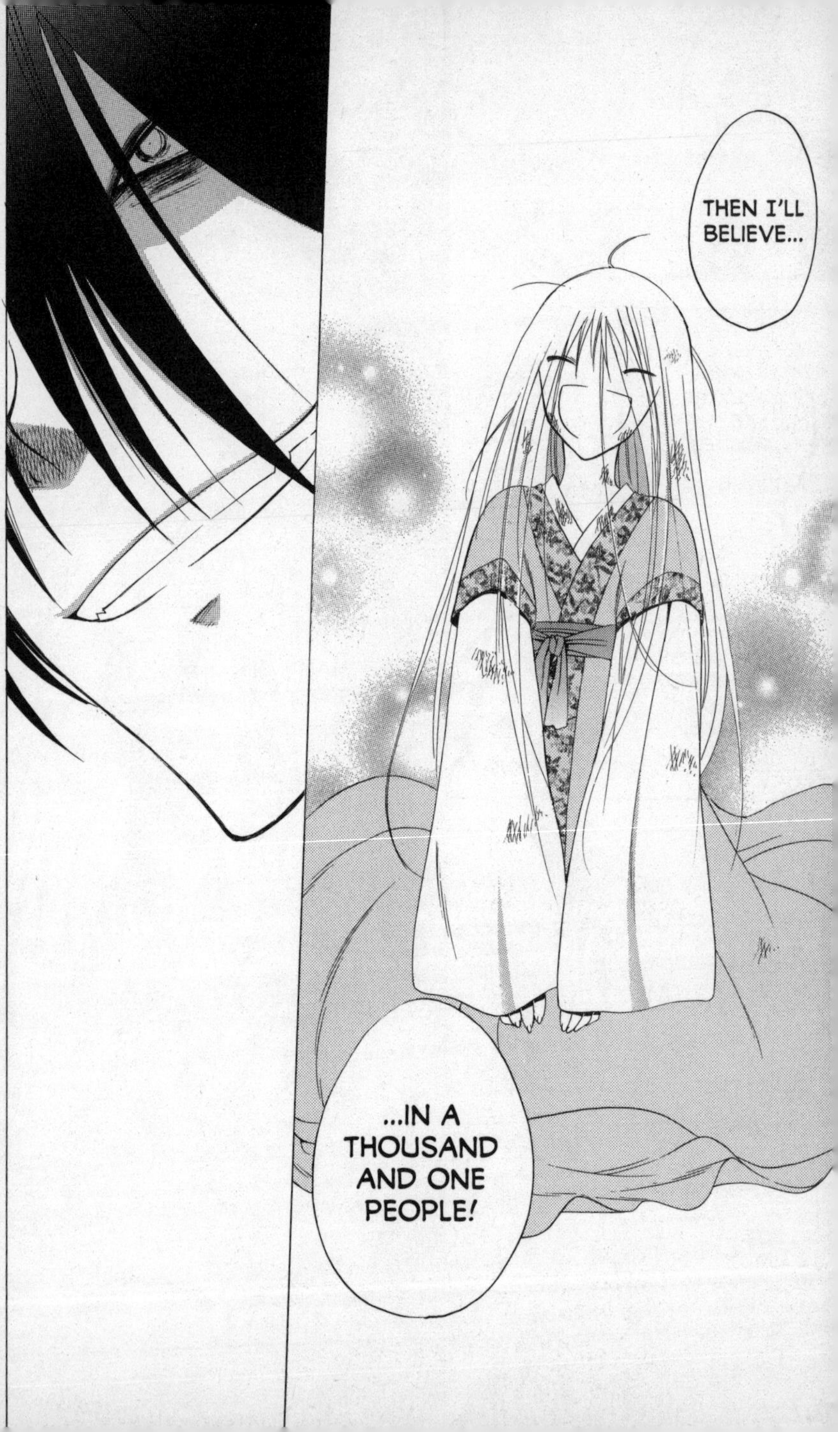
THEN I'LL BELIEVE...
...IN A THOUSAND AND ONE PEOPLE!

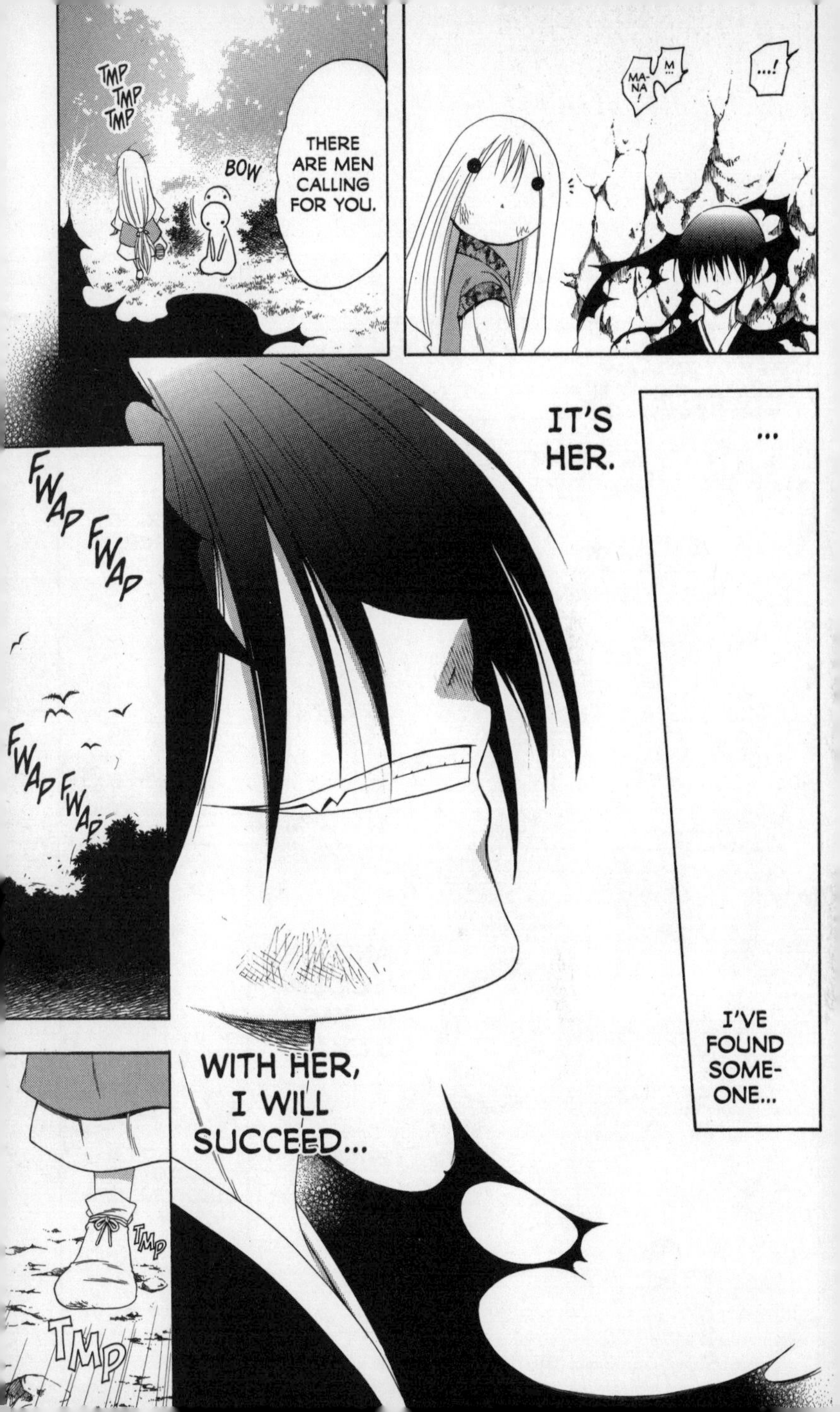

...!
M...
MA-NA!
TMP TMP TMP
BOW
THERE ARE MEN CALLING FOR YOU.
...
I'VE FOUND SOME-ONE...
IT'S HER.
WITH HER, I WILL SUCCEED...
FWAP FWAP
FWAP FWAP
TMP
TMP

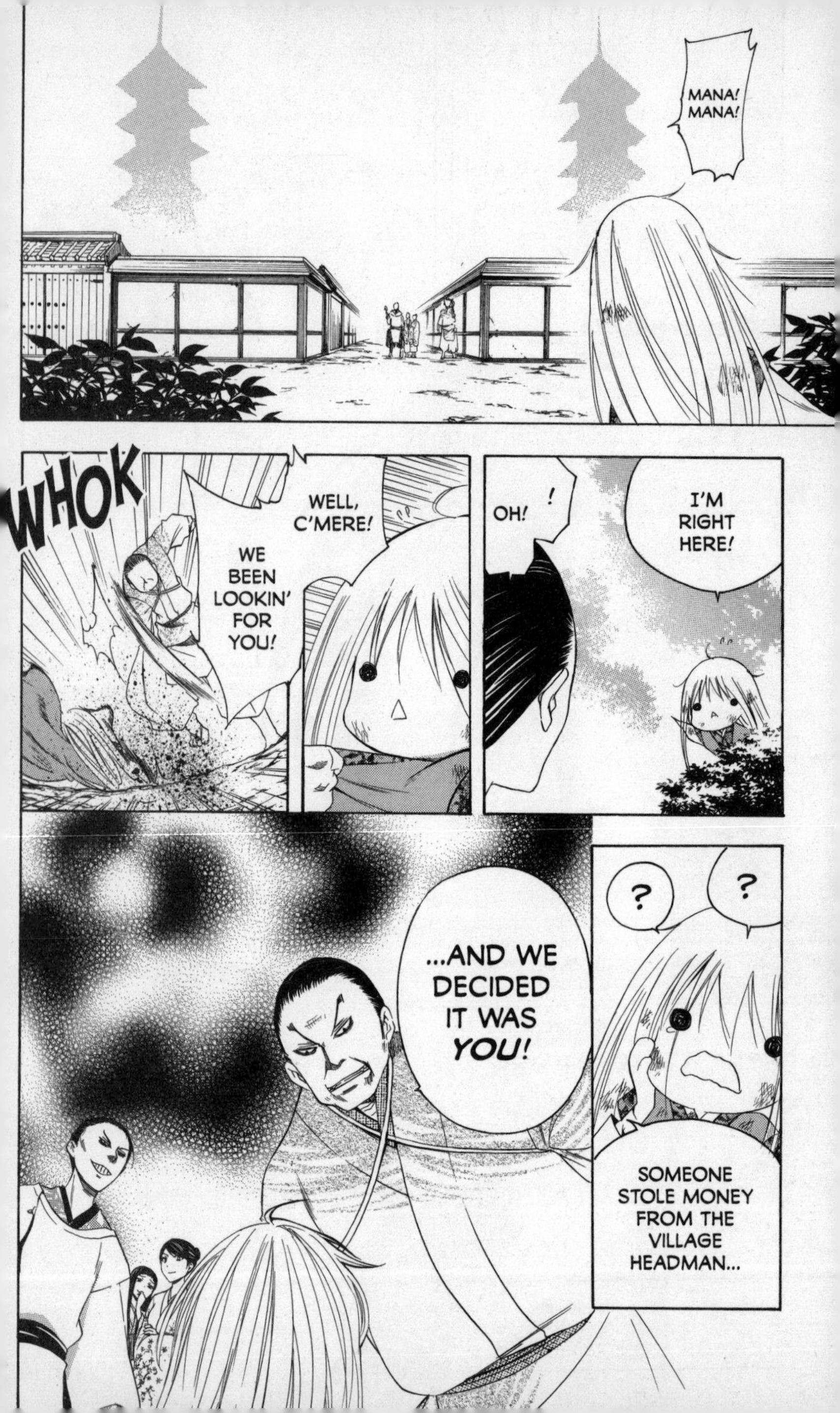
MANA! MANA!
I'M RIGHT HERE!
!
OH!
WELL, C'MERE!
WE BEEN LOOKIN' FOR YOU!
WHOK
?
?
SOMEONE STOLE MONEY FROM THE VILLAGE HEADMAN...
...AND WE DECIDED IT WAS *YOU*!

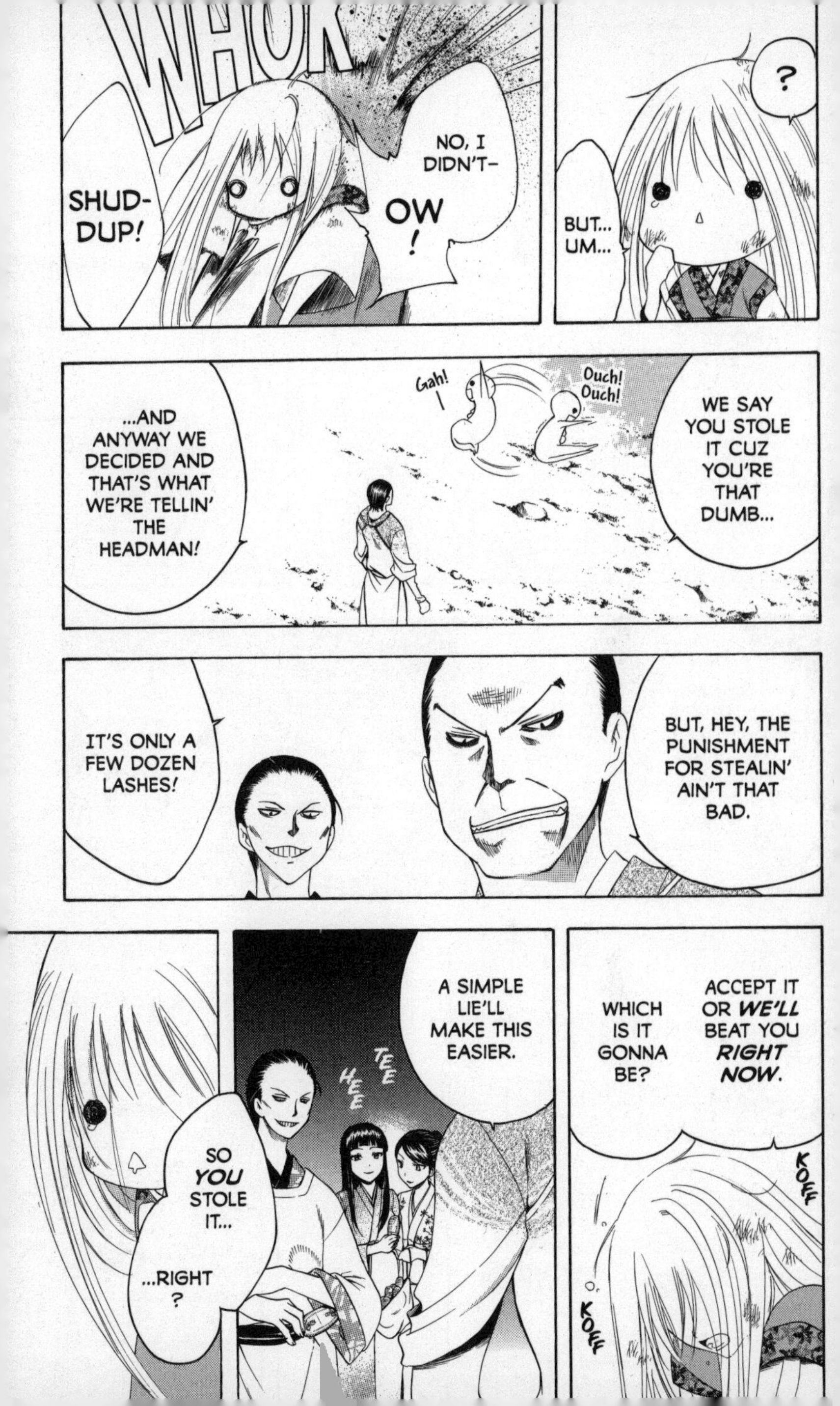
?
BUT... UM...
NO, I DIDN'T-
WHOK
OW!
SHUD-DUP!
WE SAY YOU STOLE IT CUZ YOU'RE THAT DUMB...
Ouch! Ouch!
Gah!
...AND ANYWAY WE DECIDED AND THAT'S WHAT WE'RE TELLIN' THE HEADMAN!
BUT, HEY, THE PUNISHMENT FOR STEALIN' AIN'T THAT BAD.
IT'S ONLY A FEW DOZEN LASHES!
ACCEPT IT OR *WE'LL* BEAT YOU *RIGHT NOW*.
WHICH IS IT GONNA BE?
KOFF
KOFF
A SIMPLE LIE'LL MAKE THIS EASIER.
TEE HEE
SO *YOU* STOLE IT...
...RIGHT?

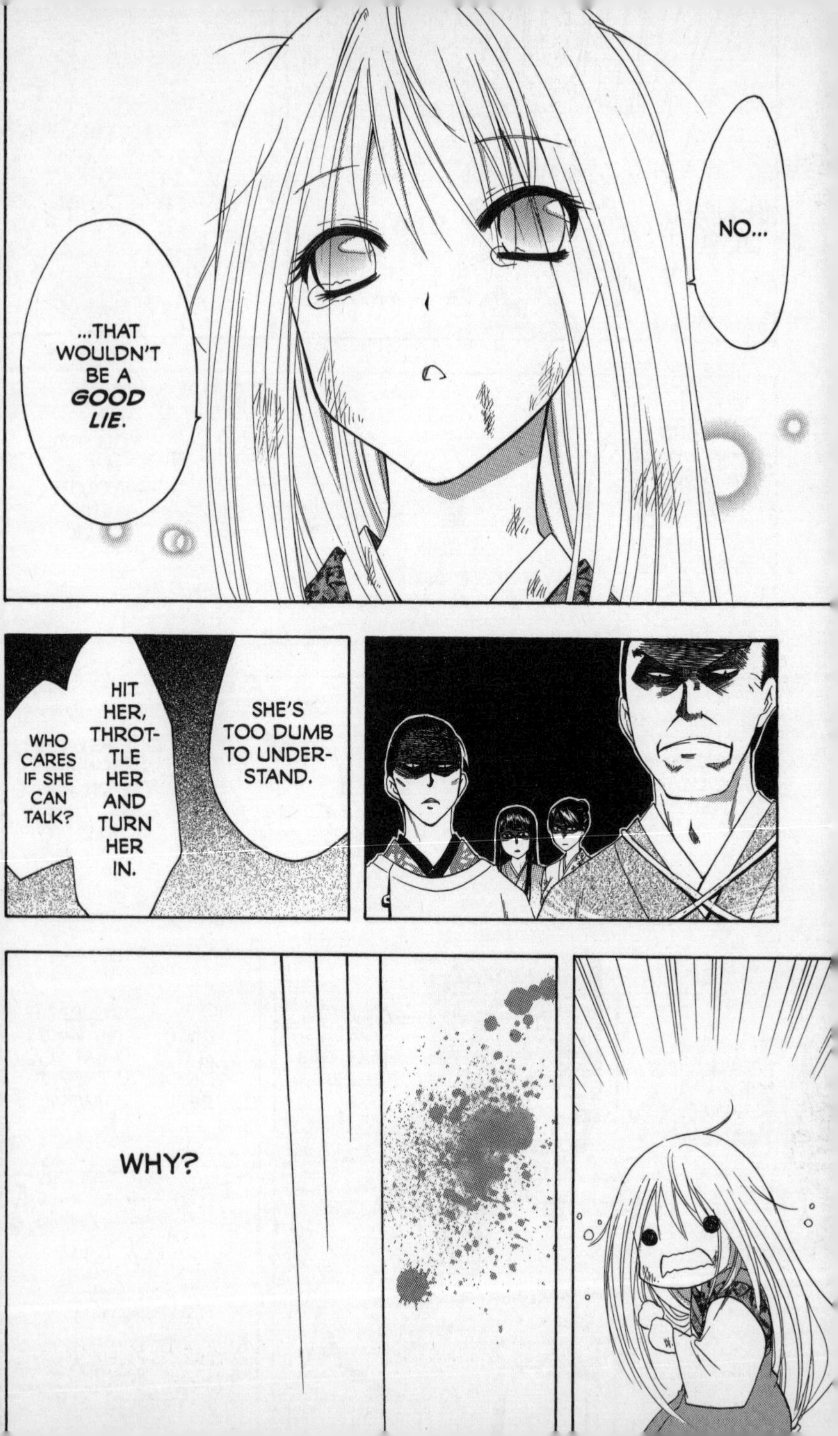
NO...
...THAT WOULDN'T BE A *GOOD LIE*.
SHE'S TOO DUMB TO UNDER-STAND.
HIT HER, THROT-TLE HER AND TURN HER IN.
WHO CARES IF SHE CAN TALK?
WHY?

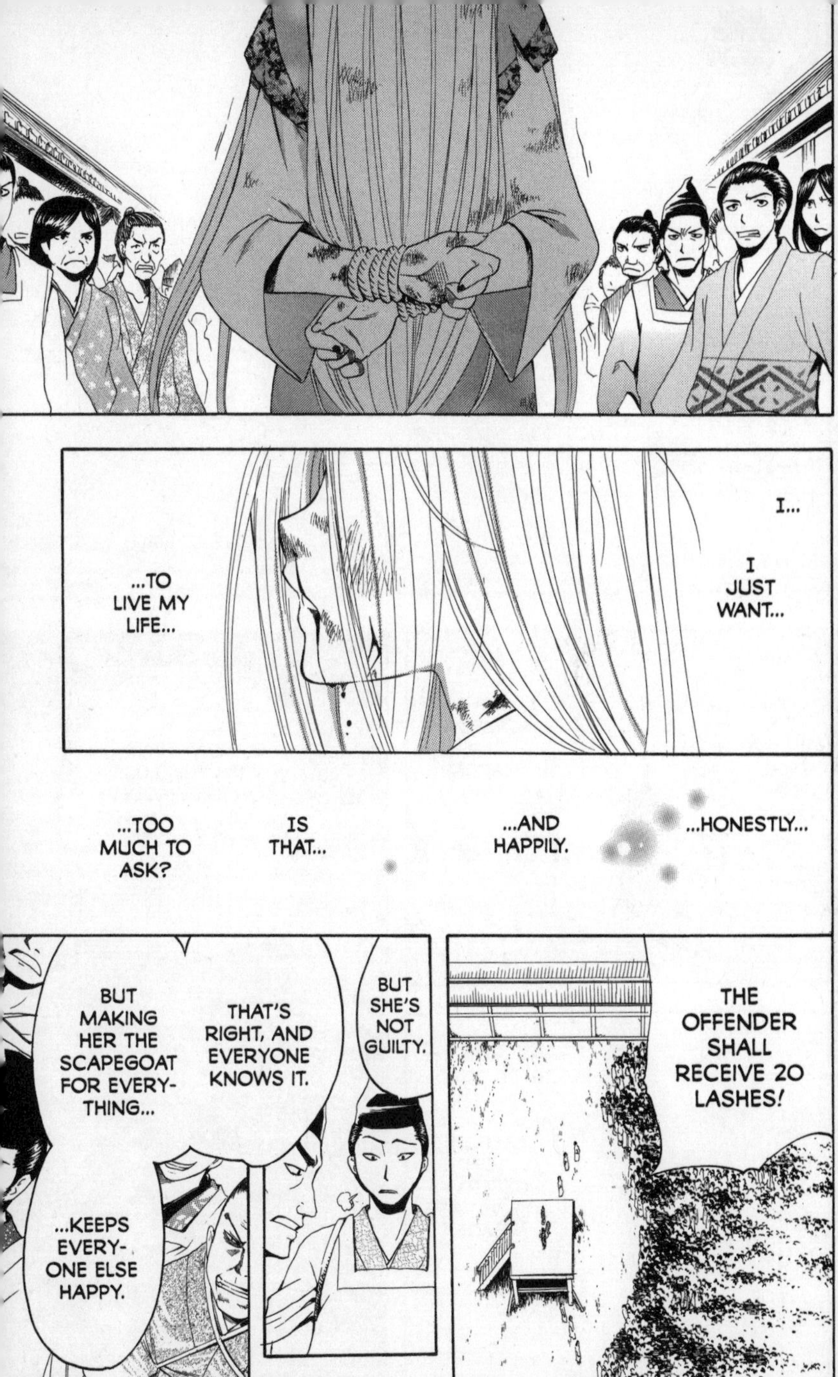
I...
I JUST WANT...
...TO LIVE MY LIFE...
...HONESTLY...
...AND HAPPILY.
IS THAT...
...TOO MUCH TO ASK?
THE OFFENDER SHALL RECEIVE 20 LASHES!
BUT SHE'S NOT GUILTY.
THAT'S RIGHT, AND EVERYONE KNOWS IT.
BUT MAKING HER THE SCAPEGOAT FOR EVERY-THING...
...KEEPS EVERY-ONE ELSE HAPPY.

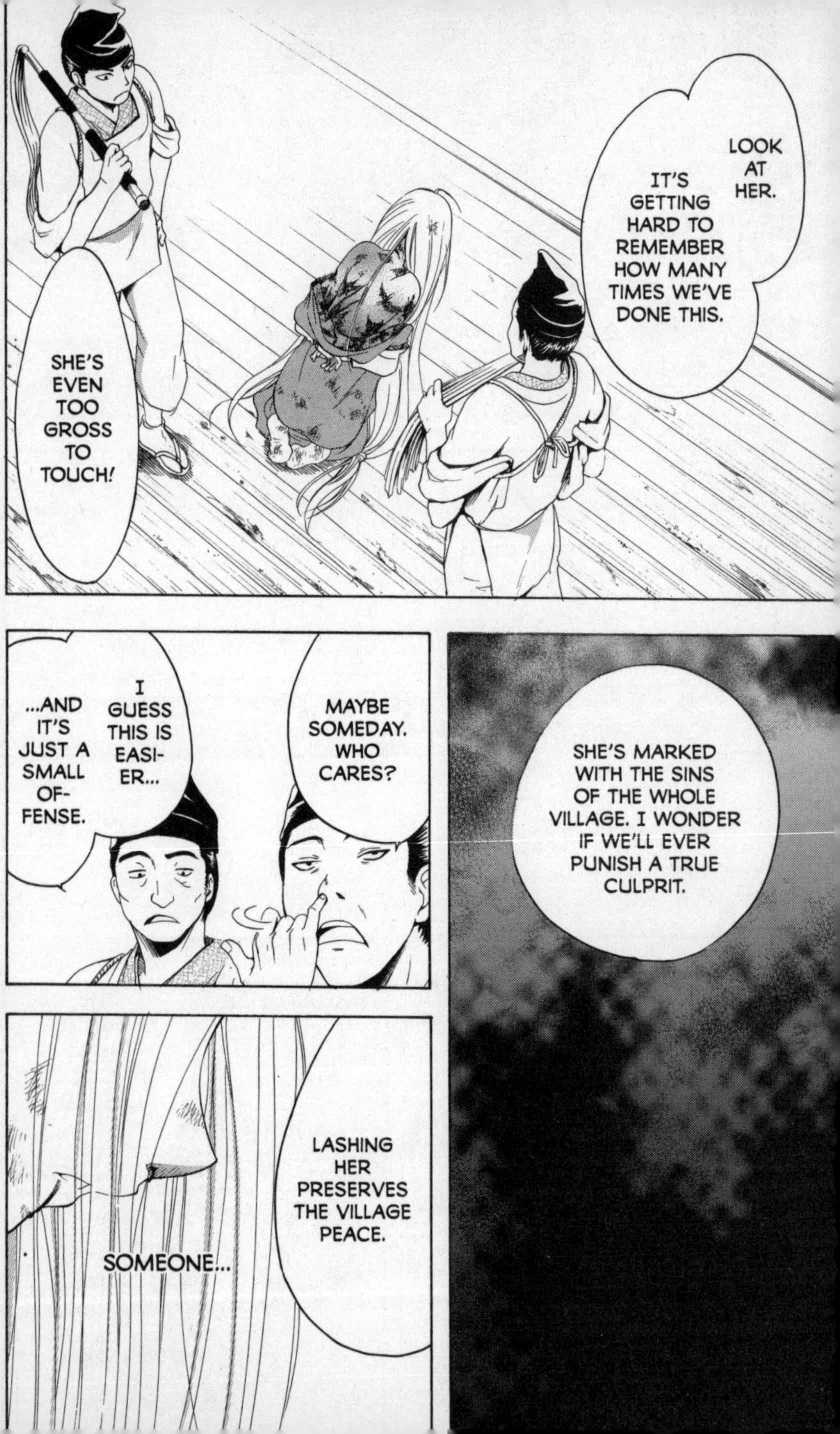
LOOK AT HER.
IT'S GETTING HARD TO REMEMBER HOW MANY TIMES WE'VE DONE THIS.
SHE'S EVEN TOO GROSS TO TOUCH!
SHE'S MARKED WITH THE SINS OF THE WHOLE VILLAGE. I WONDER IF WE'LL EVER PUNISH A TRUE CULPRIT.
MAYBE SOMEDAY. WHO CARES?
I GUESS THIS IS EASI- ER...
...AND IT'S JUST A SMALL OF- FENSE.
LASHING HER PRESERVES THE VILLAGE PEACE.
SOMEONE...

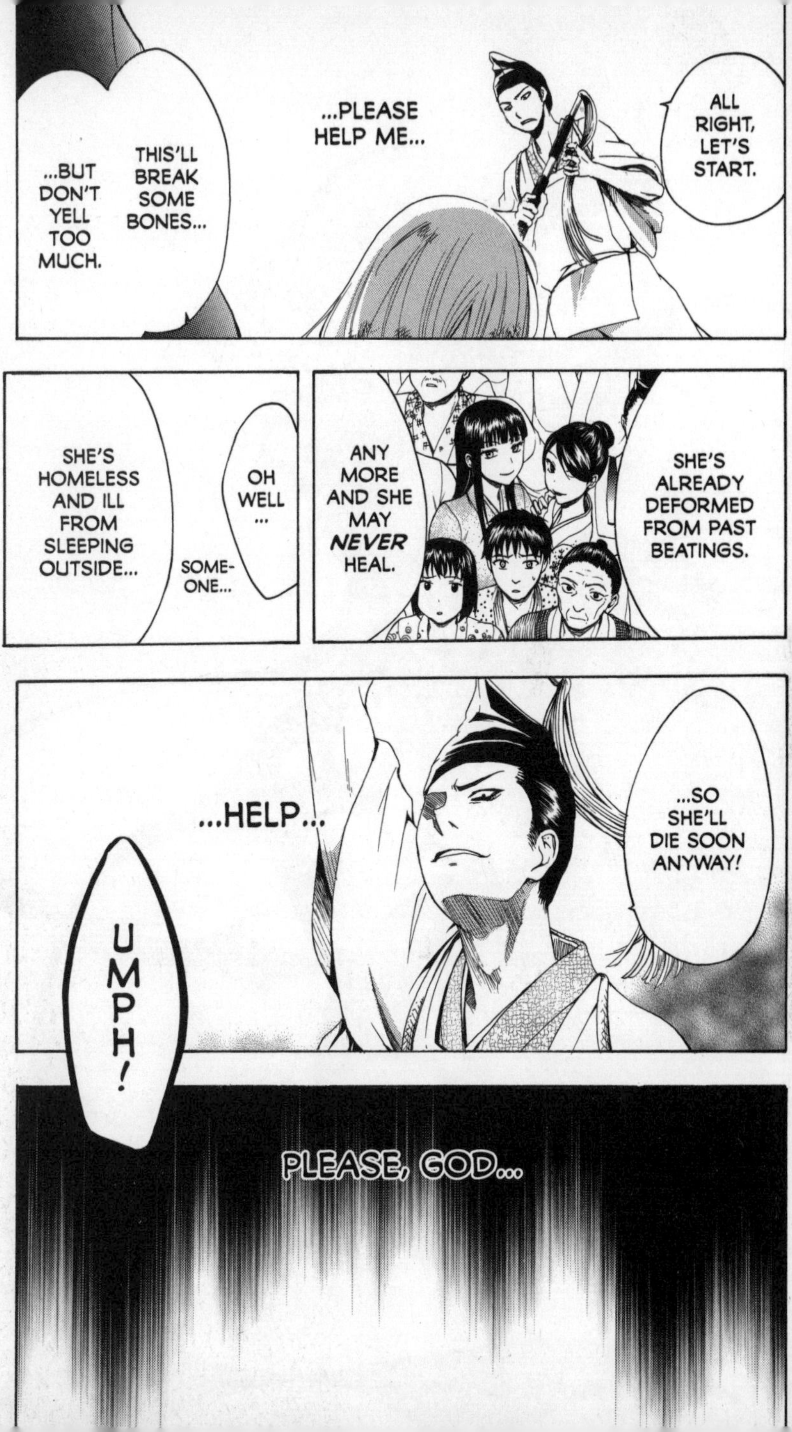
ALL RIGHT, LET'S START.
...PLEASE HELP ME...
THIS'LL BREAK SOME BONES...
...BUT DON'T YELL TOO MUCH.
SHE'S ALREADY DEFORMED FROM PAST BEATINGS.
ANY MORE AND SHE MAY *NEVER* HEAL.
OH WELL...
SOME-ONE...
SHE'S HOMELESS AND ILL FROM SLEEPING OUTSIDE...
...SO SHE'LL DIE SOON ANYWAY!
...HELP...
UMPH!
PLEASE, GOD...

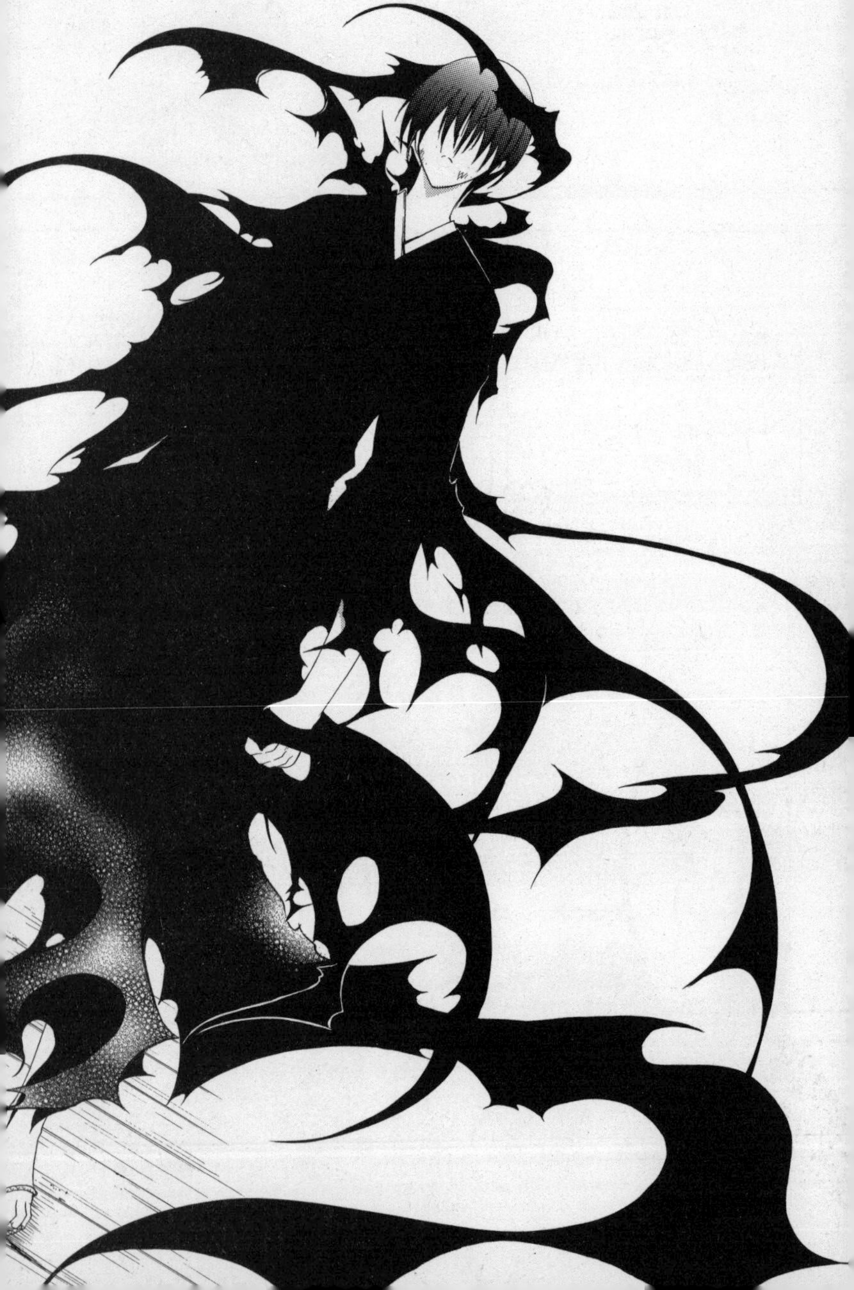

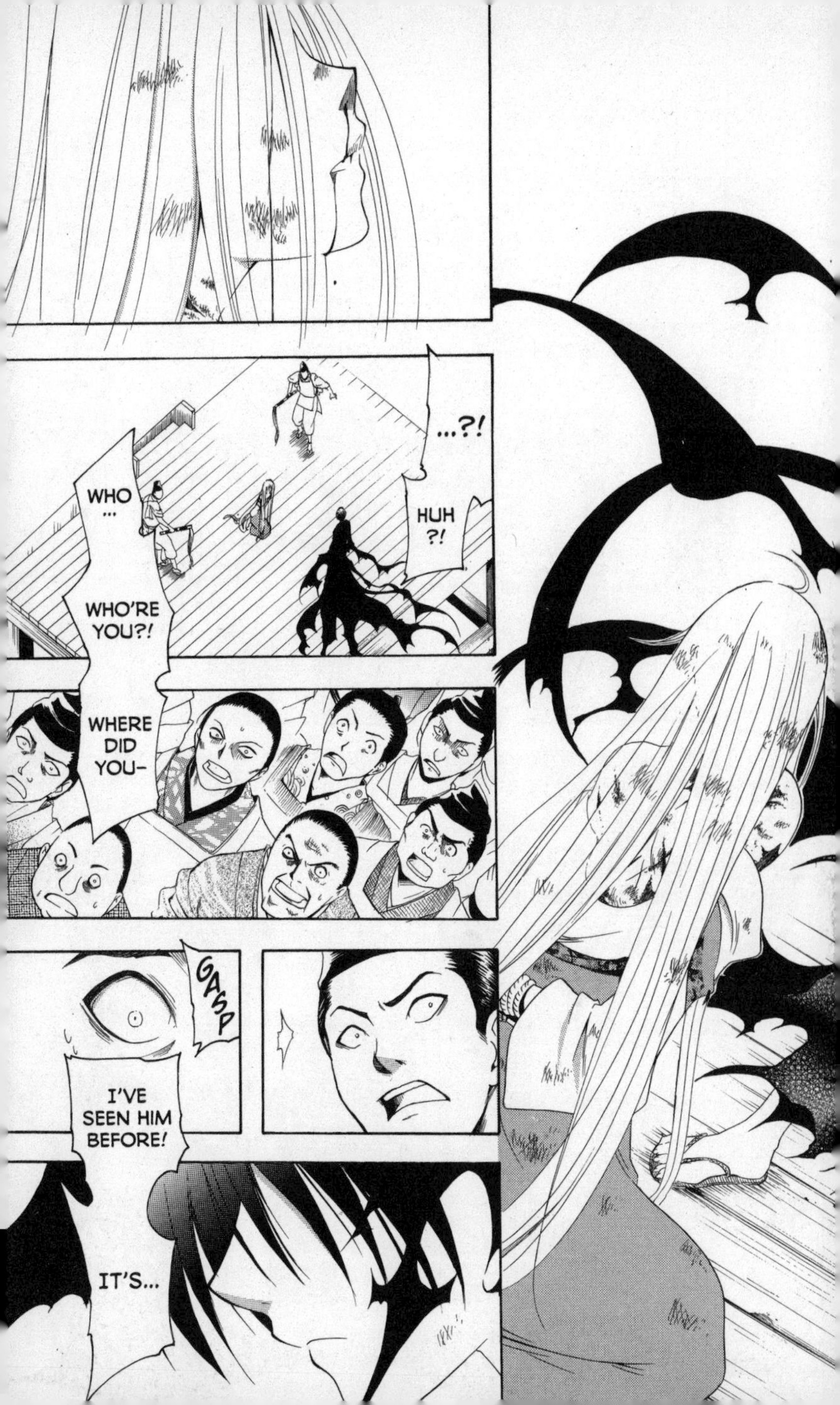

...?!
HUH ?!
WHO ... WHO'RE YOU?! WHERE DID YOU-
GASP
I'VE SEEN HIM BEFORE!
IT'S...

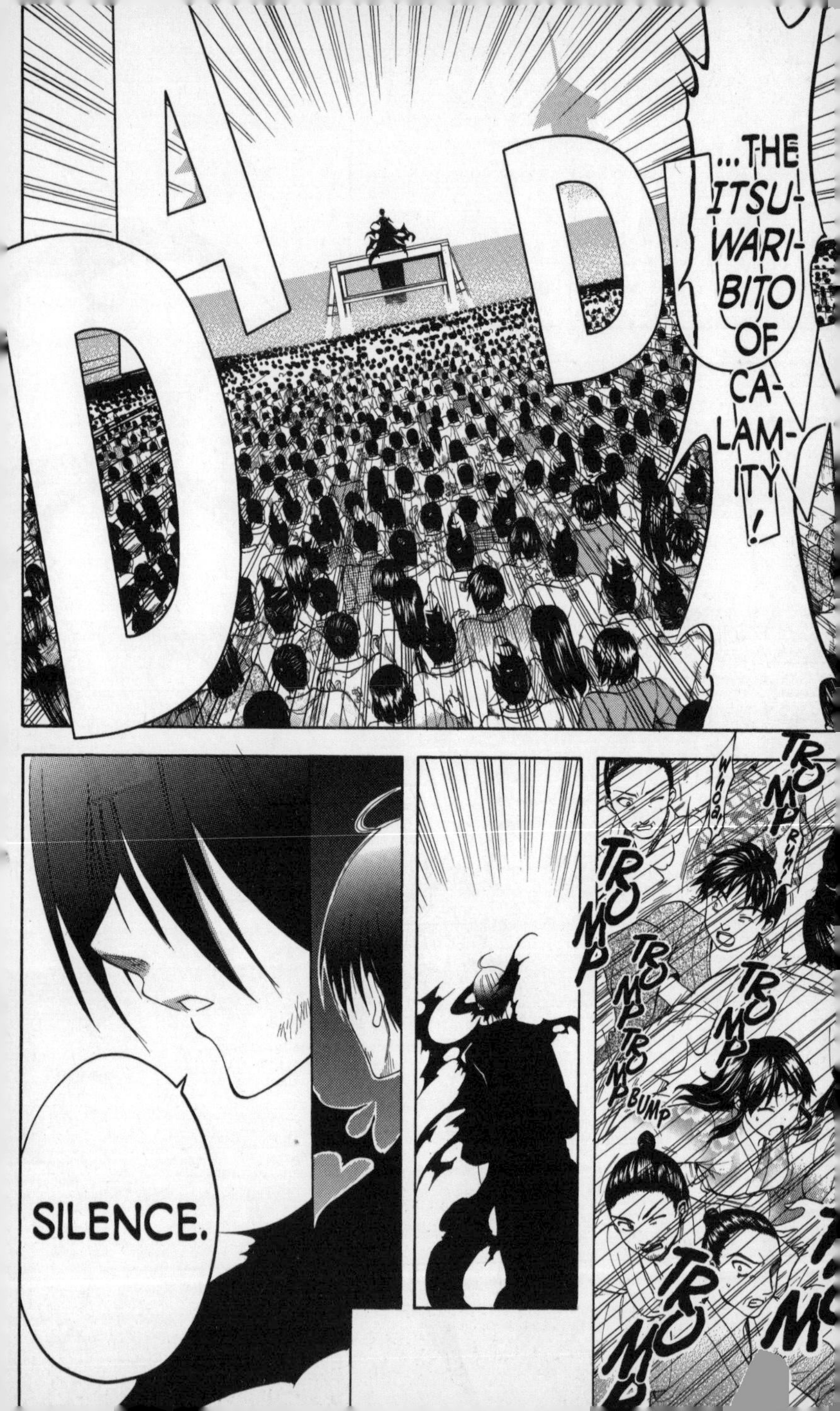
...THE ITSU-WARI-BITO OF CA-LAM-ITY!
DUM
DA
TROMP
whoa!
run!
TROMP
TROMP
TROMP
TROMP
TROMP
BUMP
TROMP
TROMP
SILENCE.

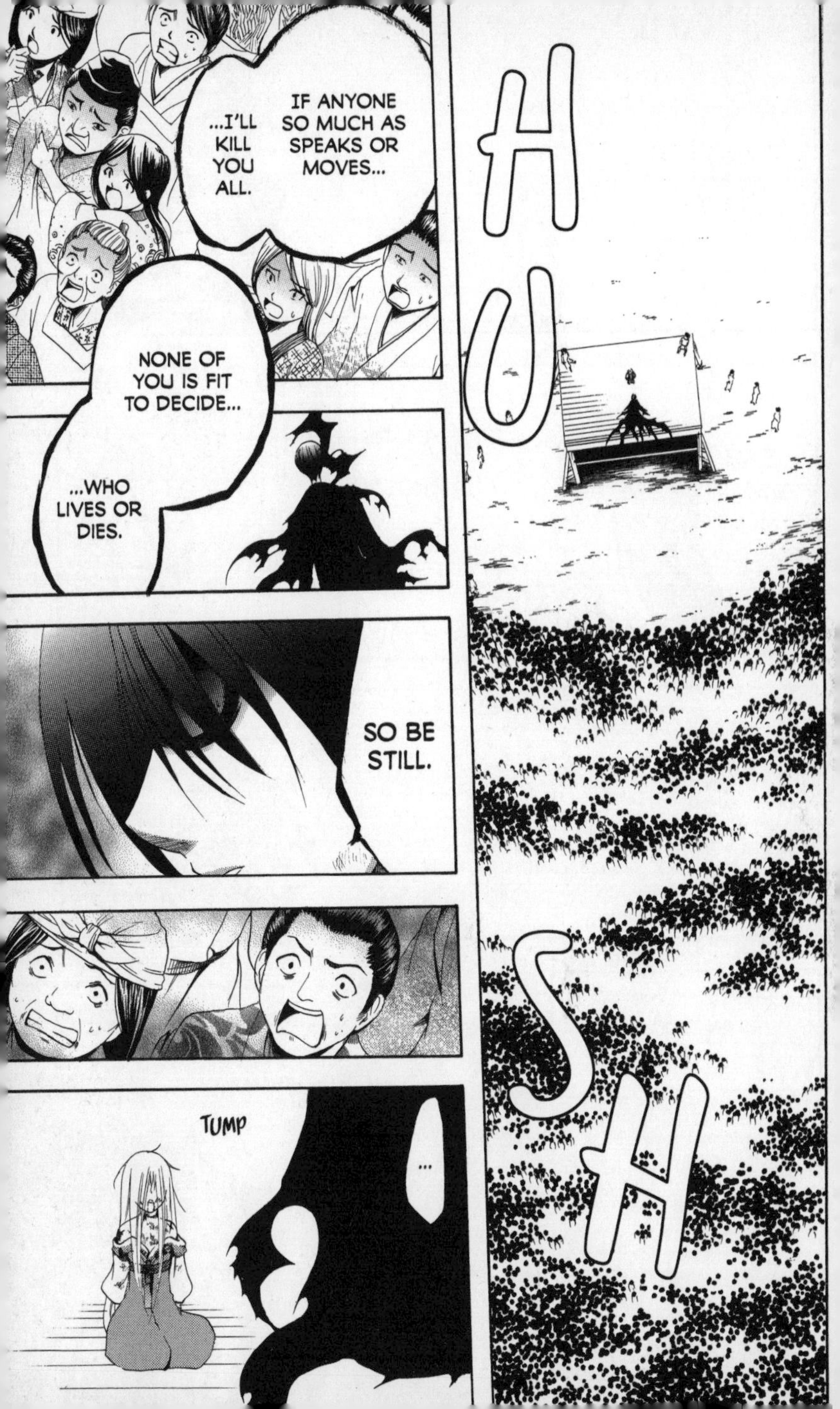
HUSH
IF ANYONE SO MUCH AS SPEAKS OR MOVES...
...I'LL KILL YOU ALL.
NONE OF YOU IS FIT TO DECIDE...
...WHO LIVES OR DIES.
SO BE STILL.
TUMP
...

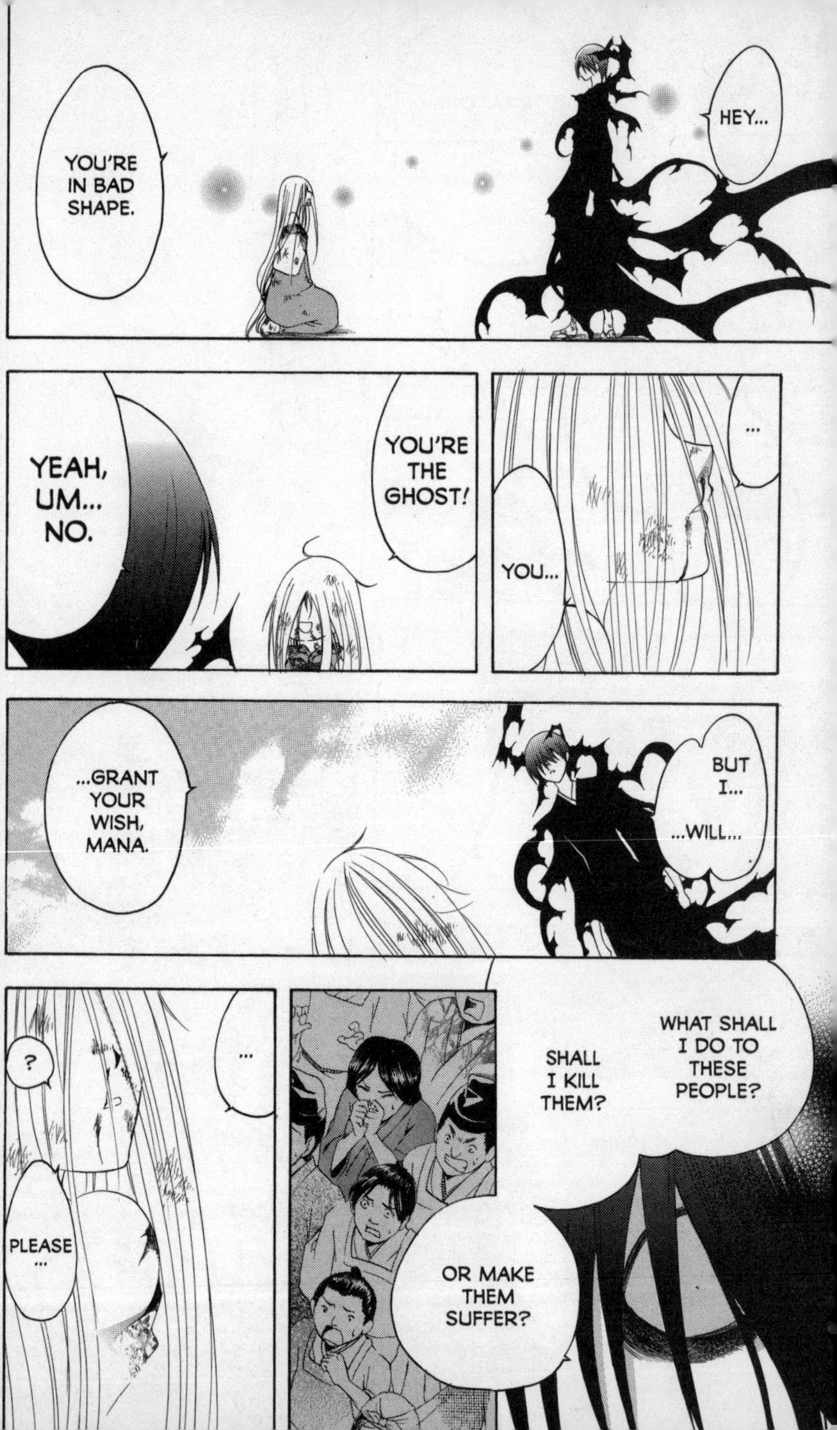
HEY...
YOU'RE IN BAD SHAPE.
...
YOU...
YOU'RE THE GHOST!
YEAH, UM... NO.
BUT I...
...WILL...
...GRANT YOUR WISH, MANA.
WHAT SHALL I DO TO THESE PEOPLE?
SHALL I KILL THEM?
OR MAKE THEM SUFFER?
...
?
PLEASE ...

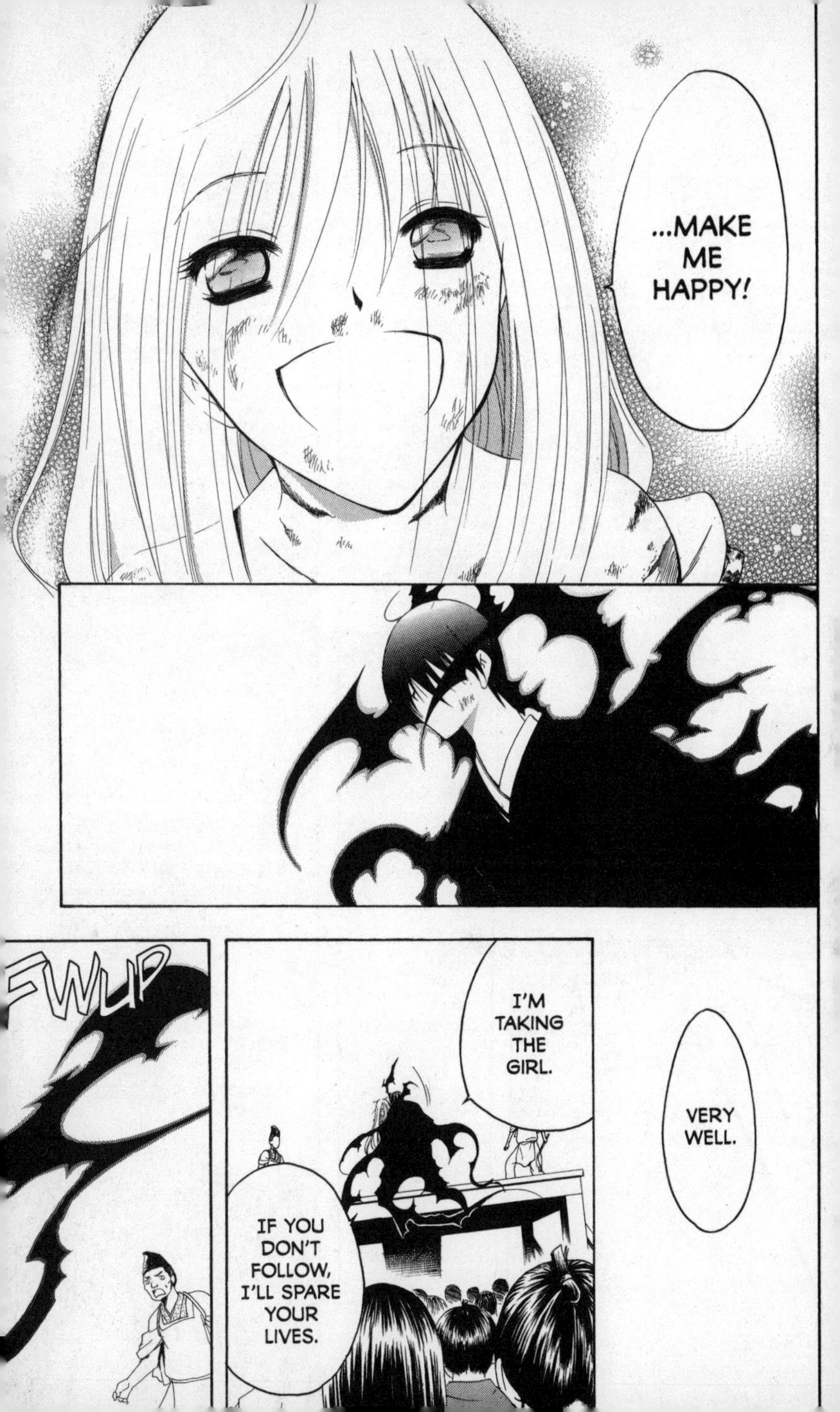
...MAKE ME HAPPY!
I'M TAKING THE GIRL.
VERY WELL.
IF YOU DON'T FOLLOW, I'LL SPARE YOUR LIVES.
FWUP

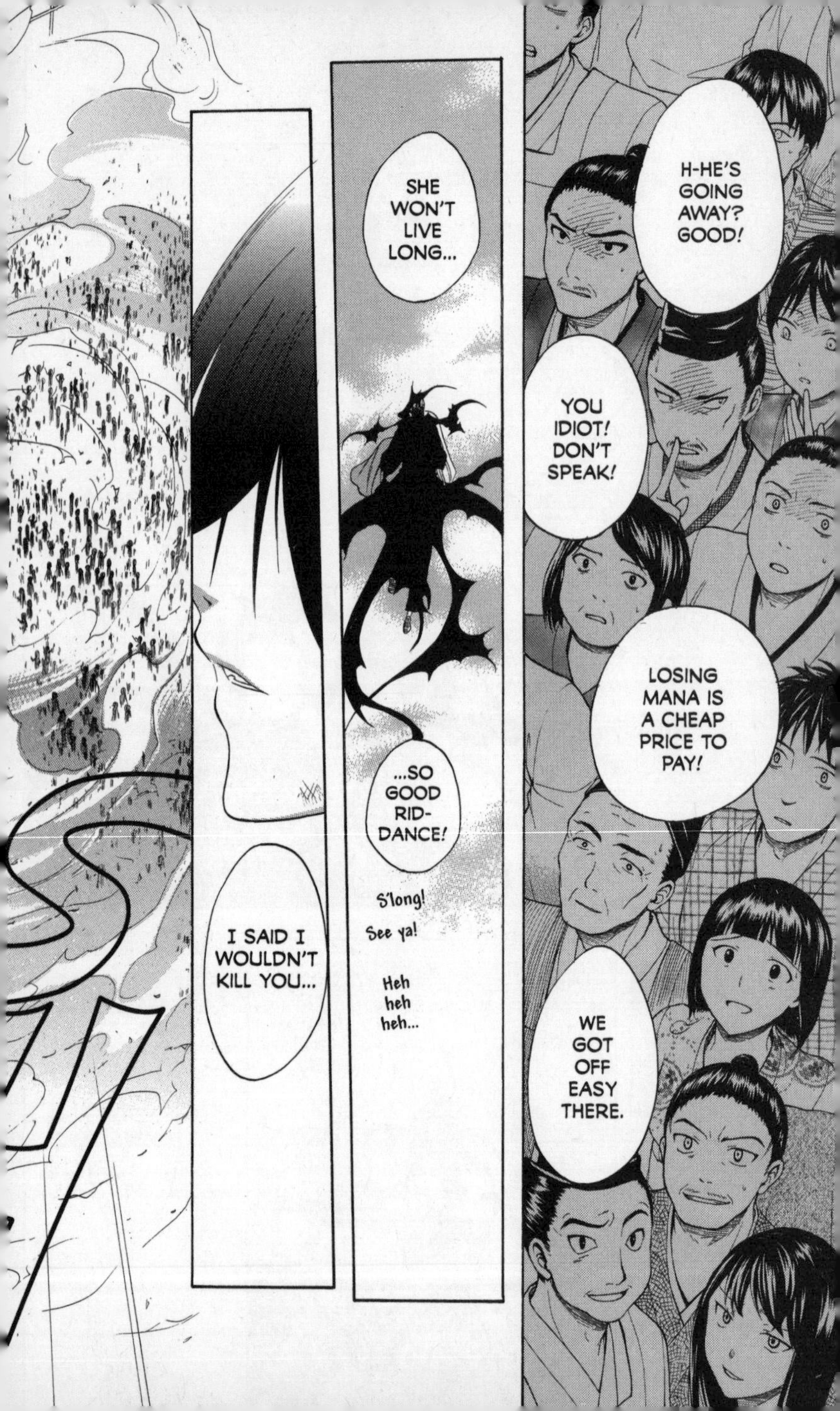
H-HE'S GOING AWAY? GOOD!
YOU IDIOT! DON'T SPEAK!
LOSING MANA IS A CHEAP PRICE TO PAY!
WE GOT OFF EASY THERE.
SHE WON'T LIVE LONG...
...SO GOOD RID-DANCE!
S'long!
See ya!
Heh heh heh...
I SAID I WOULDN'T KILL YOU...

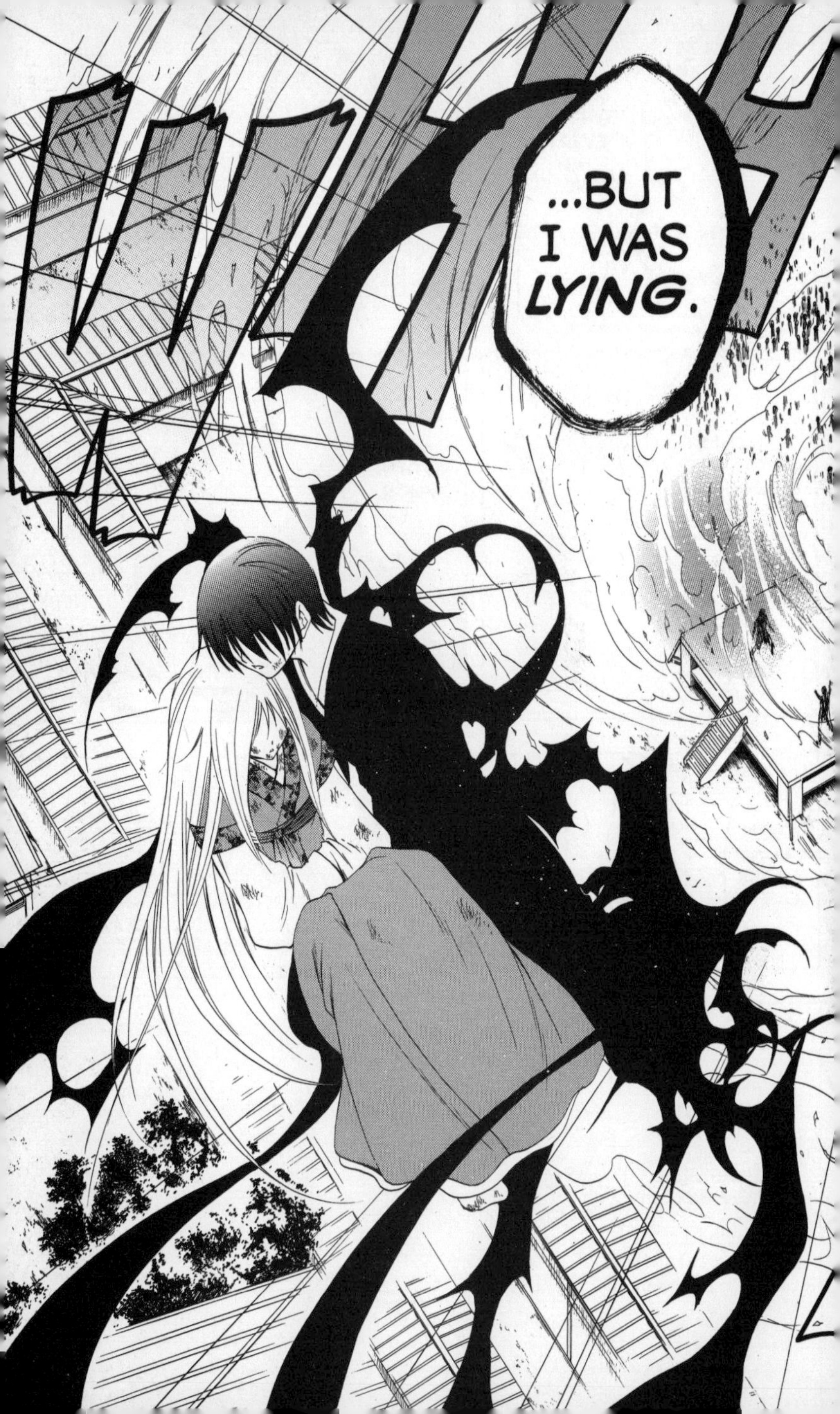
...BUT I WAS *LYING*.

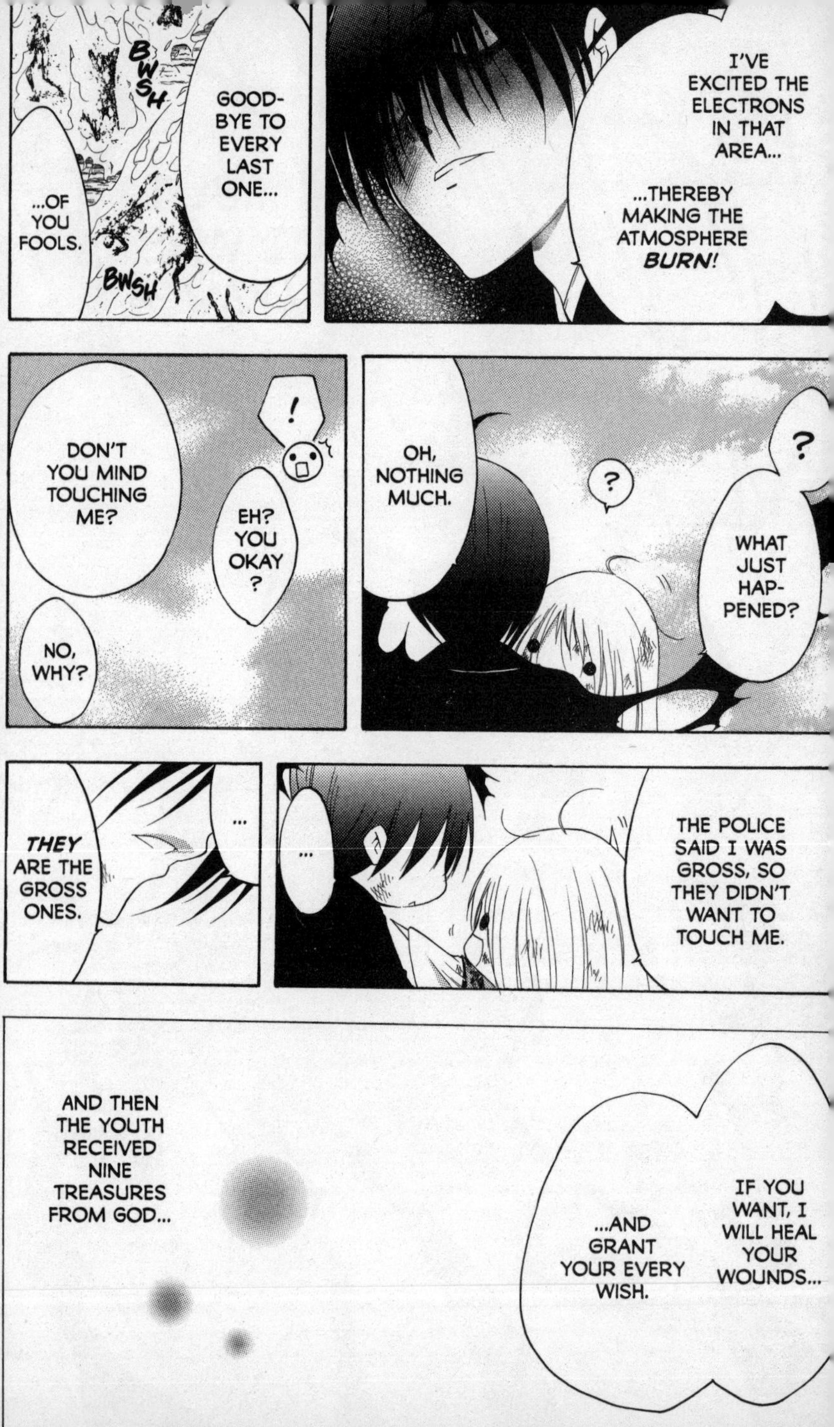
I'VE EXCITED THE ELECTRONS IN THAT AREA...
...THEREBY MAKING THE ATMOSPHERE *BURN*!
GOOD-BYE TO EVERY LAST ONE...
BWSH
...OF YOU FOOLS.
BWSH
?
WHAT JUST HAP-PENED?
?
OH, NOTHING MUCH.
!
EH? YOU OKAY?
DON'T YOU MIND TOUCHING ME?
NO, WHY?
THE POLICE SAID I WAS GROSS, SO THEY DIDN'T WANT TO TOUCH ME.
...
...
THEY ARE THE GROSS ONES.
IF YOU WANT, I WILL HEAL YOUR WOUNDS...
...AND GRANT YOUR EVERY WISH.
AND THEN THE YOUTH RECEIVED NINE TREASURES FROM GOD...

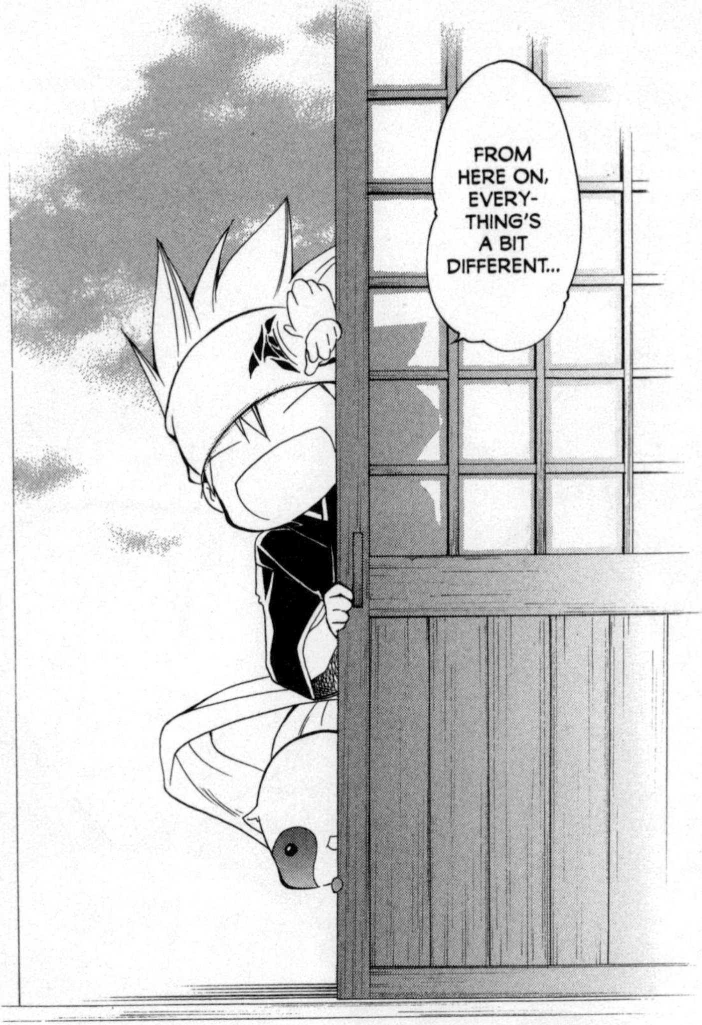
FROM HERE ON, EVERY-THING'S A BIT DIFFERENT...

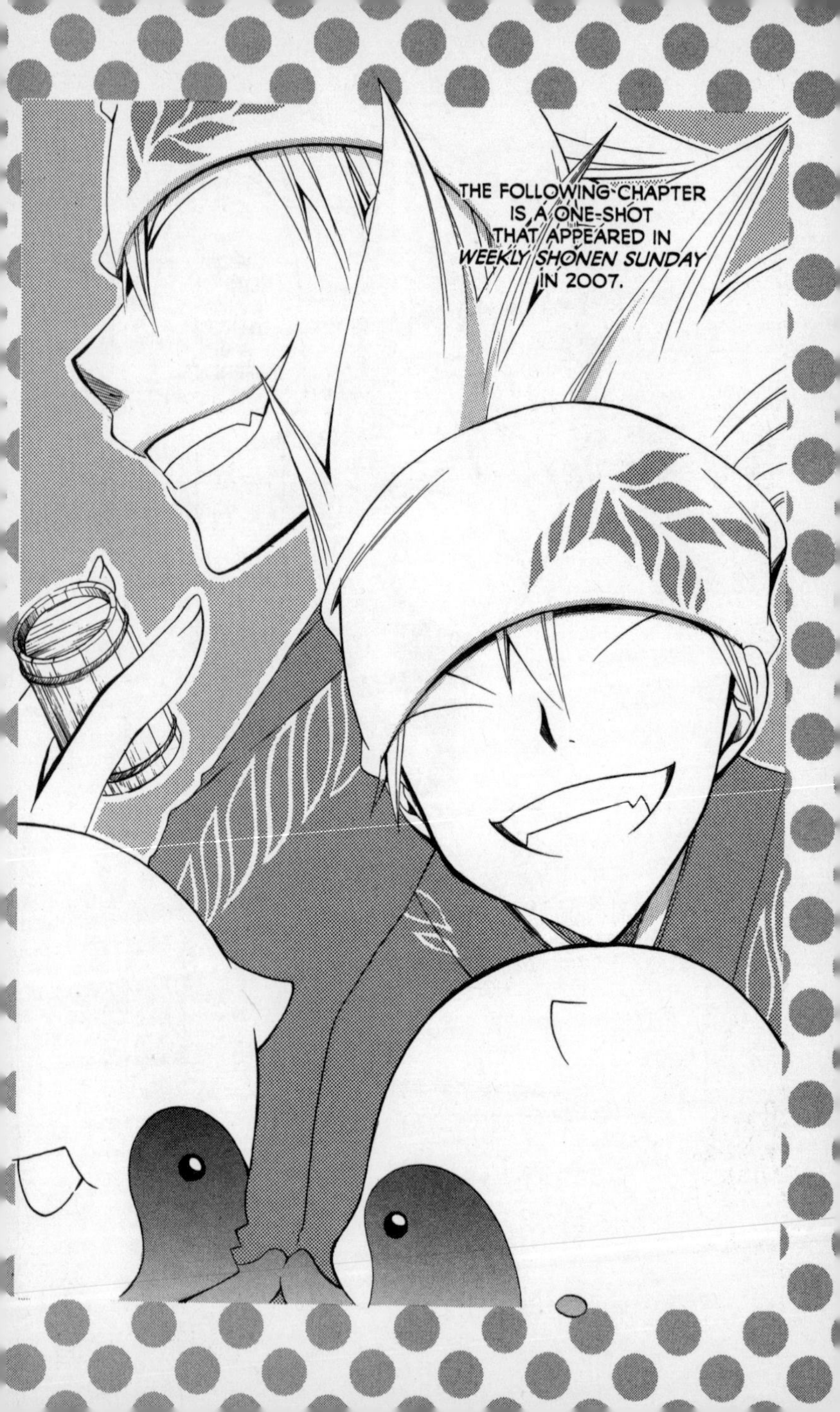
THE FOLLOWING CHAPTER IS A ONE-SHOT THAT APPEARED IN *WEEKLY SHONEN SUNDAY* IN 2007.

Special One-Shot The Honest Tanuki and the Mountain Treasure

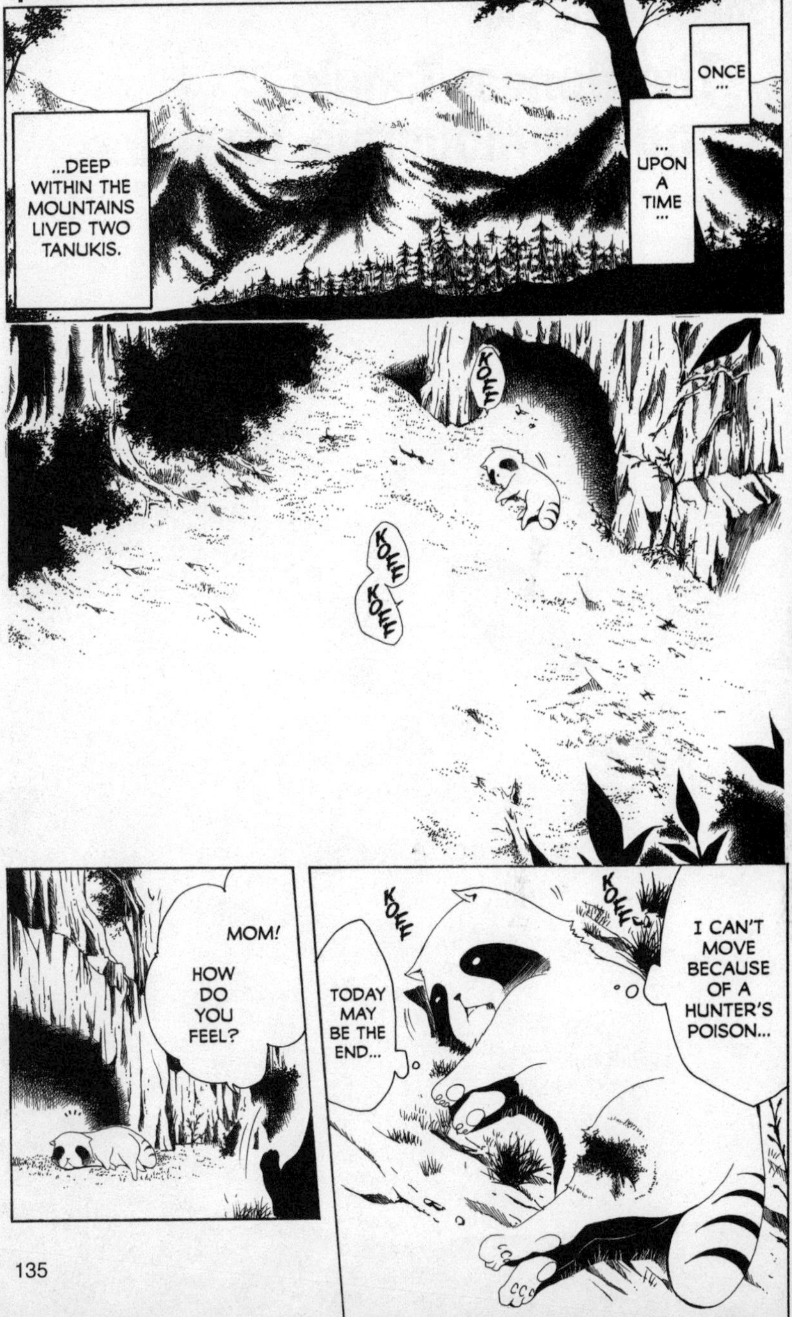
ONCE...
...UPON A TIME...
...DEEP WITHIN THE MOUNTAINS LIVED TWO TANUKIS.
KOFF
KOFF
KOFF
KOFF
I CAN'T MOVE BECAUSE OF A HUNTER'S POISON...
KOFF
TODAY MAY BE THE END...
MOM!
HOW DO YOU FEEL?

Special One-Shot

The Honest Tanuki and the Mountain Treasure

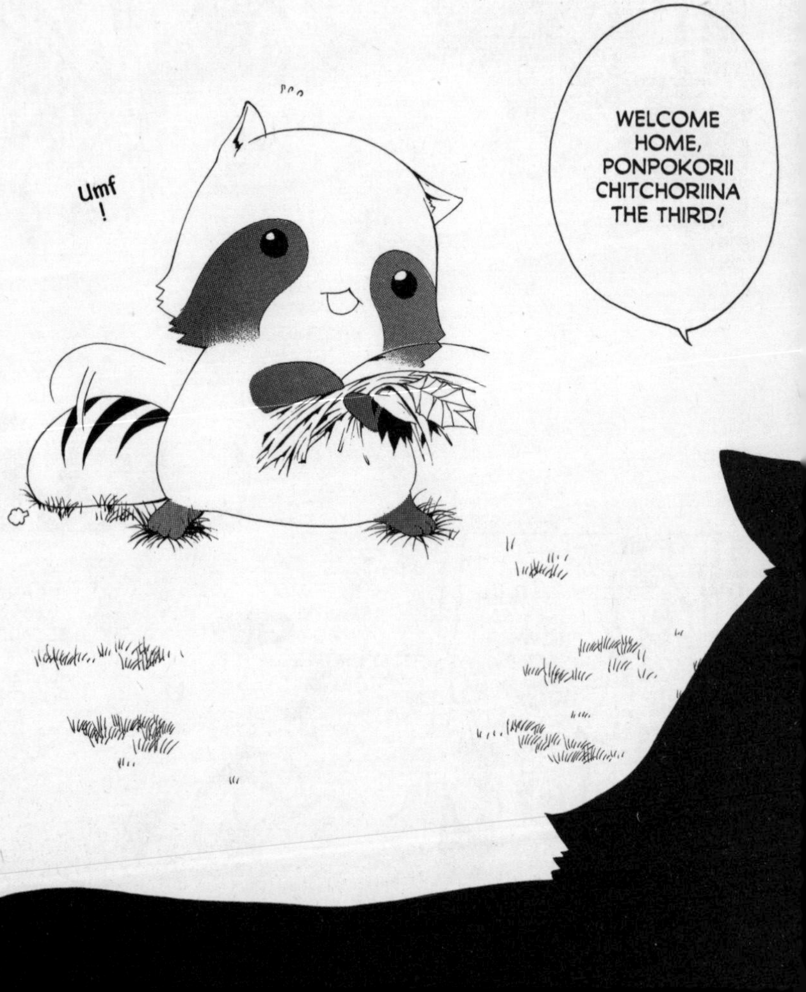

WELCOME HOME, PONPOKORII CHITCHORIINA THE THIRD!
Umf!

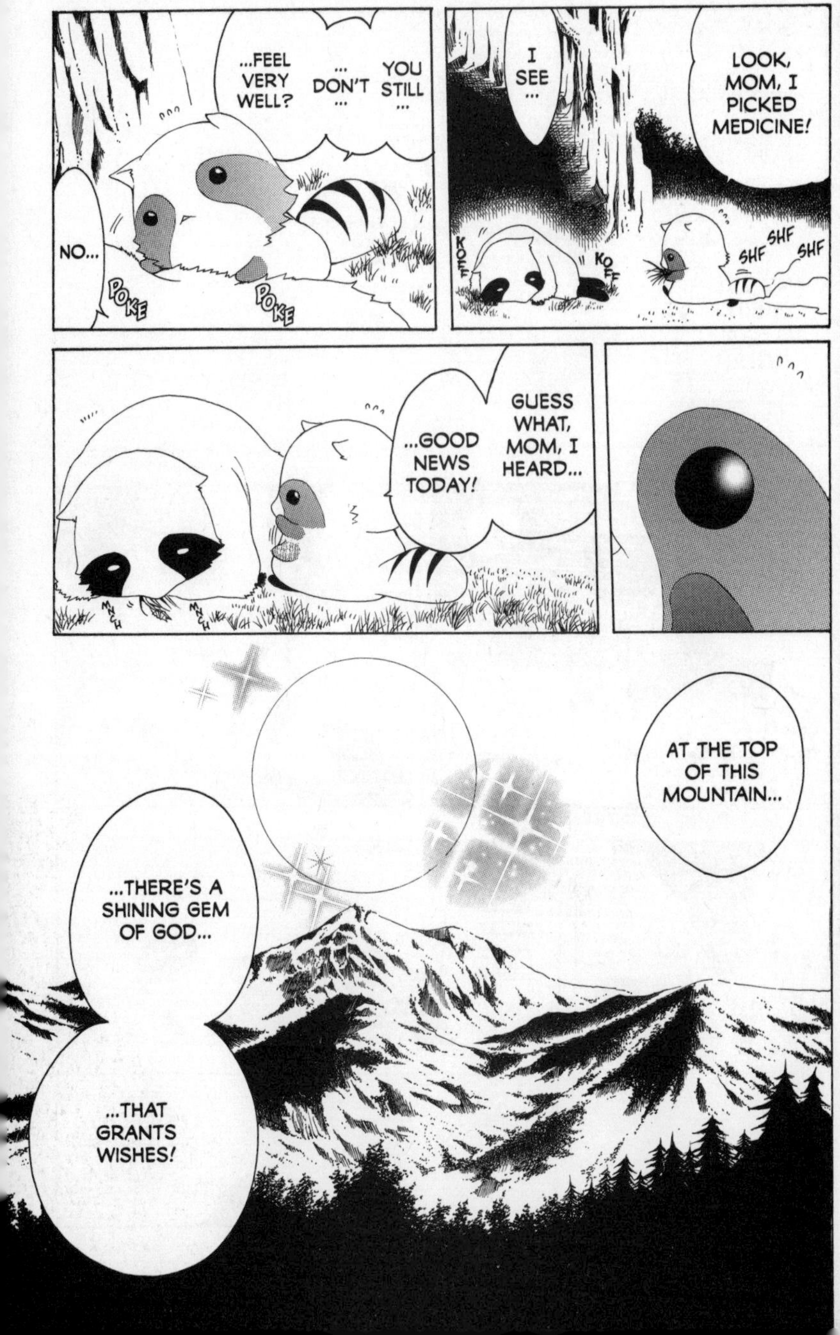
LOOK, MOM, I PICKED MEDICINE!
I SEE ...
SHF SHF SHF
KOFF KOFF
YOU STILL ...
... DON'T ...
...FEEL VERY WELL?
NO...
POKE POKE
GUESS WHAT, MOM, I HEARD...
...GOOD NEWS TODAY!
MNCH MNCH
AT THE TOP OF THIS MOUNTAIN...
...THERE'S A SHINING GEM OF GOD...
...THAT GRANTS WISHES!

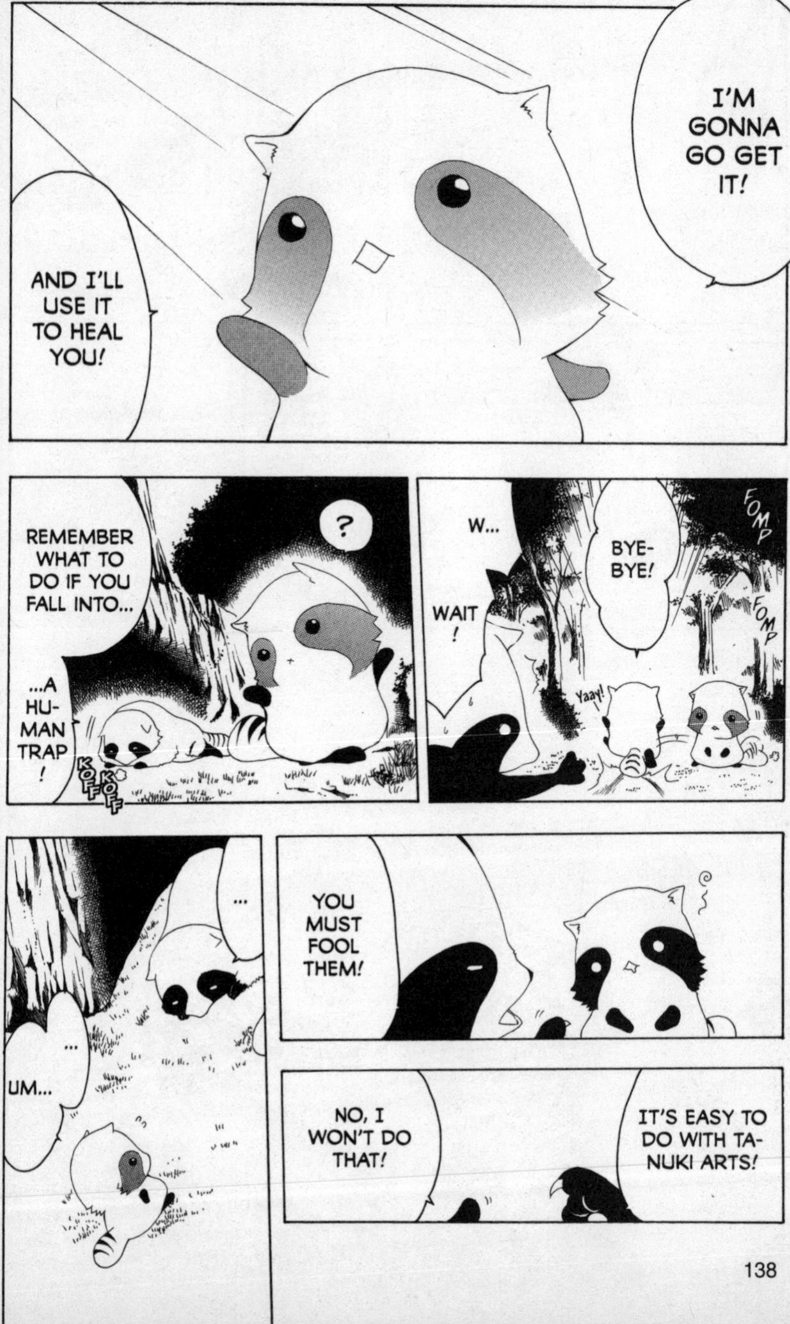
I'M GONNA GO GET IT!
AND I'LL USE IT TO HEAL YOU!
FOMP
BYE-BYE!
W...
FOMP
WAIT!
Yaay!
?
REMEMBER WHAT TO DO IF YOU FALL INTO...
...A HU-MAN TRAP!
KOFF KOFF
YOU MUST FOOL THEM!
IT'S EASY TO DO WITH TA-NUKI ARTS!
NO, I WON'T DO THAT!
...
...
UM...

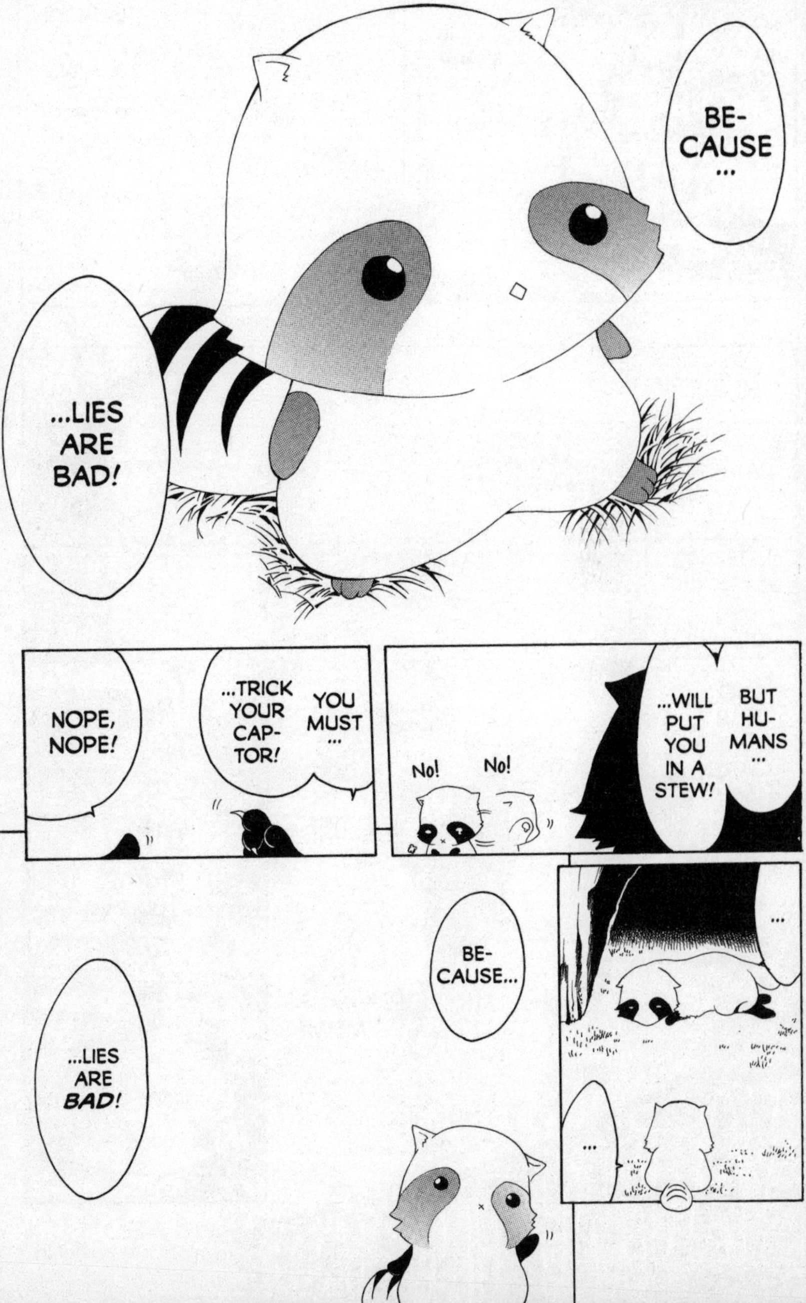
BE-CAUSE...
...LIES ARE BAD!
BUT HUMANS...
...WILL PUT YOU IN A STEW!
No!
No!
YOU MUST...
...TRICK YOUR CAPTOR!
NOPE, NOPE!
...
...
BE-CAUSE...
...LIES ARE *BAD!*

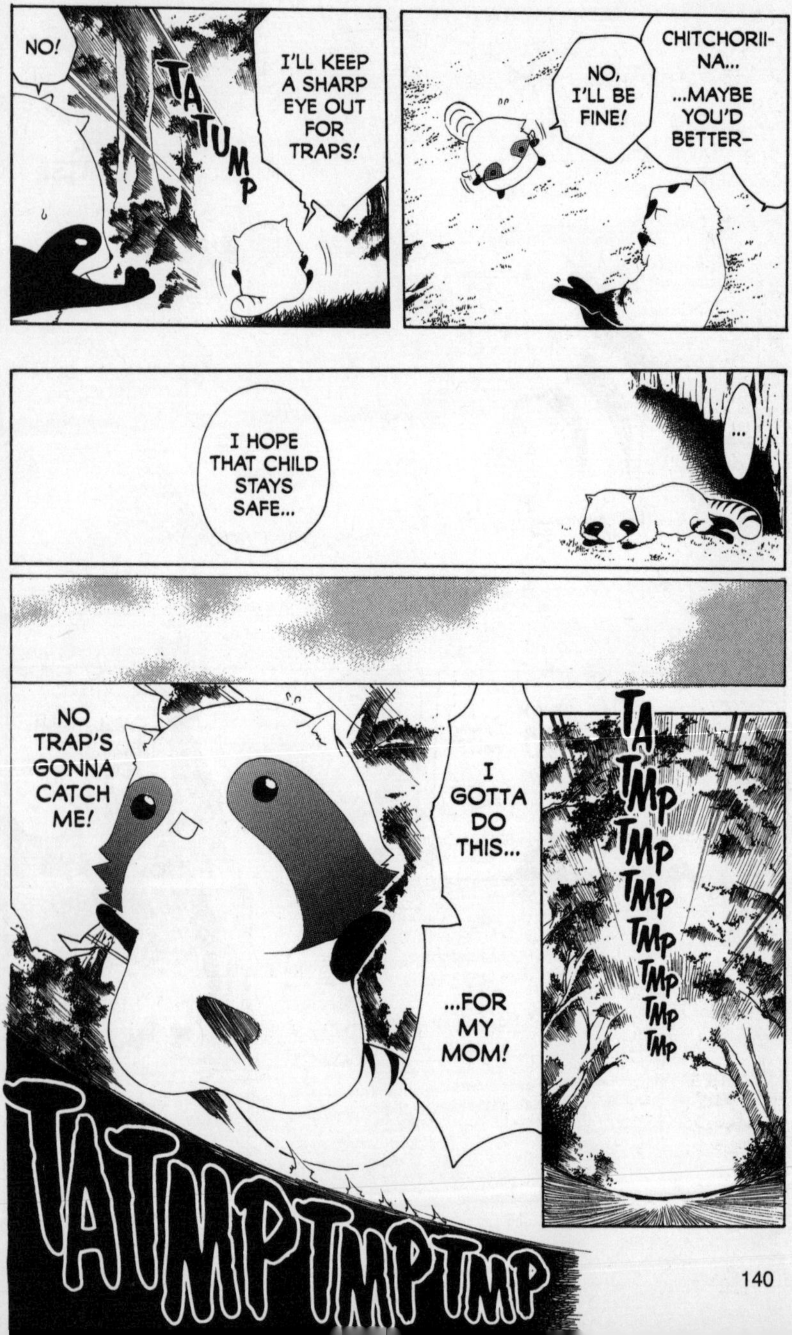
CHITCHORII-NA... ...MAYBE YOU'D BETTER-
NO, I'LL BE FINE!
I'LL KEEP A SHARP EYE OUT FOR TRAPS!
TATUMP
NO!
...
I HOPE THAT CHILD STAYS SAFE...
TA TMP TMP TMP TMP TMP TMP TMP
I GOTTA DO THIS...
...FOR MY MOM!
NO TRAP'S GONNA CATCH ME!
TATMPTMPTMP

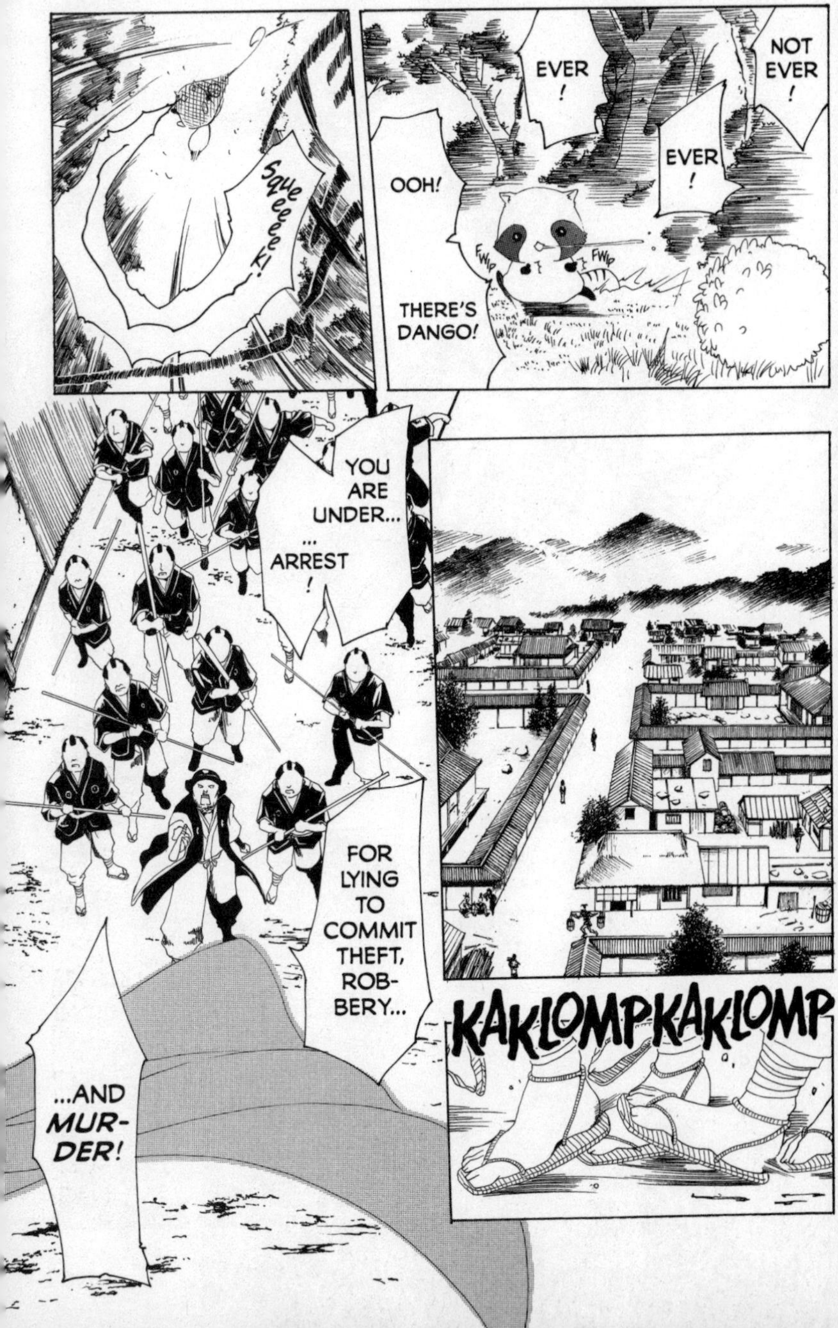
NOT EVER!
EVER!
EVER!
OOH!
THERE'S DANGO!
Squeeeeeek!
KAKLOMPKAKLOMP
YOU ARE UNDER...
...ARREST!
FOR LYING TO COMMIT THEFT, ROBBERY...
...AND MURDER!

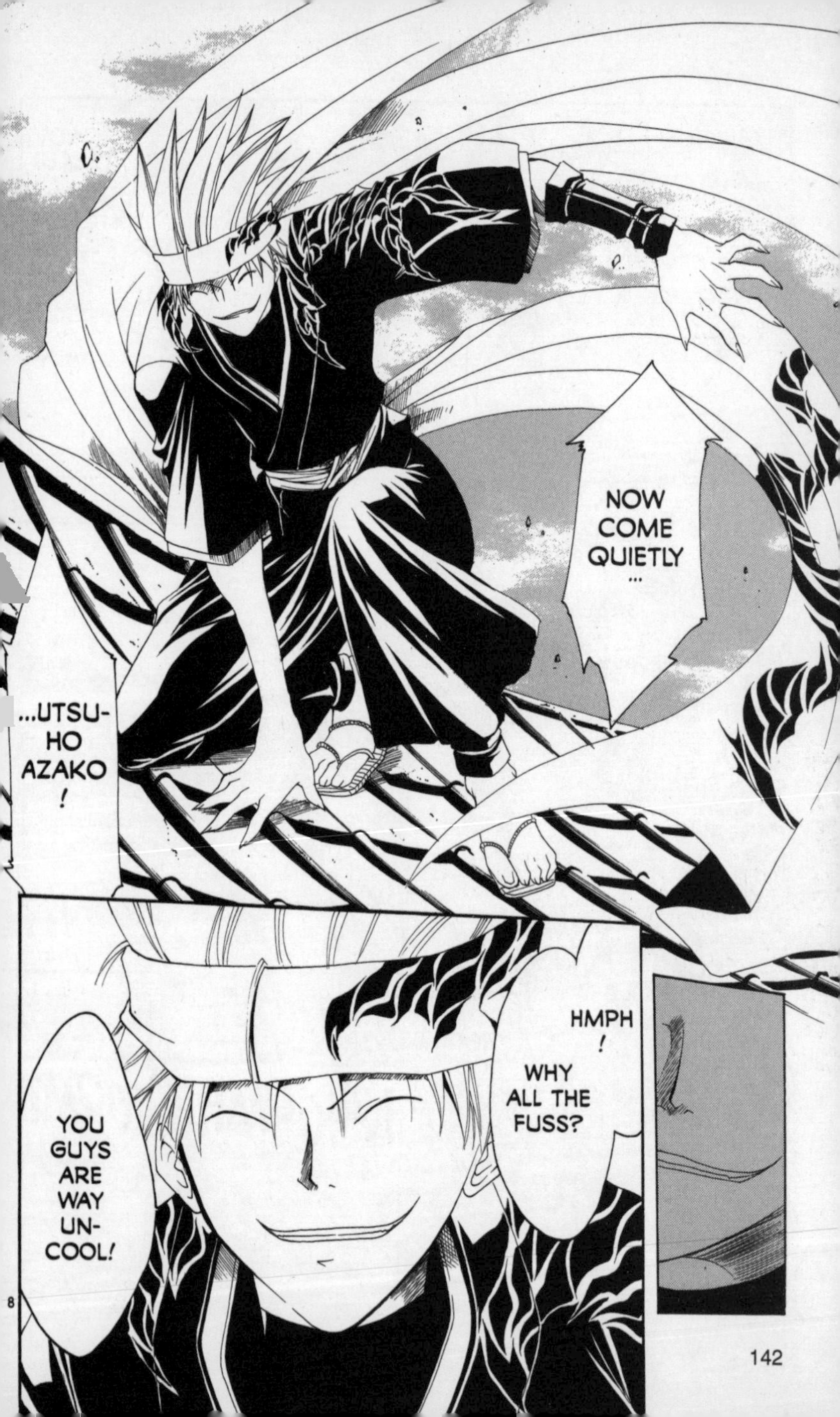

NOW COME QUIETLY ...
...UTSU-HO AZAKO!
HMPH! WHY ALL THE FUSS?
YOU GUYS ARE WAY UN-COOL!

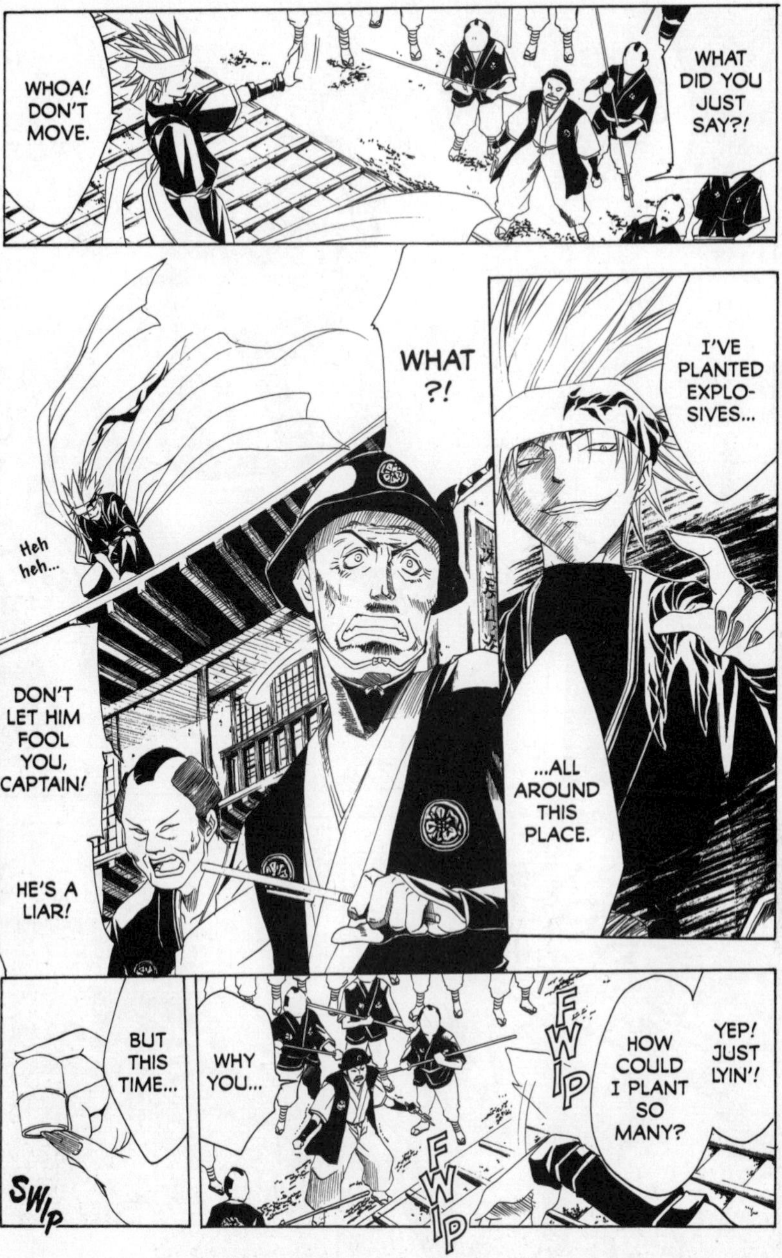
WHAT DID YOU JUST SAY?!
WHOA! DON'T MOVE.
I'VE PLANTED EXPLOSIVES...
...ALL AROUND THIS PLACE.
WHAT ?!
Heh heh...
DON'T LET HIM FOOL YOU, CAPTAIN!
HE'S A LIAR!
YEP! JUST LYIN'!
HOW COULD I PLANT SO MANY?
FWIP
FWIP
WHY YOU...
BUT THIS TIME...
SWIP

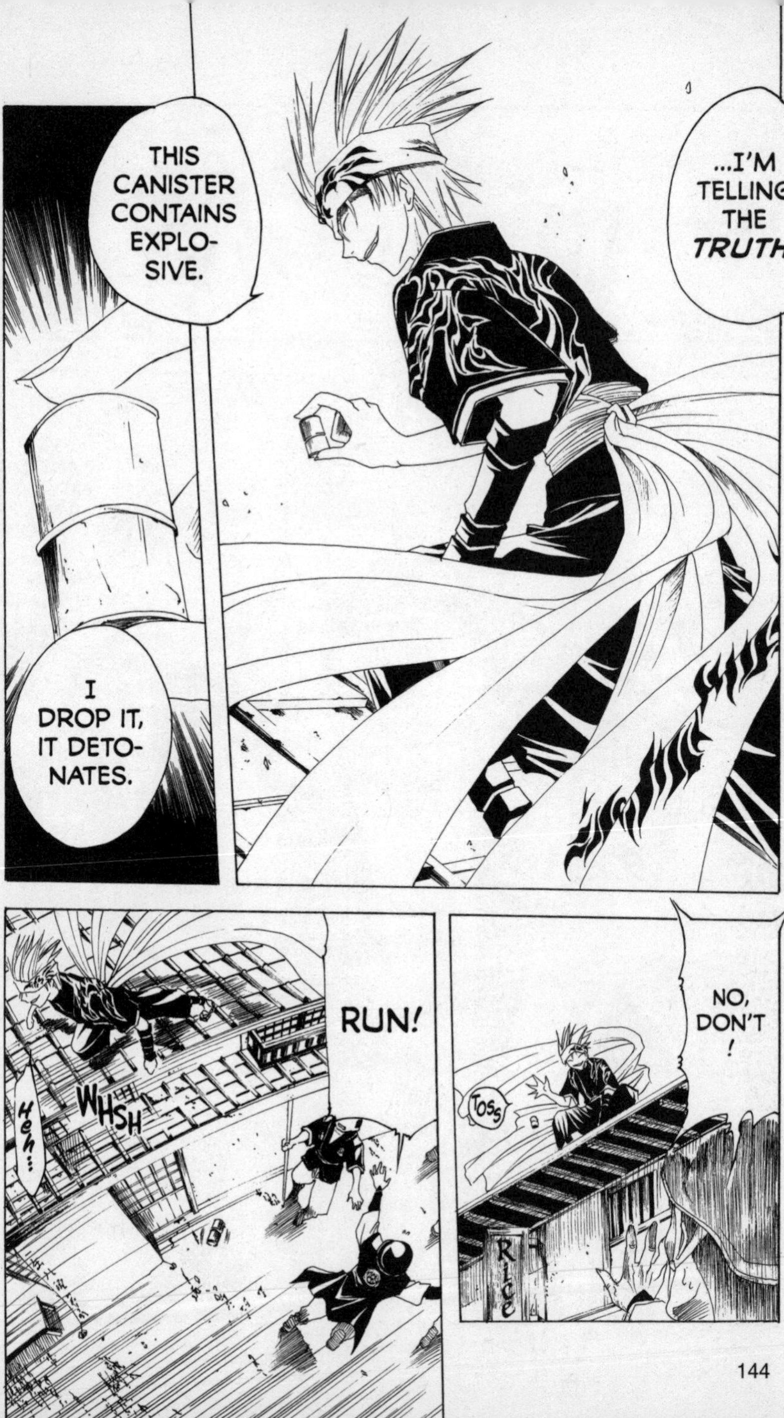
...I'M TELLING THE *TRUTH*.
THIS CANISTER CONTAINS EXPLOSIVE.
I DROP IT, IT DETONATES.
NO, DON'T!
TOSS
RICE
RUN!
WHSH
Heh...

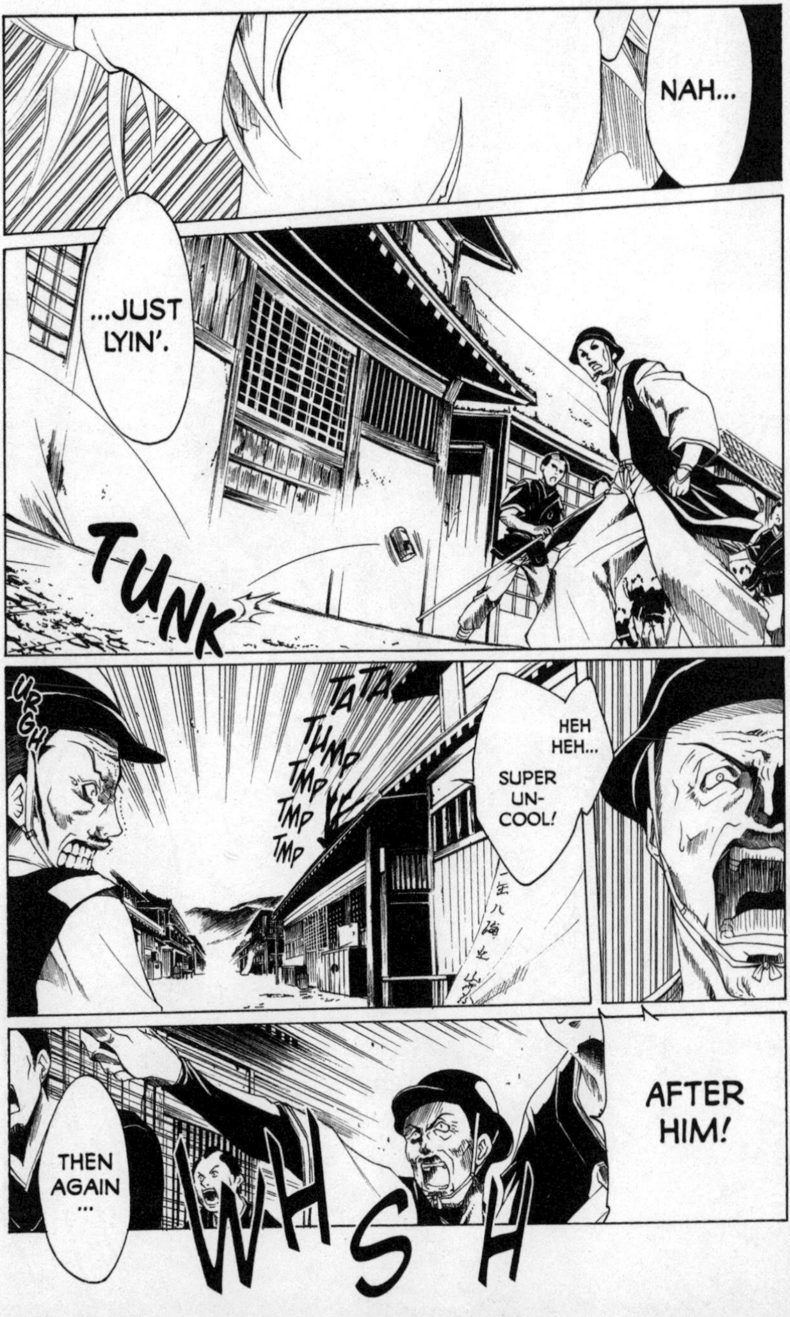
NAH...
...JUST LYIN'.
TUNK
HEH HEH...
SUPER UN-COOL!
TATA
TUMP TMP TMP TMP
URGH
AFTER HIM!
WHSH
THEN AGAIN...

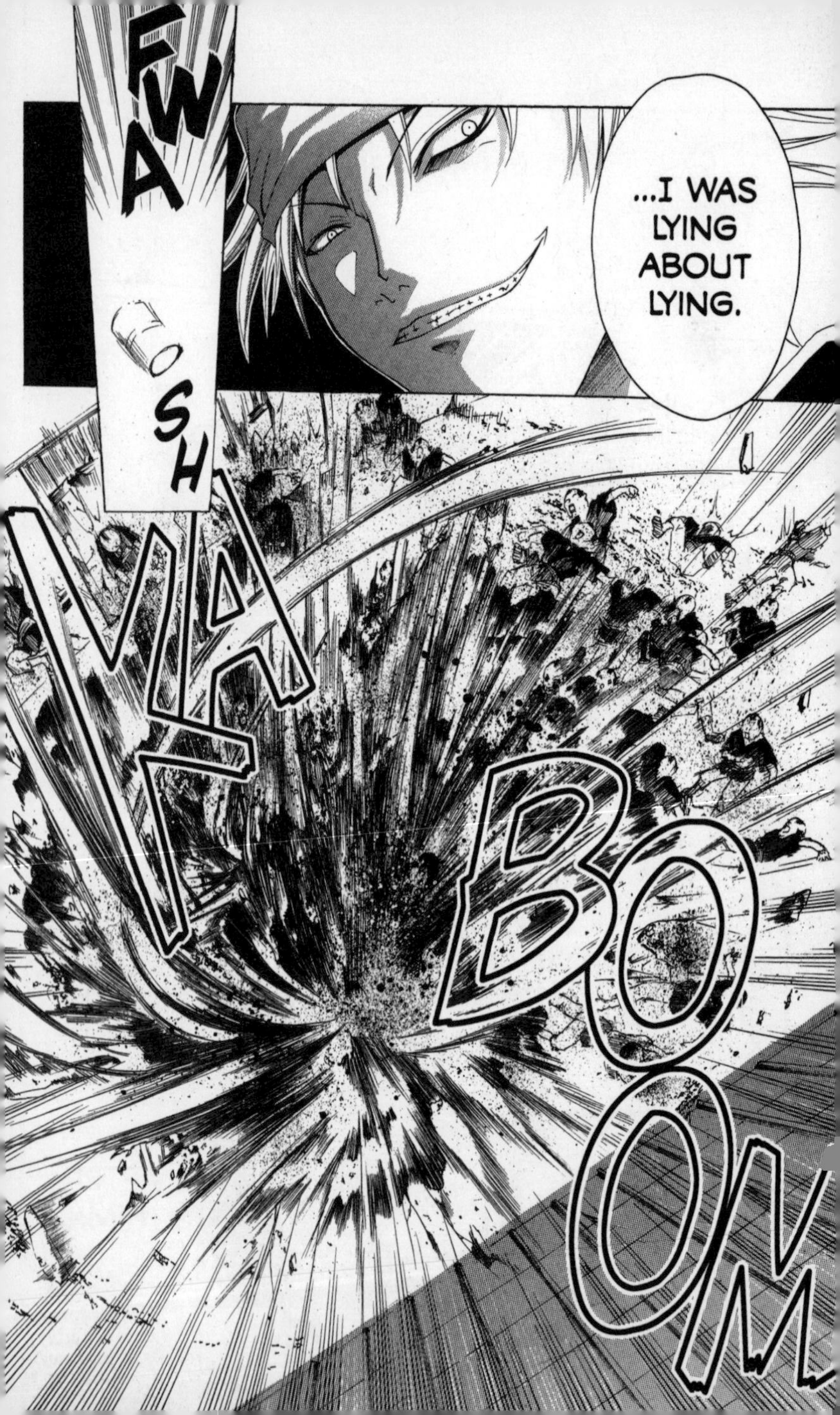
...I WAS LYING ABOUT LYING.
FWA
BOOM

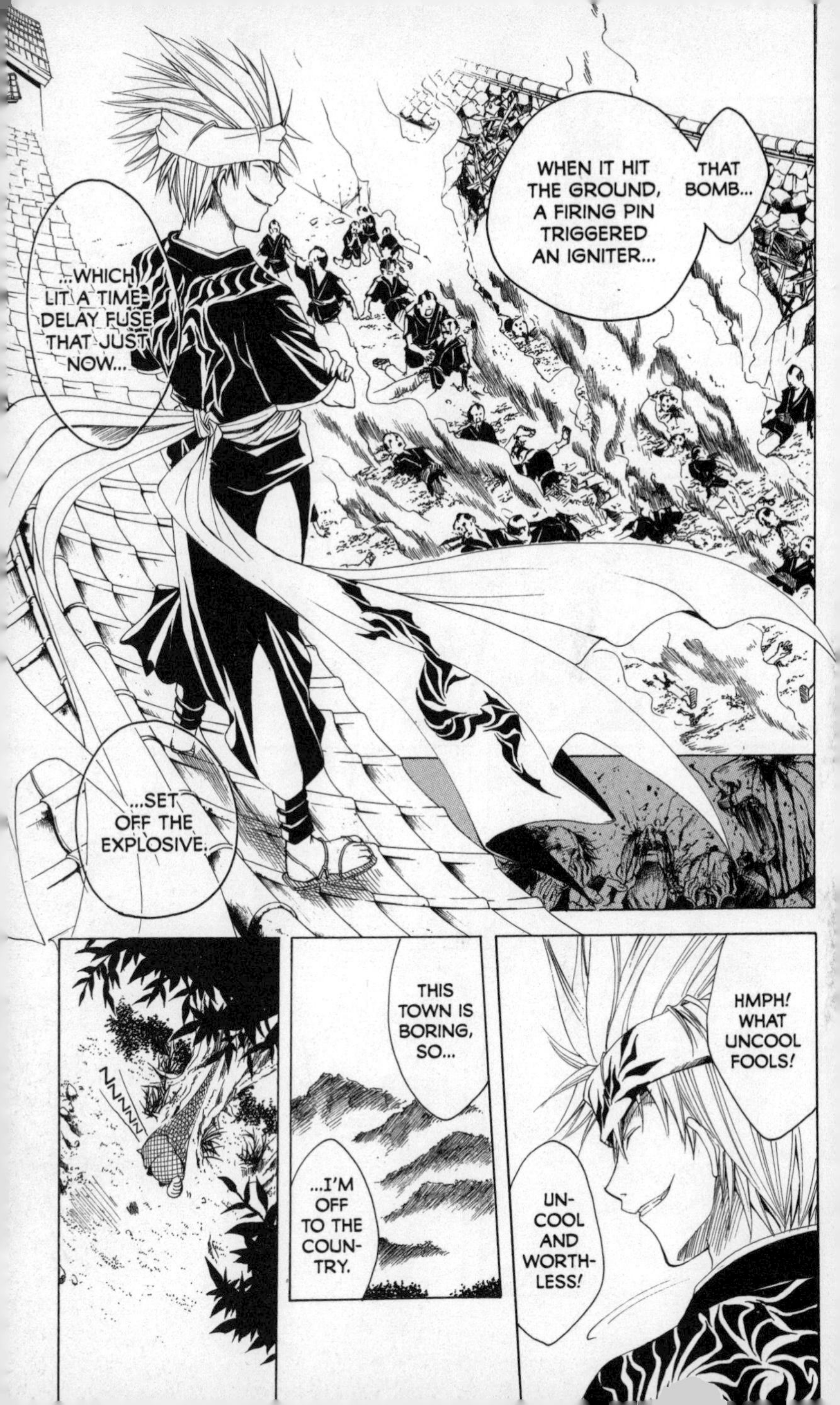
THAT BOMB...
WHEN IT HIT THE GROUND, A FIRING PIN TRIGGERED AN IGNITER...
...WHICH LIT A TIME-DELAY FUSE THAT JUST NOW...
...SET OFF THE EXPLOSIVE.
HMPH! WHAT UNCOOL FOOLS!
UN-COOL AND WORTH-LESS!
THIS TOWN IS BORING, SO...
...I'M OFF TO THE COUN-TRY.

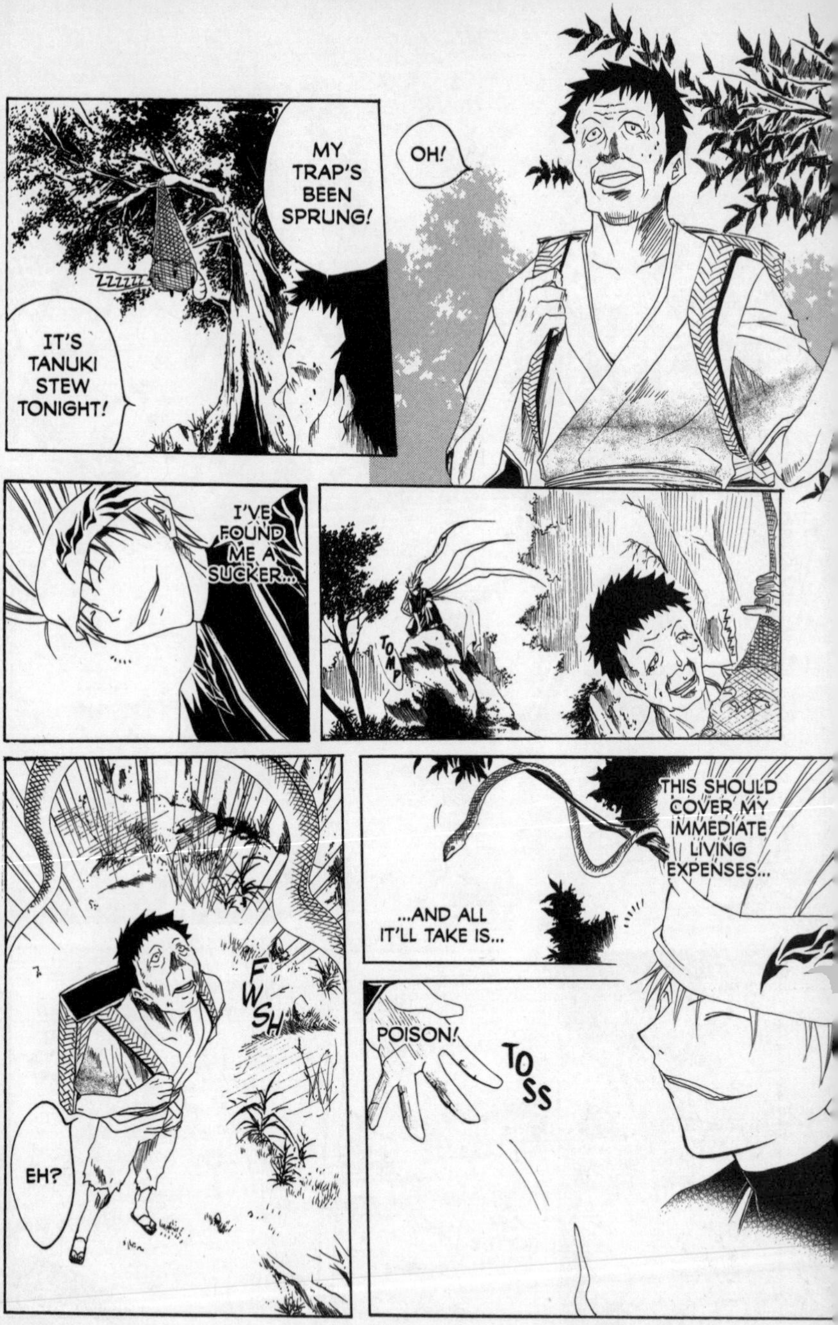
OH!
MY TRAP'S BEEN SPRUNG!
IT'S TANUKI STEW TONIGHT!
TOMP
I'VE FOUND ME A SUCKER...
THIS SHOULD COVER MY IMMEDIATE LIVING EXPENSES...
...AND ALL IT'LL TAKE IS...
POISON!
TOSS
FWSH
EH?

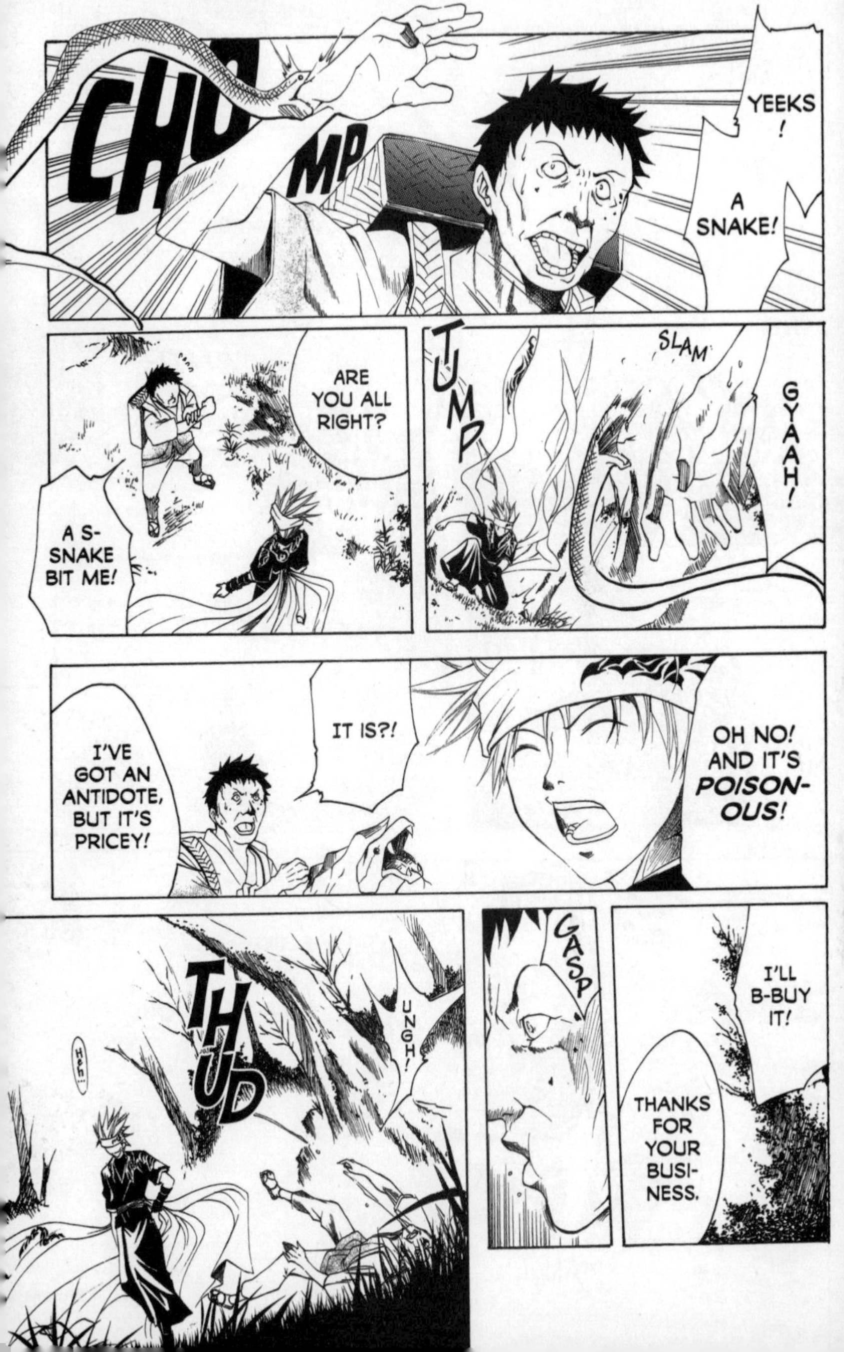
YEEKS!
A SNAKE!
CHOMP
GYAAH!
SLAM
TUMP
ARE YOU ALL RIGHT?
A S-SNAKE BIT ME!
OH NO! AND IT'S *POISON-OUS*!
IT IS?!
I'VE GOT AN ANTIDOTE, BUT IT'S PRICEY!
I'LL B-BUY IT!
THANKS FOR YOUR BUSI-NESS.
GASP
UNGH!
THUD
Heh...

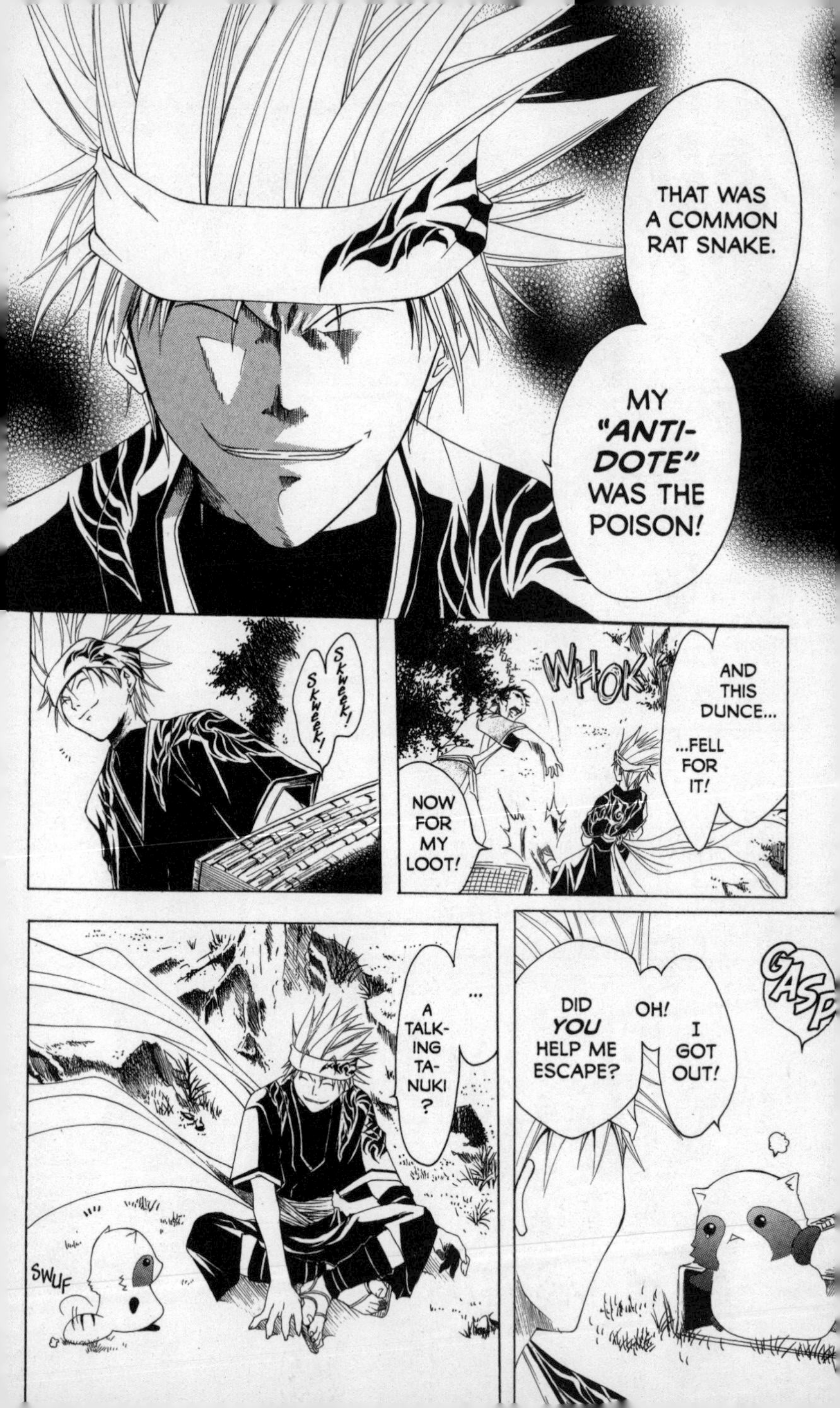
THAT WAS A COMMON RAT SNAKE.
MY "ANTI-DOTE" WAS THE POISON!
WHOK
AND THIS DUNCE...
...FELL FOR IT!
NOW FOR MY LOOT!
Skweek! Skweek!
GASP
OH! I GOT OUT!
DID YOU HELP ME ESCAPE?
...
A TALKING TANUKI?
SWUF

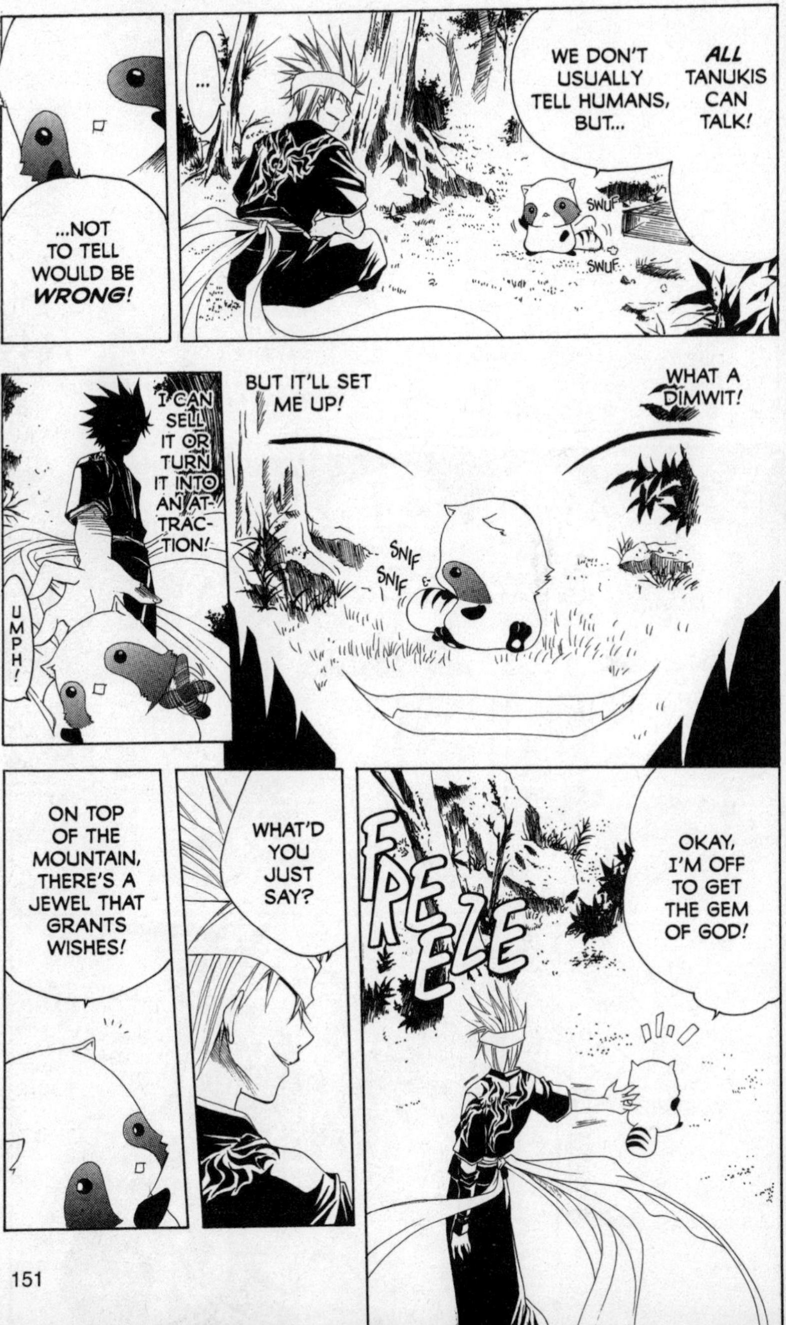
WE DON'T USUALLY TELL HUMANS, BUT... ALL TANUKIS CAN TALK!
SWUF
SWUF
...
...NOT TO TELL WOULD BE WRONG!
WHAT A DIMWIT!
BUT IT'LL SET ME UP!
SNIF
SNIF
I CAN SELL IT OR TURN IT INTO AN ATTRACTION!
UMPH!
OKAY, I'M OFF TO GET THE GEM OF GOD!
FREEZE
WHAT'D YOU JUST SAY?
ON TOP OF THE MOUNTAIN, THERE'S A JEWEL THAT GRANTS WISHES!

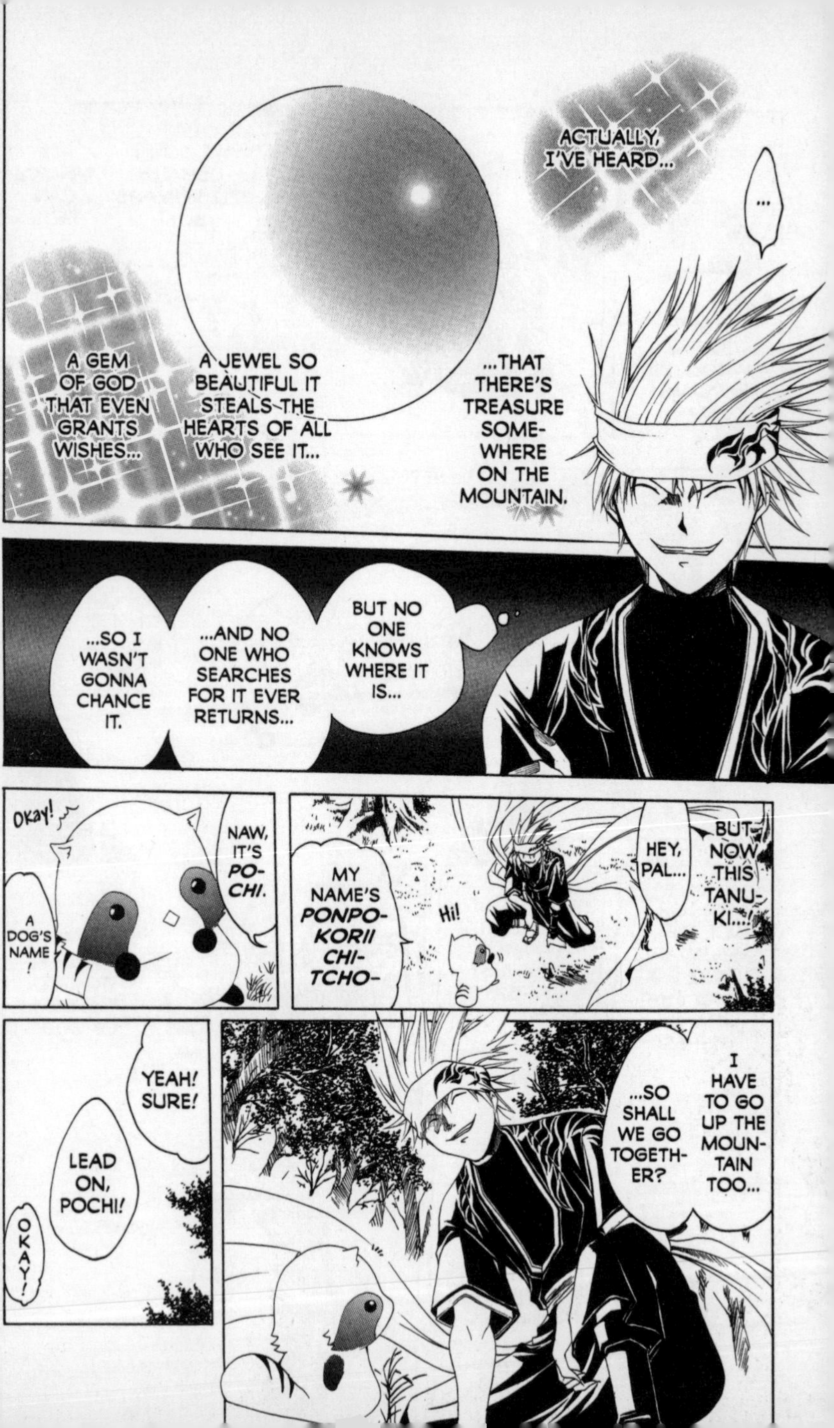
...
ACTUALLY, I'VE HEARD...
...THAT THERE'S TREASURE SOME-WHERE ON THE MOUNTAIN.
A JEWEL SO BEAUTIFUL IT STEALS THE HEARTS OF ALL WHO SEE IT...
A GEM OF GOD THAT EVEN GRANTS WISHES...
BUT NO ONE KNOWS WHERE IT IS...
...AND NO ONE WHO SEARCHES FOR IT EVER RETURNS...
...SO I WASN'T GONNA CHANCE IT.
BUT NOW THIS TANU-KI...!
HEY, PAL...
Hi!
MY NAME'S *PONPOKORII CHITCHO-*
NAW, IT'S *POCHI.*
Okay!
A DOG'S NAME!
I HAVE TO GO UP THE MOUN-TAIN TOO...
...SO SHALL WE GO TOGETH-ER?
YEAH! SURE!
LEAD ON, POCHI!
OKAY!

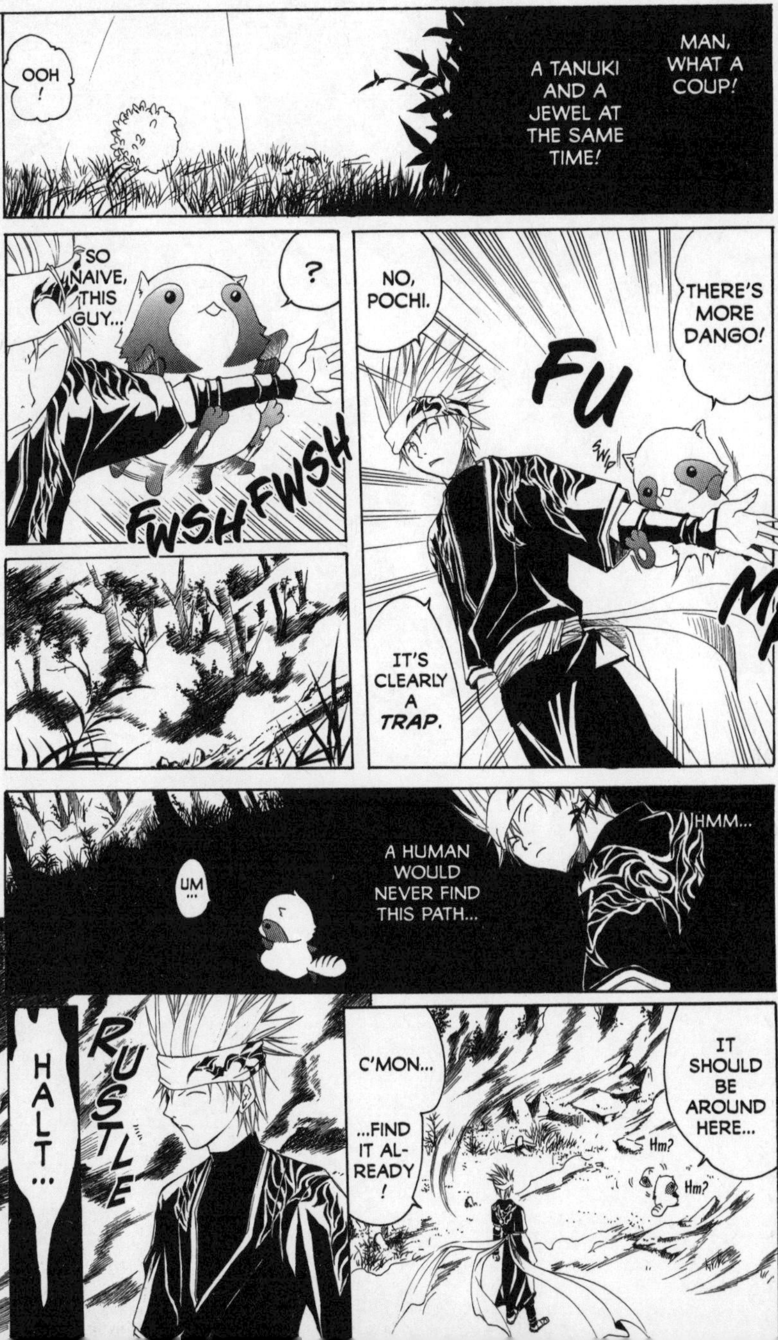
MAN, WHAT A COUP!
A TANUKI AND A JEWEL AT THE SAME TIME!
OOH!
THERE'S MORE DANGO!
NO, POCHI.
FU
SWIP
MY
IT'S CLEARLY A *TRAP*.
?
SO NAIVE, THIS GUY...
FWSH FWSH
HMM...
A HUMAN WOULD NEVER FIND THIS PATH...
UM...
IT SHOULD BE AROUND HERE...
Hm?
Hm?
C'MON...
...FIND IT AL-READY!
RUSTLE
HALT...

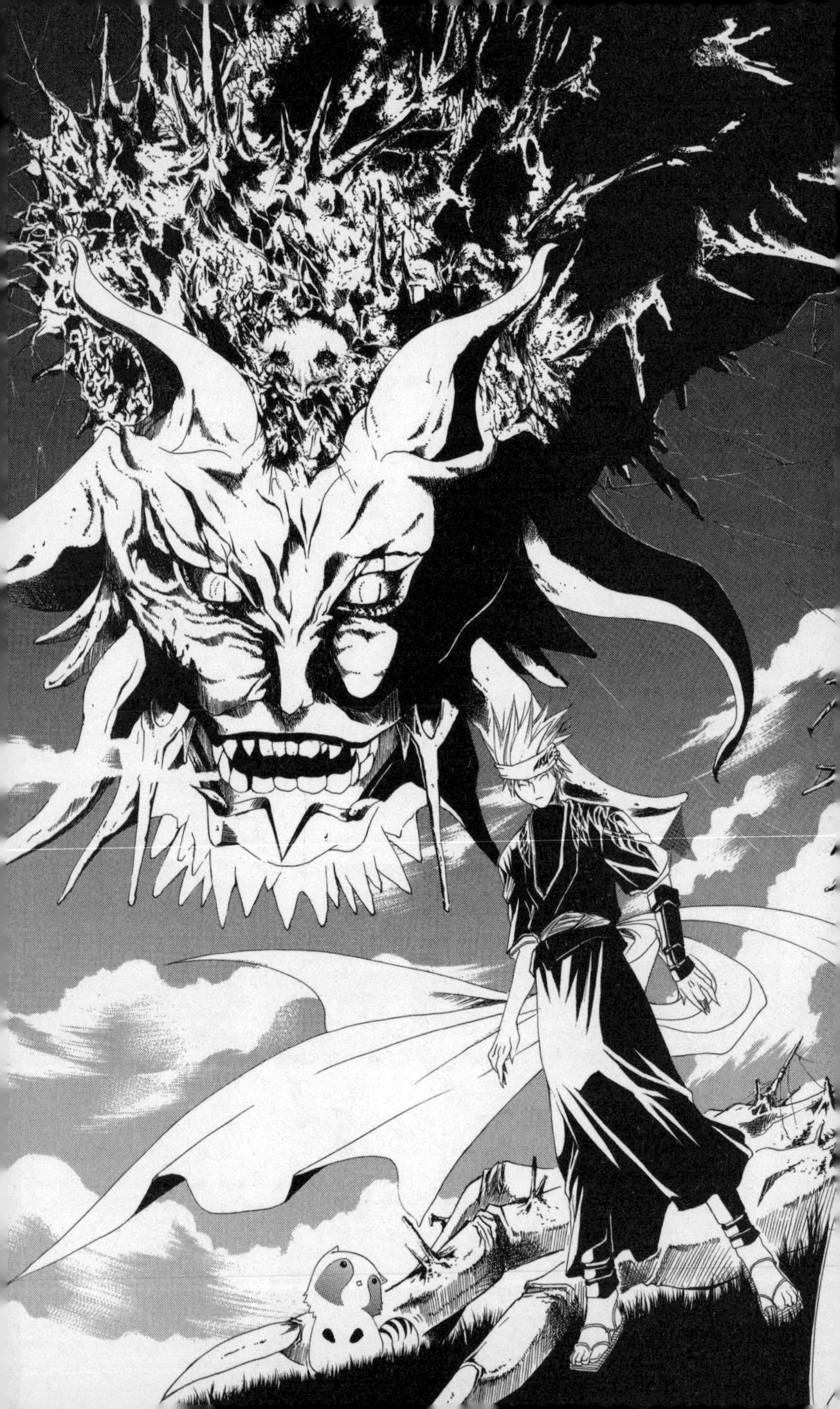

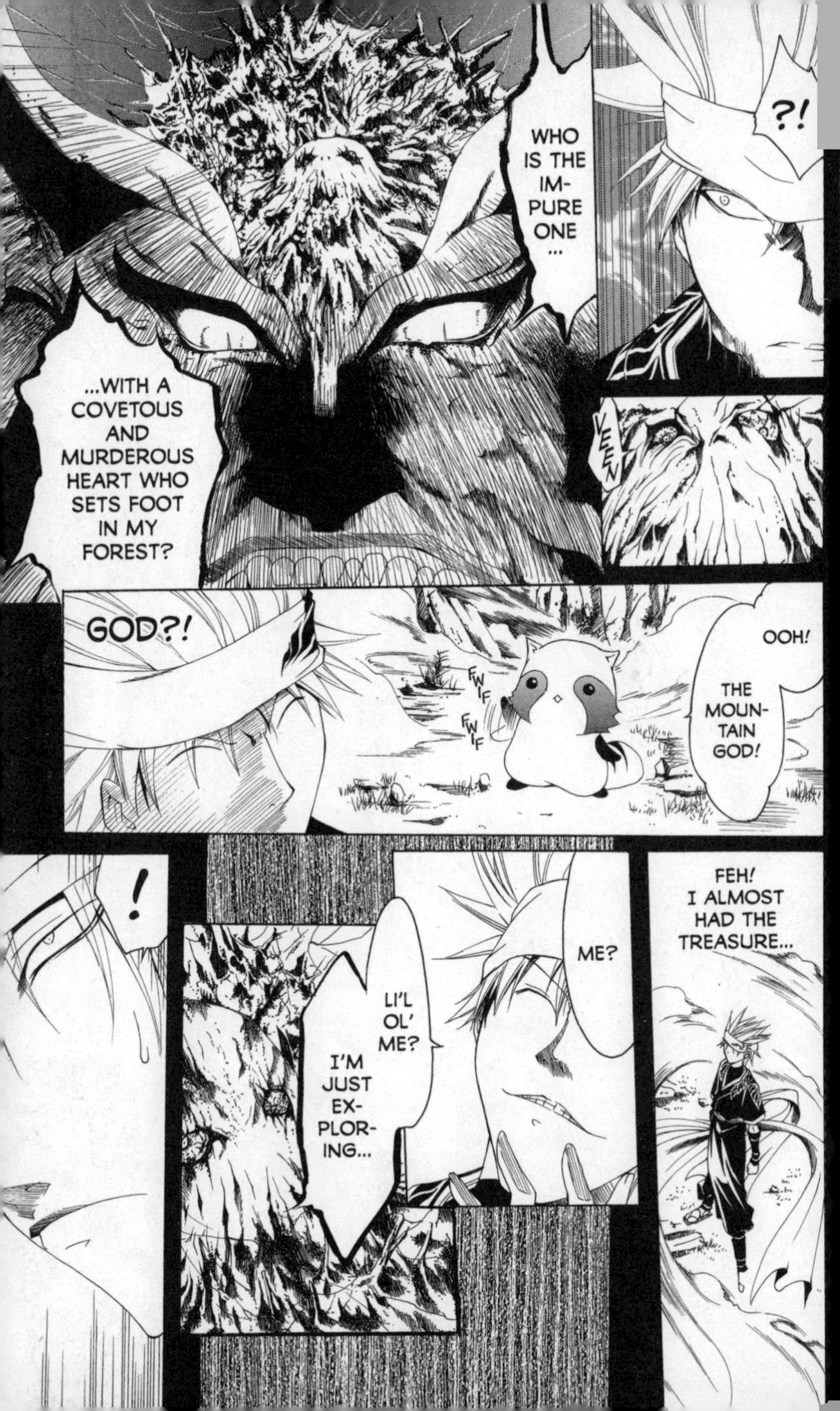
?!
VEEN
WHO IS THE IM-PURE ONE ...
...WITH A COVETOUS AND MURDEROUS HEART WHO SETS FOOT IN MY FOREST?
OOH!
THE MOUN-TAIN GOD!
FWIF
FWIF
GOD?!
FEH! I ALMOST HAD THE TREASURE...
ME?
LI'L OL' ME?
I'M JUST EX-PLOR-ING...
!

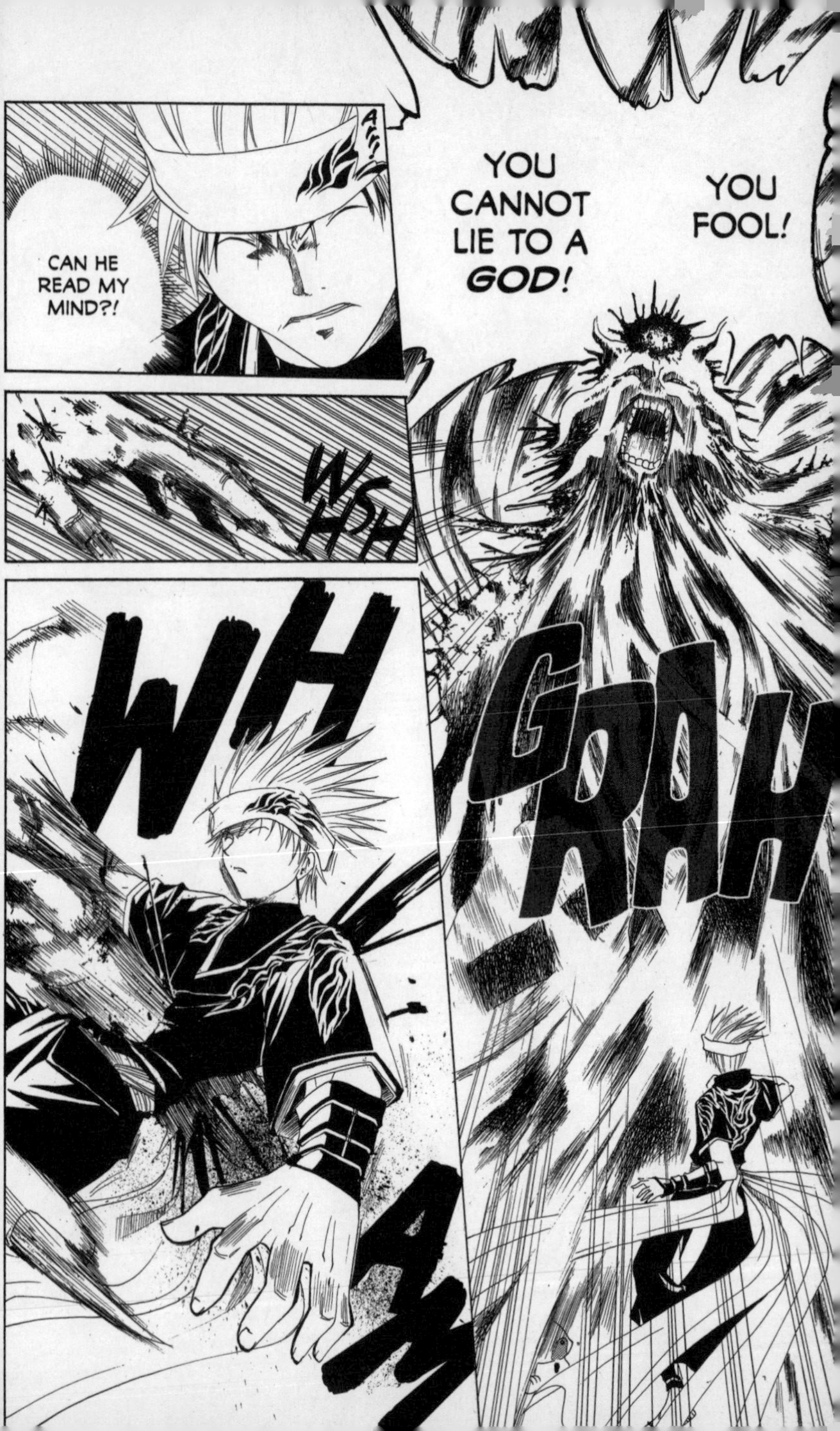
YOU FOOL!
YOU CANNOT LIE TO A *GOD*!
CAN HE READ MY MIND?!
WSHH
WHAM

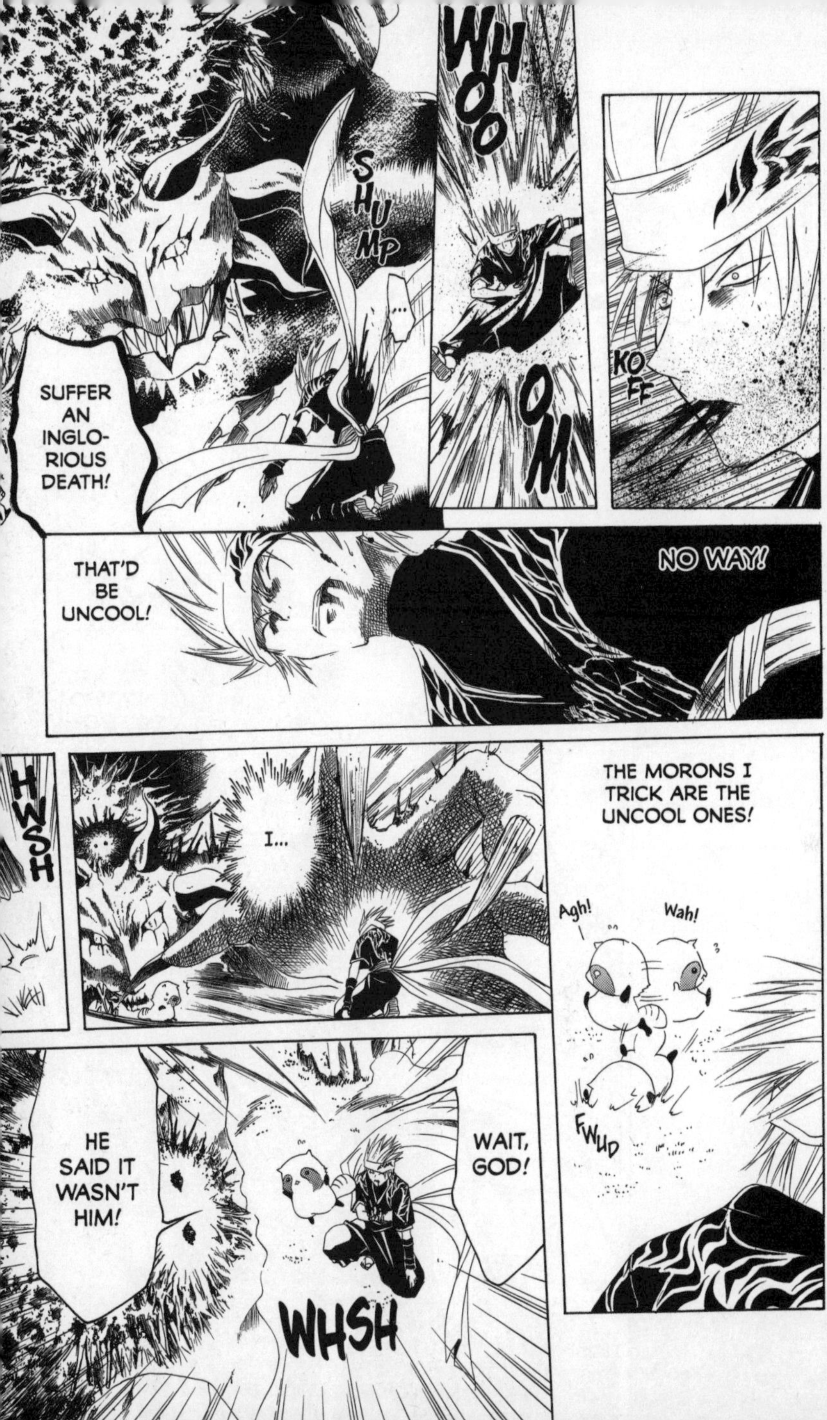

KOFF
WHOOOM
SHUMP
...
SUFFER AN INGLORIOUS DEATH!
NO WAY!
THAT'D BE UNCOOL!
THE MORONS I TRICK ARE THE UNCOOL ONES!
Wah!
Agh!
FWUD
I...
HWSH
WAIT, GOD!
HE SAID IT WASN'T HIM!
WHSH

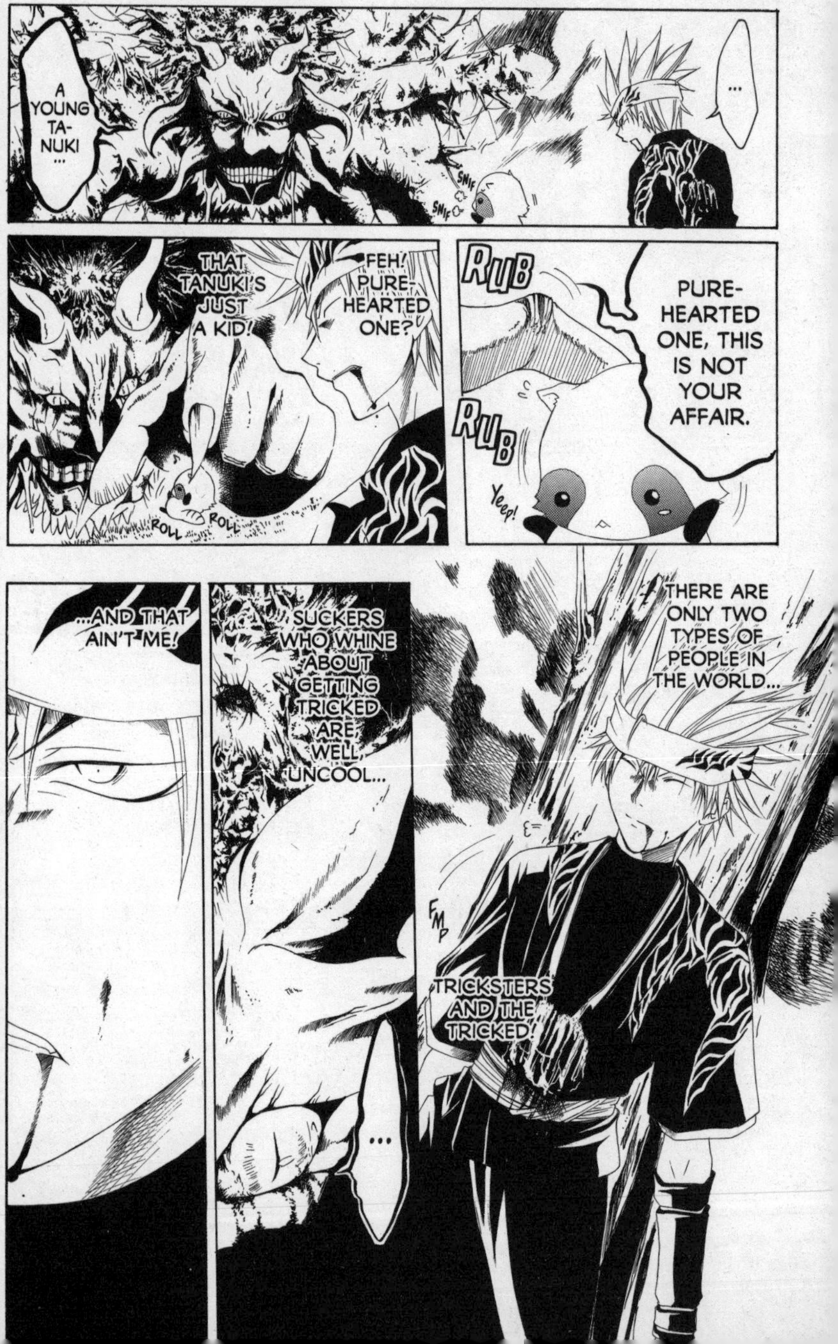

...
SNIF
SNIF
A YOUNG TA-NUKI ...
RUB
RUB
PURE-HEARTED ONE, THIS IS NOT YOUR AFFAIR.
Yeep!
FEH! PURE-HEARTED ONE?
THAT TANUKI'S JUST A KID!
ROLL
ROLL
THERE ARE ONLY TWO TYPES OF PEOPLE IN THE WORLD...
FMP
TRICKSTERS AND THE TRICKED!
SUCKERS WHO WHINE ABOUT GETTING TRICKED ARE WELL UNCOOL...
...
...AND THAT AIN'T ME!

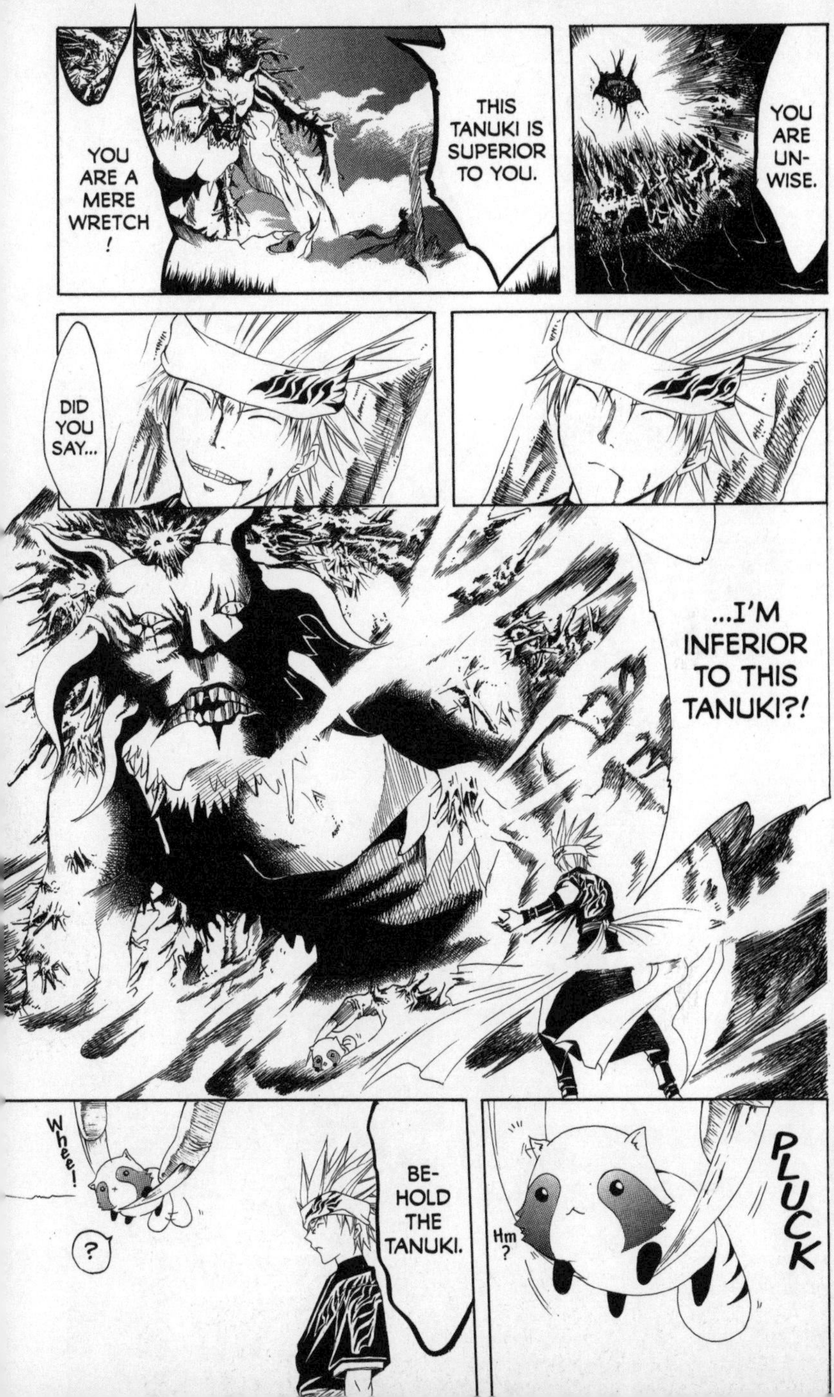
YOU ARE UN-WISE.
THIS TANUKI IS SUPERIOR TO YOU.
YOU ARE A MERE WRETCH!
DID YOU SAY...
...I'M INFERIOR TO THIS TANUKI?!
PLUCK
Hm?
BE-HOLD THE TANUKI.
Whee!
?

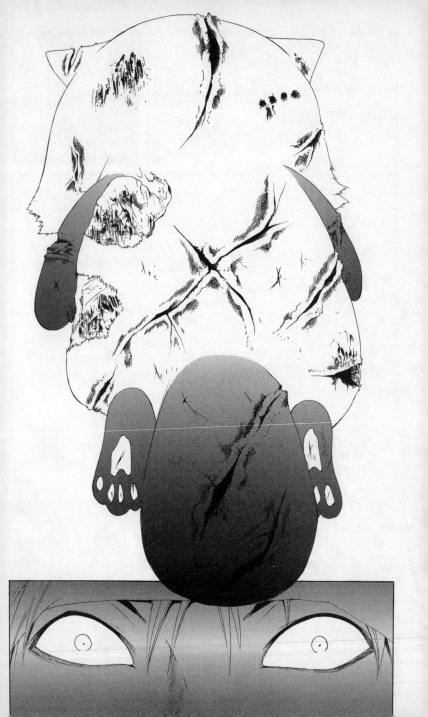

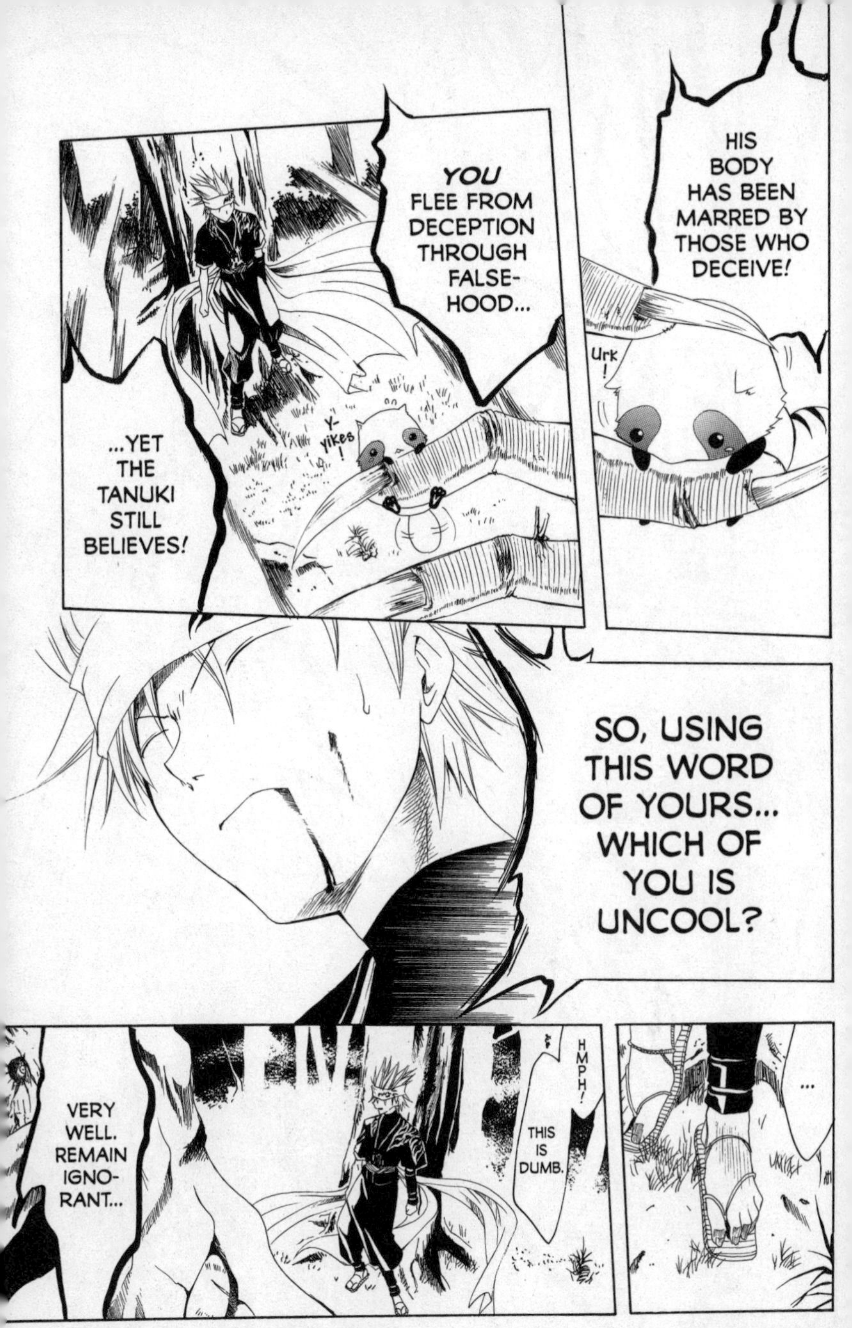
HIS BODY HAS BEEN MARRED BY THOSE WHO DECEIVE!
Urk!
YOU FLEE FROM DECEPTION THROUGH FALSE-HOOD...
Y-yikes!
...YET THE TANUKI STILL BELIEVES!
SO, USING THIS WORD OF YOURS... WHICH OF YOU IS UNCOOL?
...
HMPH!
THIS IS DUMB.
VERY WELL. REMAIN IGNO-RANT...

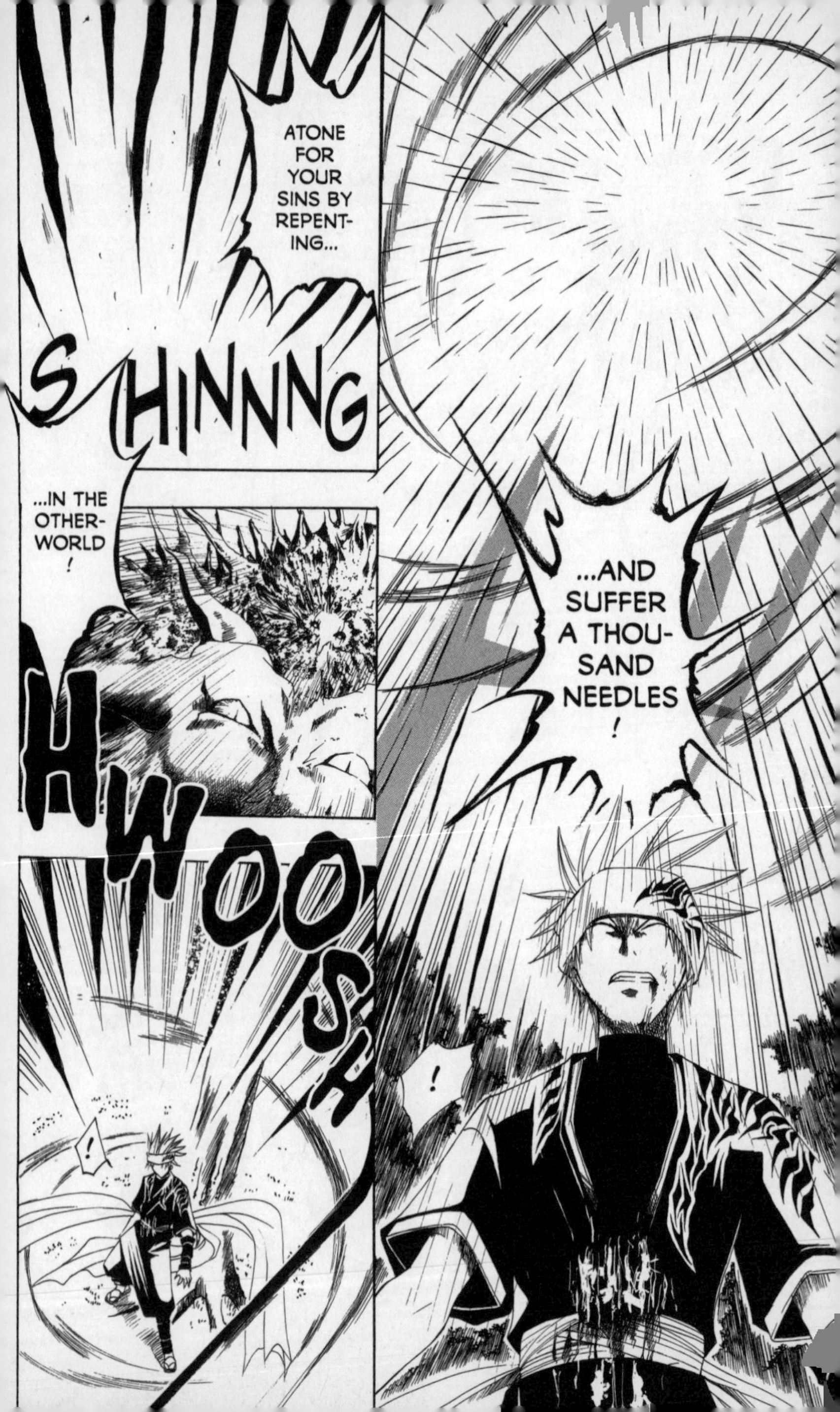
ATONE FOR YOUR SINS BY REPENT- ING...
SHINNNG
...IN THE OTHER- WORLD !
HWOOSH
!
...AND SUFFER A THOU- SAND NEEDLES !
!

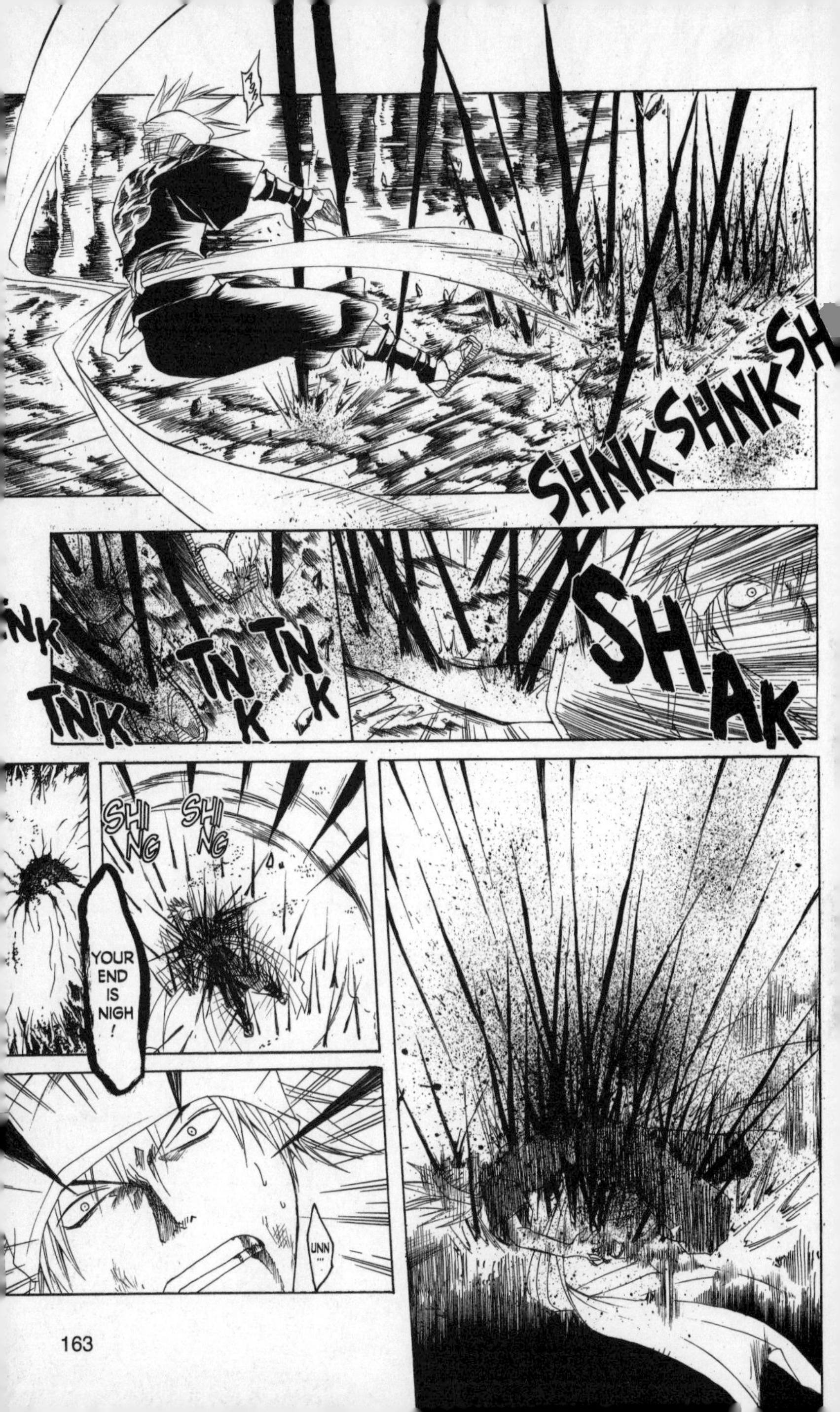
Agh!
SHNK SHNK SHNK SH
SHAK
NK
TNK
TNK
TNK
SHING
SHING
YOUR END IS NIGH!
UNN...

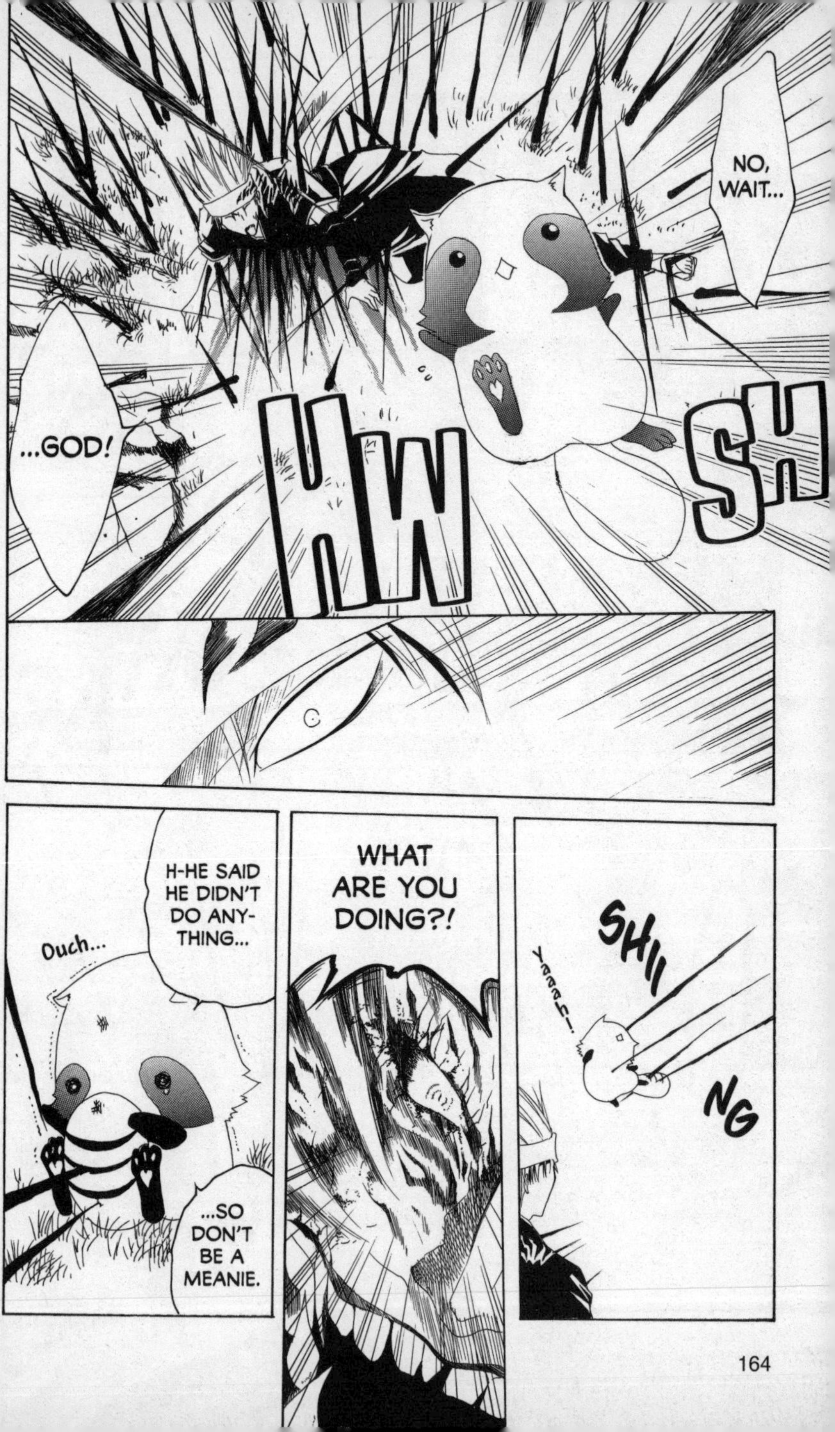
NO, WAIT...
...GOD!
HWSH
SHING
Yaaah!
WHAT ARE YOU DOING?!
H-HE SAID HE DIDN'T DO ANYTHING...
Ouch...
...SO DON'T BE A MEANIE.

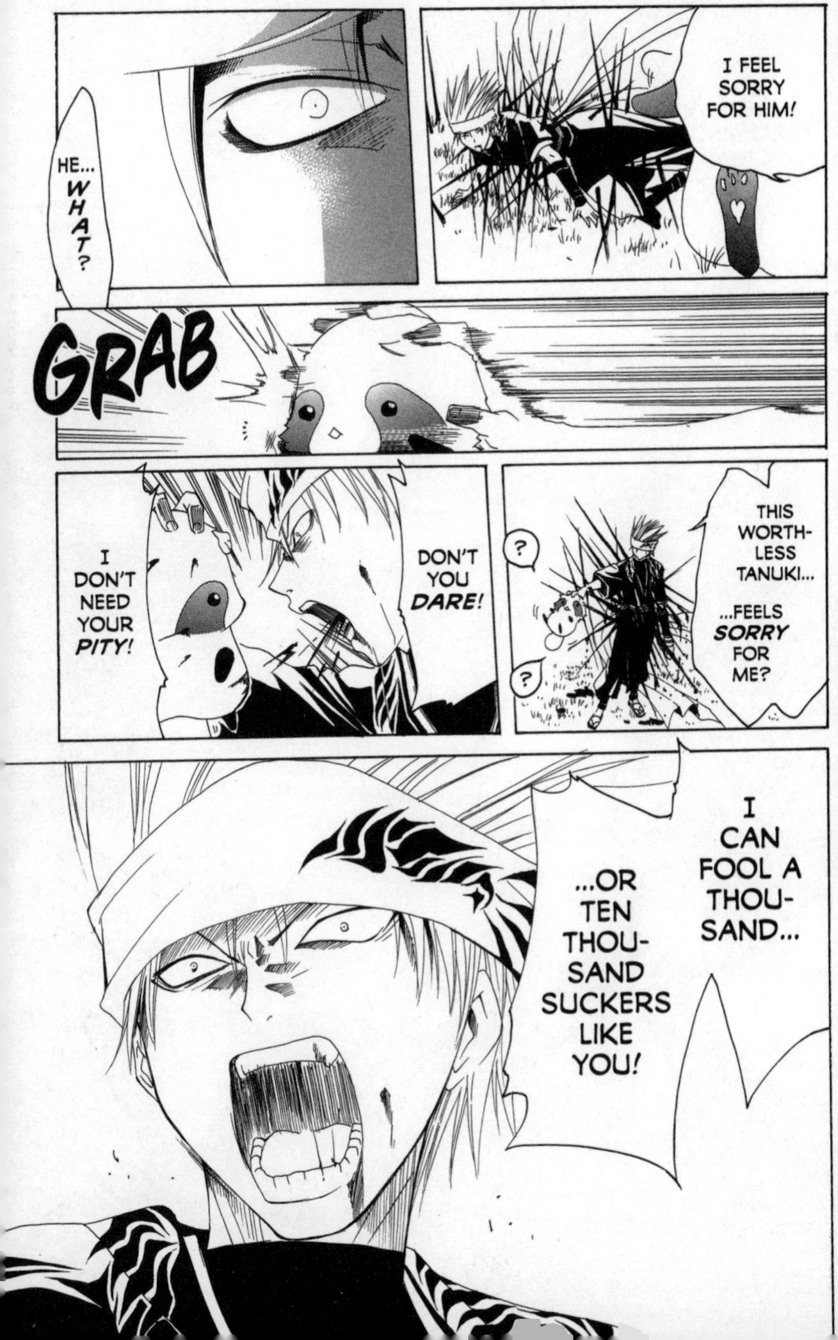
I FEEL SORRY FOR HIM!
HE... WHAT?
GRAB
?
?
THIS WORTHLESS TANUKI...
...FEELS SORRY FOR ME?
DON'T YOU DARE!
I DON'T NEED YOUR PITY!
I CAN FOOL A THOUSAND...
...OR TEN THOUSAND SUCKERS LIKE YOU!

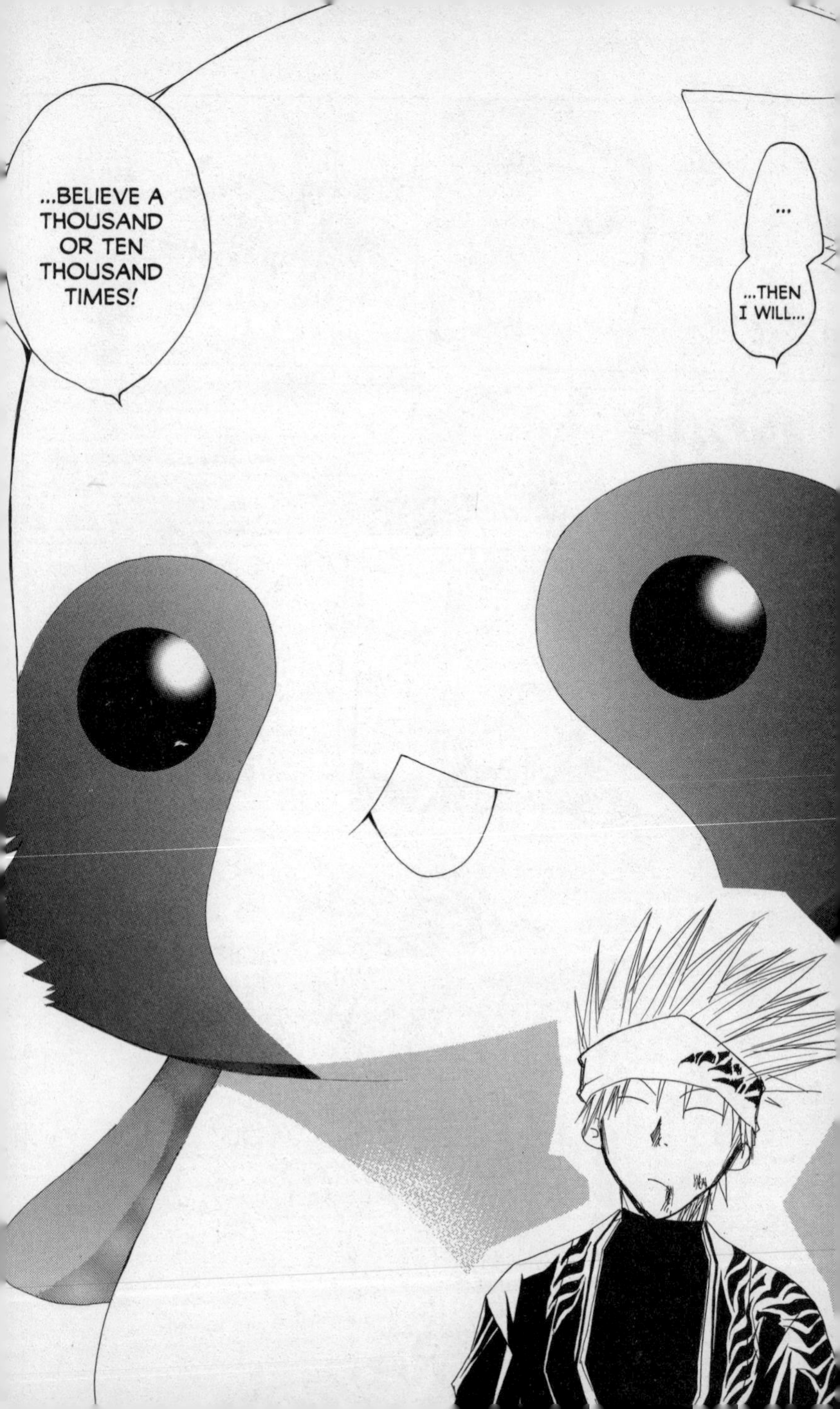
...
...THEN I WILL...
...BELIEVE A THOUSAND OR TEN THOUSAND TIMES!

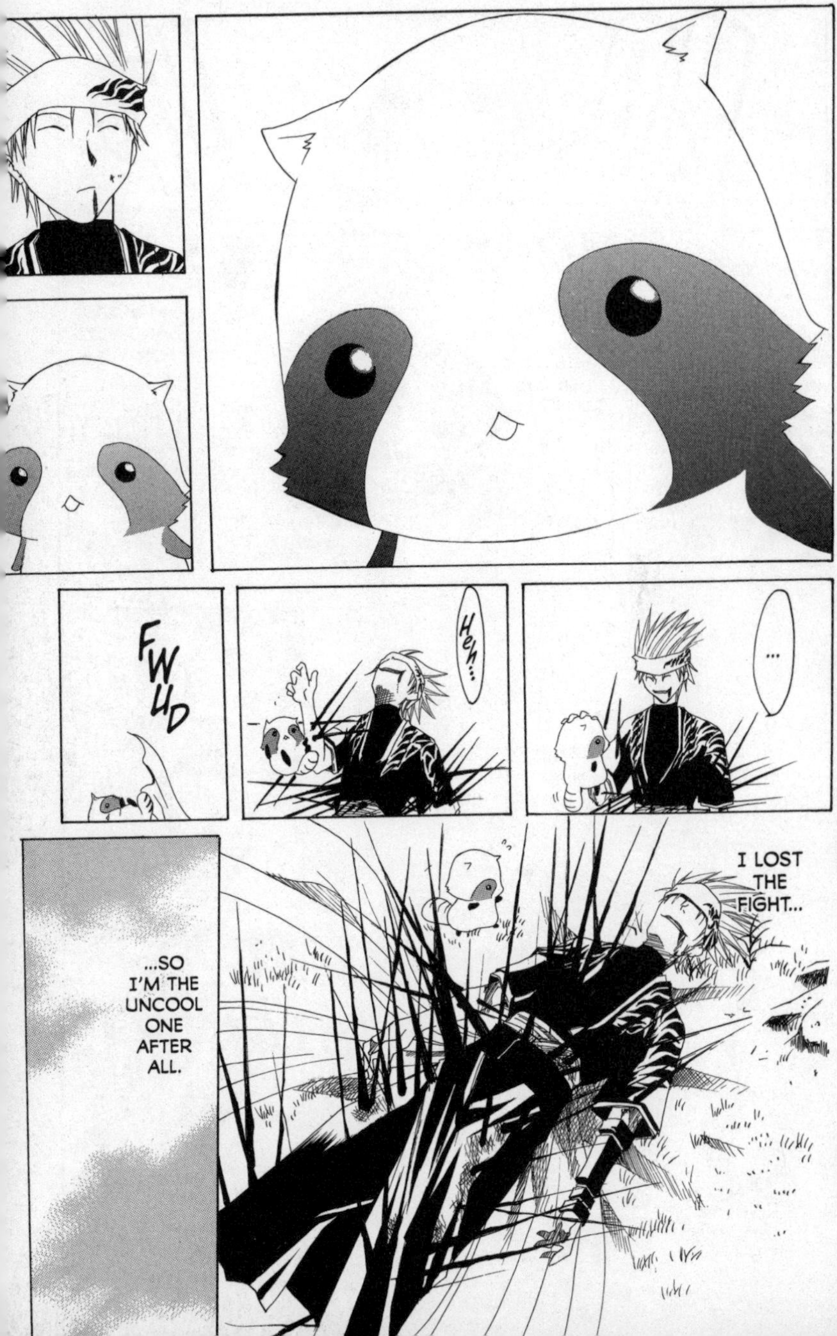
...
Heh...
FWUD
I LOST THE FIGHT...
...SO I'M THE UNCOOL ONE AFTER ALL.

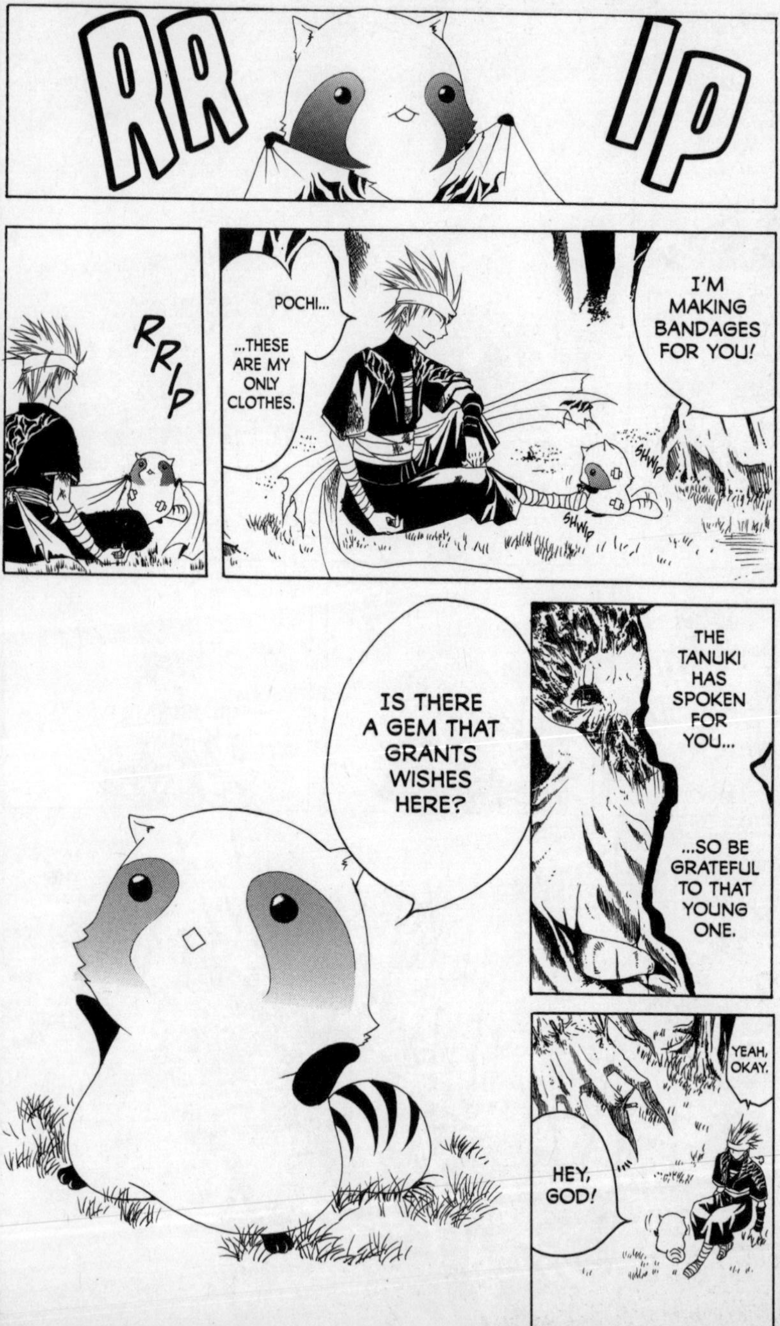
RRIP
I'M MAKING BANDAGES FOR YOU!
POCHI...
...THESE ARE MY ONLY CLOTHES.
SHWIP
SHWIP
RRIP
THE TANUKI HAS SPOKEN FOR YOU...
...SO BE GRATEFUL TO THAT YOUNG ONE.
YEAH, OKAY.
HEY, GOD!
IS THERE A GEM THAT GRANTS WISHES HERE?

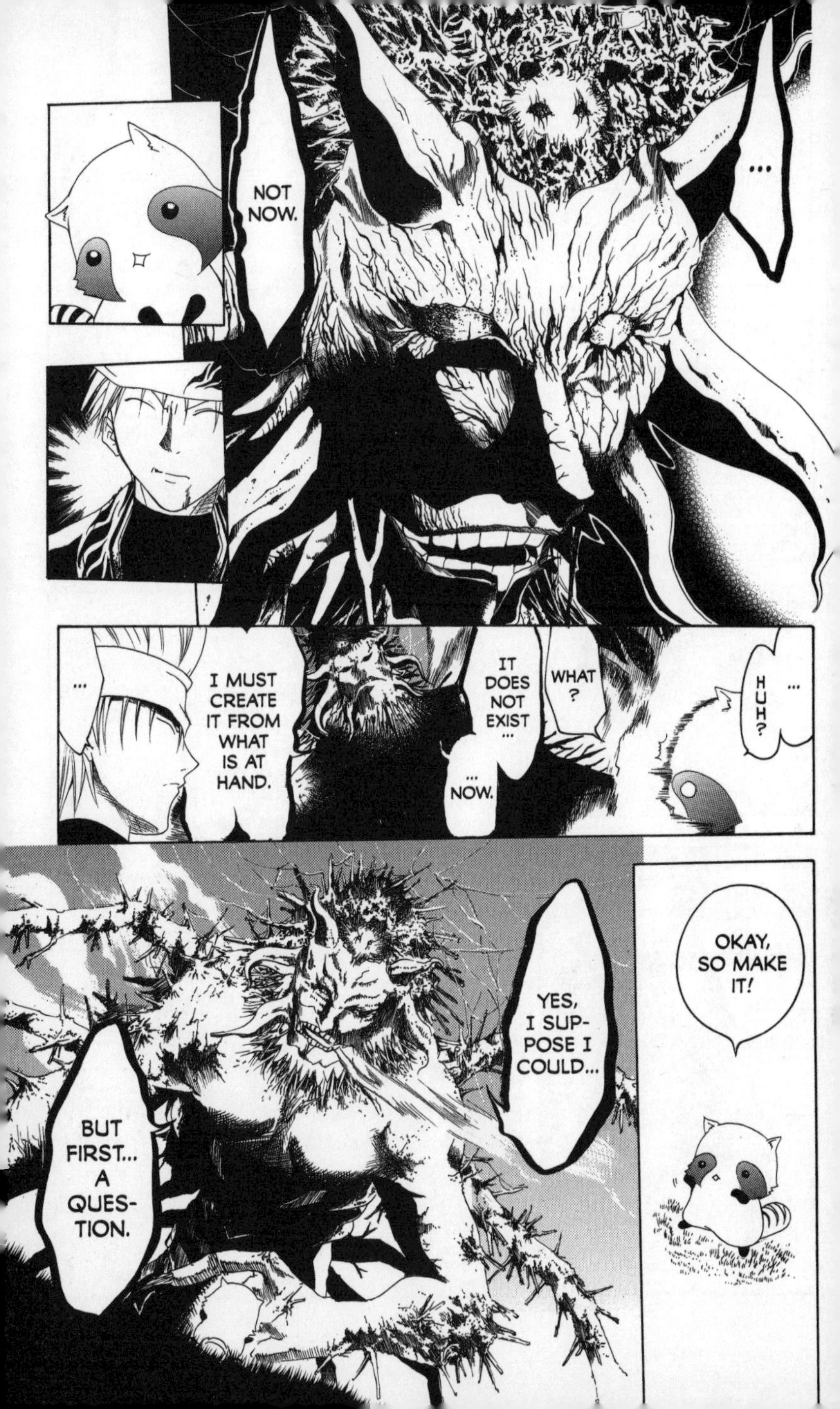
...
NOT NOW.
...
HUH?
WHAT?
IT DOES NOT EXIST...
...NOW.
I MUST CREATE IT FROM WHAT IS AT HAND.
...
OKAY, SO MAKE IT!
YES, I SUPPOSE I COULD...
BUT FIRST... A QUESTION.

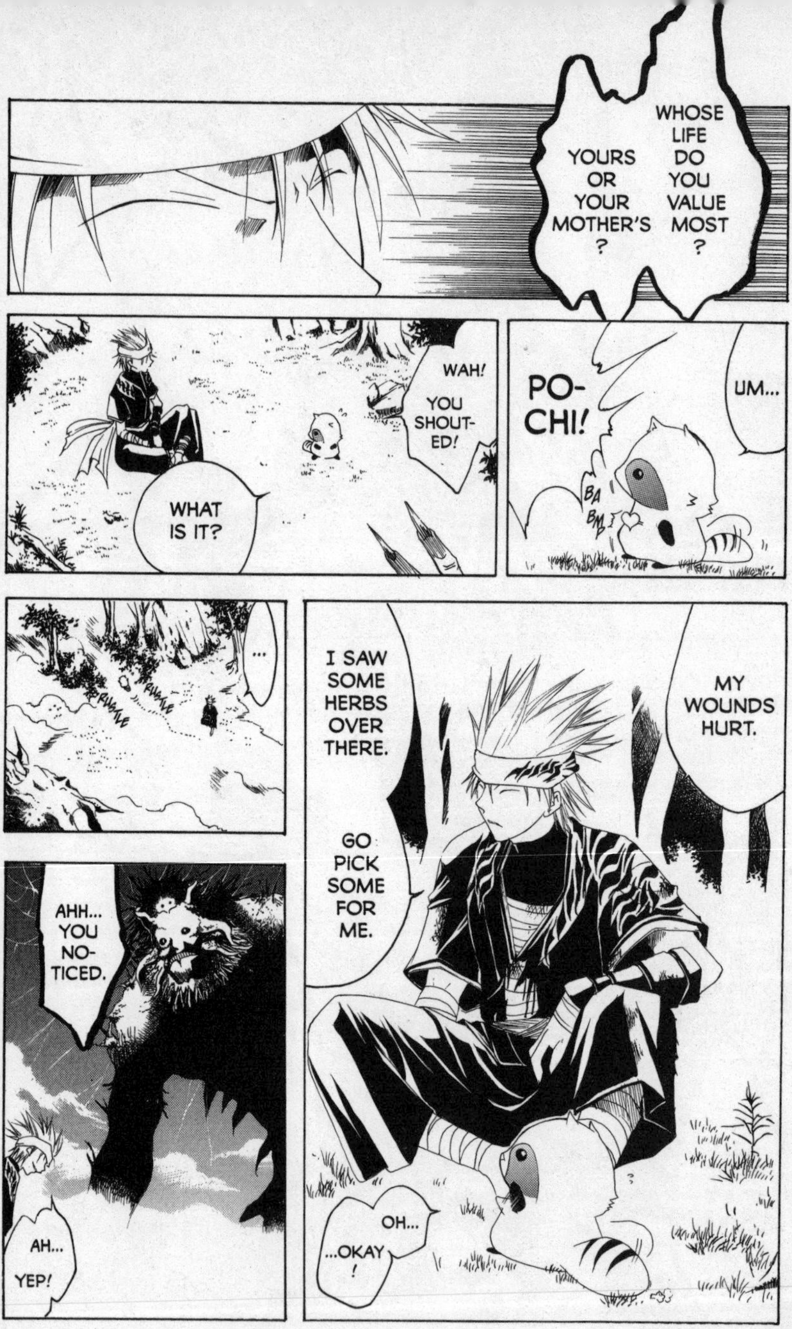
WHOSE LIFE DO YOU VALUE MOST ?
YOURS OR YOUR MOTHER'S ?
UM...
PO-CHI!
BA BM
WAH!
YOU SHOUT-ED!
WHAT IS IT?
MY WOUNDS HURT.
I SAW SOME HERBS OVER THERE.
GO PICK SOME FOR ME.
OH...
...OKAY !
...
RUSTLE
RUSTLE
AHH... YOU NO-TICED.
AH...
YEP!

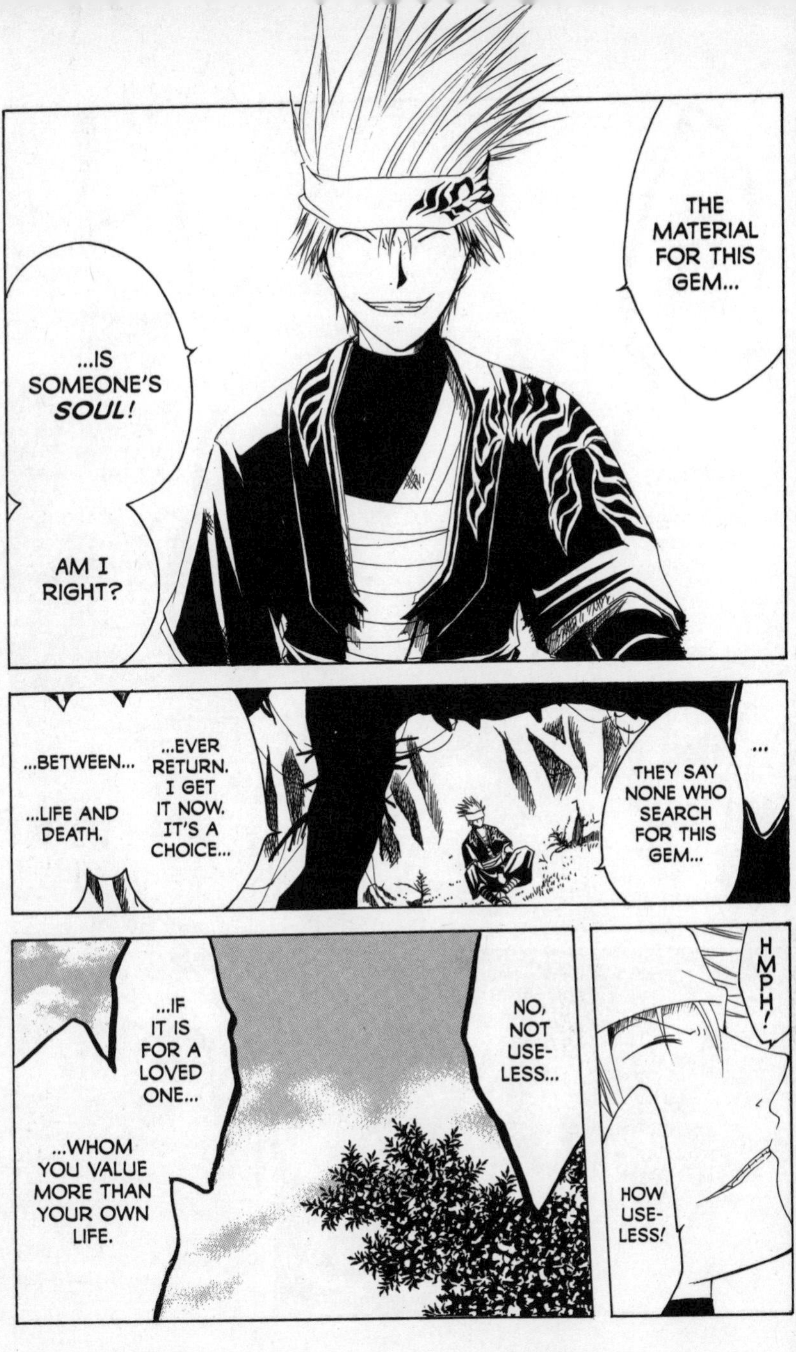

THE MATERIAL FOR THIS GEM...
...IS SOMEONE'S *SOUL*!
AM I RIGHT?
...
THEY SAY NONE WHO SEARCH FOR THIS GEM...
...EVER RETURN. I GET IT NOW. IT'S A CHOICE...
...BETWEEN...
...LIFE AND DEATH.
HMPH!
HOW USE-LESS!
NO, NOT USE-LESS...
...IF IT IS FOR A LOVED ONE...
...WHOM YOU VALUE MORE THAN YOUR OWN LIFE.

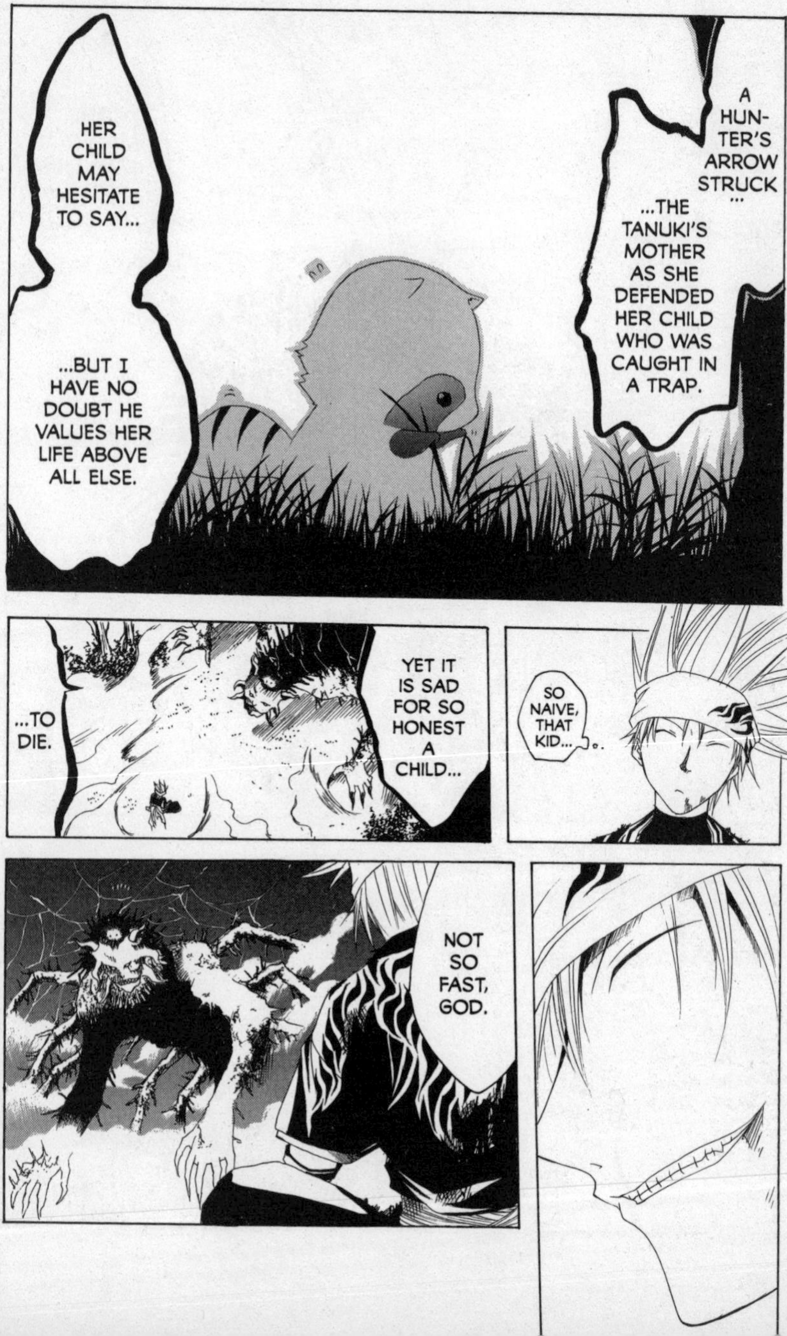
A HUNTER'S ARROW STRUCK...
...THE TANUKI'S MOTHER AS SHE DEFENDED HER CHILD WHO WAS CAUGHT IN A TRAP.
HER CHILD MAY HESITATE TO SAY...
...BUT I HAVE NO DOUBT HE VALUES HER LIFE ABOVE ALL ELSE.
SO NAIVE, THAT KID...
YET IT IS SAD FOR SO HONEST A CHILD...
...TO DIE.
NOT SO FAST, GOD.

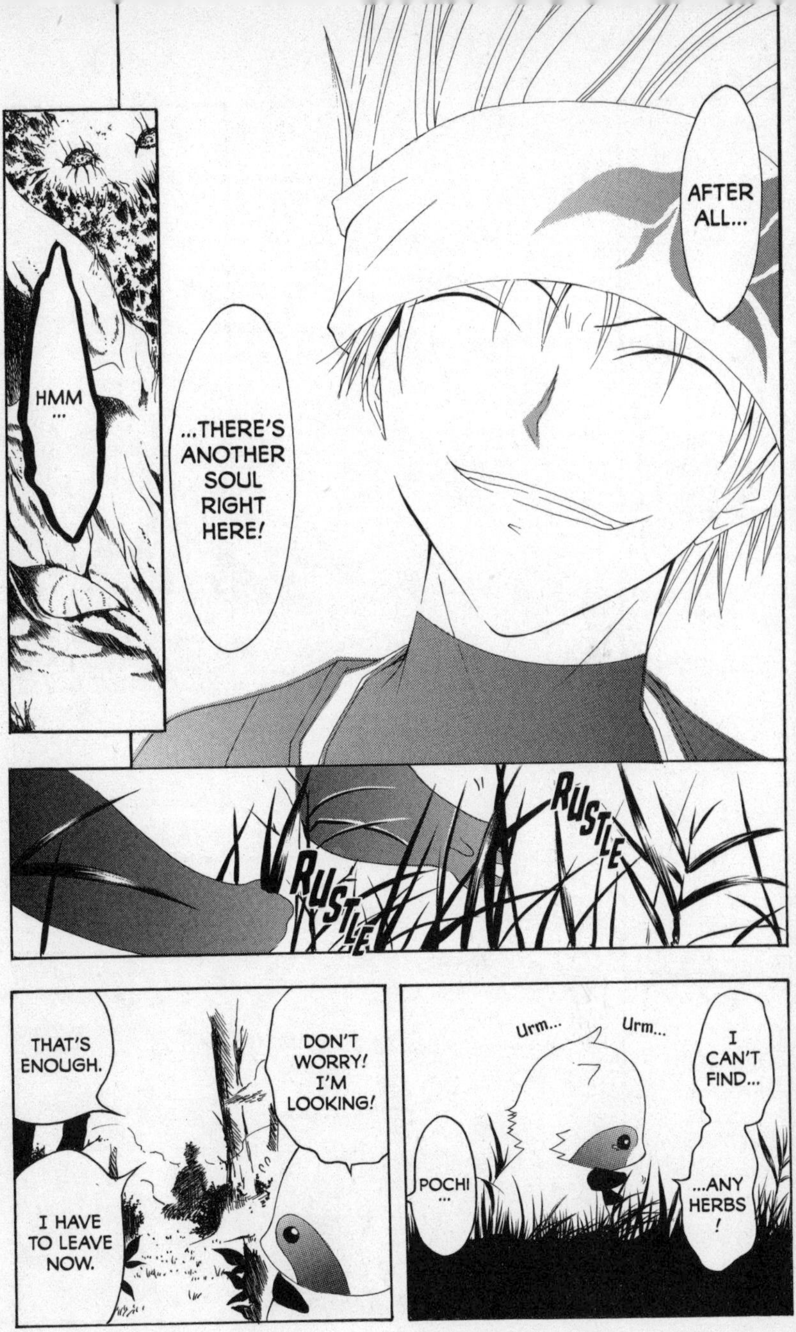
AFTER ALL...
...THERE'S ANOTHER SOUL RIGHT HERE!
HMM...
RUSTLE
RUSTLE
Urm... Urm...
I CAN'T FIND...
...ANY HERBS!
POCHI...
DON'T WORRY! I'M LOOKING!
THAT'S ENOUGH.
I HAVE TO LEAVE NOW.

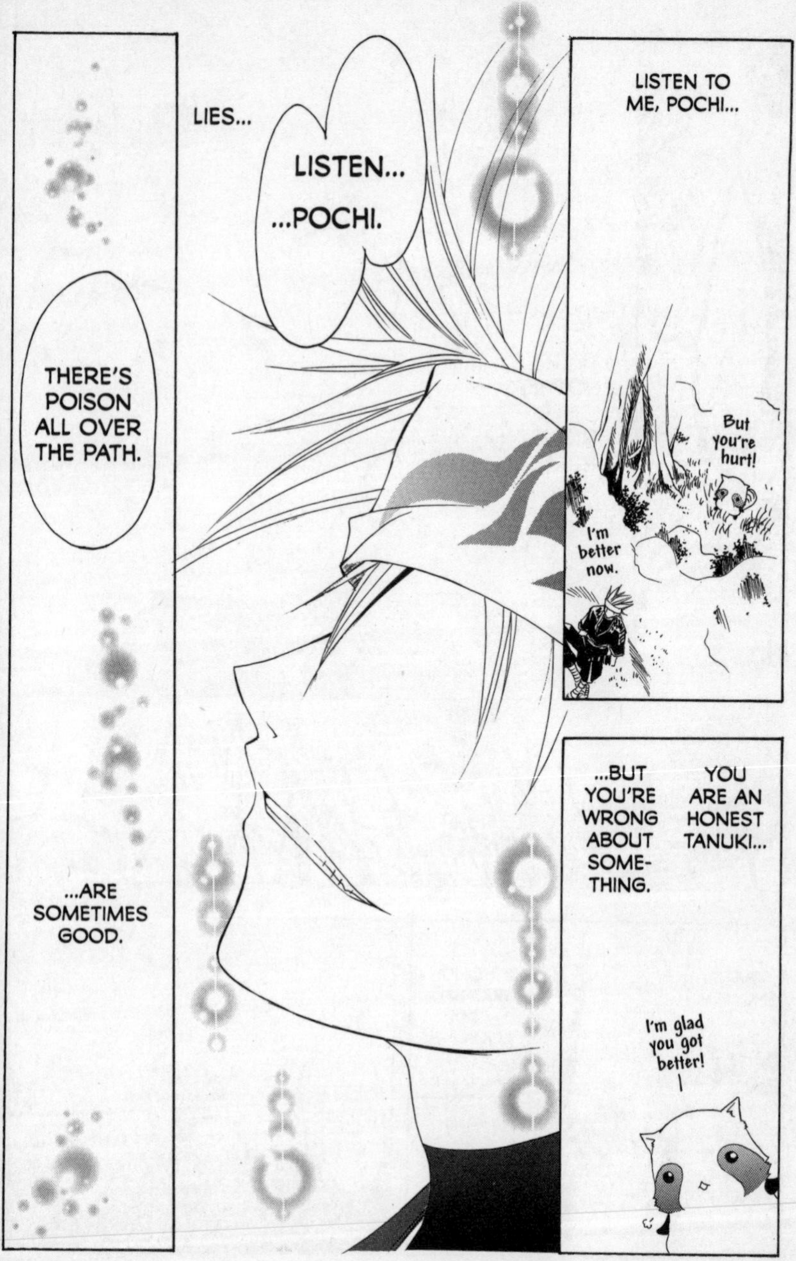
LISTEN TO ME, POCHI...
But you're hurt!
I'm better now.
YOU ARE AN HONEST TANUKI...
...BUT YOU'RE WRONG ABOUT SOMETHING.
I'm glad you got better!
LISTEN... ...POCHI.
LIES...
THERE'S POISON ALL OVER THE PATH.
...ARE SOMETIMES GOOD.

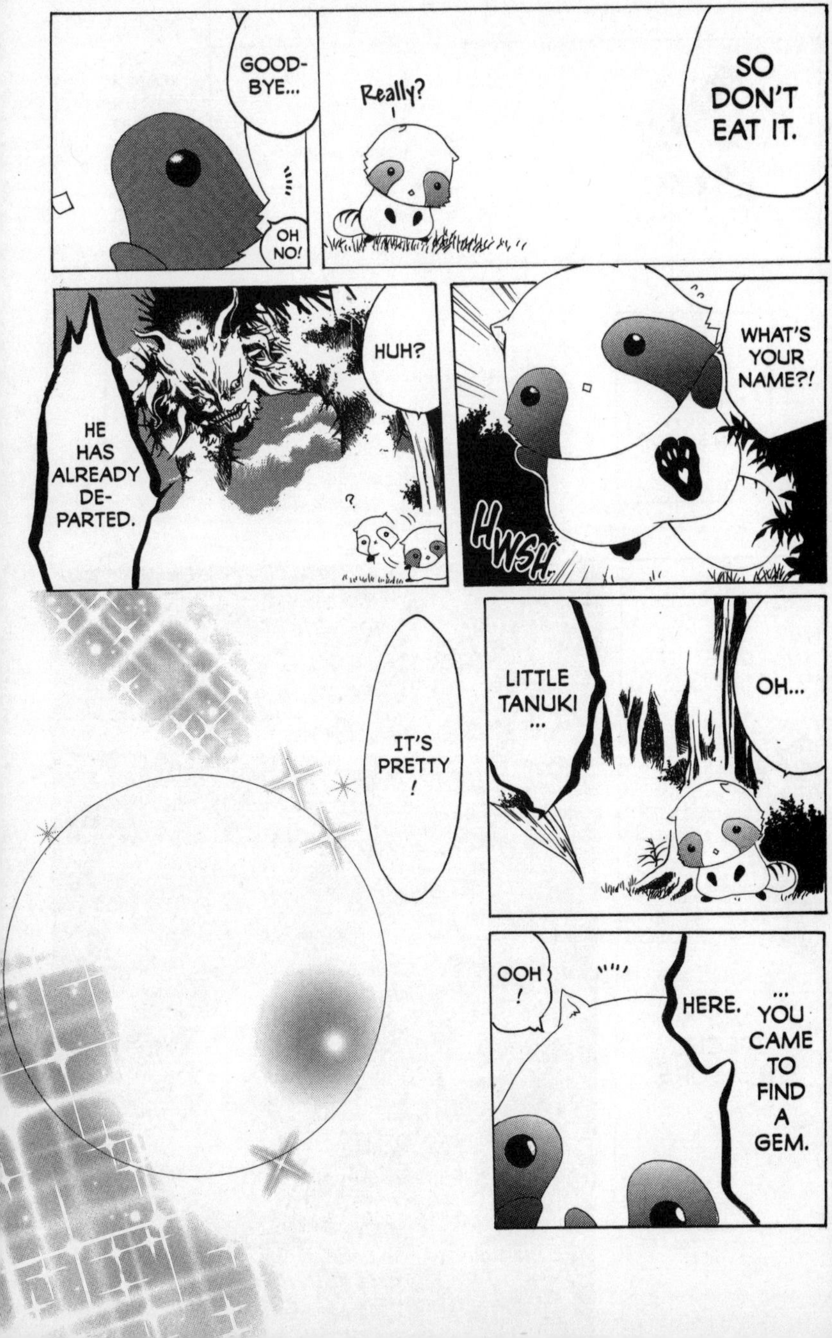
SO DON'T EAT IT.
Really?
GOOD-BYE...
OH NO!
WHAT'S YOUR NAME?!
HWSH
HUH?
HE HAS ALREADY DE-PARTED.
?
OH...
LITTLE TANUKI ...
... YOU CAME TO FIND A GEM.
HERE.
OOH!
IT'S PRETTY!

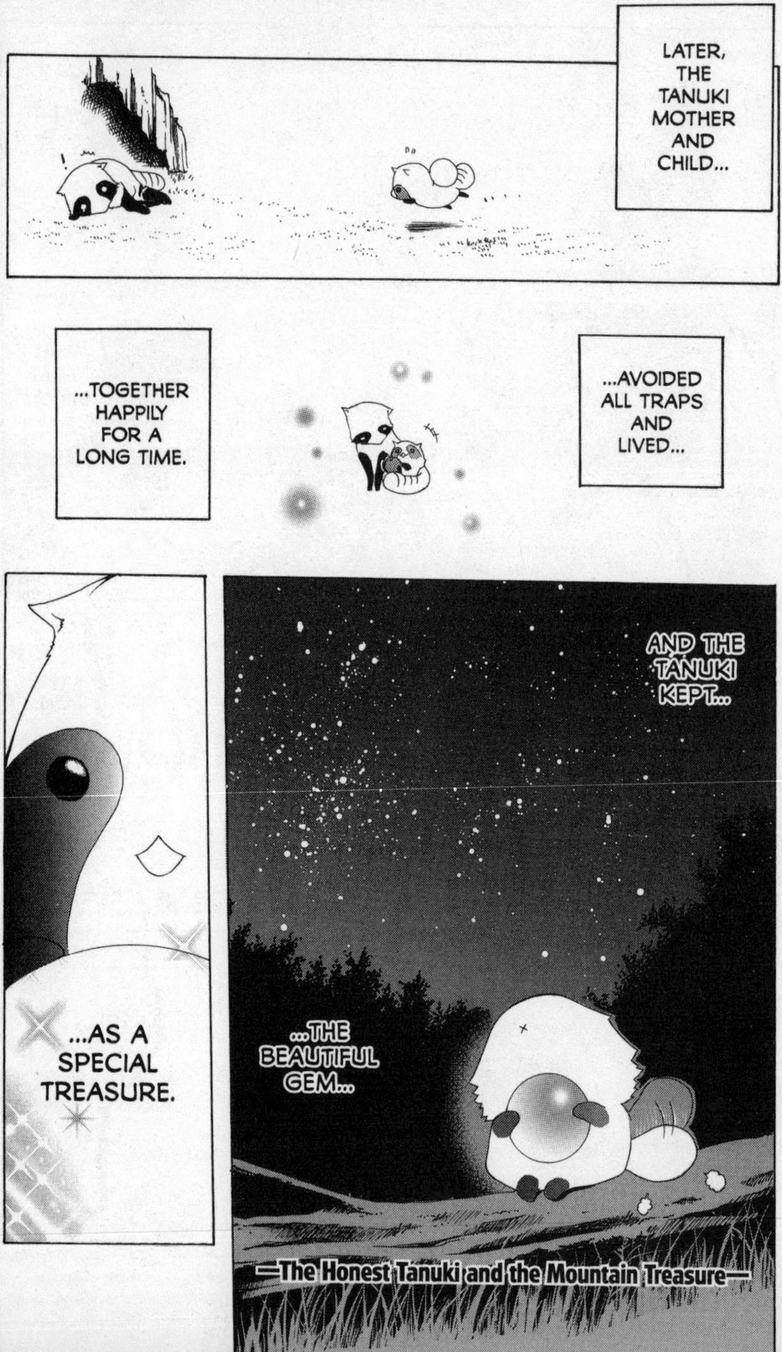
LATER, THE TANUKI MOTHER AND CHILD...
...AVOIDED ALL TRAPS AND LIVED...
...TOGETHER HAPPILY FOR A LONG TIME.
AND THE TANUKI KEPT...
...THE BEAUTIFUL GEM...
—The Honest Tanuki and the Mountain Treasure—
...AS A SPECIAL TREASURE.

Bonus Manga

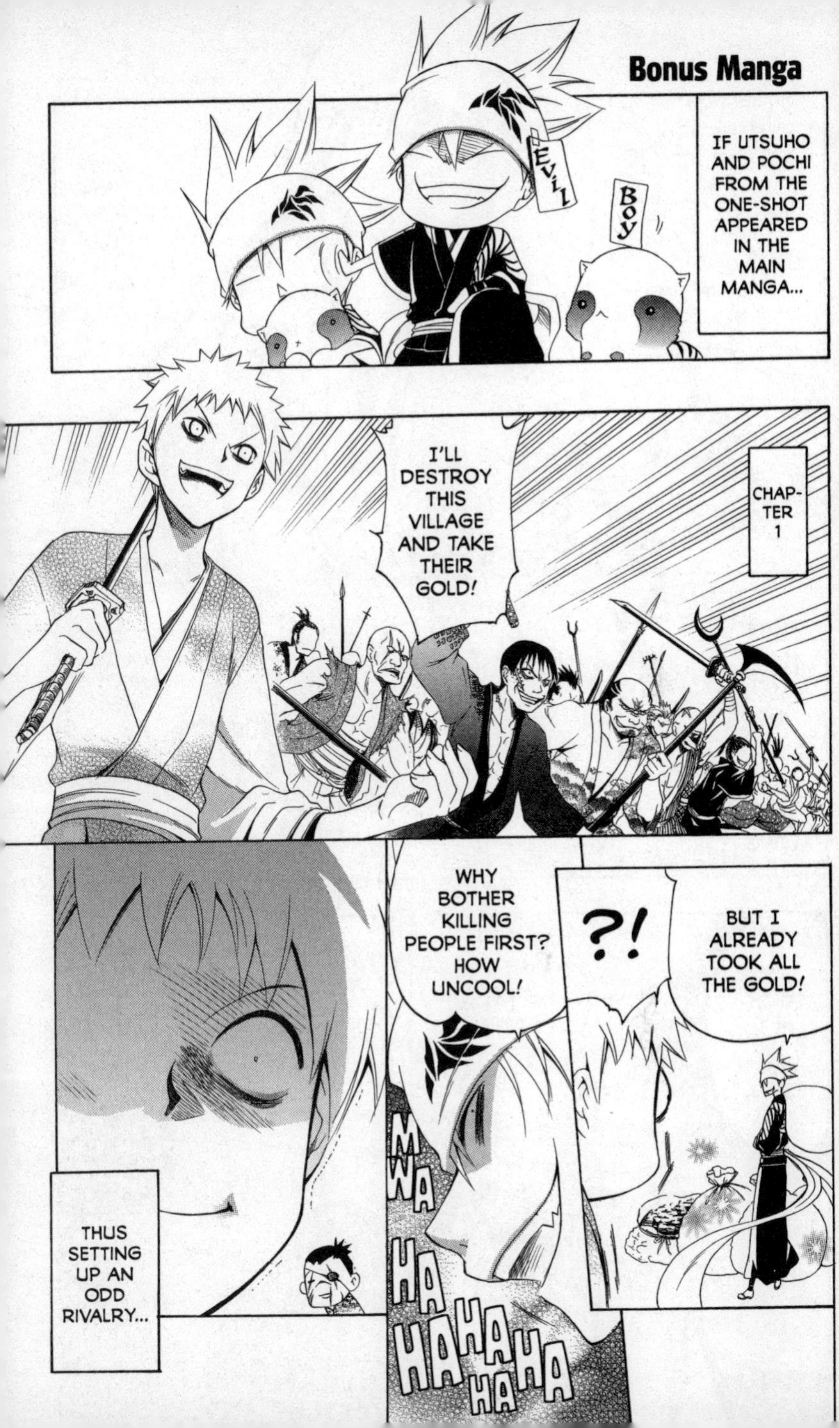
IF UTSUHO AND POCHI FROM THE ONE-SHOT APPEARED IN THE MAIN MANGA...
Boy
Evil
CHAPTER 1
I'LL DESTROY THIS VILLAGE AND TAKE THEIR GOLD!
BUT I ALREADY TOOK ALL THE GOLD!
?!
WHY BOTHER KILLING PEOPLE FIRST? HOW UNCOOL!
MWAHAHAHAHAHA
THUS SETTING UP AN ODD RIVALRY...

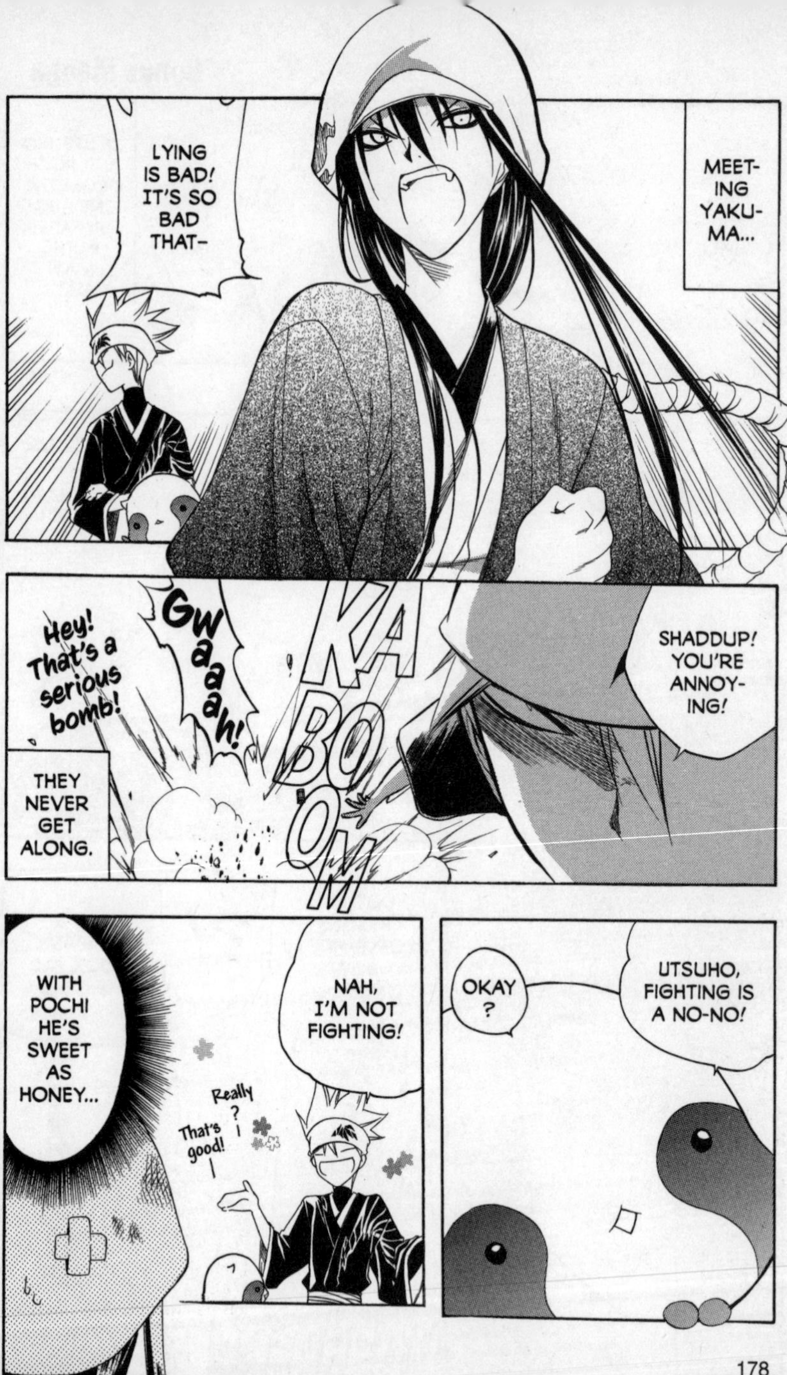
MEET-ING YAKU-MA...
LYING IS BAD! IT'S SO BAD THAT—
SHADDUP! YOU'RE ANNOY-ING!
KA BOOM
Gwaaaah!
Hey! That's a serious bomb!
THEY NEVER GET ALONG.
UTSUHO, FIGHTING IS A NO-NO!
OKAY?
NAH, I'M NOT FIGHTING!
Really?
That's good!
WITH POCHI HE'S SWEET AS HONEY...

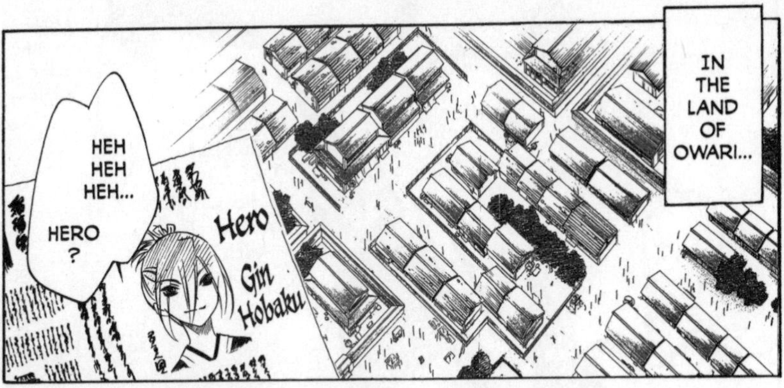
IN THE LAND OF OWARI...
HEH HEH HEH...
HERO?
Hero
Gin Hobaku

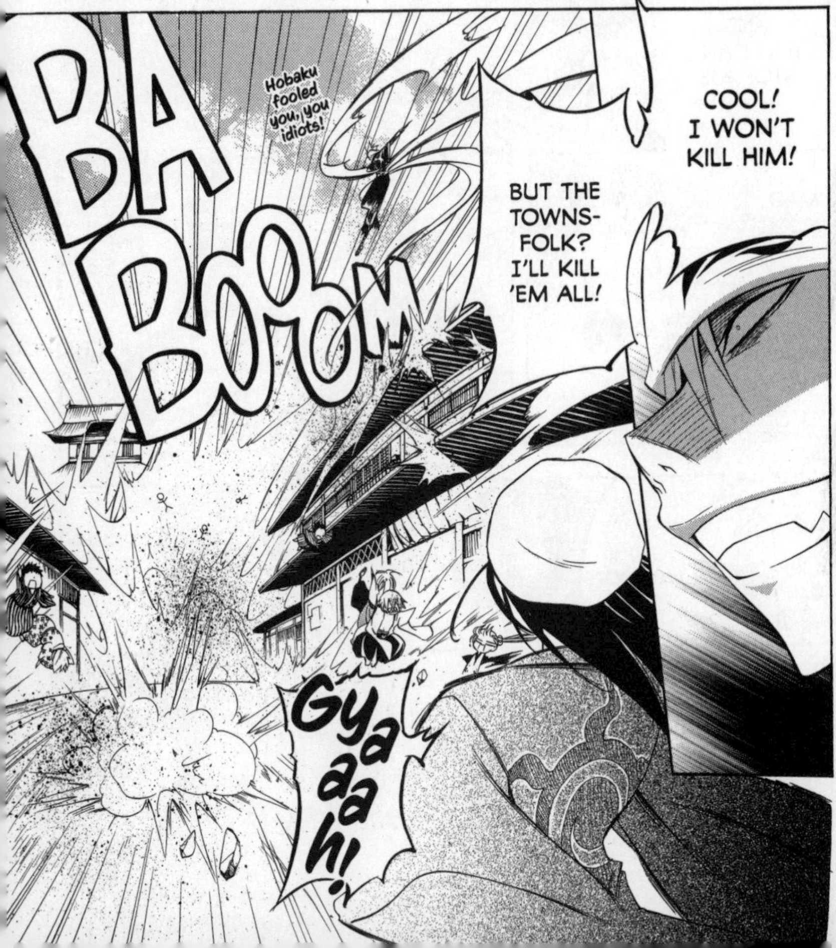
COOL! I WON'T KILL HIM!
BUT THE TOWNS-FOLK? I'LL KILL 'EM ALL!
Hobaku fooled you, you idiots!
BA BOOOM
Gyaaaah!

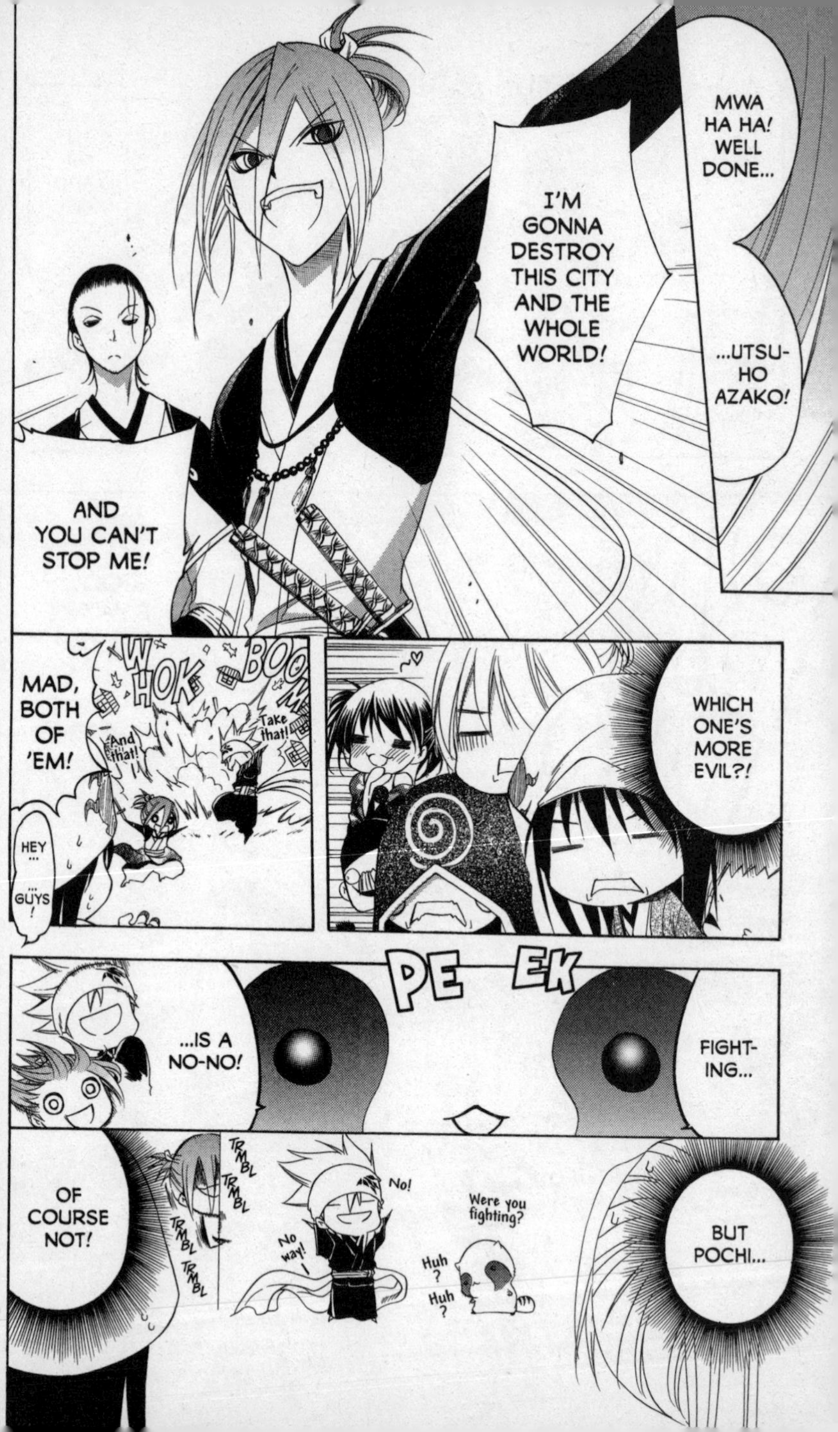
MWA HA HA! WELL DONE...
...UTSU-HO AZAKO!
I'M GONNA DESTROY THIS CITY AND THE WHOLE WORLD!
AND YOU CAN'T STOP ME!
WHICH ONE'S MORE EVIL?!
BOOM
WHOK
Take that!
And that!
MAD, BOTH OF 'EM!
HEY...
...GUYS!
PE EK
FIGHT-ING...
...IS A NO-NO!
BUT POCHI...
Were you fighting?
Huh?
Huh?
No!
No way!
TRMBL
TRMBL
TRMBL
TRMBL
OF COURSE NOT!

Chapter 199 Bonus Manga 2

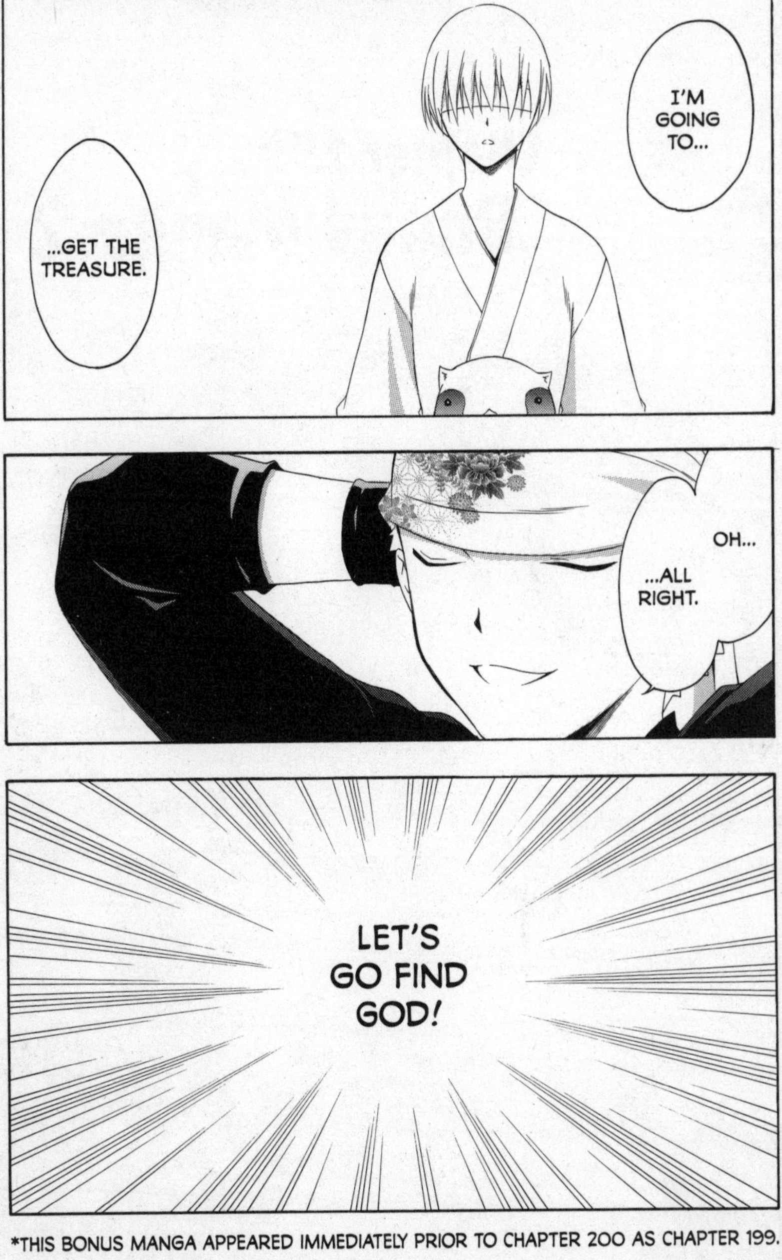

I'M GOING TO...
...GET THE TREASURE.
OH...
...ALL RIGHT.
LET'S GO FIND GOD!

*THIS BONUS MANGA APPEARED IMMEDIATELY PRIOR TO CHAPTER 200 AS CHAPTER 199.

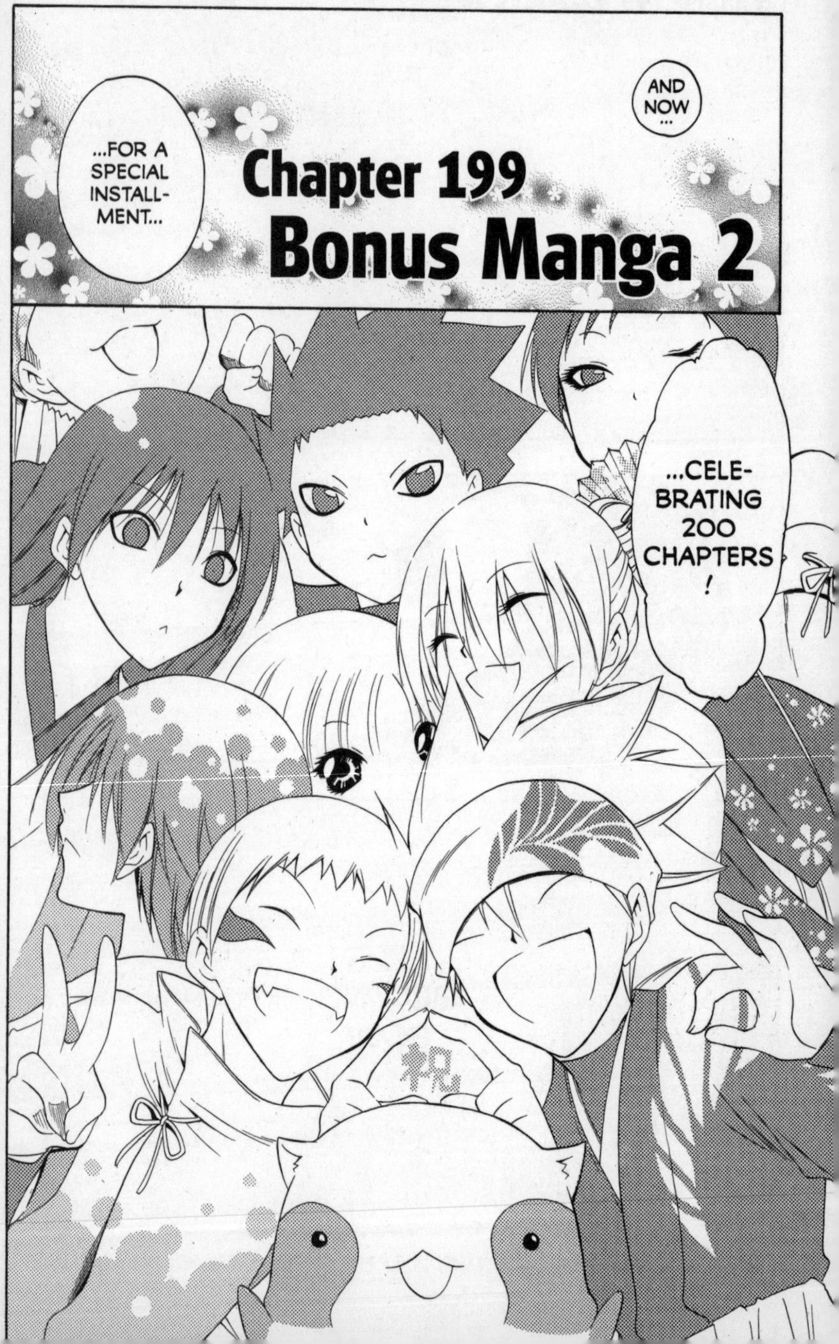
AND NOW …
…FOR A SPECIAL INSTALL-MENT…
Chapter 199
Bonus Manga 2
…CELE-BRATING 200 CHAPTERS !

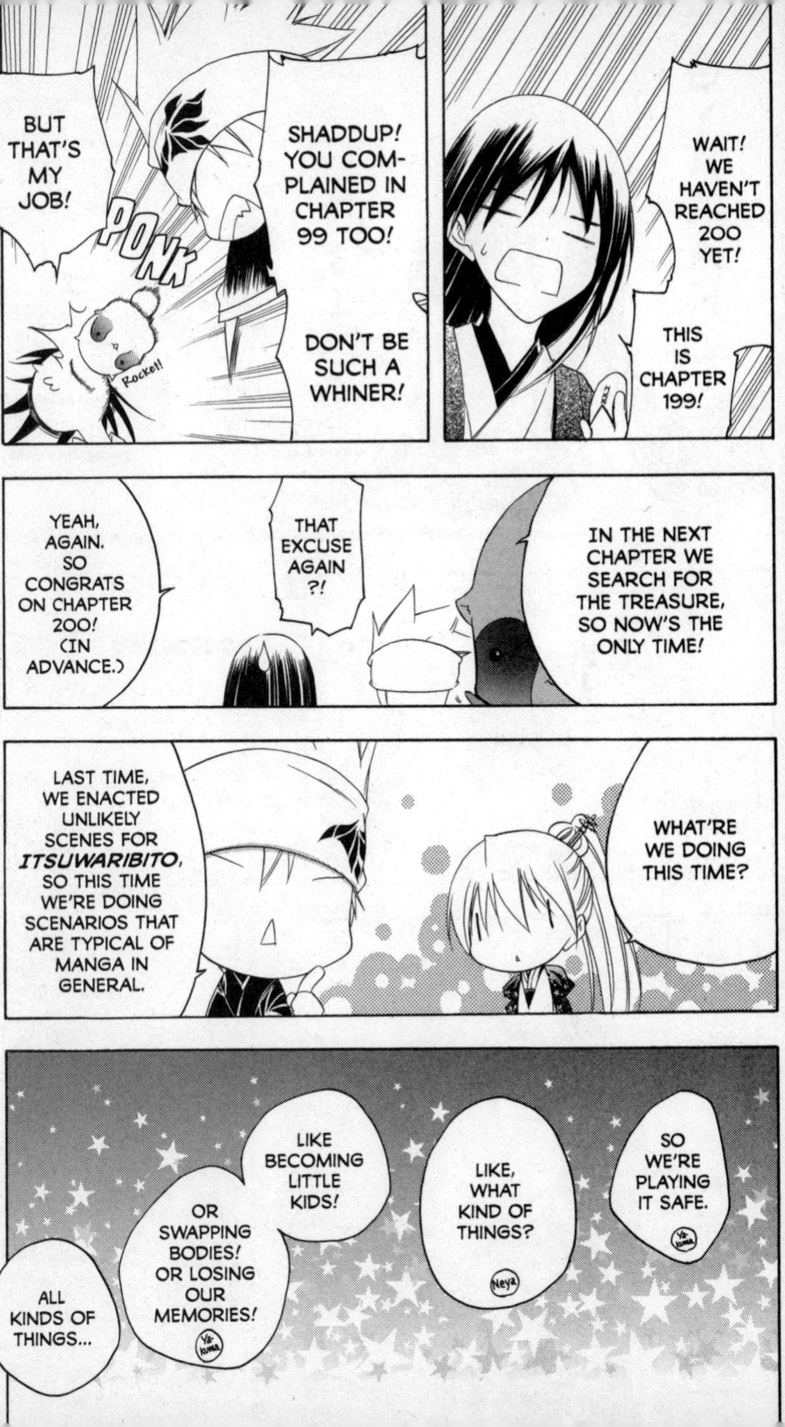
WAIT! WE HAVEN'T REACHED 200 YET!
THIS IS CHAPTER 199!
SHADDUP! YOU COMPLAINED IN CHAPTER 99 TOO!
DON'T BE SUCH A WHINER!
PONK
Rocket!
BUT THAT'S MY JOB!
IN THE NEXT CHAPTER WE SEARCH FOR THE TREASURE, SO NOW'S THE ONLY TIME!
THAT EXCUSE AGAIN?!
YEAH, AGAIN. SO CONGRATS ON CHAPTER 200! (IN ADVANCE.)
WHAT'RE WE DOING THIS TIME?
LAST TIME, WE ENACTED UNLIKELY SCENES FOR ITSUWARIBITO, SO THIS TIME WE'RE DOING SCENARIOS THAT ARE TYPICAL OF MANGA IN GENERAL.
SO WE'RE PLAYING IT SAFE.
Ya-kuma
LIKE, WHAT KIND OF THINGS?
Neya
LIKE BECOMING LITTLE KIDS!
OR SWAPPING BODIES! OR LOSING OUR MEMORIES!
Ya-kuma
ALL KINDS OF THINGS...

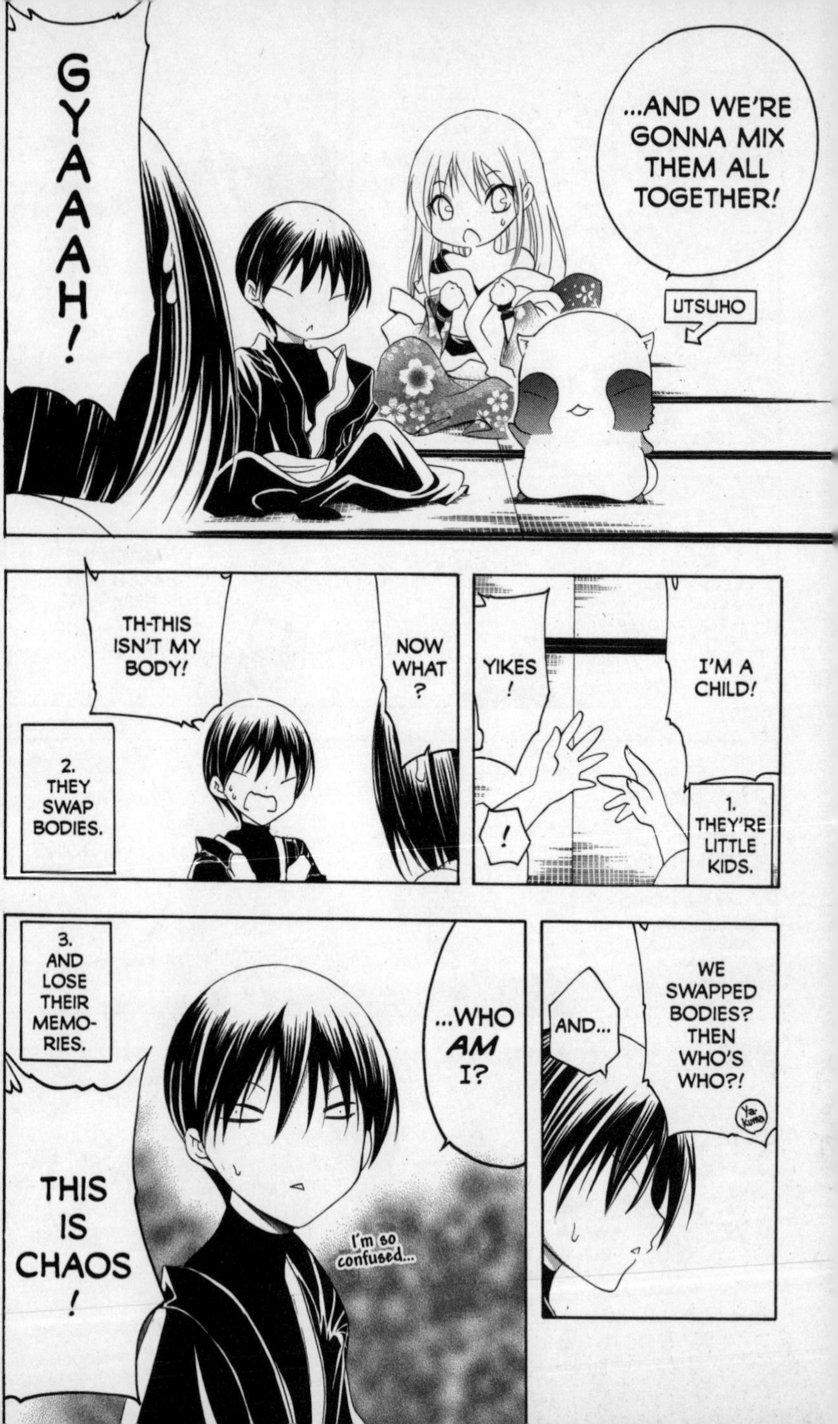
...AND WE'RE GONNA MIX THEM ALL TOGETHER!
UTSUHO
GYAAAH!
I'M A CHILD!
1. THEY'RE LITTLE KIDS.
YIKES!
!
NOW WHAT?
TH-THIS ISN'T MY BODY!
2. THEY SWAP BODIES.
WE SWAPPED BODIES? THEN WHO'S WHO?!
Ya-kuma
AND...
...WHO AM I?
3. AND LOSE THEIR MEMORIES.
THIS IS CHAOS!
I'm so confused...

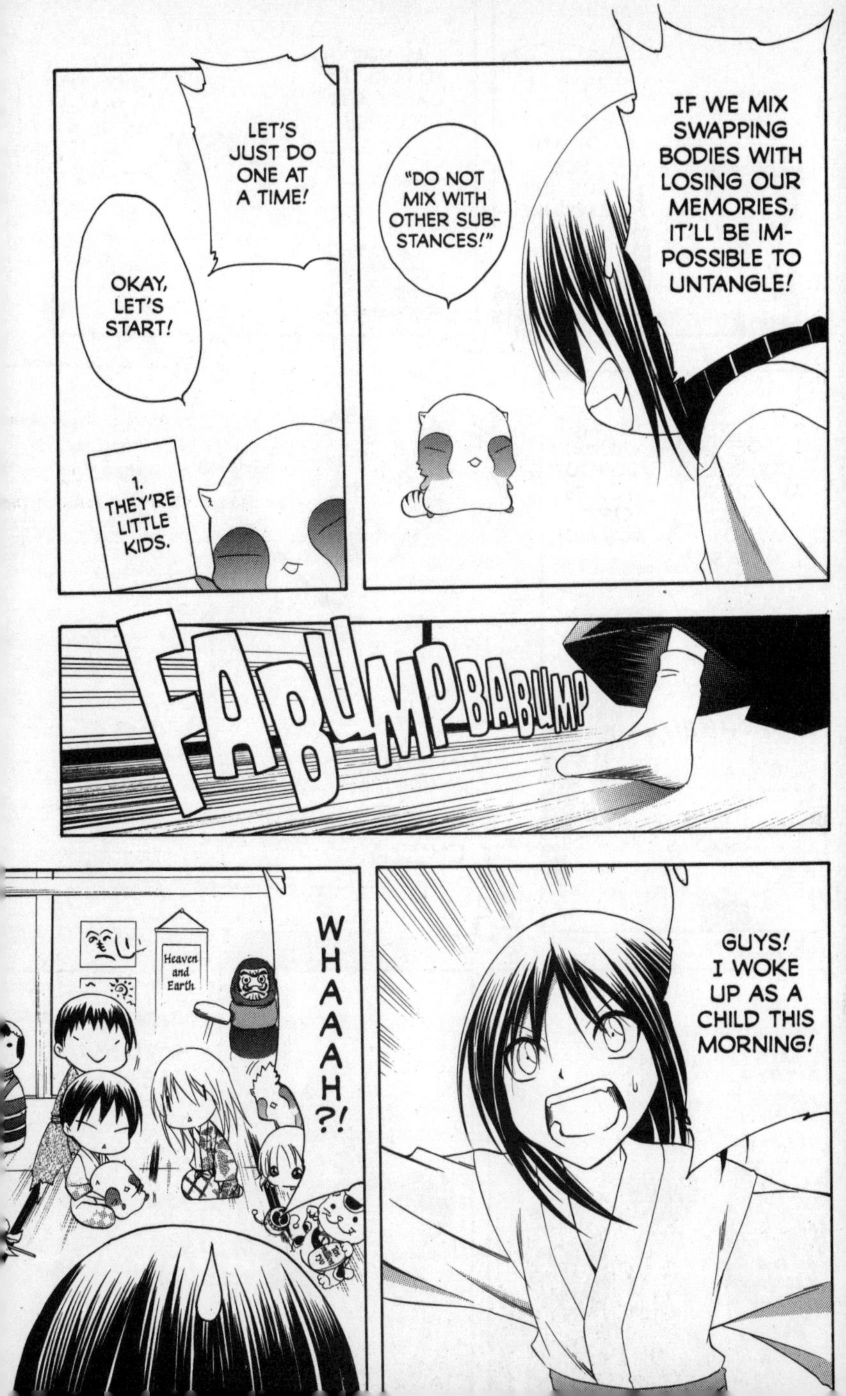
IF WE MIX SWAPPING BODIES WITH LOSING OUR MEMORIES, IT'LL BE IMPOSSIBLE TO UNTANGLE!
"DO NOT MIX WITH OTHER SUBSTANCES!"
LET'S JUST DO ONE AT A TIME!
OKAY, LET'S START!
1. THEY'RE LITTLE KIDS.
FABUMPBABUMP
GUYS! I WOKE UP AS A CHILD THIS MORNING!
WHAAAAH?!
Heaven and Earth

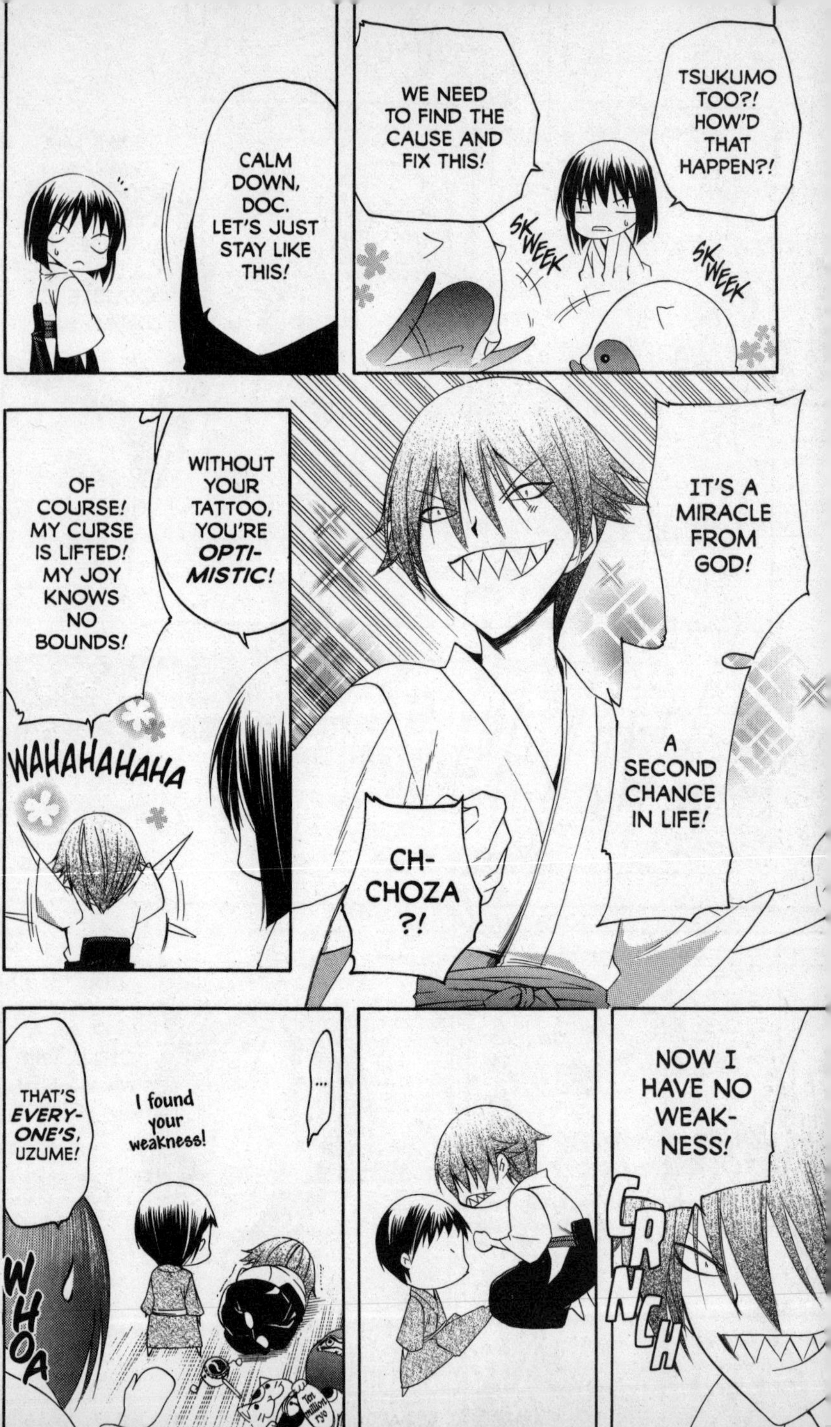
TSUKUMO TOO?! HOW'D THAT HAPPEN?!
WE NEED TO FIND THE CAUSE AND FIX THIS!
SKWEEK
SKWEEK
CALM DOWN, DOC. LET'S JUST STAY LIKE THIS!
IT'S A MIRACLE FROM GOD!
A SECOND CHANCE IN LIFE!
CH-CHOZA?!
WITHOUT YOUR TATTOO, YOU'RE *OPTIMISTIC*!
OF COURSE! MY CURSE IS LIFTED! MY JOY KNOWS NO BOUNDS!
WAHAHAHAHA
NOW I HAVE NO WEAKNESS!
CRNCH
...
I found your weakness!
THAT'S *EVERYONE'S*, UZUME!
WHOA
Ten million ryo

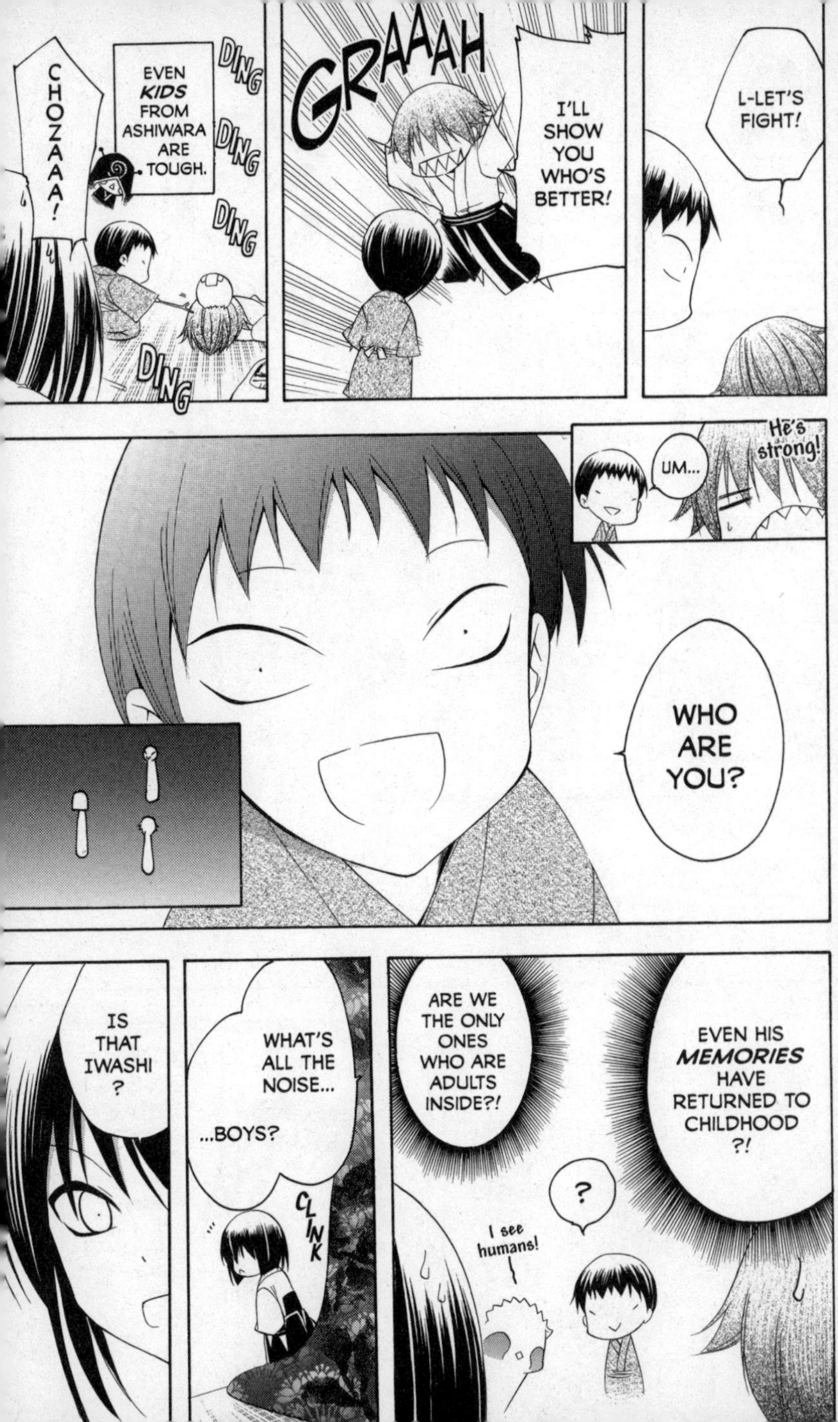
L-LET'S FIGHT!
GRAAAH
I'LL SHOW YOU WHO'S BETTER!
DING
DING
DING
EVEN *KIDS* FROM ASHIWARA ARE TOUGH.
CHOZAAAA!
DING
He's strong!
UM...
WHO ARE YOU?
EVEN HIS *MEMORIES* HAVE RETURNED TO CHILDHOOD?!
ARE WE THE ONLY ONES WHO ARE ADULTS INSIDE?!
?
I see humans!
WHAT'S ALL THE NOISE...
...BOYS?
CLINK
IS THAT IWASHI?

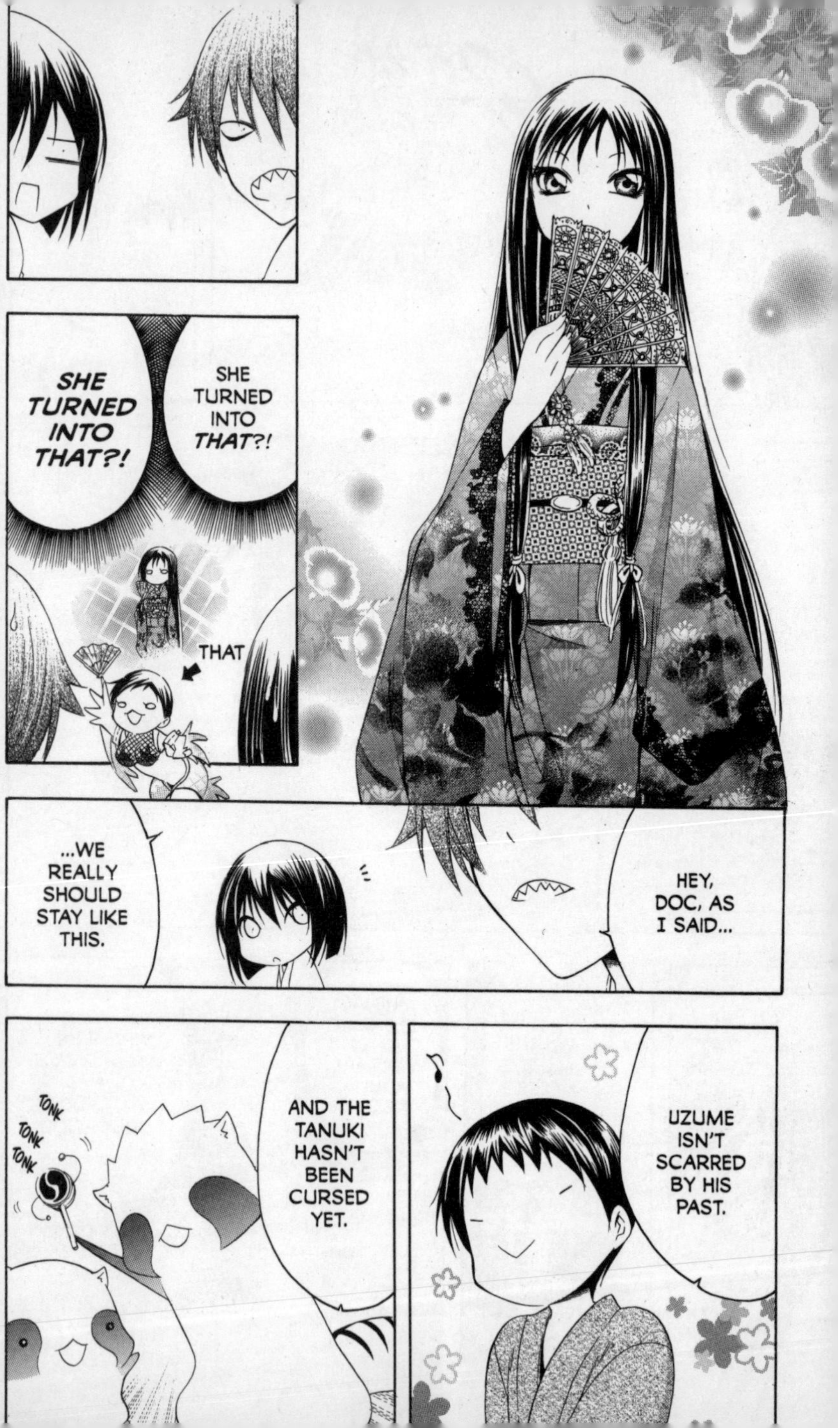
SHE TURNED INTO THAT?!
SHE TURNED INTO THAT?!
THAT
HEY, DOC, AS I SAID...
...WE REALLY SHOULD STAY LIKE THIS.
UZUME ISN'T SCARRED BY HIS PAST.
AND THE TANUKI HASN'T BEEN CURSED YET.
TONK TONK TONK

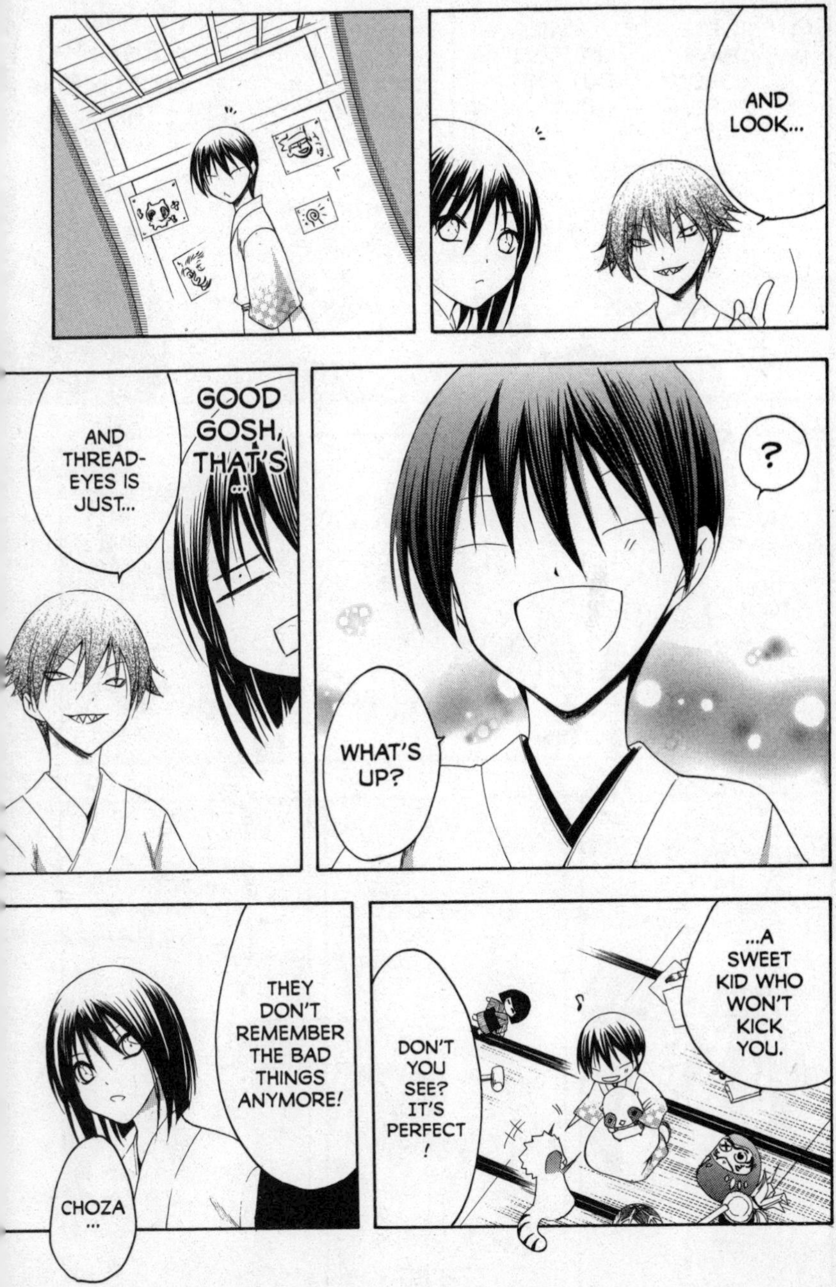
AND LOOK...
?
WHAT'S UP?
GOOD GOSH, THAT'S...
AND THREAD-EYES IS JUST...
...A SWEET KID WHO WON'T KICK YOU.
DON'T YOU SEE? IT'S PERFECT!
THEY DON'T REMEMBER THE BAD THINGS ANYMORE!
CHOZA...

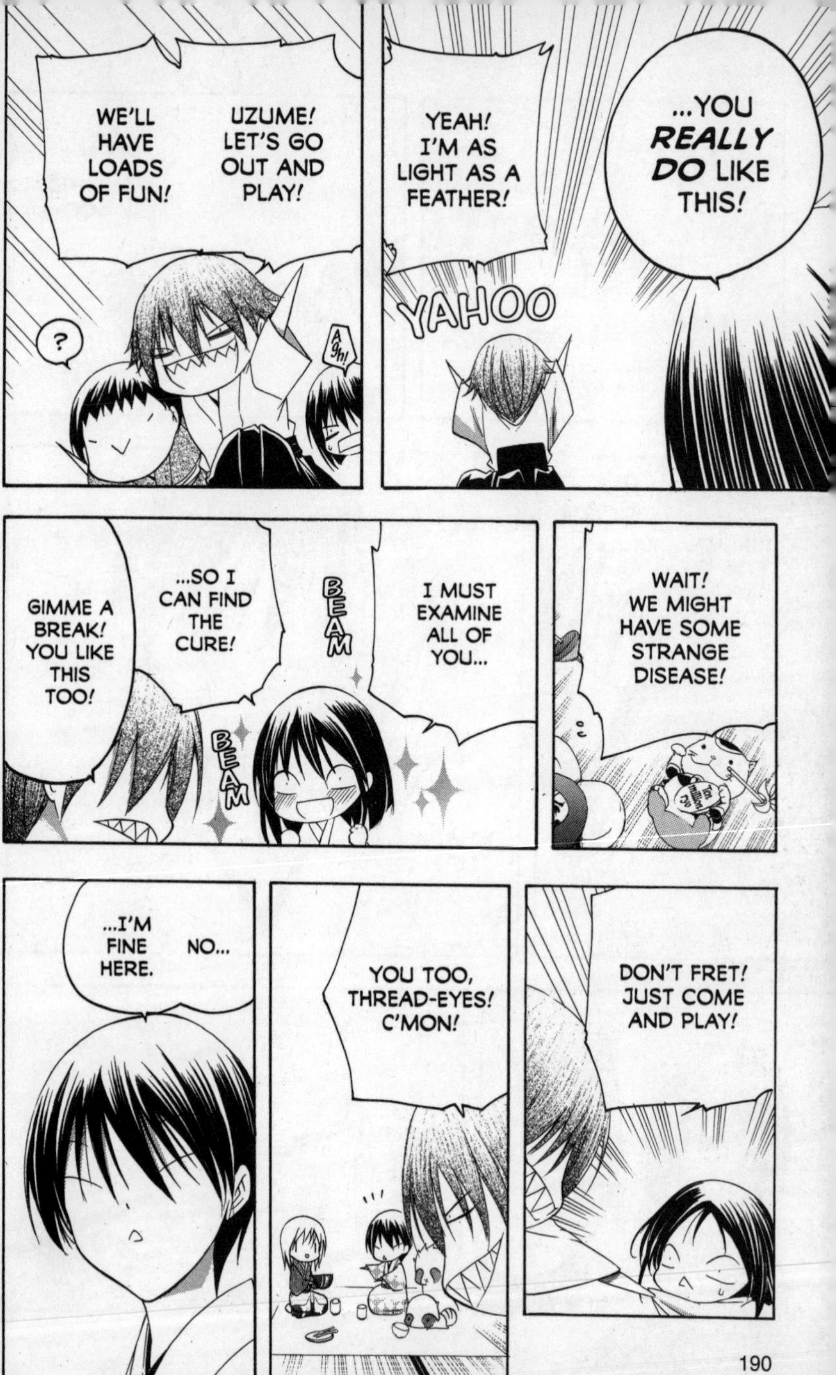
...YOU *REALLY* *DO* LIKE THIS!
YEAH! I'M AS LIGHT AS A FEATHER!
YAHOO
UZUME! LET'S GO OUT AND PLAY!
WE'LL HAVE LOADS OF FUN!
Agh!
?
WAIT! WE MIGHT HAVE SOME STRANGE DISEASE!
I MUST EXAMINE ALL OF YOU...
BEAM
...SO I CAN FIND THE CURE!
BEAM
GIMME A BREAK! YOU LIKE THIS TOO!
DON'T FRET! JUST COME AND PLAY!
YOU TOO, THREAD-EYES! C'MON!
NO...
...I'M FINE HERE.

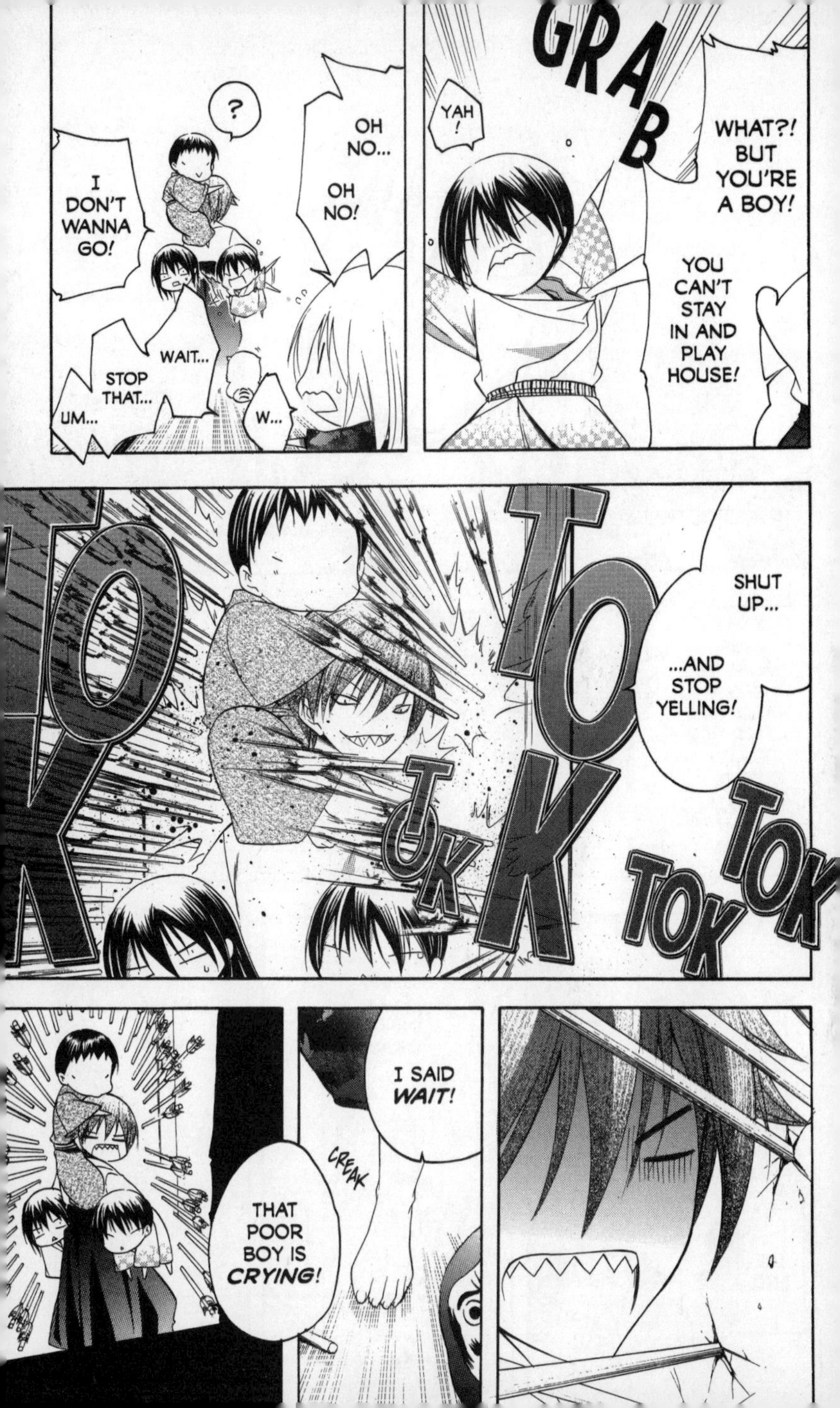
WHAT?! BUT YOU'RE A BOY!
GRAB
YAH!
YOU CAN'T STAY IN AND PLAY HOUSE!
OH NO...
OH NO!
?
I DON'T WANNA GO!
WAIT...
W...
STOP THAT...
UM...
SHUT UP...
...AND STOP YELLING!
TOK
TOK
TOK
TOK
TOK
TOK
I SAID *WAIT*!
CREAK
THAT POOR BOY IS *CRYING*!

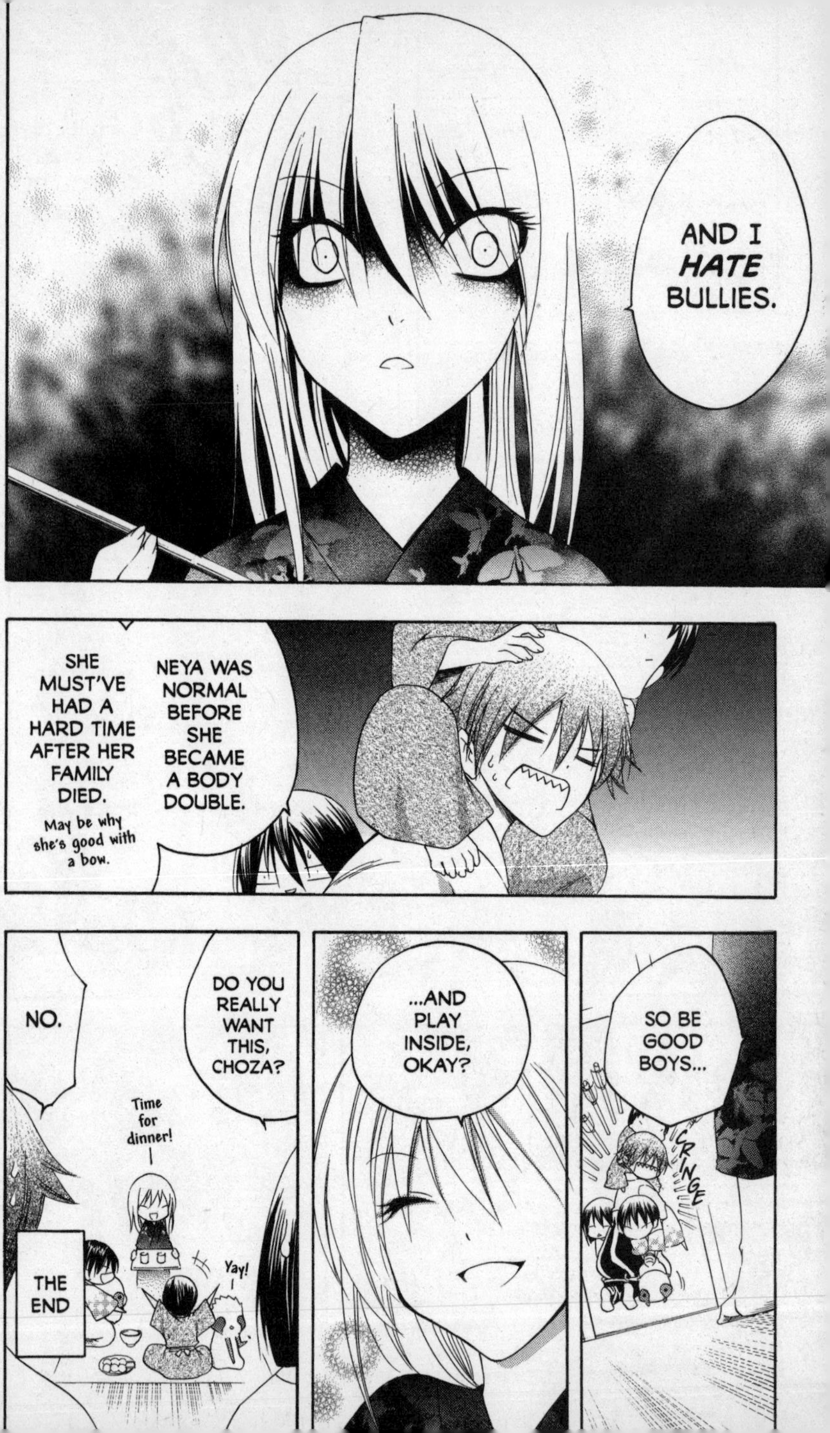
AND I *HATE* BULLIES.
NEYA WAS NORMAL BEFORE SHE BECAME A BODY DOUBLE.
SHE MUST'VE HAD A HARD TIME AFTER HER FAMILY DIED.
May be why she's good with a bow.
SO BE GOOD BOYS...
CRINGE
...AND PLAY INSIDE, OKAY?
DO YOU REALLY WANT THIS, CHOZA?
NO.
Time for dinner!
Yay!
THE END

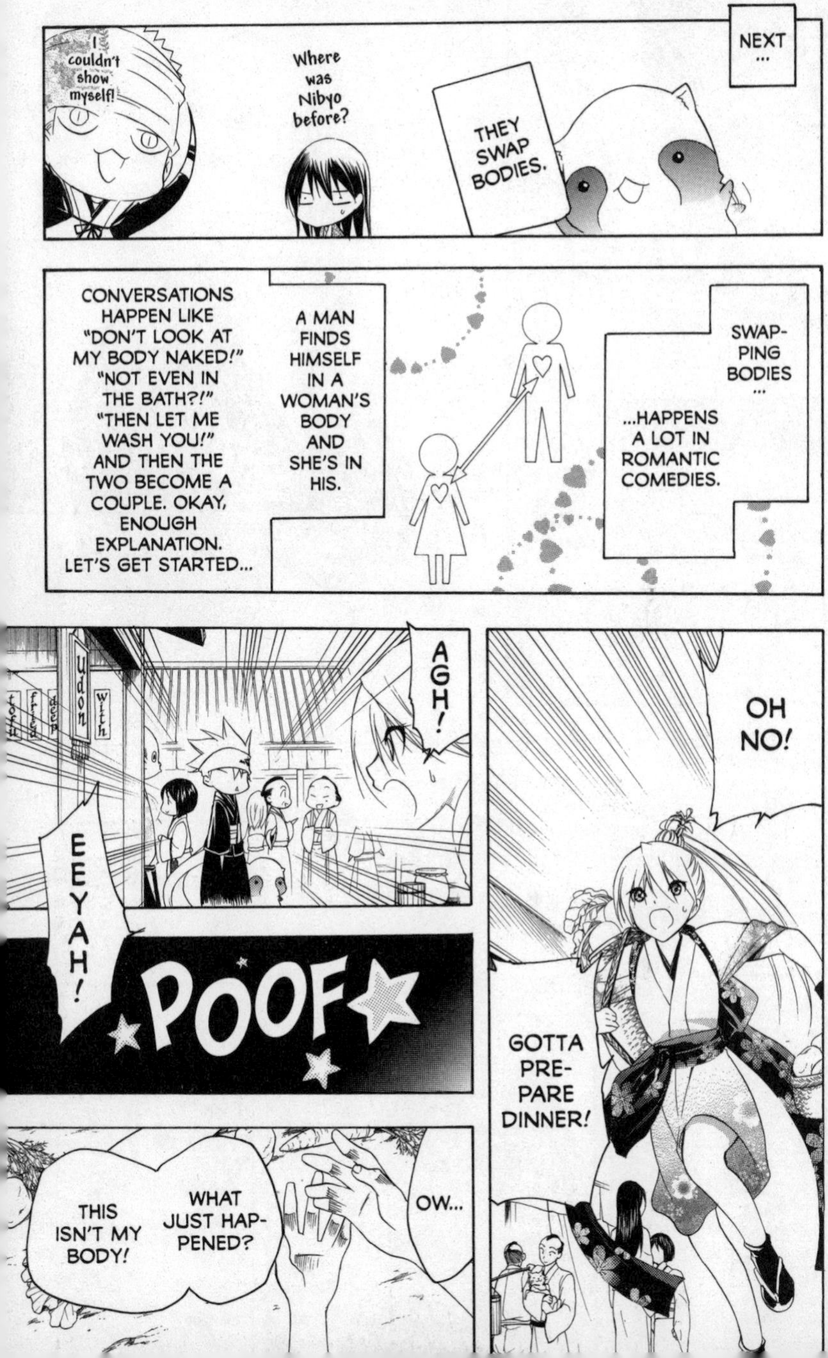
NEXT...
THEY SWAP BODIES.
Where was Nibyo before?
I couldn't show myself!
SWAPPING BODIES...
...HAPPENS A LOT IN ROMANTIC COMEDIES.
A MAN FINDS HIMSELF IN A WOMAN'S BODY AND SHE'S IN HIS.
CONVERSATIONS HAPPEN LIKE "DON'T LOOK AT MY BODY NAKED!" "NOT EVEN IN THE BATH?!" "THEN LET ME WASH YOU!" AND THEN THE TWO BECOME A COUPLE. OKAY, ENOUGH EXPLANATION. LET'S GET STARTED...
OH NO!
GOTTA PREPARE DINNER!
AGH!
udon with deep fried tofu
EEYAH!
POOF
OW...
WHAT JUST HAPPENED?
THIS ISN'T MY BODY!

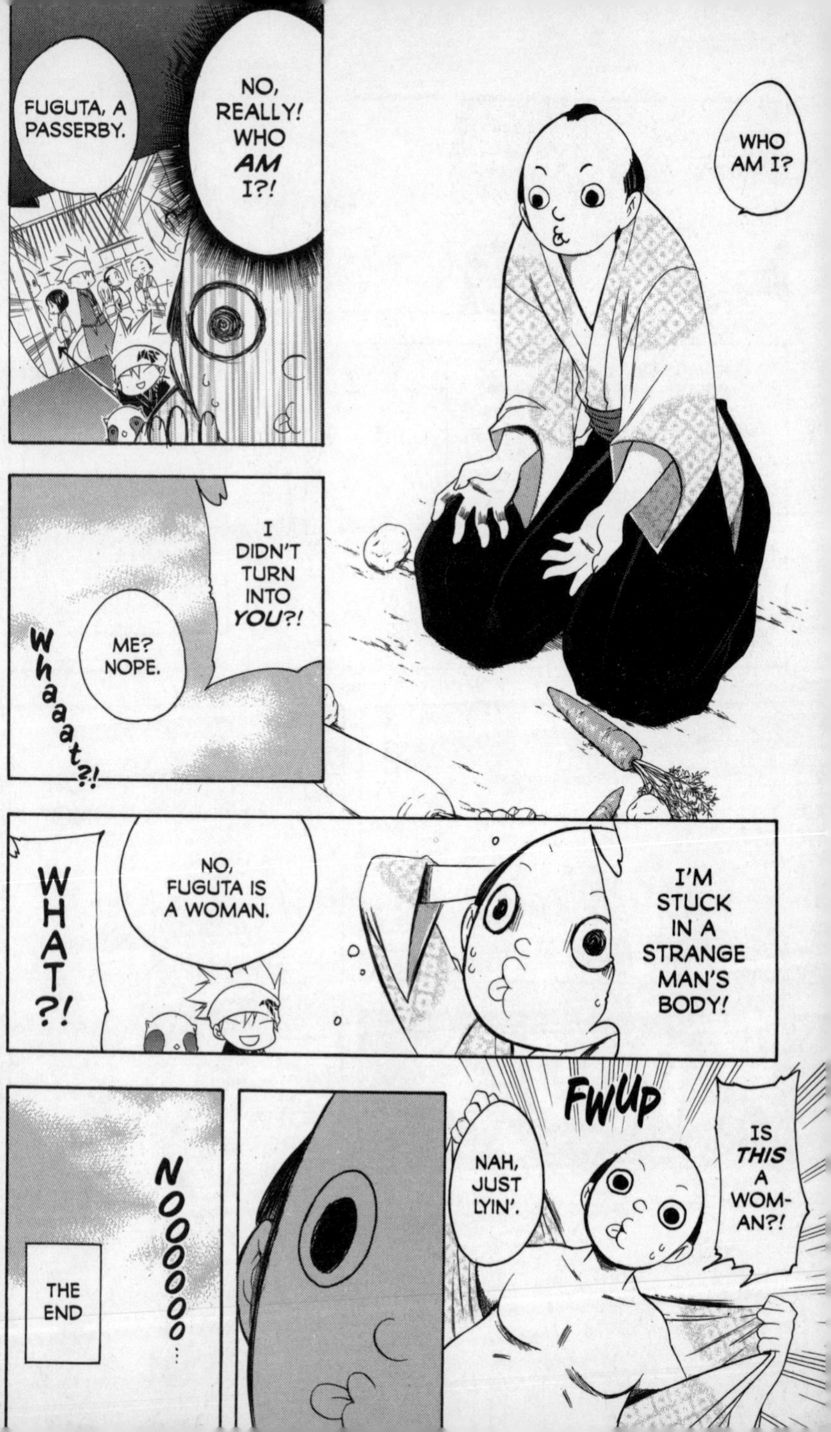
WHO AM I?
NO, REALLY! WHO *AM* I?!
FUGUTA, A PASSERBY.
I DIDN'T TURN INTO *YOU*?!
ME? NOPE.
Whaaaat?!
I'M STUCK IN A STRANGE MAN'S BODY!
NO, FUGUTA IS A WOMAN.
WHAT?!
IS *THIS* A WOM-AN?!
FWUP
NAH, JUST LYIN'.
NOOOOOOO...
THE END

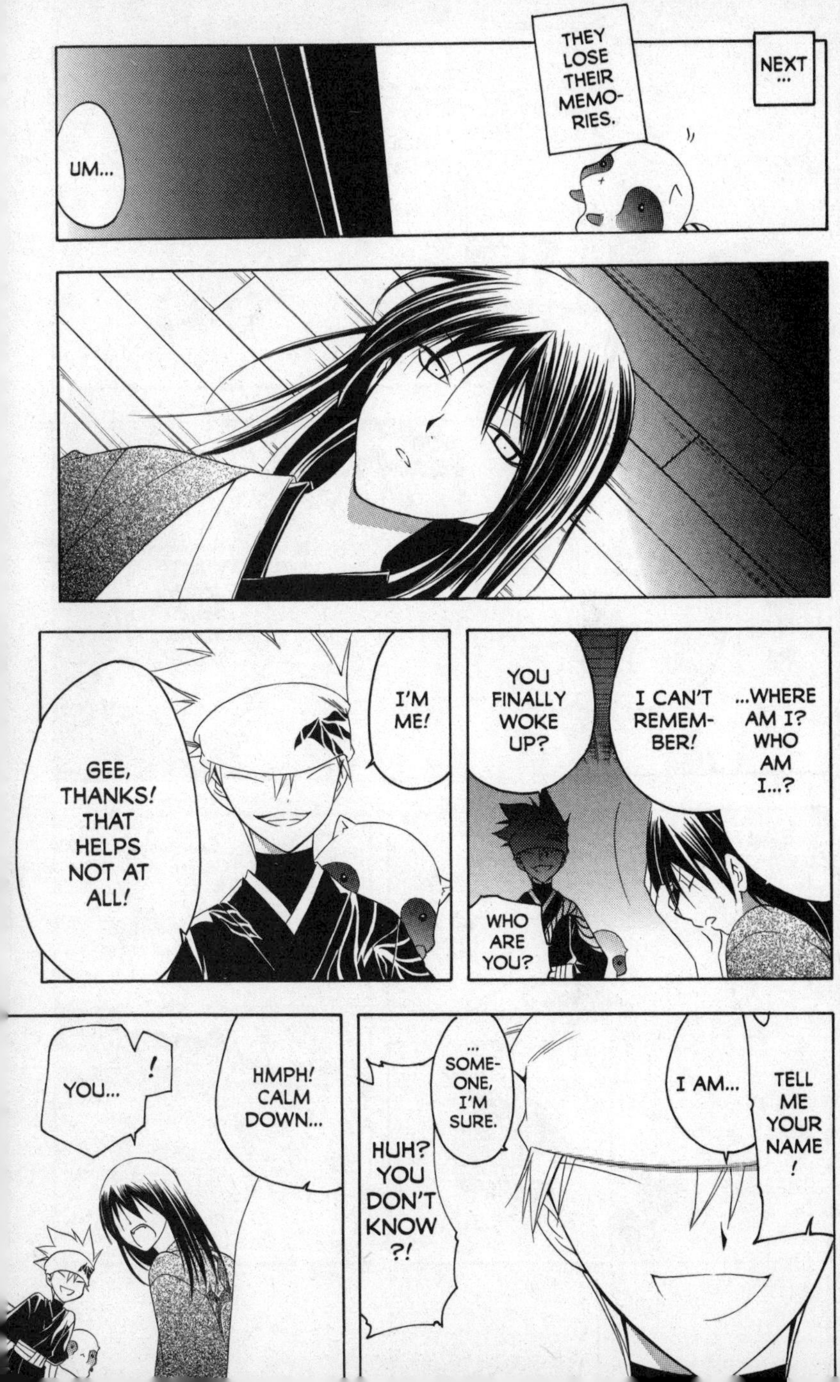
NEXT...
THEY LOSE THEIR MEMORIES.
UM...
...WHERE AM I? WHO AM I...?
I CAN'T REMEMBER!
YOU FINALLY WOKE UP?
WHO ARE YOU?
I'M ME!
GEE, THANKS! THAT HELPS NOT AT ALL!
TELL ME YOUR NAME!
I AM...
...SOMEONE, I'M SURE.
HUH? YOU DON'T KNOW?!
HMPH! CALM DOWN...
YOU...!

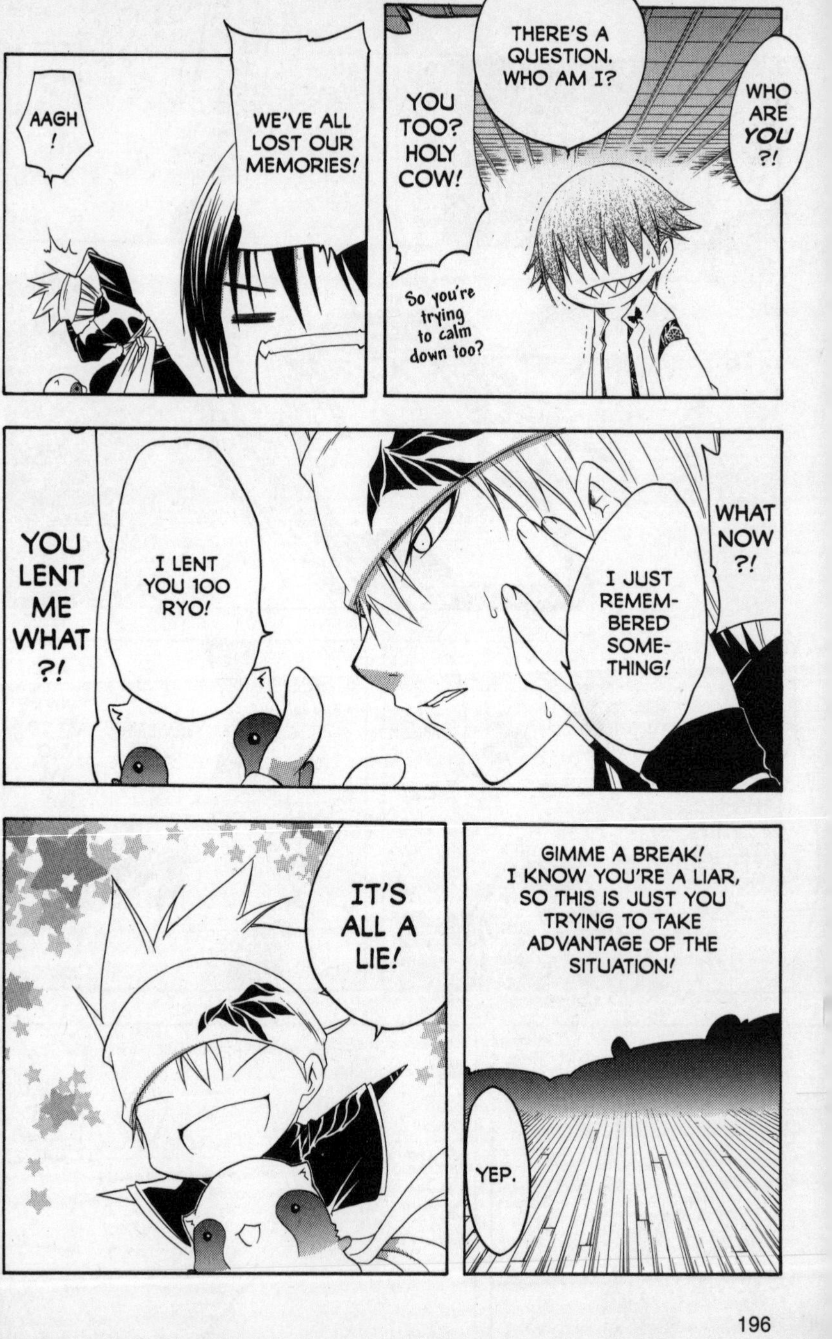
THERE'S A QUESTION. WHO AM I?
WHO ARE YOU?!
YOU TOO? HOLY COW!
So you're trying to calm down too?
WE'VE ALL LOST OUR MEMORIES!
AAGH!
WHAT NOW?!
I JUST REMEMBERED SOMETHING!
I LENT YOU 100 RYO!
YOU LENT ME WHAT?!
GIMME A BREAK! I KNOW YOU'RE A LIAR, SO THIS IS JUST YOU TRYING TO TAKE ADVANTAGE OF THE SITUATION!
YEP.
IT'S ALL A LIE!

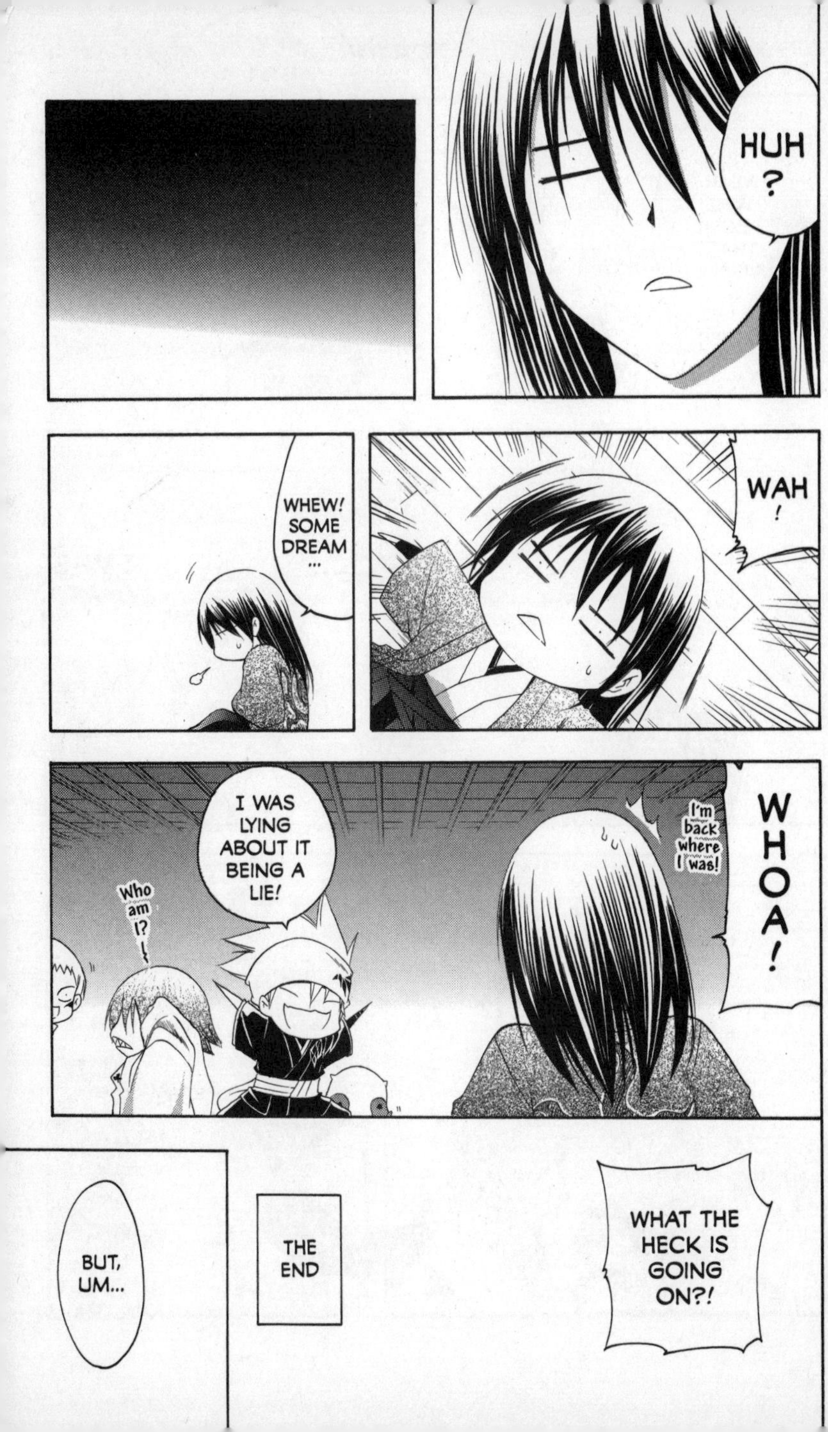
HUH?
WAH!
WHEW! SOME DREAM...
WHOA!
I'm back where I was!
I WAS LYING ABOUT IT BEING A LIE!
Who am I?
WHAT THE HECK IS GOING ON?!
THE END
BUT, UM...

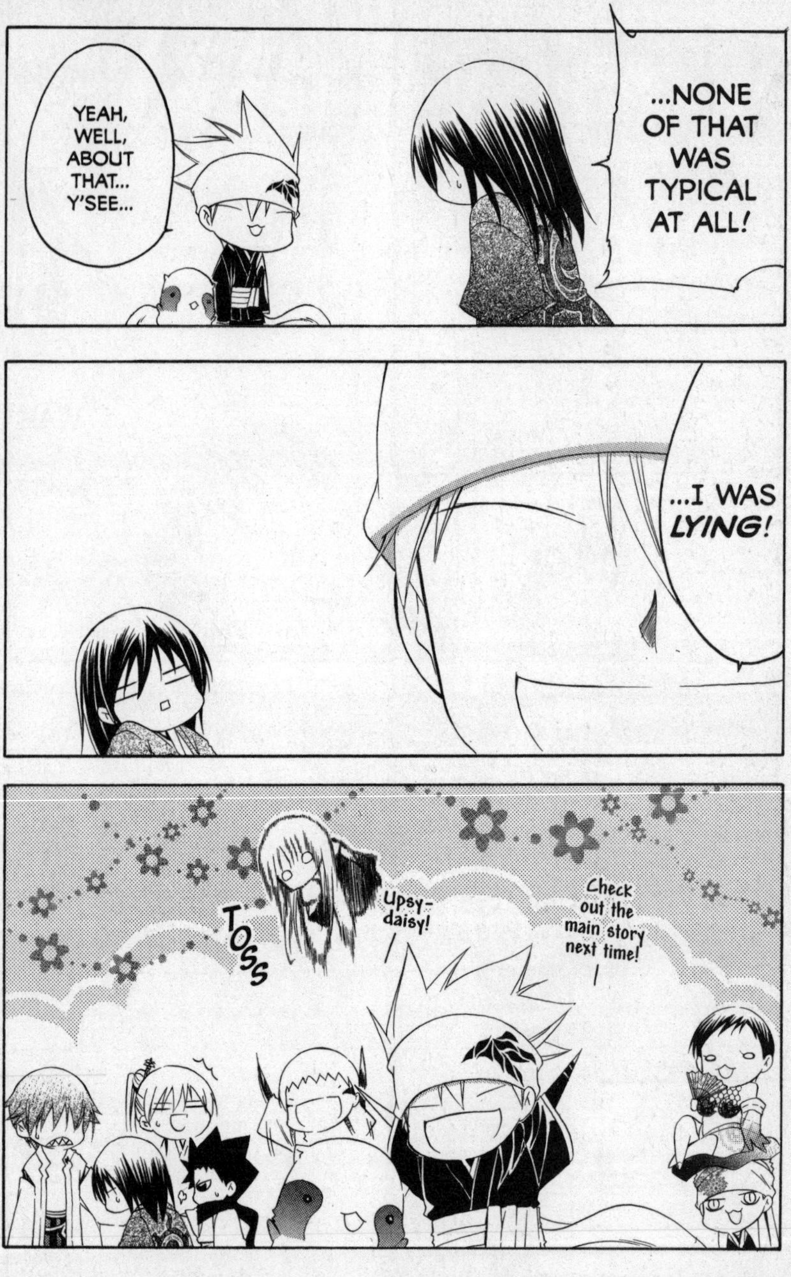
...NONE OF THAT WAS TYPICAL AT ALL!
YEAH, WELL, ABOUT THAT... Y'SEE...
...I WAS *LYING*!
Check out the main story next time!
Upsy-daisy!
TOSS

ITSUWARIBITO
Volume 21
Shonen Sunday Edition

Story and Art by
YUUKI IINUMA

ITSUWARIBITO ◆ UTSUHO ◆ Vol. 21
by Yuuki IINUMA
© 2009 Yuuki IINUMA
All rights reserved.
Original Japanese edition published by SHOGAKUKAN.
English translation rights in the United States of America and Canada
arranged with SHOGAKUKAN.

Translation/John Werry
Touch-up Art & Lettering/Susan Daigle-Leach
Design/Matt Hinrichs
Editor/Gary Leach

The stories, characters and incidents mentioned
in this publication are entirely fictional.

No portion of this book may be reproduced or transmitted
in any form or by any means without written permission
from the copyright holders.

Printed in the U.S.A.

Published by VIZ Media, LLC
P.O. Box 77010
San Francisco, CA 94107

10 9 8 7 6 5 4 3 2 1
First printing, August 2017

NEWPORT PUBLIC LIBRARY

www.viz.com   WWW.SHONENSUNDAY.COM

PARENTAL ADVISORY
ITSUWARIBITO is rated T+ for
Older Teen and is recommended
for ages 16 and up.
ratings.viz.com
FOR OLDER TEEN

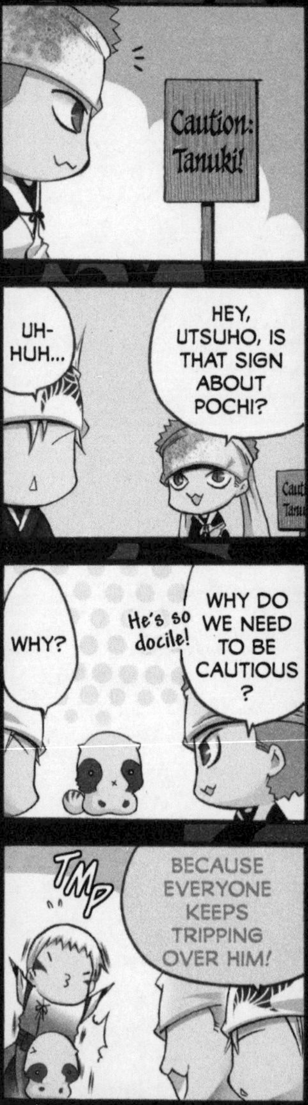
Caution: Tanuki!
HEY, UTSUHO, IS THAT SIGN ABOUT POCHI?
UH-HUH...
WHY DO WE NEED TO BE CAUTIOUS?
He's so docile!
WHY?
BECAUSE EVERYONE KEEPS TRIPPING OVER HIM!
TMP